THE SOUTHERN CENTURY:
GEORGIA SOUTHERN UNIVERSITY
1906 – 2006

THE SOUTHERN CENTURY:
GEORGIA SOUTHERN UNIVERSITY
1906 – 2006

Delma Eugene Presley

Georgia Southern University
Statesboro, Georgia

The Southern Century:

Georgia Southern University, 1906 – 2006

Delma Eugene Presley

Georgia Southern University

Statesboro, Georgia 30460

Book production and design by Regina Neville

Copyediting supervised by Kelly Caudle

In-house copyediting by Kelley Callaway

Typeset in Hoefler Text and Myriad,
display typeface in Trajan Pro and Viva.

Printed in Canada by Friesens, Inc.

Presley, Delma Eugene.

The Southern Century: Georgia Southern University 1906-2006

Includes source notes.

Includes index.

ISBN - 13: 978-0-9788650-0-9 (hardcover)

ISBN - 10: 0-9788650-0-6 (hardcover)

First published 2006

With appreciation to those fabulous fifty
who on December 1, 1906, gave to the
future a gift many know and love as
Georgia Southern University

CONTENTS

Foreword

Vision has driven Georgia Southern University through its first century. Sometimes that vision has been common and unified. Sometimes it has come from a single leader; at other times, from a group within the campus or the communities we serve.

That vision—tied to a drive to always reach higher and serve our community better—has created a powerful bond. It's what so clearly links today's research university back to Georgia Southern's founders, who were focused on a brilliant future and knew the sweet triumph of landing the First District A&M School.

That kind of focus on the future is critical, but as we look ahead, we must never forget to also look back, to fully understand what it is that we're building on. As generations pass, details of our heritage can fade.

That's why *The Southern Century* is so important: not only to mark the completion of our first 100 years, but to infuse context into our vision of what's next for Georgia Southern. Throughout these pages are countless indicators of the continuum onto which the future will be built.

When freshmen make that first approach to Sweetheart Circle, the Herty Pines greet them. But will they have an opportunity to understand the breakthrough work of Professor Charles Herty, carried out on the site of our campus, to modernize resin extraction and in turn preserve the pine forests of the South?

They'll see the Pittman Administration Building, but how much richer will their experience be if they know the story of Marvin Pittman, who stood his ground against a governor bent on destroying him?

They'll see Anderson Hall, but will they appreciate its origins as East Hall, the girls' dormitory, and the challenges that came with pioneering coeducation in the region?

They'll likely walk by Hanner Field House without realizing that, through those doors, in early 1965, passed the first African-American student to register for classes at Georgia Southern, or that, in that same building later in the year, the Rolling Stones stumbled through their first American college performance.

Del Presley's account of Georgia Southern's history, three years in the making, examines political intrigue and alliance building, naysayers astonished by results, and the overcoming of powerful social and economic forces. It is enhanced by a rich collection of archival photographs and other significant images.

This is a book for everyone with a connection to Georgia Southern. It's also for anyone interested in the remarkable development of an educational institution in the context of Georgia and American history.

Long after the celebration of our Centennial has passed, *The Southern Century* will serve as an enduring source of enlightenment. Could the second century parallel—or even surpass—the first in its progress?

I believe it will. My perspective is not just that of one who is privileged to be the university's president at this historic time. My confidence comes from subscribing to the overarching message of *The Southern Century*, that greatness is attainable if greatness is the vision we share.

Bruce Grube, President

Georgia Southern University

PREFACE

This centennial history of Georgia Southern University is a gift, but it is not the one I originally picked out for you, my reader. When I began working on this book three years ago, I was thinking in terms of a typical institutional history—a tribute to past leaders, illustrated with historic photographs and heart-tugging campus scenes. That volume would have included a guarantee backed by the faith and credit of nostalgia.

The Southern Century turned into a different kind of book, and let me tell you how that happened. It all started as conversations with two people who recently have accepted greater responsibilities elsewhere: Associate Vice President for Academic Affairs Robert Haney and Provost Vaughn Vandegrift. We talked about ways to write university histories.

We appreciated the work of 1982 by a faculty member and historian, Ray Shurbutt, *Georgia Southern: Seventy Five Years of Progress and Service*. Should I update that book with a survey of the last twenty-five years, adding a fourth layer to the centennial birthday cake? That would have been the simplest solution, although the entire cake would have required a new icing. We rejected that idea, because historians, like bakers, know the importance of starting big projects from scratch.

Our final topic of conversation was how to write the ideal university history. I recall optimistically saying it must be accurate, interesting, documented, and illustrated profusely. The author should tell the university's story in the context of the larger history of Statesboro, Bulloch County, the State of Georgia, and, for good measure, the American South.

The centennial history should be truthful, I continued. The reader should be able to reach out and feel this place. Words on the page should come from the pen and through the lips of both living and deceased faculty, staff, and alumni. Supporters and opponents should have their say. Finally, that ideal history should be packed with images of people, places, and events. Some pictures, in fact, are worth a thousand words.

The three of us—Haney, Vandegrift, and I—talked about such a book, convincing ourselves that I, a retired English professor/museum director, could complete it within three short years. That assumption at times proved ambitious, bordering on foolhardiness.

After Provost Vandegrift recommended and President Bruce Grube authorized the centennial history project, I spent the next two years reading much more than I had imagined would be necessary. The book began to fall into place when I combined my reading with my listening. A good story lingers in my memory like a worn jacket hanging in the closet, reminding me of places traveled or people encountered on the journey through life.

I started by gathering episodes stored in my mental closet, beginning with 1969– the year I joined the faculty. I merged these into a database of several thousand stories gleaned from newspapers, articles, and books.

Since 2003 I have worked in seven archives, read my way through seventy-five years of local newspapers, digested several dozen books and articles, and talked with scores of individuals. At last count my centennial database contained 4,285 stories, not counting many more from sixty interviews and numerous serendipitous conversations. Alumni have been especially generous. Within this great collection of opinions and observations, I have tried to locate the true story of this place.

When the citizens of Bulloch County made the winning bid for their college in 1906, they capped it with a promise to provide telephone service, water, and lights. Their priceless gift, one that continues to this day, is a greater promise of that light of learning on a hill south of Statesboro. Over the years it has flickered at times, but that light has never gone out.

The founders called it "the people's school," because they knew their college meant hope for each new generation. They envisioned here a brighter horizon for Georgia and the nation. *The Southern Century* is the story about this light, this hill, and the people of this place—Georgia Southern University. I am honored to share it with you.

D. E. P.

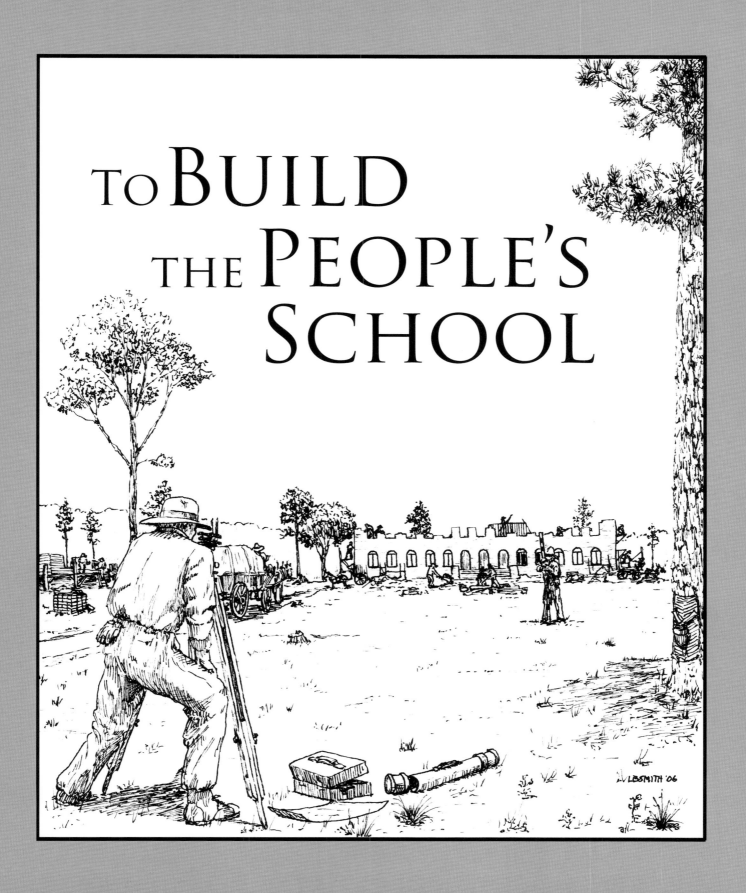

TO BUILD THE PEOPLE'S SCHOOL

TO BUILD THE PEOPLE'S SCHOOL
1889-1906

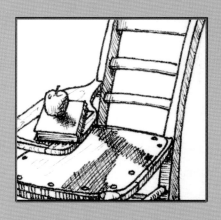

1889 – Citizens organize the Statesboro Academy on the corner of Church and North Main Streets.

1889 – Statesboro connected to the Central of Georgia Railway after building a new railroad line to Dover, Georgia.

1899 – The Savannah & Statesboro Railroad is completed and provides access to Savannah via Cuyler, Georgia. (5/30)

1900 – Two percent of Americans between the ages of eighteen and twenty-four, approximately 157,000 students, attend college.

1901 – Chemist Charles Holmes Herty completes ground-breaking turpentine research project on land that five years later became the campus of First District A&M School.

1901 – Former mayor Lonnie Brannen urges citizens to work together to build a college in Statesboro. (9/6)

1901 – Assassin kills U.S. President William McKinley. Vice President Theodore Roosevelt becomes president of the United States.

1902 – Scientists discover that mosquitoes transmit malaria.

1902 – Lonnie Brannen writes in the *Statesboro News* that the town's pioneer days have passed, and the new era calls for young people trained in "diversified agriculture." (2/28)

1901 – The Statesboro Normal Institute and Business College opens on Institute, College, and Grady Streets.

1903 – Wilbur and Orville Wright make the first heavier-than-air flight.

1904 – The Republican presidential candidate, Theodore Roosevelt, wins national election.

1905 – J. Randolph Anderson becomes president of the Savannah & Statesboro Railroad and names Lonnie Brannen of Statesboro the company's secretary.

1905 – Professor Joseph Spencer Stewart of the University of Georgia proposes a plan for rural high schools in Georgia. (6/1)

1905 – The State of Georgia receives funding from the General Education Board of the Rockefeller Foundation to study a system of rural high schools. (9/1)

1906 – Earthquake in San Francisco, California, destroys 28,000 buildings and claims 3,000 lives, leaving 225,000 people homeless. (4/18)

1906 – Representative Henry H. Perry of Hall County introduces legislation to organize a network of agricultural and mechanical schools in Georgia. (7/11)

1906 – Governor Joseph M. Terrell signs a bill creating district A&M schools and appoints J. Randolph Anderson as trustee of the First District School. (8/18)

1906 – Citizens of Statesboro and Bulloch County organize a "college committee." (8/24)

1906 – Bulloch County grand jury recommends using public funds to support bid for A&M school. (10/30)

1906 – Theodore Roosevelt becomes the first U.S. president to take an official trip abroad when he travels to Central America to review the construction of the Panama Canal. (11/9)

1906 – Statesboro becomes home of the First District A&M School after offering the highest bid and receiving Governor Terrell's tie-breaking vote. (12/1)

THE MEANING OF THE FIRST DAY

The early morning temperature dropped into the thirties, and dim streetlights illuminated a bizarre scene on the streets of Statesboro. Galloping horses appeared on four streets, all named Main. In the misty air above the action, five sharp sounds from the courthouse bell tower punctuated the first sentence of this day's grand story.

From all parts and around each corner, in buggies and on horseback, people joined in this predawn parade. The men wore fine suits, vests, silk ties, and bowler hats. Women bundled up in coats and shawls and wore pantaloons underneath long dresses. All were perfectly attired for a Sunday meeting. But this was a Saturday, in fact, the first Saturday as well as the first day of December 1906. Within thirty minutes, a line of horses and buggies encircled the block of the Jaeckel Hotel and continued eastward to the Savannah & Statesboro Railroad (S&S) depot at the corner of Railroad and Vine.

The "college special" soon would arrive at the station, and these delegates with their supporters would be on their way to Savannah, some fifty miles away. There they hoped to witness what they expected would be the turning point in the history of this town called Statesboro. Expectation mounted with the growing sound of hoof beats.

This scene from December 1, 1906, is part of the collective memory of a university and a community. It belongs to a larger drama, a *magnum opus*, which began well before the action of that day unfolded.

The remarkable event that took place in Savannah on that Saturday early in the twentieth century would shape Statesboro in ways the delegates could not possibly have imagined. Most of them well remembered how far the town had come since the census taker in 1880 tallied only twenty-five residents. They knew the town only recently had cast off its reputation as a nonentity, a reputation it clearly once deserved.

The town simply did not grow during its first seventy-five years. Founded as Statesborough in 1803, it was merely the place where, for most of the nineteenth century, the Bulloch County Superior Court met a few times each year. Change, in name only, began in 1866 when the state gave the town a new

Statesboro reborn

A progressive town in 1906, Statesboro boasted modern utilities. This view of downtown's North Main Street includes structures built after 1885.

Looking East, Showing East Main St. and Jaekel Hotel, Statesboro, Ga.

Hotel Jaeckel, Statesboro, Ga.

The Jaeckel—a grand hotel

Built in 1905, the Jaeckel was the area's finest hotel for dining and social events. Gustave Jaeckel, proprietor, was a delegate to the Savannah bidding meeting. Such well-known personalities as Henry Ford, William Jennings Bryan, and Cornelius Vanderbilt stayed at the hotel.

JAMES ALONZO "LONNIE" BRANNEN

Brannen, Statesboro's first mayor, moved to Statesboro from Bryan County in 1879. The visionary attorney and newspaperman represented Bulloch County as both state representative and senator. He was the first treasurer of the A&M school's board of trustees.

charter and revised its name—replacing the archaic "borough" with an up-to-date "boro." But it was not until the late 1880s that merchants, lawyers, bankers, and farmers jointly envisioned Statesboro as a regional hub of commerce.

The once-isolated community sponsored its first railroad, built an impressive courthouse, set up telephone lines, and installed water and electric utilities. Entrepreneurs built up the town that boasted of four major downtown streets—North Main, West Main, South Main, and East Main. In quick time new leaders, who had grown up on farms in Bulloch and other counties, created southeast Georgia's leading agricultural center. Its name was Statesboro. By 1900 all wagon trails in the region seemed to lead there.

On Saturdays surreys, from surrounding hamlets lined the streets, and customers patronized neat shops and stores operated efficiently by savvy merchants, both Gentile and Jew. Long before the chamber of commerce came on the scene, local boosters on every corner talked up the town's bright prospects. Georgians who attended state fairs after 1902 took note of prize-winning displays by the city and Bulloch County.

A community cannot live on enterprise alone, and Statesboro's leaders understood this. A particularly insightful early leader was an attorney named James Alonzo "Lonnie" Brannen. Operating under a new charter that called for an elected mayor and council, citizens chose him as their first mayor in 1889. Later, he promoted the town's prospects as both a representative and a senator in the state legislature.

At the turn of the century, Brannen founded and edited one of the town's early newspapers, the *Statesboro News,* and he would later hire James R. Miller as editor. In his weekly column of September 6, 1901, Brannen put into print what others had only discussed. Namely, the community needed a college:

We hope the time is even at hand, when the money spent in sending our young people off to complete their education can be kept at home and put into a system of higher education right here in Statesboro. If our people do not work to this end, as a matter of course such will not be the case; but with well-directed efforts the much-desired end can be reached. We are not isolated, cut off from the world. Our transportation facilities are first-class; our people are progressive and it only requires organized effort to reach out and grasp our opportunity to become the educational center of this section of Georgia. We can do it. Why not?

Brannen wanted Statesboro to become a model town, a mature community. In his eyes a college would send a signal to all of Georgia—

Statesboro was becoming a hub of commerce *and* culture. Brannen's proposal was ambitious but not unrealistic. After all, Bulloch County had learned to reach far, and everything it touched seemed to glitter. But the next move, organizing a college for Statesboro, did not follow quickly.

What deferred, almost defeated, the dream was a series of events that began in the heat of August 1904. The crucial episode played out in the Bulloch County Courthouse in downtown Statesboro. Two black men had been charged with the murder of five members of a prominent family, Mr. and Mrs. Henry Raiford Hodges and their three young children. After a sensational and controversial trial, the two—Will Cato and Paul Reed—were convicted and sentenced to death. Governor Joseph M. Terrell had ordered the militia to preserve order at gunpoint, but the commander, Robert M. Hitch, told his soldiers not to resist a mob of white men that charged the courthouse after Cato and Reed were sentenced. Dozens of men seized the two prisoners and led them in chains to a pine thicket just outside of town. There they bound Will Cato and Paul Reed to a pine stump and burned them to death.

On that day, August 16, 1904, local citizens betrayed a decade of hard-won victories. The shameful events overshadowed the town's once bright image as a progressive community of the "New South." National newspapers easily linked the name *Statesboro* with lynching and racial injustice.

An influential southern politician even laid blame for the defeat of the Democratic Party's presidential candidate at the doorstep of Statesboro. U.S. Senator John Sharp Williams of Mississippi told an audience in Spartanburg, South Carolina, that the Statesboro lynching resulted in a shift of half a million votes. Williams claimed the event provoked anti-southern sentiment nationwide and allowed the Republican candidate, Theodore Roosevelt, to win the presidential election. Senator Williams concluded, "I feel it is my duty to say to a southern audience that things like the Statesboro affair must stop."[1]

Statesboro mayor Greene Sharpe Johnston hoped a grand jury would act to redeem matters and bring to justice the mob's leaders; when it failed to do so, he lamented, "If our grand jury won't indict these lynchers . . . what are we coming to?"[2] The unwanted attention both embarrassed and frustrated local leaders. One individual who rose to the occasion was the Reverend Whitley Langston, pastor of the town's Methodist church. He called for the dismissal of two church members who had participated in the mob. The pastor's action, supported by the church's administrative board, led to the departure of twenty-five members who disapproved of Langston's brand of discipline.[3]

Statesboro grew defensive. Black men felt threatened, and dozens pulled up stakes and moved

Savannah & Statesboro Railroad

Completed in 1899, the S&S Railroad helped connect rural communities in southeast Georgia. In 1905 J. Randolph Anderson of Savannah purchased the railroad and opened an office in the Jaeckel Hotel. He named as S&S secretary the former mayor of Statesboro Lonnie Brannen.

JEFFERSON RANDOLPH ANDERSON

> " I have just received a telegram from the Commissioner of Agriculture in Atlanta saying that the Governor has appointed me as the member from Chatham on the Board of Trustees for the school. All of the counties in the district are anxious to get this school located in their borders. This position will add greatly to my strength in the district. It will do so particularly in Bulloch County which is crazy for the school. "

J. Randolph Anderson,
letter to his wife, 21 September 1906

A Bill by
Hon. Henry H. Perry,
of Hall Co.

To be entitled an Act to provide for the establishment and maintenance of schools of agriculture and the mechanic arts in the respective congressional districts of this state.

Section 1. Be it enacted by the General Assembly of the State of Georgia, and is hereby enacted by authority of the same, that the Governor is hereby authorized to establish and cause to be maintained in each congressional district of the State an industrial and agricultural school in accordance with the further provisions of this Act. Said schools shall be branches of the State College of Agriculture, a department of the University of Georgia. The general board of trustees of the University shall exercise such supervision as in their judgment may be necessary to secure unity of plan and efficiency in said schools.

"District Agricultural Schools of Georgia,"
Bulletin of the University of Georgia,
71:11 (July 1907 Supplement)

away with their families, thereby creating a labor shortage. The crisis was real, and the impact was noticeable. Merchants and local leaders no longer walked around town with that trademark "Statesboro swagger."

The distracted community forgot important lessons it had mastered during the last decade of the nineteenth century.[4] Editor James R. Miller of the *Statesboro News* tried to boost local confidence by organizing exhibitions prepared by local farmers. Some were quite impressive and won recognition at the annual state agricultural fair. Despite walking away with the prizes in 1905 and 1906, the town had not yet recovered its earlier luster.

What Statesboro needed was another chance to prove itself. Opportunity arrived in the form of a news report from Atlanta. In the spring of 1906, Governor Terrell gave Statesboro a reason to hope. Terrell had proposed once again his idea of expanding state-supported education beyond the university in Athens and a technical school in Atlanta. (At that time the only other state educational institutions were an institute for "colored youths" in Savannah, two normal schools in Athens and Milledgeville, and a small agricultural school in Dahlonega.) Although he had sent a similar bill to several sessions of the legislature, this time he believed it would pass. The news set Statesboro astir.

Terrell's dream—to build a system of agricultural and mechanical, or A&M, schools in Georgia—was as bold as it was brilliant. In 1902 , in his very first message to the state legislature, the new chief executive, then only forty-one years old, spoke of his education vision with youthful idealism. The creation of these schools had nothing to do with politics. Like Thomas Jefferson, Joseph Terrell simply believed that public education was a privilege of citizenship. A state-supported A&M system would provide a source of better-educated and more productive citizens.

Governor Terrell pointed out that Georgia's Constitution of 1777, the state's first, included a provision for public education. Georgia "was first in the union, and probably the first in the world, to incorporate in its organic law a provision for public schools," Terrell said.[5] Legislators might have agreed with his ideals, but few of them were willing to support such a bold measure in 1902. Although he was equally unsuccessful in intervening sessions, the governor persisted, eventually succeeding with what became his education bill of 1906.

This time around Governor Terrell left nothing to guesswork. He enlisted Senator J. Randolph Anderson, president of the Savannah and Statesboro railroad, as a strategist. He obtained a grant from the General Education Board of the Rockefeller Foundation. And he persuaded U. S. Secretary of Agriculture James Wilson to authorize soil studies of each congressional district. Wilson, in turn, commissioned a curriculum specialist, Dick J. Crosby, to help develop the legislative proposal. Crosby worked with a knowledgeable educator at the University of Georgia, Professor Joseph Spencer Stewart. Stewart was president of the North Georgia Agricultural

College in Dahlonega until 1903, when he was hired by the University of Georgia to serve as a high school agent.[6] Crosby and Stewart gave the governor all the documentation he needed to prepare his A&M proposal.

Alabama had already organized a system of agricultural schools, beginning in 1889, placing one school in every congressional district. Each school was related to an agricultural experiment station. A state board supervised eleven district schools. Georgia had an opportunity to become the second state to develop and support agricultural schools in congressional districts.[7]

Recent history suggested to Crosby and Stewart a future trend: the economic growth of the state would continue to depend upon those who tilled the soil. The schools would offer traditional subjects for boys and girls, as well as practical classes in agricultural science, mechanics, and homemaking. The schools would do more than provide high school classes. They would increase Georgia's farm production.

Governor Terrell found the work of Crosby and Stewart persuasive, and he encouraged the legislature to approve schools for each of the eleven congressional districts. A town in each district would host a school, and tax receipts from fertilizer inspection fees would cover the annual cost of operating the new schools. The finished product would be a statewide network of A&M schools.

Terrell knew better than to ask the legislature for funds to acquire property and construct school buildings. Such a request would have torpedoed his bill. Instead, the governor cleverly devised a plan to allow the legislature to construct eleven new A&M schools at no cost to the state. He decided to announce bidding contests in each district. Then, he believed firmly, local citizens would realize the long-term advantage of winning rights to a new school. Competition and local pride would do for education what the Georgia legislature could not dream of funding.

A representative from Hall County, Henry H. Perry, introduced the governor's A&M bill, and it easily passed in both the House of Representatives and the Senate. Unlike Alabama's special supervisory board, Georgia's legislative act stated that "schools shall be branches of the state College of Agriculture, a department of the University of Georgia."[8] As soon as the governor signed the bill, one of the proposal's architects, Dick J. Crosby, said the state of Georgia was preparing to set into motion "the most complete and comprehensive system of agricultural education of any state in the Union."[9]

JOSEPH MERIWETHER TERRELL
After serving ten years as attorney general, Terrell (1861-1912) was elected governor of Georgia, a position he held from 1902 to 1907. He championed the cause of public education and supported A&M schools. Later, he was appointed U.S. Senator.

Statesboro Normal Institute & Business College

Built in 1901, the elementary and high school stood on the corner of College and Grady Streets, the site of the Statesboro Police Department at the turn of the twenty-first century.

MEETING A LOCAL NEED

At the beginning of the twentieth century, most rural schools in Georgia served only primary and elementary grades. Rarely did a boy or girl advance beyond grade six. Young teenagers usually began working full-time on the family farm. If parents could afford it, they sent their children away to a high school, often designated an "academy," and made local arrangements for room and board. Few local high schools offered classes of standard quality. In all of southern Georgia in 1905, for example, only two schools had applied for accreditation, South Atlantic Institute in Guyton and Savannah High School.

During the 1890s—its boom decade—the citizens of Statesboro had supported public schools for white children.[10] In 1891 they built the Statesboro Academy on the corner of North Main and Church Streets. Ten years later the town's growing population required a larger facility. In the fall of 1901 a new brick structure appeared on the southwest side of town, ambitiously named the Statesboro Normal Institute and Southeastern Business College. Loosely speaking, Statesboro had its own college on the corner of College and Grady streets. The business "college," in fact, was a makeshift operation; its curriculum consisted of occasional accounting and secretarial classes. Some of the teachers themselves had not completed college. The Statesboro Normal Institute was a fancy name for an ordinary but good school for white children.

Black children might have attended a school on the west side of town as early as 1903. Lonnie Brannen had asked all citizens to support an "industrial or high school," which the town organized in July 1902. In November the *Statesboro News* reported on the progress of a school building. However, newspapers printed little information about educational opportunities for African Americans before 1907. Then William James, a young college-trained black educator moved to town. He mobilized support among both blacks and whites for what became Statesboro High and Industrial School.[11]

A&M schools, as the state planned them, were not colleges. They were boarding schools with collegelike facilities. Professor Stewart described them as a combination of the common high school and the university.[12] Each school would have a distinct campus with classrooms, dormitories, offices, and farm buildings. The curriculum would also be appropriate for graduates who desired to enroll at the state university. Locals realized, perhaps, that a state-supported vocational school might eventually be transformed into a state-supported college. Thus it was easy for residents of Statesboro to speak of the new "A&M college."

David Turner's new press

David Turner, *right*, a native of Florida, began his journalistic career in 1885. He moved to Statesboro early in the twentieth century and edited the *Bulloch Times* until the 1950s.

Another reason for the claim, as one historian has noted, is that in popular usage a rural high school typically was called a "college" from the 1890s to the 1920s.[13]

Inspired by the governor's A&M proposal in 1906, both local newspapers, the *Statesboro News* and the *Bulloch Times*, published articles about the progressive idea and the need to locate the "college" in Statesboro. The concept caught fire among local leaders. Bulloch County's Superintendent of Schools, J. Ewell Brannen, championed the cause and made sure the board of education supported it unanimously. The county commissioners, city council, and business leaders pledged both moral and monetary support. Governor Terrell signed the legislation on August 18, 1906. Immediately, the buzz on the Main streets concerned the new "A&M college."

Almost every edition of the local newspapers contained hints and rumors about the competition for the location of the new school within the First Congressional District. James R. Miller considered geography alone sufficient reason to award the school to Bulloch County. Miller argued that Statesboro was "almost the geographical center of the First Congressional District" and had "as good if not better railroad facilities than any town in the First District. She has four passenger trains daily." Miller's *News* headline left no doubt about his preference: "Let Statesboro have the Agricultural College."

By October several landowners had offered potential campus sites, and cash contributions had begun to flow. David Turner, editor of the *Bulloch Times,* wrote this headline for October 3, 1906: "Time is at hand to pull for it if Statesboro is to get the District College." Noting accrued cash donations of $3,500, Turner also speculated about a location:

A most admirable site of two hundred acres, almost in the edge of town, has been promised by J. S. Mikell at the very reasonable price of $32 per acre, with the promise of a handsome donation from Mikell in the event his land is found suitable. Besides this tract, the Gould estate embracing 200 acres, is understood to be accessible at a price aggregating $5,000 and various other convenient locations have been offered in the neighborhood of $50 per acre. Everything considered, the Mikell tract seems to be by far, the best offer so far had.[14]

These locations were on the east side of town. The James Simon Mikell property was more than two miles east of the courthouse, and the William Patrick Gould estate was nearly three miles northeast.[15]

When the Bulloch County grand jury met on October 30, 1906, its members unanimously recommended "that our board of county commissioners pay out the sum of Twenty-five Thousand Dollars ($25,000) or more if necessary, for this

A geographical advantage

The twelve counties of the first district in 1906 were Bryan, Bulloch, Burke, Chatham, Effingham, Emanuel, Jenkins, Liberty, McIntosh, Screven, Tattnall, and Toombs. (Evans and Candler counties had not yet been created.) *Statesboro News* editor James R. Miller noted that Statesboro was "almost the geographical center" of the district.

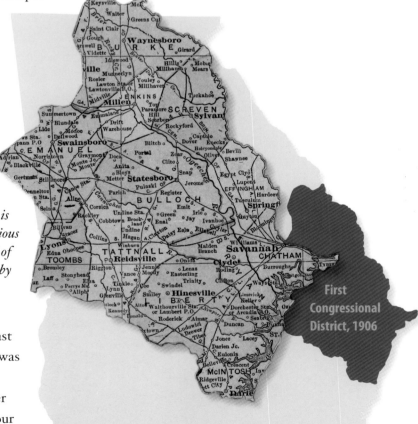

First Congressional District, 1906

enterprise if it can be secured for Bulloch County, the payments to be made in such manner and at such time as the county commissioners may determine."[16]

Local attorneys immediately challenged the legality of using county funds to enter a state-sponsored contest. The challenge was short-lived, because newspapers printed accounts of how counties in other districts had successfully used tax revenues to supplement their winning bids. Bulloch County eventually decided it could do the same. Miller applauded the idea and urged the county commissioners and board of education to be generous, and they were.[17]

Leaves of autumn fell on an uncharacteristically active citizenry that year. They attended hearings, wrote letters, raised funds, and collectively "pulled together" as Lonnie Brannen had urged in his pro-college editorial five years earlier. Once again the town was beginning to resemble the Statesboro of the 1890s, the local version of the Gilded Age. Allowing enthusiasm to overwhelm his logic, Miller declared in his October 30 editorial for the *Statesboro News*, "The entire state expects Bulloch County to get this college. This county is regarded as the best county in the entire state, and a failure to land this college here would be a disappointment to every section of the state."

On Tuesday, November 11, downtown merchants closed their doors at 11 a.m. so they could attend a town meeting at the courthouse. The agenda had only one item—to raise funds for the A&M school. News circulated among the crowd that Savannah did not appear enthusiastic about entering the competition. Even though the governor had scheduled bidding for December 1 in Savannah, local leaders in that city had not mustered support.

Miller reminded his readers that only four inland counties wanted to place bids: Bulloch, Burke, Emanuel, and Tattnall. With a sense of alarm, he wrote that George Brinson of Emanuel County was ready to offer a fine brick school building and hundreds of acres of land in the town of Stillmore. Brinson also had said that once the college was theirs, he promised the new "college town" would become the seat of government of a new county to be carved from Bulloch, Emanuel, and Tattnall counties.

Meanwhile, citizens of Waynesboro, an agricultural center, were said to be working hard behind the scenes to build a convincing case. A few miles south of the Bulloch County line, the Claxton-Hagan community, then in Tattnall County, enthusiastically backed their bid. They expected to become home of First District A&M.

With unconcealed anxiety, Miller wrote on November 16, 1906 that "we ... cannot afford to let this thing slip by. It means more for the social and industrial life of the county than any other one thing or any combination of things." He continued, "We have no one to fear but ourselves. If we are true to ourselves and give as liberally as we ought, then the college will be located here."

On the eve of bidding day, November 30, the *Statesboro News* prominently featured an announcement for December 1: "The Savannah & Statesboro railway will run a special train . . . [passing] straight through to Savannah with only one stop at Brooklet. A committee of one hundred citizens is expected to go down to see that Bulloch takes care of her interest." According to the *News,* the goal, simply, was to "land this college for Bulloch County." That is exactly what everyone wanted. So they made plans for what they hoped would be the first day of the "Southern" century.

DECEMBER 1, 1906

5:00 AM

On streets virtually unfamiliar to automobiles, the delegates depended on conventional transportation to their gathering point downtown. Lonnie Brannen, formerly mayor, would walk from his home on Zetterower Avenue. Greene Johnston, recently mayor, would walk along with newspaper editor David Turner, school superintendent J. Ewell Brannen, and others who lived on East Main, Savannah, and Zetterower. Some, especially women and older men, would use their handy buggies. Raymond Jimmerson Kennedy, the dentist who bought an automobile earlier that year, probably drove his newfangled machine. At that time Dr. Kennedy was one of a handful of residents who owned a car. Within a few years, most of those who arrived in buggies that morning would be proud owners of "horseless carriages."

Albert Mitchell Deal, as usual, rode horseback, as did many other men. Perhaps Deal marveled at streams of vapor rushing from the nostrils of the powerful animals as stable boys guided them to snug hay-lined quarters for the day. Deal, a youthful and energetic attorney, carried with him a satchel stuffed with copies of deeds, agreements, petitions, and newspapers—all relevant for an event he considered the most important in the history of Statesboro. The headline in Friday's paper had said it all: "Bulloch County Must Have That College." This ambitious goal inspired him and other citizens to rise so early that Saturday. Everyone in Statesboro seemed eager to succeed in Savannah.

People who knew each other well bantered as they hurried up the steps of the Jaeckel Hotel. County commissioners, city councilmen, school board members, judges, lawyers, and doctors were there. Farmers, merchants, teachers, and preachers also entered the hotel and went straight to the dining room. There were women—wives, daughters, and well-wishers—who eagerly listened and talked, one imagines, as everyone sat down to eat.

The hotel proprietor, Gustave Jaeckel, had arranged a splendid, old-fashioned southern breakfast of grits, eggs, bacon, gravy, hot biscuits with cane syrup, and steaming cups of just-brewed coffee. As the early risers finished their hearty meal, they heard the train. Quickly Jaeckel bundled up and joined the group, walking briskly those forty yards from the hotel's back door to the railway depot across Vine Street. As he climbed on board that morning, he must have been grateful that J. Randolph Anderson, owner of the Savannah &

ALBERT MITCHELL DEAL
The attorney was elected to several terms in the state House of Representatives. He provided legal and financial guidance to the First District A&M School for dozens of years. Deal Hall, originally the boys' dormitory, was named in his honor. Throughout his life (1868-1951) he preferred to ride a horse or drive a horse-drawn buggy in the city and county.

JEFFERSON RANDOLPH ANDERSON

Every alumnus of this institution and every citizen of the community and surrounding counties should be grateful. His efforts many years ago were largely responsible for the existence of this great institution we know as Georgia Southern College.

Julian K. Quattlebaum at the naming of Anderson Hall, 12 April 1970

Local leaders thought highly of J. Randolph Anderson (1861-1950). The representative and senator from Chatham County had friends in high places, and he knew how to influence governors and national politicians. He seconded the nomination of Oscar W. Underwood for president of the United States at the Democratic National Convention of 1912.

What impressed the farmers and merchants of Bulloch County most of all was Anderson's belief in the institution they nurtured from the beginning – the First District A&M School. They came to know him well, especially after he purchased the Savannah & Statesboro Railroad in 1905.

Many leading citizens in Georgia asked him to assist worthwhile causes, and he was attentive to their concerns. But he picked the school in Statesboro as his major project in the field of education.

From 1906 to 1922 he was chairman of the board of trustees, and he continued to assist the school afterward. On several occasions he convinced banks the struggling school in Statesboro deserved major loans. He intervened with governors, seeking special allocations necessary for the school's survival.

He sincerely believed President Thomas Jefferson was correct about public education. A democratic society depended on "enlightened and responsible citizens," he once told the students and faculty of the A&M school. Anderson found at a rural boarding school in Statesboro a way to implement his ancestor's commitment to education.

Born in Savannah in 1861, J.R. Anderson, or J. Randolph Anderson, as friends knew him, was the son of Edwin C. Anderson Jr., foreign agent for the government of the Confederate States of America and twice mayor of Savannah. He studied at the University of Virginia and the University of Göettingen, Germany, before completing his liberal arts education at the University of Virginia.

He developed a major law practice, representing mainly railroads and corporations. His firm continues today under the name of Hunter Maclean. With more than fifty lawyers, it is the largest law firm in Georgia outside of Atlanta.

Page Wilder Anderson, left, wife of J. Randolph Anderson and mother of two sons and a daughter, became the first Girl Scout leader in America in 1912. In 1906 J. Randolph Anderson championed two great causes in the legislature: creating a statewide system of A&M schools and funding a monument to honor the founder of Georgia, General James Edward Oglethorpe. Anderson, below, speaks in Savannah at the dedication of the monument on Bull Street in Chippewa Square on November 23, 1910.

Statesboro Railroad, had volunteered to arrange this train to Savannah.

Anderson, known locally as "J. R.," had located his S&S Railroad office in Jaeckel's handsome, new three-story hotel. Although Anderson lived in Savannah, he kept an office in Statesboro, where he regularly worked and discussed business with friends. Statesboro's citizens had come to depend on Anderson's railway, and he realized how important the town was to him, both economically and politically.[18]

Anderson was also one of Savannah's brightest lawyers (local newspapers noted he was "well-connected") and a popular legislator from Chatham County who was currently serving as Speaker of the Georgia House of Representatives. He was an ally and confidant of Governor Joseph Terrell who had championed the A&M school bill in the legislature.[19] A month earlier Terrell had appointed Anderson to the future school's board of trustees.

7:00 AM

Anderson's passenger trains normally made a dozen stops between Statesboro and Savannah, but this train was a "special." Those on board, of course, thought of it as the "college special." The steam locomotive broke its strong and steady rhythm long enough to pick up a group of Bulloch County delegates from Brooklet. Wasting no time, the travelers prepared for the task of this day. As the train swayed and rocked, they plotted for the showdown in Savannah.

For the better part of two hours school board members could compare notes with county commissioners, consulting documents in Deal's stuffed satchel. There also was news to pass around the passenger car, including a recent bit of gossip that Waynesboro had experienced trouble mounting a successful fund drive. If true, that meant the only competitors vying against Bulloch would be the counties of Emanuel and Tattnall. All three would see in this day the very same opportunity to put their county on the educational map of Georgia.

The train ride would have given participants time to select their spokesman. They needed an experienced debater who used words well—a man who could think clearly on his feet. He also should be a diplomat who could argue for Statesboro rather than against opposing speakers. The delegates chose Robert Lee Moore.

Moore was a youthful attorney and the current mayor, who for sixteen years had won friends on the bench and bar of southeast Georgia. He also had developed his own special brand of spontaneous humor. In short, he was the perfect antidote to Emanuel County's George Brinson, the magnate of Stillmore who had earned a reputation for arranging deals behind the scenes. Mayor Moore also would go head-to-head with a Tattnall County delegation whose pockets reputedly

ROBERT LEE MOORE
Moore (1867-1940) was mayor of Statesboro when the Bulloch County "college delegation" asked him to serve as their spokesman in Savannah on December 1, 1906. Also known as R. Lee Moore, the attorney was elected to the U.S. House of Representatives in 1923 and served one term.

Union Station

The delegates from Statesboro arrived early at Savannah's Union Station on December 1, 1906. Designed by Washington, D. C., architect Frank P. Milburn, the handsome building stood until 1962, when a highway construction crew demolished it and built an exit ramp for Interstate Highway 16. The historic station was located on West Broad Street (renamed Martin Luther King Jr. Boulevard in 1990).

were deep. Tattnall had earlier selected its spokesman—John Patrick Moore, a smooth-talking, quick-witted lawyer, (unrelated to Mayor Moore) who was one of the best public speakers in the region.

The governor had signed the bill creating A&M schools on August 18, 1906. In the very next issue of the *Statesboro News*, its editor James R. Miller acknowledged that other communities desired the college, notably the city by the sea: "Savannah and Chatham County want this college, and if we sleep they will get it." Miller concluded his editorial by hinting at Statesboro's strategy: "Governor Terrell has been written to for information as to the best steps to be taken to secure this school."[20] Both local newspapers, the *News* and the *Times*, championed the idea. Miller, a well-known booster who had organized Bulloch's prize-winning state fair entries, had written columns supporting the A&M school almost each week that autumn.

Bulloch County must wake up and support the "college fund," Miller had proclaimed: "To the man who gives liberally to this good cause, the blessings of posterity will be his and to the clam who shuts himself up in his shell and refuses to give anything, the curses of ignorant country boys who are eager for learning will be his only reward."[21]

Spurred by Miller and his younger counterpart, David Turner, of the *Bulloch Times*, the Bulloch County Grand Jury had met in October and recommended a sum of $25,000 be "set aside for the procurement of the First District Agricultural College for Bulloch County." Miller considered the amount proposed by the jury to be a "most generous one and is to be commended. As an investment, none better could be made by the county; not that the school will pay it back in a few years, but because, when once established, the school will be a permanent institution that will advertise the county continuously and benefit the agricultural interests every day of its existence."[22]

Miller's presence on the train constantly reminded the delegates this was no ordinary train ride. They recalled, perhaps, that their champion of progress could also be a harping critic. So Statesboro's delegates knew they had better "walk the line" Miller had drawn indelibly in newsprint. Three weeks earlier he had issued this dire warning:

It may be well for the people to know what they have got to go up against in bidding for this college. Stillmore is backed by George Brinson. Our sworn enemy is making all sorts of frantic efforts to get the school. At a mass meeting Saturday they

Historic DeSoto Hotel

The Romanesque hotel was built in Savannah in 1890, complete with five stories and 206 rooms. Located on Bull Street near Madison Square, the grand hotel included a restaurant, drugstore, solarium, and barbershop along with musical entertainment and dancing.

In 1968 the hotel was razed to make way for the DeSoto Hilton Hotel and the Citizens and Southern Bank.

raised the sum of $10,000 outside of the big mogul Brinson who says that the balance will be forthcoming out of his great store of filthy lucre. Then Waynesboro is making a quiet but determined effort to secure the school. Hagan-Claxton is also bidding for it, and so the people had just as well look these facts in the face when they go to raising subscriptions. . . . This is an appeal primarily to the county and town spirit. The man who has not enough spirit to give to a cause like this when he is able is a poor specimen of manhood.[23]

His front-page story on November 30 set the stage for this critical day: "A committee of one hundred citizens is expected to go down to see that Bulloch takes care of her interest. Everyone who will go is expected to be on hand and be a part of the party that will land this college for Bulloch County."[24]

9:00 AM

As the "college special" arrived at Savannah's Union Station, some of the older delegates and women probably caught the equivalent of the modern taxi—a horse-drawn buggy known as a "hack." Most of the Statesboro men would walk, side by side, to the DeSoto Hotel some four blocks away. Carrying collectively the future of Bulloch County on their shoulders, they strode toward their appointment with destiny. Savannah residents who ventured outside their city homes to pick up the Saturday morning newspaper might have wondered about this early morning processional of men from the country. On Sunday they would read the *Savannah Morning News* and wonder no more.

By 1906 the DeSoto had claimed the title as Savannah's largest and best "full-service" hotel—a suitable choice for the governor of Georgia. The event scheduled for this first Saturday in December lured both partisans who came to win as well as the merely curious who wanted to catch a glimpse of the governor and observe the spectacle. Bystanders found little room that day, however. If Bulloch's delegates were eager and earnest, they met their match in those energetic delegates from Tattnall and Emanuel. The bustling crowd spilled out of the DeSoto's drawing room and into the lobby. The hotel offered delegates the headquarters of Company B in the Volunteer Guard's Armory nearby on Bull Street. Meanwhile, members of the school's board of trustees, consisting of one representative for each of the district's twelve counties, remained in the drawing room.

Site of bidding contest: Volunteer Guard armory

This Romanesque red-brick structure, still standing in the twenty-first century, was designed in 1893 by William Gibbons Preston. The building, located on Bull Street south of the DeSoto Hotel, served as an armory for the Savannah Volunteer Guards.

10:00 AM

As the delegates gathered at the armory, they quickly confirmed the rumor that Burke County, indeed, would not participate in the bidding. Competitors from Bulloch, Emanuel, and

The Delegates

Fifty individuals represented Statesboro as official delegates on this historic day, December 1, 1906:

Jefferson Randolph Anderson (moderator)
James R. Miller (secretary)
Robert Lee Moore (spokesman)
Julian J. E. Anderson
J. Gordon Blitch
Alfred J. Bowen
Moses J. Bowen
Cecil Williams Brannen
James Alonzo Brannen
James Ewell Brannen
Joshua G. Brannen
William J. Brannen
Morgan Brown
Daniel Buie
Albert Mitchell Deal
William H. DeLoach
James Hobson Donaldson
William Henry Ellis
Bedford Everett
Joshua Everett
Alton Jerome Franklin
George Bruce Franklin
Jason Franklin
Jasper Franklin
Stephen Hill Franklin
Noah D. Hendrix
Gustave Jaeckel
James Z. Kendrick
Perry Kennedy
Raymond Jimmerson Kennedy
Wallace D. Kennedy
James B. Lee
S. H. Lichtenstein
D. E. McEachern
Samuel Lowndes Moore
Edwards Conyers Oliver
William Cling Parker
Jakle Z. Patrick
Albert W. Quattlebaum
Hunter Marshall Robertson
Milledge J. Rushing
Egbert Andrew Smith
Millard Fillmore Stubbs
Thomas B. Thorne
George R. Trapnell
Leon Jackson Trapnell
David Benjamin Turner
Remer Warnock
Madison Warren
John William Williams

NOTE: Newspapers took note of female supporters but did not list the names of those who might have accompanied the delegation from Bulloch County.

Tattnall then began to size up one another. Opposing parties threw verbal barbs from the start, according to newspaper accounts. Quickly the chatter ceased.

Governor Terrell entered the room. The man who had championed the formation of A&M schools had come to oversee the bidding—the approved method for awarding a state-supported institution to serve Georgia's sprawling First Congressional District. He introduced special guests, including Professor Joseph Spencer Stewart of the University of Georgia, who had helped develop the plan for the A&M system.[25]

The professor outlined the academic program of the new school as "a compromise between the common school and the university." Like the university, an A&M school would offer a four-year curriculum consisting of classroom work, but it would also provide hands-on instruction in agricultural science and mechanics.[26]

Delegates had reason to chatter again when the governor reported the trustees had elected two "J. R.'s" as officers of the meeting. J. Randolph Anderson would moderate and James R. Miller would serve as secretary. Anderson might have been somewhat neutral, but everyone knew Miller had but one goal—to place the new A&M school in Statesboro.

Immediately before opening the discussion and debate, Anderson, the moderator, silenced the room with an eloquent testimony on behalf of his friend: "History will place upon the brow of Governor Terrell a wreath for the energy with which he has worked toward the establishment of these congressional district colleges and for his success in getting them. To him is due the credit of originating this grand plan."[27]

A photographer appeared and asked the delegates to stand outside the armory for a group photograph, which would accompany a blow-by-blow account in Sunday's edition of the *Savannah Morning News*.[28] Pleasant facial expressions must have melted afterward, as everyone returned to a respective corner inside the armory, awaiting Anderson's cue.

George Brinson of Stillmore in Emanuel County rose and went straight to the point. He spoke not of the future but of the present. The town of Stillmore had commissioned the architect Louis F. Goodrich of Augusta to design a building for what he called Stillmore College. In fact, the building already had been built atop a hill some 497 feet above sea level—the highest spot in the entire first district, Brinson claimed. He said Tattnall and Bulloch had nothing to offer but promises. Emanuel, on the other hand, had a well-equipped facility that could be used for A&M classes immediately. In addition, his county would contribute three hundred acres of choice land, most of which was under cultivation. (A month earlier Brinson had promised that once the school was settled in Stillmore, the tiny village would become the seat of a new county.) Finally, Brinson proclaimed, Emanuel County had established a bank account for the school in the amount of $22,500. Brinson tallied up his county's bid at $67,300.

The moderator next recognized Mayor Robert Lee Moore of Statesboro. Neither he nor the spokesman for Tattnall referred directly to Brinson's proposal, according to newspaper accounts. The delegations from Tattnall and Bulloch were prepared to escalate the bids well beyond the amount offered by Brinson. They speculated, perhaps, that the winner that day would set forth a bid in the neighborhood of $90,000. After all, in November the city of Tifton had won the rights to the Second District A&M School by offering $95,000.[29]

Eloquently the mayor reviewed the agricultural achievements of Bulloch County. A recent accomplishment appeared in the national survey published by the U.S. government. Moore might have referred to the survey to support his claim that Statesboro was "the best cotton market in this part of the country, as well as the largest Sea Island cotton market in the world."[30] Moore maintained his county's farmers were superior. Delegates from Tattnall cried foul. When he reminded the audience that Bulloch County had won the top prize at the 1906 statewide agricultural exposition in Atlanta, attorney John Patrick Moore of Claxton begged to be heard.

The widely respected spokesman from Tattnall County resonated with rich tones and injected his own brand of humor, which surely provoked at least a smile from Terrell: "We have captured no prizes at fairs, but, between you and me, Governor, I understand that the Bulloch men took to Atlanta Irish potatoes from Indiana and grain from Illinois." Laughter and retorts echoed from each side of the room. The *Savannah Morning News* recounted Moore's skill:

Silver-haired and silver-tongued [J. P. Moore] championed the cause of Tattnall, and his remarks . . . fairly bristling with spicy adjectives, were enjoyed fully as well by the Bulloch adherents as by the Tattnall delegates. . . . Often, during Moore's remarks, there were tilts between the speaker and the Bullochs and several times the entire assemblage, trustees, delegates and spectators made the hall ring with their laughter and cheers.[31]

2:00 PM

After several hours of bidding, boasting, and bickering, the moderator announced the preliminary bidding results: Emanuel County, $67,300; Bulloch County, $95,500; and Tattnall County, $95,500 - $100,000.[32]

The results shocked the audience, especially those from Statesboro. Bulloch County's delegation reminded Anderson that Tattnall had placed a value on water and sewerage that tilted the total in Tattnall's favor. Bulloch needed more time to make certain its delegates had not overlooked valuable in-kind and cash contributions. Responding to this and other appeals from the audience, Anderson permitted each side one last chance to bid. Each delegation could firm up its total, making sure the amounts were based on either cash or real values of property and services.

JOHN PATRICK MOORE

John Patrick Moore, a native of Enal in Bulloch County, grew up in Groveland, a town in Bryan County. After receiving a law degree from the University of Georgia in 1882, Moore practiced his profession for twenty years in the western United States, before returning to Georgia. The "silver-haired and silver-tongued" Mr. Moore was the uncle of Maud Moore Benson, a dietitian at Georgia Normal College.

GEORGE MATTHEW BRINSON

" Stillmore is backed by George Brinson. Our sworn enemy is making all sorts of frantic efforts to get the school. At a mass meeting Saturday they raised the sum of $10,000 outside of the big mogul Brinson who says that the balance will be forthcoming out of his great store of filthy lucre. Then Waynesboro is making a quiet but determined effort to secure the school. Hagan-Claxton is also bidding. "

James R. Miller,
Statesboro News, 9 November 1906

Emanuel County must have believed the attractive existing building and choice location in Stillmore would overcome empty promises by their competitors. Brinson and the Emanuel County delegates contentedly resubmitted their original bid. The other parties did not find it so easy to settle on their final figures.

The Bulloch and Tattnall delegations conferred, spied upon each other, and negotiated. There was "considerable excitement among the contending delegations," David Turner of the *Times* wrote.

Albert Deal opened his satchel and reviewed deeds he had gathered from the old Peter Brannen estate and adjoining lands south of Statesboro. Two Brannens currently held 211 acres.

The larger plot, 115 acres, belonged to the unacknowledged leader of the bidding team, J. Ewell Brannen. Combined with his cousin Richard's 96 acres, Brannen controlled 211 acres, the bulk of the property. Brannen and Deal eventually confirmed approximately three hundred acres, including property owned by Glen Bland, T. E. Fields, and others.[33]

Once Deal could verify that bidders controlled some three hundred acres, Superintendent J. Ewell Brannen caucused with the school board, and Mayor Robert Lee Moore convened the city council. Meanwhile, Chairman Moses Bowen asked the county commissioners to review current assets and future revenue that might be used to bolster Bulloch's bid. After an hour, both Bulloch's and Tattnall's caucuses signaled they were ready to submit final offers.

Anderson gaveled the meeting to order and reminded the delegates their bids were final. He also made clear the highest bidder did not necessarily win the contest. Rather, the twelve members of the board of trustees would vote to elect the winner, taking into account the amount of each county's bid and other relevant factors.

Using information from results posted at the armory, Turner reported the conclusion of this tense and historically important session in the *Times*: "Spurred by the knowledge that Tattnall was in earnest in her fight, the Bulloch County commissioners decided to make an appropriation of $45,000. The city council of Statesboro agreed to give $5,000. The other $10,000 cash was promised by the county board of education. Private individuals agreed to contribute the 300 acres of land."[34] Thus, Bulloch's final bid was worth $125,500.

The final bids reflected serious efforts by both Tattnall and Bulloch counties to walk away as winners. Although Tattnall increased its cash bid by $2,500, its final offer was only slightly different from the original amount, perhaps because its delegates might have been forced to recalculate the value of such in-kind services as water and sewerage.

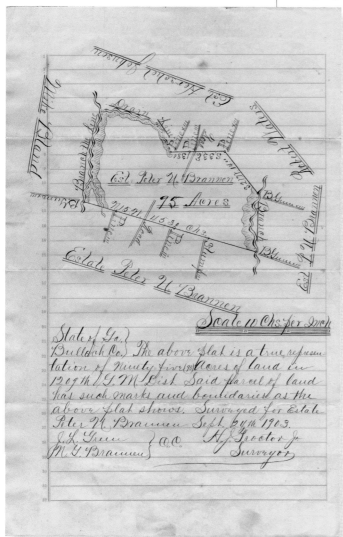

Original plat of a portion of the A&M campus.

A fter verifying each county's figures, the governor announced that the trustees would adjourn to the DeSoto Hotel and compare the real value of each bid. Afterward the twelve trustees would cast votes, taking into consideration all pertinent information. Emanuel's bidders continued to hope their choice location and new brick building would impress the trustees. Tattnall's bidders believed trustees would be moved by the powerful presentation of John Patrick Moore and by their "ideal site"—halfway between Claxton and Hagan. (These towns became part of Evans County when the legislature created it in 1914.) Bulloch's bidders trusted the axiom "money talks" as they planned a celebratory train ride back to Statesboro.

The governor and the trustees retreated to the drawing room of the DeSoto Hotel for what Bulloch's delegation assumed would be a swift decision in their favor. After fifteen minutes, delegates among the three parties began to stir, making an environment ripe for rumors. After thirty minutes rumors likely multiplied. Some began to wonder whether Bulloch County would win a majority of the votes. The Bulloch delegates had reason to fear the outcome of discussions behind closed doors. Only a few months earlier, Lonnie Brannen of Statesboro saw the jaws of defeat snatch away his victory in the congressional election. In that contest Brannen easily won the popular vote and tied in the electoral vote. Yet he lost the election when the first district's politicians met in closed caucuses.

Inside the drawing room, trustees from Tattnall and Emanuel counties lobbied their fellows from adjoining counties. They urged trustees to look beyond Bulloch's bid, although it was significantly higher than its closest rival. Four "neutral" trustees were swayed by these arguments and refused to accept Bulloch County's significantly higher bid.

After an hour the twelve trustees apparently had not awarded the majority of its votes to Bulloch. David Turner's account only hints at the drama. He reminded his *Times* readers that Governor Terrell was "an ex-officio member of the board." The twelve had given Bulloch just six votes. Finally, the trustees forced the governor to provide the majority. Almost ninety minutes after the closed-door deliberations began, the group returned to the armory, where the governor delivered the results to an anxious audience: Emanuel County, 2; Tattnall County, 4; and Bulloch County, 7.

A single vote, cast by the governor, had brought the competition to a close. Governor Terrell then formally awarded the First District A&M School to Statesboro and Bulloch County.

The big secret in Albert Deal's satchel

Albert Deal stuffed deeds, notes, and scraps of paper inside his satchel. The attorney assured Bulloch County's delegation he controlled more than 300 acres of land. A note pad found among his papers reveals a major error in addition. In the heat of the bidding war, someone miscalculated the acreage at 302 acres. The note pad clearly reveals the delegates had access to only 287 acres, thirteen less than their official bid of 300.

Robert M. Benson Jr. found this evidence in 2006 as he reviewed the files of the Cone Realty Company. This company handled Deal's real estate transactions in behalf of the A&M School.

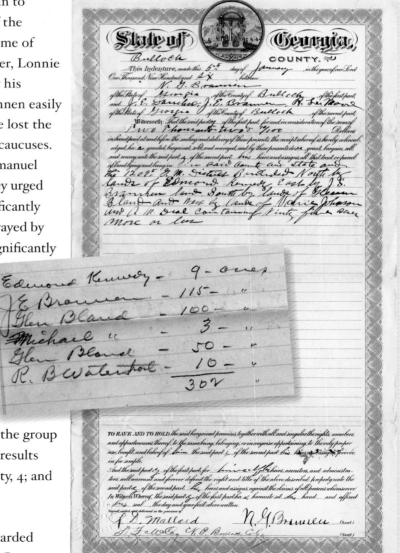

Turner recalled in the *Times* the impact of the decision on the delegations:

When the result was made public, there was great rejoicing among the Bulloch crowd and sorrow among those from Tattnall and Emanuel. Defeat was taken good naturedly, however, by the losers who congratulated Bulloch upon her success. County School Commissioner J. E. Brannen, who was indefatigable in his fight for the school, went before the board of trustees and extended the thanks of the county for the honor which had been bestowed by the award.[35]

5:00 PM

Delegates from Statesboro had begun this first day of December in Savannah by marching earnestly from Union Station toward the DeSoto Hotel. They ended it with a swift and joyous return to the S&S "College Special." Both the engine and the passengers were fired up and ready to go home. The leading citizens of Bulloch County shared in the celebration of a hard-fought victory. Each delegate surely realized how easily the A&M school could have been snatched away in that agonizingly long and final meeting of trustees. They could thank Governor Terrell, the moderator Anderson, Lady Luck, Gentleman Cash, or all of the above. They also could thank one another and the people back home for working so diligently that autumn to make sure Statesboro came away from the contest as the winner. For fifty-three miles the passenger cars of the S&S train rocked back and forth without stopping at the local stations, as was customary.

The college special pulled the happy band of Bulloch's bidders nonstop through pine forests and cypress swamps, whizzing past Cuyler, Blitchton, Eldora, Olney, Ivanhoe, Hubert, Stilson, Arcola, and Shearwood. The good times rolled all the way home. The train stopped only once, briefly. At Brooklet several smiling travelers shook hands with others on board and bade farewell. After breezing past Pretoria Station, the conductor decided to join the mirth. Unexpectedly, he pulled hard on the steam handle and held it down for the last mile home. The mellow-toned whistle split the cool evening air. Turner described the sound in *the Bulloch Times* as "deafening." Passengers roared their approval. Within moments the ecstatic crowd reached its destination—the S&S depot on the corner of Railroad and Vine streets, back home in the heart of Statesboro.

7:00 PM

The conductor's gesture created a commotion throughout town; housewives exchanged aprons for warm coats and scarves, joining husbands who donned their winter jackets. Sons and daughters tagged along in this impromptu parade to the depot. Some swung lanterns as they walked, casting over the scene a glimmering spectacle of light. The crowd clapped its approval as the delegates poured out of the train and onto the boardwalk, shouting out their names, beginning with Bulloch County Superintendent of Schools, the "indefatigable" J. Ewell Brannen, followed by his cousin and Statesboro's first mayor, Lonnie Brannen; the recent mayor, Greene Johnston, and the current mayor and champion of that day's contest

---

Final & binding bids

Emanuel County

Cash	$ 22,500
Land, 300 acres	$ 30,000
School building	$ 14,800
TOTAL	$ 67,300

Tattnall County

Cash	$ 27,500
Tax levy	$ 25,000
Land, 200 acres	$ 20,000
Electricity, water, sewerage, 10 yrs	$ 25,000
TOTAL	$ 97,500

Bulloch County

Cash	$ 60,000
Land, 300 acres	$ 40,000
Electricity, water, 10 yrs.	$ 25,000
Telephone service, 10 yrs.	$ 500
TOTAL	$125,500

Savannah Morning News, 2 December 1906
Statesboro News, 7 December 1906
Bulloch Times, 5 December 1906

in Savannah, Robert Lee Moore. Surely someone began a chant that rose to a crescendo: "We won! We won! We won the college!"

Rival newspaper editors James R. Miller of the *News* and David Turner of the *Times* strode the boardwalk, undoubtedly, with smiles on their faces and pages of notes on their pads—eyewitness accounts of what Miller said was Statesboro's greatest day. The headline of Miller's front page story in the *Statesboro News* said it all: "Bulloch wins the college: Committee went down after it and brought it back with them." He announced the chairman of the new board of trustees, Bulloch County's loyal friend J. Randolph Anderson. The two elected to top administrative positions lived in Statesboro: James R. Miller, secretary, and Lonnie Brannen, treasurer. The leadership of the new school now rested in the hands of those who helped bring it to life.

Bulloch wins the college

Townspeople braved the chilly December air to welcome home the Statesboro delegates after they successfully bid for a college to be located in Bulloch County.

All the way home

In 1906 the S&S railway normally stopped at these stations:

Savannah • Culyer • Blitchton • Eldora • Olney • Ivanhoe • Hubert • Stilson • Arcola • Shearwood • Brooklet • Pretoria • Statesboro

On December 1, 1906, the "college special" ran to and from Savannah, stopping only at the station in Brooklet to accommodate a number of delegates who lived in that vicinity.

S&S railway between
Statesboro and
Savannah

Miller reprinted a thoughtful appraisal of events of that Saturday from an editorial in the *Savannah Press:*

It is very gratifying to know that the First District made such a fine showing. Three counties put in bids which would have carried off the prize in any other district. The delegations of ladies and gentlemen showed how wide the interest was and the arguments made before the board left no doubt of the fact that the people were in earnest and that the agricultural high school would not have suffered in any of three of those bidding for its location. Some of the best men of the district were here to back up their home counties.[36]

The amount of the winning bid, incidentally, was the largest offered for A&M schools in Georgia. On the following Saturday, December 8, delegates from the fourth district met for their bidding session in Columbus. The two highest bidders were Muscogee and Carroll counties. Carroll County's package of $70,000 was the winning bid.[37] Local newspapers did not compare Bulloch County's winning bid with other successful bidders in the state. Had they done so, readers would have learned that the two lowest bids were from the seventh district at Powder Springs, which offered an academic building and a dormitory, and from the ninth district, in which Clarkesville pledged $25,000 in cash plus three hundred acres of land. Both of these schools, incidentally, failed, and the state eventually dissolved them and three other A&M schools.[38]

This decisive moment in time—December 1, 1906—marks the beginning of Georgia Southern University. Remarkably, one hundred years later, several locations historically significant in the university's history survive in mint condition. The elegantly restored three-story brick building downtown still bears the stone marker "Jaeckel Hotel." Today, it functions as Statesboro's city hall. The depot on the corner of Railroad and Vine streets is an attractive business office. The ground on which the cheering spectators and delegates stood is today the beginning segment of a mile-long greenway designed for walkers and bikers.

Although a developer razed Savannah's historic DeSoto Hotel, a large, modern building bearing the name DeSoto Hilton Hotel now stands in its place. The armory on Bull Street where the bidding contest unfolded is part of the historic downtown campus of the Savannah College of Art and Design. Union Station no longer stands, but an historic terminal nearby has become the Savannah History Museum and Visitors Center, a major tourist attraction.

Within these walls and around these places echo the voices of ambition and courage—the ancestral voices of December 1, 1906. The Statesboro delegation bargained for and won the right to be the home of the First District Agricultural and Mechanical School. It was their gift to the future. Today that gift is known as Georgia Southern University.

IF WALLS COULD TALK . . .

The Courthouse clock chimed the hour as delegates gathered at the hotel on East Main Street for breakfast. Later they walked from the hotel to the "college special" at the depot on the corner of Railroad and Vine Streets.

Three structures in downtown Statesboro contain memories of December 1, 1906—the Bulloch County Courthouse, *right*, the Jaeckel Hotel, *below*, and the Savannah & Statesboro railroad depot, *bottom*.

On August 20, 2000, the Bulloch County Commission rededicated the Bulloch County Courthouse after completely renovating the building, restoring it to its appearance of the early twentieth century. The county erected the building in 1896.

On February 13, 1996, the City of Statesboro dedicated the Jaeckel Hotel as its new City Hall. The restoration preserved the exterior and interior of the Jaeckel, erected in 1905.

Savannah & Statesboro Railway depot 100 years later

Users of the Willie McTell Trail walk through time as they pass by the white wooden building with a red roof at the corner of Railroad and Vine Streets. A restored S&S depot, an emblem of the past, was a business office in 2006.

One hundred years earlier, Statesboro's citizens stood nearby and cheered local delegates who bargained successfully for the First District A&M School on December 1, 1906.

To Build the People's School
1906-1909

1906 – The Board of Trustees elects officers: J. Randolph Anderson of Savannah, chairman; James R. Miller of Statesboro, secretary; and Lonnie Brannen of Statesboro, treasurer. (12/1)

1907 – Trustees approve bid by Nicholas Ittner for three buildings at a cost of $47,657, to be completed by September 15. (1/17)

1907 – Trustees select first principal, J. Walter Hendricks, a native of Bulloch County and graduate of the University of Georgia. (2/12)

1907 – City landscapes entrance to campus and creates future "Eagle Creek" and "Southern Drive." (2/19)

1907 – National economic depression or "panic" forces individuals and companies to reduce expenditures. (6/30)

1907 – Trustees postpone opening of school until 1908, because facilities are not ready for occupancy. (9/1)

1907 – First faculty under contract for first term in 1908: Otto Tauber Harper, agriculture; Frank M. Rowan, mechanics and mathematics; Josephine Schiffer, domestic science; Principal J. Walter Hendricks, English and physics. (10/17)

1908 – First District A&M begins classes; forty-two students are enrolled after seven weeks. (2/5)

1908 – Trustees grapple with 30 percent shortfall in state funding; principal reconsiders earlier decision to resign. (5/14)

1908 – After trustees and principal decide to cancel school for fall term, alarmed citizens successfully petition them to continue operations. (9/1)

1908 – Professor Otto Harper receives donation of 700 books and publications for the library from the U. S. Department of Agriculture. (10/20)

1908 – Principal Hendricks organizes successful "open house" on campus for the community. (12/15)

1909 – A&M baseball team plays first extramural game against Brooklet. (4/3)

1909 – A knife-wielding man attacks James R. Miller, trustee, after Miller defends the behavior of A&M students. (6/1)

1909 – Trustees intervene in school operations and monitor closely fiscal affairs and agricultural operations of the school. (7/8)

1909 – Contractor Nicholas Ittner sues trustees for failure to pay final 12 percent of bill for construction of the administration building and two dormitories. (9/13)

1909 – Principal Hendricks resigns and leaves the teaching profession. (11/4)

AN ASPIRATION SET IN A PINE FOREST

People long remembered and often discussed the events of December 1, 1906. They recalled how the audience in Savannah applauded Mayor Robert Lee Moore's well-crafted speech about a college-on-the-hill south of Statesboro. Moore, educated in the Victorian era, knew how to paint a bright picture, using broad oratorical strokes.

The honorable mayor probably brushed over some details known only to Bulloch County residents. One detail, in truth, was huge. Moore's glowing image of Statesboro's three-hundred-acre campus concealed a stark reality. He and his band of determined delegates actually had promised to build a school and farm on property that was far from ready for school buildings. The land, furthermore, was unsuitable for farming.

The future campus of the First District A&M School was an aspiration set in the middle of a pine forest. The delegates had donated the peak portion of a typical south Georgia sand ridge. Filled with tall evergreens and scrub oaks, the would-be campus was an "ideal location," perhaps, for harvesting resin.

The land was ready neither for school buildings nor for growing cotton, corn, peanuts, and vegetables. In 1906 J. A. McDougald and Jesse Outland used much of the property to support a profitable turpentine distillery they had set up on the eastern side of the ridge.

Five years before the forest became the site of a campus, it was this distillery that attracted a thirty-four-year-old chemist who had earned his PhD at Johns Hopkins University. His name was Charles Holmes Herty, a member of the faculty of the University of Georgia. An early developer of naval stores in the region, Jesse Parker Williams, referred Herty to McDougald and Outland. The two were eager to support the research of the energetic Professor Herty.[1] He built within this lush hillside forest an outdoor laboratory. Here he conducted scientific experiments that proved beneficial both to industry and to the ecosystem.

Turpentine harvesters traditionally cut holes or "boxes" deep into the trunks of pine trees in order to gather resin. Their methods eventually destroyed the trees and ruined ancient forests. Among these pines Herty experimented with a cup and gutter system. He found that trees would produce more resin over a longer period if harvesters nailed a quart-sized clay cup to a tree. Using a small hatchet, a workman hacked away the bark above the cup, making the v-shaped pattern of a chevron and forcing the resin into the exposed area (called a "catface"). Then the resin dripped

CHARLES HOLMES HERTY
In 1901 the noted chemist, a native of Milledgeville, conducted research in a pine forest that became First District A&M School. While leading the chemistry department at the University of North Carolina from 1905-1917, Herty developed new ways to harvest and use pine resin. Before starting his research project in Statesboro, Herty taught chemistry at the University of Georgia in the 1890s. He introduced collegiate football to the South and served as the Bulldogs' first football coach. Herty later donated his two hand-written notebooks, below, to the library of South Georgia Teachers College.

Outdoor education

Wearing stylish A&M sweaters and caps around 1919, members of a forestry class learned the subject first-hand. The instructor taught them to identify different kinds of trees and to analyze bark for evidence of insects. At this time pine trees were important sources of income, because the naval stores industry paid a premium for pine resin and a by-product, turpentine.

into the cup and gradually filled it over a period of time. Workers could collect the resin and replace the cup. Trees remained healthy and productive.[2]

Forest historians maintain that Herty's experiments in Statesboro literally saved the great southern pine forests from devastation. Later, Herty demonstrated how pulp from pine trees could be processed into paper and used for containers and newsprint.

Five years after Herty concluded his experiments here, the trustees of the A&M school faced the task of carving a campus out of the forest. They selected the highest ground for the three main buildings. Then they staked out a fertile area near some lowlands south of the ridge. That section would become the school's demonstration farm. To accomplish what they envisioned, trustees arranged swiftly for a project of tree felling and stump clearing—the kind of work pioneers had done throughout the piney woods of Bulloch County during the past century.

What concerned the trustees most was whether the school would be ready for students by September 1907. James R. Miller, secretary of the board of trustees, called a meeting of the executive committee for December 19, 1906. His agenda was to review the state's architectural plans for all district A&M schools, establish a completion date, and solicit bids from contractors.[3] Trustees found the cookie-cutter plans attractive: three stately red brick buildings with arched windows and porches with columns.

State officials suggested two dormitories should flank the larger central classroom-administration building. The larger building in the middle featured impressive Tuscan columns. In early January committee members opened the bids and awarded the contract to Nicholas Ittner from Macon in the amount of $47,657. (A local contractor who had built the Jaeckel Hotel, A. J. Franklin, had submitted a bid in excess of $60,000.) The contract called for the project to be finished by September 15, 1907.[4] Ittner ambitiously promised in nine months to deliver the keys to the brand-new First District A&M School.

When Governor Joseph M. Terrell visited Statesboro near the end of January 1907, he observed workmen clearing the land for the new school. The popular governor wanted to see this work in progress, while attending a meeting of the new school's board of trustees. A local newspaper reported that "Governor Terrell was the guest of the Jaeckel Hotel, where many courtesies were shown the distinguished citizen and chief executive of the state." He learned the buildings on the campus "are to be fitted up with facilities for steam heating. They will be modern in every sense of the word."[5]

More positive information about the school came in February 1907 when the *Statesboro News* announced that trustees had nominated as principal a man who was born and reared in western Bulloch County:

Prof. J. Walter Hendricks, of Douglas, has accepted the position of principal of the First District Agricultural College. He was elected to this position at the meeting of the trustees of the college in January. . . . Mr. Hendricks is a man of wide and varied experience in the teaching world. He is a man of broad and liberal culture to which is added a large amount of native ability that fits him peculiarly to head an institution where foresight and good judgment are quite as necessary as scholarship.[6]

James Walter Hendricks (he preferred "J. Walter") then was principal of an independent normal school in Douglas and would continue his work there through the summer. The local newspaper in nearby Millen greeted the announcement enthusiastically. The editor noted that Hendricks was married to a member of the Lively family of that town.[7] Citizens of Statesboro already were familiar with Mrs. Nina Hendricks' sister, Mattie Lively, a popular teacher at the Statesboro Institute located on South College Street.

The editors of the local newspapers peppered their pages weekly with announcements about "our" campus that was beginning to take shape over the creek and up the hill. In glowing words James R. Miller, editor of the *Statesboro News* described the proposed avenue leading to the three buildings:

South Main Street will be extended and will run through the college grounds. It will be made eighty feet wide, with rows of trees on either side, and a row of evergreens in the middle, affording driveways on each side of this row of trees. This will be by far the most beautiful street in the city. Another street will be opened through the college grounds in front of the residence of Col. A. M. Deal.[8]

At the time of the announcement, local backers of the school assumed it would be ready to open in mid-September. That assumption did not take into account the Herculean task of clearing the land. Farmers who had planned to send their sons and daughters to the school that autumn began to have second thoughts.

Doubters looked at the plans and then looked at the site. They concluded the new school had little chance of success, primarily because there were so many trees to fell and stumps to remove. Once the land was cleared, some argued, the soil itself would not be suitable for farming. David Turner, editor of the *Bulloch Times*, faulted the disbelievers, not for their arguments but for their lack of confidence in the community's willpower:

There are some few skeptics, as there ever will be, who prophesy that it will be a failure. If our people waited on such as these, it would have failed already. But there are enough who have faith in the future and confidence in our own county, who have rallied to the school when a strong effort was needed, that there is no chance for failure.[9]

Turner's optimism notwithstanding, success was by no means assured. Within the nation and state, economic conditions had deteriorated. By summer several national banks and major industries tottered on the edge of bankruptcy. The failure of the Knickerbocker Trust that year sent shock waves through Wall Street, and investors lost millions of dollars. The collapse of the stalwart Westinghouse Electric Company eroded public confidence.

Tree saving methods for harvesting pine resin

A modern demonstration of Herty's cup-and-gutter system of harvesting pine resin, *above*.

Three different types of resin-catching cups, *below*.

HERTY CUP Hand Book

1905

Issued by CHATTANOOGA POTTERY CO.
Sole Manufacturers
JACKSONVILLE, FLORIDA.

EAST HALL

ACADEMIC BUILDING

WEST HALL

First buildings on campus

East Hall was a thirty-six-room dormitory for the girls. West Hall had forty-two rooms for the boys. The residence halls included all the modern conveniences, new and substantial furniture, electric lights, hot and cold baths, and telephone connections.

The bulletin boasted, "no better health advantages are offered in Georgia. Our School is located upon a high sand hill and with our complete system of sewerage and care in sanitation, the accumulation of disease germs is practically impossible. Our school grounds and buildings are furnished with the finest artesian water from the City of Statesboro."

This rapid financial downturn, known as the Panic of 1907, caused some local citizens to reconsider their pledges of support to the new school. Communities building A&M schools in other districts felt the downturn as well. A report by the Georgia Department of Education acknowledged a widespread loss of enthusiasm in the new building projects: "The panic came on at about this time and many honest subscribers to the building funds were unable to meet their promises. Many of the trustees took little interest in their welfare and even the most optimistic began to shake their heads."[10]

Laborers found the work of clearing the grounds challenging, and some wondered whether the school possibly could be ready for the first class that September. Black employees, especially, took note of the danger of working so hard and so fast. In the middle of March, a young black man named Eugene Fulton labored with a mule while clearing the land. Somehow his feet became entangled in lines attached to the hames (part of the mule's bridle). Fulton's death was the first, perhaps only, recorded during construction.[11]

In spite of the contractor Nicholas Ittner's efforts to meet the deadline, he was unable to complete the buildings by September 15. Less than a month later, the buildings, at least, were ready to be used. Trustees met on October 17, 1907, ratified the selection of the principal and elected the first faculty. Trustees thought it wasteful to let the new buildings sit empty for the better part of a year. They probably knew the Fourth District A&M School in Carrollton also had missed its September opening date and was planning to open its doors early in 1908.[12] The trustees decided to do the same at First District A&M.

During the intervening months, the principal-elect, J. Walter Hendricks, toured the countryside and talked with farmers about the advantages of sending their sons and daughters to the new school in Statesboro. He also made arrangements for faculty and staff to move to town and settle into their new quarters before school began. Meanwhile, Otto Tauber Harper, an agriculturalist, prepared a plot to serve as a demonstration farm. The trustees later set the opening date for February 5, 1908.[13]

PRINCIPAL JAMES WALTER HENDRICKS

Publicity about the new principal and faculty quelled public doubts about the new school. Considering the scarcity of university-educated men and women in rural Georgia, the trustees realized they would need to cast a wide net. Their choice for principal, J. Walter Hendricks, happened to be a native of Bulloch County, but he had accumulated some experience as an educator. At age thirty-four, he was both a teacher and principal at a school in Douglas, Georgia.

Hendricks graduated from the University of Georgia in Athens in 1897. As a student he took classes in agriculture and traditional subjects, in addition to military training. The studious Hendricks ranked third in his graduating class. At Athens he made some lifelong friends who also excelled in academics. One college companion who corresponded with Hendricks for many years was Roland Harper, who became an influential naturalist and ethnographer specializing in the rural South. While Harper focused his research and became a well-published regional authority, Hendricks was what his grandson once dubbed "a Victorian intellectual, a generalist." [14]

Hendricks, the "generalist," began his teaching career at age twenty-four. He returned to teach in the rural Georgia schoolroom in Millen where he had completed his public schooling in 1893. It was not a position he would settle into, but the experience helped him discover what he might do for a living.

Hendricks enjoyed his first job in Millen, and he made plans to pursue a career in the field of education. After teaching for a year, he learned of a faculty position opening at Holbrook Normal College, located in a suburb of Knoxville, Tennessee, for the fall of 1898. He applied for a job there and was appointed to the faculty. As a "normal college," Holbrook prepared elementary teachers and offered classes for high school students. The curriculum emphasized the standards or "norms" of instruction.[15] In Georgia he had taught children. In Tennessee he would be teaching teachers. He knew his subject matter well, but he realized he needed further instruction.

During the summer of 1898 he signed up for an intensive session at a highly regarded summer institute offered by the Northern Indiana Normal School. Henry Baker Brown and O. P. Kinsey taught the course. Their school became successful and influential among boards of education, particularly in the Midwest. In 1900 the school's trustees elevated its status, giving it a new name, Valparaiso University.[16] Among a student body of 2,500, Hendricks was the only Georgian. He said he enjoyed meeting "young people from the North, and . . . came to know them and understand them better." He described what he learned there in one plain sentence: "I enjoyed this experience and got the lowdown on many school methods." [17]

In Tennessee Professor Hendricks taught Latin, Greek, and other subjects. During his two years at Holbrook, he grew to enjoy his work on the edge of the Great Smoky Mountains. During his second year there, however, the school fell onto hard times and faced closure. Hendricks looked for a job nearer his native Bulloch County. He accepted a position on the small faculty of Southern Normal Institute in Douglas, Georgia. While there, he renewed his acquaintance with Nina Lively, the daughter of Dr. M. M. Lively, and in 1901 the two were married. Hendricks had met Nina and sister, Mattie, in 1893, when he lived briefly in Millen while completing his schooling.

From 1902 until 1907 he settled into both the marriage and the role of teacher and principal at Southern Normal Institute, an "independent normal school." Clearly he enjoyed living there, and the community honored him

South Main Street Extension

The view down South Main extended, as it looked from the Administration Building steps around 1920. A postcard, *below*, captured a neighborhood section of South Main Street in 1906.

1st View South Main Street, Statesboro, Ga.

as an educational leader. Locals probably noticed that Hendricks, already a dyed-in-the-wool Primitive Baptist, refused to attend Methodist services with the wife he recently had married. They also observed, perhaps, the young couple living together devotedly, while worshipping separately.[18]

ORIGINAL FACULTY AND STAFF

When the trustees formally appointed J. Walter Hendricks principal in October 1907, they also approved the first three faculty members—an agriculturalist, a home economist, and a mechanics instructor. The trustees searched for prospective faculty members, but Hendricks probably nominated the agriculture teacher. Hendricks learned that his friend from college, Roland Harper, had a brother named Otto who possessed practical knowledge as a farmer as well as academic training. The *Savannah Morning News* described Otto Harper as follows:

[He] was born in Massachusetts, but moved early in his life with his father to Georgia. He graduated from the University of Georgia a few years ago in the agricultural department, and since that time has been operating a farm in Whitfield County. He is a farmer by choice and profession and will doubtless be of inestimable benefit to the school and to the First district at large.[19]

Frank M. Rowan was the second faculty member named. The graduate of Cornell University recently had been managing a cotton mill in Tennessee. Rowan applied for the position in mechanics at First District A&M, following the advice of a mentor at the Georgia Institute of Technology.[20]

Josephine Schiffer became the third member of the faculty. She was hired to teach young women "domestic science." Schiffer brought to the new school an academic background equal or perhaps superior to that of other faculty members, including the principal. A graduate of the Drexel Institute of Philadelphia, she had successfully completed post-graduate classes at Columbia University.

JAMES WALTER HENDRICKS

Hendricks, the first principal of First District A&M School, was a native of Bulloch County. He graduated third in his class at the University of Georgia. After serving as principal for less than two years, he resigned and took up farming full-time. Later he became a successful and influential elder in the Primitive Baptist Church.

Students arriving

In 1908 the prevalent modes of transportation—trains and buggies—carried students to Statesboro's new A&M school. The East Hall dormitory, *left*, had only two stories.

Screven County, northeast of Bulloch County, provided many students for the school. They rode the train from Dover to Statesboro, using the Central of Georgia Depot on the northeast corner of Railroad and East Main Streets.

The early female faculty members deserved special praise, according to one first-hand observer. Writing in 1933, on the twenty-fifth anniversary of the institution, the original secretary of the board of trustees, James R. Miller, evaluated the first two female faculty members. Schiffer, he said, was "the hot brick of the whole organization." [21] He recalled she was "a smart German woman, an old maid." Miller was equally impressed with the woman who succeeded Schiffer: "Miss Estelle Bozeman [was] one of the best women in the world. Hundreds of women are scattered all over this country who were taught by her how to run a home in the proper manner." [22]

The first staff members to be appointed by trustees were matrons for the dormitories—Nina Hendricks for the girls of East Hall, and Ila Crumpler of Latta, South Carolina, for the boys of West Hall. Viola C. Adams of Bulloch County would operate the dining hall. A newspaper described her as "one of the best cooks within the confines of the state." The farm foreman, also a native of Bulloch County, was G. W. Kicklighter.[23]

Local citizens relished each bit of news about the administration, faculty, and staff of the First District A&M School. Some who went up the hill to observe the new buildings came back down amazed at the classic lines and stately columns of the red brick structures. Nothing else was equal to this arrangement of buildings in all of Bulloch County. Newspaper stories kept enthusiasm at a peak.

To others, however, the school appeared more promising in newsprint than in real life. Such was the experience of Professor Frank M. Rowan, who, encouraged by oral and written accounts of the school, had moved to Statesboro.

On a cold, blustery, wintry day, January 1, 1908, Mr. Hendricks met me at the depot in the "surrey." When we drove out to the school, I looked over the poor sand hill with scrub oak and pine bushes growing on it and was not particularly impressed. The school grounds were unswept, and the fields beyond had numbers of recently pulled pine stumps scattered over them.[24]

OTTO TAUBER HARPER
Harper was the first faculty member. He taught agriculture from 1908 until 1914.

FRANK M. ROWAN
Rowan, the second faculty member to be hired, was the first faculty member to go on to serve as principal.

The campus had an unfinished look. Students and laborers would work for several years to dig up stumps, remove them, and level the soil.

THE FIRST DAY OF THE FIRST SEMESTER

On Wednesday, February 5, 1908, students lined up at their dormitories upon completing after-breakfast chores and their rooms. Young men and women who arrived by horse and buggy (the first nonresident students) joined them. Expecting to attend opening exercises, they walked to the classroom and administration building. But inexplicably Principal Hendricks called off a formal opening convocation that day and informed professors to begin classes at the usual hour. First District Congressman Charles Edwards told the *Savannah Morning News* he would release to the press what he had intended to announce at the opening exercise. He was endowing an academic award in the form of a medal to be presented each year to "the student, girl or boy, who has the best general average for the year. This, I hope, will stimulate effort and be of some help to the college. This medal will be given at your commencements each year to the girl or boy making the best general average. It will be a gold medal and will be worth winning. I give this medal and wish it to be known as the Edwards Medal. I dedicate the gift in favor of my beloved father and mother, Hon. and Mrs. T. J. Edwards, and for that reason wish it known as the 'Edwards Medal.'" [25]

Although lacking in pomp and circumstance, Principal Hendricks' plans for the first day did include an assembly. The chairman of the board of trustees, J. Randolph Anderson, made a brief talk, followed with comments by J. B. Cone, a dentist and community leader. According to the *Savannah Morning News* on February 6, the most memorable remarks came from a faculty member, Josephine Schiffer, who "gave a full description of the work she hopes to accomplish, and during her interesting talk gave evidence that she will make a strong member of the faculty which the trustees have chosen."

How many students enrolled for the first term? Not as many as the trustees had wanted, according to the *Savannah Morning News*. The newspaper attributed the small attendance to the school's inconvenient opening date in February.[26] Published enrollment figures range from fifteen to seventy-five. Principal Hendricks recalled "some fifty or sixty students." [27] The *Savannah Morning News* on February 6 reported in a headline: "First District School opened with about 75 students." In his historical summary in 1952, President Emeritus Marvin S. Pittman wrote of the first day's attendance: "At the opening there were fifteen pupils and four teachers." [28] An end-of-term update, "In interest of District College," in the Savannah *Morning News*, May 15, 1908, noted the attendance at that time was thirty-five.

The earliest seat of learning

Slate blackboards wrapped around classrooms in the Academic or Administration building. Desks were sturdy pieces of well-crafted furniture. The desk pictured above bears the initials of Frank Miller, a member of the first class of students at the school. He became a newspaper editor in Pembroke, Georgia. His son, Homer Miller, preserved the desk.

While there may be uncertainty about the enrollment on the first day, there is little doubt about how many were enrolled at the end of the second month of the semester. Dan Bland, who attended the first class on February 5, 1908, copied names from the principal's roll that he found in 1948. Bland's list accounts for forty-two students on March 25—thirty-four boys and eight girls. Most of the boys lived in West Hall, but only three girls lived on campus in East Hall; the other female students returned to their homes after attending classes.[29]

THE CURRICULUM: "FROM EARLY MORNING TILL 7 PM"

Faculty assignments called for Professor Schiffer to teach home economics, Professor Rowan mechanics and mathematics, and Professor Harper agriculture, chemistry, and biology. Principal Hendricks taught English and physics.[30] The courses coincided, more or less, with the state's guidelines.

Professor Joseph Spencer Stewart of the University of Georgia announced the curriculum for A&M schools, at the request of Governor Terrell. The *Statesboro News* summarized the report in a front-page article, "What Will be Taught," on January 18, 1907. Stewart made clear "the work of the school continues from early morning till 7 p.m. . . . [after which] a two hours' study period closes the day's exercise at 9:30."

All students would spend one half of each day learning in classes devoted to core subjects:

- English (grammar, composition, classics of literature)
- Mathematics (arithmetic, algebra, geometry, accounting)
- Physics and Chemistry
- History and Civics (world and national history, economics)
- Science (horticulture, botany)
- Electives (foreign languages, modern history, science)

In A&M schools, practical learning supplemented classroom instruction: "In addition to the above hours . . . one half of every secular day is given to practice work in field, shop, orchard, and laboratories in practical instruction under teachers or higher students and in work for maintenance of [the] farm in all its parts."

Boys could anticipate a "practicum" in agricultural science at the school farm. This meant they would work in the fields and on the school grounds. Girls would learn "home science, including the study of foods, cooking, dining-room service, laundry, household emergencies, gardening, dairying, hand and machine work, simple dressmaking, millinery, home ornamentation, and household science . . . . We have also arranged for a certain amount of woodwork for the girls."

By 1912 the state's curriculum chart included more details about the courses. For example, students read the following literature: American and

JOSEPH SPENCER STEWART
Stewart, a professor of secondary education at the University of Georgia, prepared the curriculum guidelines for district A&M schools in 1906.

List of students after first six weeks

In 1948 Dan Bland, a member of the original class of students, copied the names on the principal's record book for March 25, 1908.

INSIDE THE ACADEMIC BUILDING

The Academic Building could accommodate three or four hundred pupils. The "modern" building featured both electricity and running water. Telephone connections with Statesboro provided communications with the nation.

The girls "have superb advantages offered by few schools. Domestic Science, Home Economics, Domestic Art, how to cut, fit and sew, the Model Home with all its advantages, and music under the direction of competent instructors."

The Academic Building also included a library. The leaders of the A&M school believed reading books was "absolutely essential." The bulletin for 1911 states: "Through the medium of books, one may come in possession of the thoughts, motives, aims and person of all ages. In order to keep abreast of the times in which we live and be familiar with the current of modern thought it is necessary to read newspapers and magazines."

Not yet landscaped, the Academic Building in 1910 included a flagpole on the roof of the porch.

A class in drawing and building design

Food preparation class in the domestic science laboratory

Learning to sew and design clothing

A view of the cotton laboratory

With round Tuscan columns, the Academic Building of 1909 had a flagpole on top.

British poetry and prose, featuring works by Cooper, Longfellow, Thoreau, Dickens, Tennyson, Milton, and Shakespeare. Classics included Homer's *Odyssey* and selected stories from the *Old Testament*. History classes covered world, American, and Georgia history. Practical subjects in agriculture had expanded to include geography, freehand drawing, surveying, and laboratory work. "Domestic arts and science" also involved the study of hygiene, home management, nursing, and dietetics.[31]

THE PRINCIPAL AND THE STUDENTS

The young women and men reflected the population of rural youth of southeast Georgia. Principal Hendricks later characterized some of them as "not such desirable students."[32] He pointed out that some "had been incorrigible in public schools. . . . Under this idea the school received some students who were not angelic at all. . . . The question of discipline was a very serious and difficult one." Hendricks recalled how he, armed with a wooden board—"a three foot piece of quarter round"—broke up a fight in the boys' dormitory and confiscated a "hat full of all kinds of pistols."[33]

The principal's negative evaluation of some members of the original student body should be viewed in context. He was a disciplinarian—not uncommon for rural principals. He also was a stern Primitive Baptist. Instead of praising students' virtue, he tended to ruminate on their misdeeds. There was a puritanical sternness in this man who lived the hardy life and loved the *Holy Bible*. His grandson recalled hearing Hendricks preach sermons filled with "venom and brimstone."[34]

Not surprisingly, the principal was a moralist, and a strict one, but he was able to laugh at the antics of youth. Hendricks wrote about giving a chapel talk against the use of profanity. Later, he said he was "walking in the corn field where four of the boys were plowing side by side, engaged in animated conversation." Hendricks said he listened unobserved and heard the following from one of the older students: "You boys remember about the professor giving us such a lecture about cussing. Well, I'm going to quit. I don't expect to cuss another d−−n bit."[35]

STRUGGLING TO SURVIVE

The first few years of the First District A&M were among the most difficult in its history. Newspaper accounts, official school reports, letters, and memoirs together tell the same sad story: the school stumbled at the start.

On March 12, 1908, only five weeks after the school opened, an alarmed trustee, James R. Miller, took the Savannah & Statesboro Railroad to Savannah. He met with the chairman of the board of trustees, attorney

> " *Some advantages of an industrial school*
>
> . . . . In our course of study the students' experience is more varied and consequently a wider sphere of knowledge is compassed. 'We learn to do by doing,' is a common educational phrase. It is probably nearer the truth to say, We learn by doing.'
>
> The best educational thinkers are now coming to believe that more genuine culture is gained from the proper study of a growing plant than from a course of Latin and Greek. And why not? If one learns the laws that govern the growth and development of a plant, the processes through which its soil home was made, the stages through which it must pass to fulfill its destined end it does seem that no amount of research and study of the 'dead languages' could be compared to such an accomplishment.
>
> Technical training in any line of work always assists in the higher development of the minds and hearts of the people. But when that technical training is based upon and accompanied by a thorough literary training, the symmetrical development of the whole being is guaranteed.
>
> We feel that we can honestly and conscientiously claim all of the above advantages for our school, and that its graduates will be the beneficiaries of such advantages. Therefore, we earnestly appeal to the people of the First Congressional District to lend their support to the school. "
>
> First District Agricultural and Mechanical School *Catalogue*, 1911-1912

who had played key roles in the great bidding war at Savannah in 1906—Mayor Robert Lee Moore, businessman J. Gordon Blitch, and the lawyer with the satchel, Albert Deal. Within a week of the trustees' announcement of closure, Moore, Blitch, and Deal requested an emergency meeting of the trustees.

In Savannah the three men invoked the spirit of 1906 and forcefully urged the twelve trustees to reconsider their decision. Their point was that in 1906 the people of Statesboro and Bulloch County did something quite unreasonable: they gathered $125,500 and bet it on the future. Facing merely a temporary budget shortfall now, they argued, should not stop the school in its tracks. They asked the trustees to lift their eyes from the ledger and look at the calendar; within a few months the state would provide funding. In the meantime, the people of Statesboro and Bulloch County could find a way to pay the bills.

An observer summarized the impact of the presentation: "It was made plain to the board that an injustice would be done the institution by allowing it to remain closed during the fall." The trustees listened to the three men from Statesboro and promptly "decided to yield to the request of those who had, at great expense, built the school, and opened it at the earliest date possible."[45] They announced that the fall term would begin as originally scheduled, on September 30, 1908. "Bulloch County Glad School to Be Reopened" was the headline everyone wanted to read, and it appeared on September 2 in the *Savannah Morning News:* "After the board rescinded its earlier decision, the people of Bulloch County and Statesboro are behind the school as never before."

The people of Statesboro and Bulloch County acted on December 1, 1906 to win the rights to their very own "college." Then they had raised their bids and their voices, shouting a collective "YES" to the future. In August 1908, they acted again. They stood together as one, and they spoke for the future. They said with one voice, and loudly, "NO!"

The school belonged to the people. This was the meaning of the message Statesboro sent to trustees from outlying counties. Now the larger board grasped, perhaps for the first time, the spirit of 1906. The community that won the school had returned to reclaim its ownership.

To underscore Bulloch County's commitment to the school, Moore and Deal attended the opening exercises on September 30, 1908. They spoke words of encouragement to the fifty students who had enrolled.

In other important ways that autumn, the community recovered from hard times. The *Savannah Morning News* reported an especially strong cotton market in Statesboro that fall. Nationally and locally, the economic picture was the brightest it had been in several years: "The town and county begins to look like itself once

Creative borrowing saves A&M school

The state did not provide all of the money originally allocated for the school, forcing trustees to borrow from individuals and banks. On March 26, 1908 the trustees took a loan from a local grocer, W. H. Kennedy, promising to repay him on October 1; they did not pay him until December 16. This transaction shows that trustees borrowed money on that day from the Sea Island Bank to repay Kennedy.

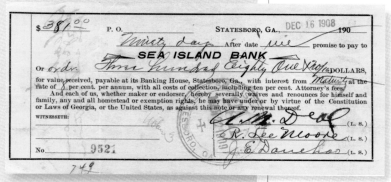

LEARNING TO GROW

Testing the Spaulding tilling machine, above. Corn breeding, below left;
student with the engine he built, middle right; young ladies preparing to plant, bottom.

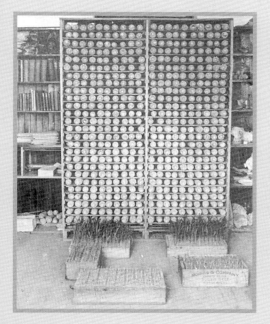 

more and memory of the panic is fast disappearing."[46] No doubt the "college on the hill," though small, shared the community's improved outlook.

THE 'CULTURE EMERGES

It works subtly, this delicate and hard-to-measure something that is the lifeblood of an academic institution. Call it "school spirit"—a tradition as old as England's Oxford and Cambridge. In this case the tradition had a name, and students probably invented it. They began to call their school the 'Culture or De 'Culture. Perhaps the expression began as early as 1907 when African American laborers casually shortened "Agriculture" and added the vernacular handle. For the next two decades students and locals alike preferred the moniker De 'Culture as a term of institutional endearment.

'Culture worked magically as a nickname for the school. The faculty all had studied Latin, and they knew the word stems from *cultus*—to till or cultivate the soil, as in "agriculture."[47] The term also carries the weight of a noble concept. Did 'Culture Hill not embody the hopes and dreams of both students and the community? Did it not symbolize the upwardly mobile aspirations of an entire generation? That must have been what Lonnie Brannen had in mind when he editorialized in 1901 about the need to establish a college. The institution would fundamentally improve the moral and intellectual quality of life—the culture—of the larger community.[48]

The late physician of Savannah, Dr. Julian Quattlebaum, grew up on North Main Street in Statesboro. He attended the Statesboro Institute from 1903 until his graduation in 1913. He recalled how he and everyone he knew used the term De 'Culture, especially, as a nickname for athletic teams.[49]

I played in many baseball games between the Statesboro Institute and De 'Culture, when I was a boy and was quarterback for the Statesboro Institute against De 'Culture in the first football game ever played in Bulloch County, and for your information we got beat 18 to 3. The boys who played for De 'Culture were from farms and used to real work and were tough, and they really gave us a working over, that I at least have never forgotten.[50]

The spirit of the 'Culture, born in hard times, symbolized the new attitude on campus and around town. Even though the enrollment in the autumn of 1908 was smaller than trustees had wanted, they surely realized the outlook for the school had changed after its poor beginning earlier that year. The First District A&M School once seemed rudderless, and all on board had sailed through rough waters. Now, however, it appeared that students and faculty, perhaps for the first time, realized the community really believed in them. Instead of bemoaning what the legislature or trustees had left undone, the

Postcard of North Main Street in 1908.

administration, faculty, and students began to take initiatives to improve the school they shared with a community.

Some farmers had ridiculed Otto Harper for sterilizing hoe handles and wearing a stiff white collar as he worked in the field.[51] But they began to change their opinion as they heard about the fruits of his students' labor. Land the farmers considered "poor" produced fifteen bales of superior cotton in the fall of 1908, under Harper's management. The harvest of sugar cane, peas, and potatoes was equally impressive.[52] Harper also endeared himself to the entire community when he obtained for the school, without cost, a seven-hundred-volume library of agricultural books.[53]

The fall session ended on a high note. The faculty and principal announced an "educational open house" during the week of December 15–19.[54] Domestic science students would serve sandwiches, hot coffee, pies, and cakes. Principal Hendricks wrote a letter to the newspapers, inviting the public to the open house and two lectures. The speakers included Professor C. L. Goodrich of Washington, D. C., and the principal's classmate at the University of Georgia, Robert John Henderson DeLoach. DeLoach, a native of Bulloch County, referred to as "our John" in the newspaper, planned to speak about problems of cultivating cotton, the selection of seeds, and the importance of bird life for agriculture. DeLoach then was preparing to publish his research conducted at the Georgia Experiment Station in Athens.[55]

The school enrolled eighty-five students on its first day of classes in 1909. The headline in the *Statesboro News* for January 19, 1909, proclaimed: "College on a Boom." The semester seemed to be packed with news of growth and progress. The students, perhaps led by Professor Schiffer, organized a debating society, called the Persephonians.[56] Principal Hendricks invited private and public schools in the first district to participate in a literary and athletic meet on the campus. The news kept getting better each week, and newspapers in Savannah and Statesboro printed a number of articles describing the school's progress.

When Governor-elect Joseph M. Brown visited Statesboro, the mayor organized a parade from the courthouse to the 'Culture. Schiffer's students in domestic science prepared a luncheon, and the governor-elect toured the farm. Brown entertained the audience afterward with some spontaneous remarks about his early experiences with agriculture: "My father said that he wanted to give me some constitution. I remember now that when I was out hoeing it seemed that he was not only going to give me a constitution but the by-laws too."[57]

Principal Hendricks began to play a more visible role in the community. He wrote a newspaper column for farmers in south Georgia. His sermonlike message was conservative by any standard. He stated that rural people are morally superior to those who live in the city. Agricultural education, he

ROBERT JOHN HENDERSON DELOACH
An early lecturer at First District A&M School, DeLoach joined the faculty of South Georgia Teachers College in 1932.

He was told to employ such means as would bring this about, and warned not to come back to the next annual meeting of the board with any excuses at all, but to bring results." The article in the *Statesboro News* concludes with a revealing comment: "This is the people's school, and they are expected to come up and assist the faculty and board of trustees in making it a success."[66]

Twice during the summer of 1909 the trustees intervened in the day-to-day operations of the A&M school. First, to defuse a highly charged scandal, and second, to respond to local critics of the school farm. None of the newspaper articles describing the interventions mentioned the role, if any, J. Walter Hendricks played. Undoubtedly the principal was at odds with the governing authority. Confessing he was upset and disillusioned, the principal decided to leave his job shortly after beginning the 1909–10 school term. Hendricks revealed his reasons in his *Autobiography*:

Soon after opening the term for 1909-1910, I became deeply disturbed and greatly dissatisfied. I could not get on very well with the local trustee from Bulloch County [J. R. Miller] who lived in Statesboro and had very much to do with the general oversight of the school. Rather than have a run in with him and maybe a general upset with the entire board which consisted of one man from each county in the First Congressional District, I decided to resign . . . This ended my career as a teacher . . . I moved back to Douglas, Georgia, in the end of 1909 and began my career as a farmer.

In Douglas Hendricks ran a farm successfully and organized agricultural clubs for young farmers. Later he felt the call to the gospel ministry and became an elder in the Primitive Baptist Church, a cause to which he was faithful until his death in 1962.

Hendricks had the mind of a moralist. When he recalled his brief tenure as principal, he tended to focus on those students who misbehaved. The youth enrolled at his school were, he said, "not such desirable students," "incorrigible," and "not angelic at all." When he reflected on the first students some twenty-five years later, he remembered them as spoiled and undisciplined:

The school had its beginning in a time of great financial depression then called a "panic." But when prosperity came, as it did come, and the first principal had resigned, it was harder than ever to carry on the school as formerly. The students not only did not want to work, but they saw no great necessity for it; their parents did not want them to work, and soon the school began to enter upon great and serious changes.[67]

James R. Miller, and perhaps others, took note of the fact that the roll book at the A&M school included the offspring of some highly regarded families in Bulloch and neighboring counties. Frank Miller, a student in the first class of 1908, was Miller's son. The student body included young women and men with such prominent family names as Anderson, Bland, Blitch, Brannen, Bunce, Donaldson, Everett, Johnson, Jones, Franklin, Kennedy, Lester, Moore, Olliff, Rigdon, Simmons, and Waters. These families were the backbone of a community that had supported the A&M school from its infancy.

The stress and tension J. Walter Hendricks acknowledged so candidly probably would have continued as long as he sat behind the principal's desk.

Elder J. Walter Hendricks

Several years after leaving the A&M school, J. Walter Hendricks felt the call to serve as an elder in the Primitive Baptist Church. In time he became a beloved leader in this denomination.

When he exchanged that desk for a pulpit, however, he came into his own. His departure was itself a form of pilgrimage. In time he found his true calling outside of academia, and in his later years, he gained a reputation as one of the progressive forces of his denomination. He neither sought nor accepted a generous salary, and he and his family lived a Spartan existence as "tenants of the Lord." [68] Often he paid his own way and personally aided the poor and needy.

After resigning from his job as principal of the A&M School, he ended his career as an educator, but at age eighty he returned to the field he long ago had abandoned. He founded a Bible college in Thomasville, Georgia. On many occasions during his career as pastor and itinerant evangelist, he visited the Statesboro campus. Then, he was a highly regarded churchman. Faculty members and administrators enjoyed meeting the first principal, and they listened to his occasional messages of inspiration and advice.

Hendricks was the first of three principals who briefly served the school before moving on to other fields of endeavor. To review his brief tenure as principal is to be reminded of the forces that shaped and nurtured the First District A&M School during its infancy. When Hendricks was principal, the school refused to crumble, in spite of several hard knocks.

A common truth for individuals and institutions is that survival precedes success. Within a relatively short time, the school on the hill became the symbol of a community's resolve. It survived because the community would not allow it to do otherwise.

During critical moments in the early history of First District A&M, someone always seemed ready to step forward and say, with James R. Miller, "This is the people's school." The character of the early institution revealed itself during those times of crisis and struggle. The people who envisioned a college for Statesboro paid a premium for it, not only in 1906 but also in subsequent years when they borrowed money and intervened to keep the school on course.

The spirit of 1906 is more than mere sentiment. It is bold, sometimes sacrificial, action. Citizens of South Georgia also believed the A&M school symbolized their aspirations. When they saw their dream slipping away, they forcibly grasped it from the hands of those all-too-reasonable advisors who would shut the doors of learning rather than incur temporary debt. They fought for the good name of the "people's school," and they deflected harsh criticism. This positive, sometimes aggressive, spirit reemerged at critical moments during the school's first decade when south Georgians nurtured the fledgling school. In those days students, faculty, and citizens together learned to share a loyalty for a special place, their very own 'Culture.

Demerits: How to keep the young folks moral

Why did the A&M school issue demerits to students who misbehaved?

First, students who received them knew their shortcomings. Second, the school received free labor at a time when there was much work to do and little funding.

Students would "work off" demerits by digging up stumps, caring for livestock, chopping firewood, and digging holes for fence posts. Students caught engaging in the most serious offense—smoking—received five demerits. Littering cost two and unauthorized visiting only one demerit.

Students who accumulated demerits could not graduate without "working them off" at a rate of one hour per demerit. The mechanics teacher, Frank M. Rowan, monitored this system of discipline in 1909.

The Campus Farm

Pigs and cattle once roamed the front campus, later known as Sweetheart Circle. This photograph of 1911, *right*, shows pigs of various ages enjoying a meal in view of the three original buildings.

Professor of Agriculture, Otto Harper, introduced students to scientific methods of farming, including a sanitary poultry house, *middle left*, and the Spaulding disc plow, *middle right*. Harper typically wore a vest and tie, covered by overalls. In this photograph, an early campus mascot, a hound dog, joins him in the field. A student operates the new deep-digging plow. The cabbage patch, *bottom*, with its king-sized plants, attracted local farmers who admired the results of the model farm.

TO BUILD THE PEOPLE'S SCHOOL
1909-1929

1909 – Students buy a "foot ball" and begin practicing a new sport. (11/30)

1909 – R. J. H. DeLoach of Statesboro inducted into Royal Society of Science. (12/20)

1910 – American humorist and novelist Mark Twain dies at the age of seventy-four. (4/21)

1910 – Three seniors make up the first graduating class. (6/2)

1910 – Enrollment of 180 is largest of the state's A&M schools. (9/1)

1911 – Crowd of three thousand hears Governor Hoke Smith at school graduation and picnic. (5/30)

1911 – Principal Emmette Charles Jones Dickens publishes first catalog of the A&M school. (7/25)

1911 – Built mostly by A&M students under the direction of Frank M. Rowan, new dining hall/dormitory is ready. (11/30)

1911 – Former students James Rogers and Elizabeth Johnson wed in Savannah— the first alumni to marry. (12)

1912 – New Mexico becomes the forty-seventh state. (1/1) Arizona becomes the forty-eighth state (2/1).

1912 – The *Titanic* strikes an iceberg, sinks, and causes more than 1,500 people to lose their lives. (4/14)

1914 – First major fire on campus destroys school barn and omnibus. (2/6)

1914 – J. Randolph Anderson, chairman of trustees, runs unsuccessful race for governor of Georgia. (6/2)

1914 – Archduke Francis Ferdinand is assassinated in Sarajevo, Bosnia. (6/28) Germany declares war on France and invades Belgium the next day. (8/03)

1914 – Emmette Charles Jones Dickens, suffering ill health, resigns as principal. Frank M. Rowan, professor of mechanical arts, becomes third principal. (12)

1915 – U.S. House of Representatives rejects bill to permit women to vote. (1/10)

1915 – First transcontinental phone call placed, from New York to San Francisco. (1/25)

1915 – Albert Deal and J. Randolph Anderson arrange loan of $12,000 from Sea Island Bank to prevent school's bankruptcy. (1/30)

1915 – Hughie Galbreath of Lyons is first student to die on campus. (4/10)

1915 – H. P. Sloan, graduate of Georgia Tech, is new coach of A&M teams. (8/26)

1915 – School introduces first teacher education classes that quickly become the most popular on campus. (9/15)

1916 – U.S. president Woodrow Wilson appoints Justice Louis Brandeis as the first Jewish supreme court justice. (1/28)

1916 – Trustees consider and reject request to sell northeast part of campus for a meat-processing plant or packinghouse. (5/18)

1916 – Voters of Montana elect pacifist Jeanette Rankin as the first woman to serve in the U.S. House of Representatives. (11/6)

1916 – Oglethorpe and Stephens literary societies hold hotly contested debate on the merits of U.S. president Woodrow Wilson. (11/6)

1916 – Football team defeats Savannah High 12–0 at annual Thanksgiving Day game. (11/23)

1917 – The military draft begins in the United States. (1/1)

1917 – Professor C. S. Folk explains benefits of new military training program. (1/25)

1917 – The United States enters World War I when it declares war on Germany. (4/6)

1917 – Bulloch County School Superintendent B. R. Olliff supports expanded program of classes for teachers at A&M. (5/10)

1918 – Largest graduation class to date (twenty-five) receives A&M diplomas. (5/23)

1918 – World War I ends when Germany signs armistice with the Allies. (11/11)

1919 – James Allen Bunce History Award begun by Allen Hamilton Bunce. (6/1)

1919 – Esten Graham Cromartie is named new 'Culture football coach, and his assistant, George H. Aull, is named director of the military science program. (8/28)

1920 – Prohibition begins after ratification of the 18th amendment to the U.S. Constitution. (1/16)

1920 – Women's basketball team, Farmettes, beats Savannah High. (2/12)

1920 – " 'Culture's Lads and Lassies" win state literary meet in Athens. (4/29)

1920 – Frank M. Rowan resigns as principal. New principal is Ernest Victor Hollis. (5/6)

1921 – Babe Ruth hits fifty-nine homeruns, setting the homerun record in U.S. baseball.

1921 – Principal Hollis organizes school's first alumni association, building on previous support by former students. Luther Zeigler of Savannah is president. (5/21)

1921 – Albert Einstein wins the Nobel Prize for Physics. (12/10)

1922 – J. Randolph Anderson resigns as chairman of trustees but continues to work for school. John E. McCroan is elected as new chairman. (5/22)

1922 – New football coach, Dan C. McKinnis of Mississippi, introduces one week of preseason football practice. (8/10)

1923 – School property now worth $125,000, says Principal Hollis. (1/1/)

1923 – Enrollment drops to 109 students. (1/10)

1923 – Alumni Association formally votes to meet each year at graduation. (5/23)

1923 – U.S. president Harding dies in office; Vice President Calvin Coolidge is inaugurated as president. (8/12)

1923 – Ex-UGA star, Mark Anthony, thrills fans when he agrees to serve as A&M football coach and athletic director. His nickname is "the noblest Roman of them all." (8/12)

1924 – Trustees ask legislature to change A&M school into a junior college, specializing in "normal subjects" for public schools. (1/17)

1924 – Alumni Association votes to plant trees bordering entrance to campus. (5/23)

1924 – Principal Hollis introduces summer normal classes for teachers. More than two hundred enroll. (6/8)

1924 – New staff includes Maud Benson, "dining hall matron," and P. L. Ivester, farm manager. (8/7)

1924 – Legislature approves Bill 514, changing A&M school to Georgia Normal School, a junior college. (8/18)

1924 – Burrus Matthews becomes first dean of Georgia Normal School.

1924 – Normal School's new newspaper, *Station G.N.S.*, replaces *'Culture Bulldog*.

1925 – Tennessee bans the teaching of evolution. (3/21)

1925 – Edith Johnson becomes the first foreign language teacher at the institution. (8/27)

1925 – Students plan first yearbook, as yet unnamed. (10/25)

1925 – George Bernard Shaw wins the Nobel Prize for Literature. (12/10)

1926 – Guy Wells, superintendent of the school system in Eastman, is named dean when Burrus Matthews becomes head of education department.

1926 – New auditorium is ready for graduation. (6/7)

1926 – Summer session for teachers attracts nearly three hundred. (6/24)

1926 – After serving one month, Dean Guy Wells becomes president when Ernest Hollis resigns to complete his PhD. Ernest Anderson is new dean. (8/26)

1926 – Bulloch County Board of Education and Georgia Normal jointly fund Sunnyside School on campus as a laboratory school for training teachers. (10/10)

1927 – President Wells begins four-year curriculum, planning to transform school into a four-year college. (1/20)

1927 – One of the earliest social clubs is formed as female students join "leading ladies" club, the "Dux Domina." (4/7)

1927 – The freshman class publishes the first *George-Anne,* the third student newspaper to serve the school. (4/12)

1927 – The baseball team is called the "Normal Nine." (4/12)

1927 – Popular dean, Ernest Anderson, dies suddenly. The new dean is Zach Suddath Henderson. (4/21)

1927 – New tennis court stimulates interest in a new campus sport. (5/2)

1927 – Annual Field Day becomes "May Day," featuring a pageant, maypole, and crowning of the "Queen of May." (5/5)

1927 – Charles Lindbergh is first person to fly solo across the Atlantic. (5/21)

1927 – Teachers attend summer school in record number of 450, creating a housing crisis on campus and in the community. (6/16)

1927 – Legislature pays off school's cumulative debt of $45,000. (9/16)

1927 – The world's first talking movie, *The Jazz Singer*, debuts in October, featuring Al Jolson. (10/6)

1927 – New nickname for football team introduced, "Blue Tide." Star players are Loy Waters and Delmas Rushing. (11/3)

1928 – Faculty Club is organized and hosts a social event at the "Teacherage." (11/23)

1928 – Georgia Normal accepted into American Association of Teachers Colleges. (2/1)

1928 – New post office for campus approved: "Studentsboro." Within a month the U. S. Post Office changes name to "Collegeboro." (8/30)

1929 – First museum on campus, located in the administration building, is named in honor of original chairman of trustees, J. Randolph Anderson. (6/29)

1929 – Georgia Normal becomes a four-year college, South Georgia Teachers College. (8/18)

1929 – Following a week of stock market declines, Wall Street crashes. The Great Depression begins as 20,000 companies and most banks go bankrupt. (10/29)

THE VIEW FROM CULTURE HILL

TRUSTEES TAKE CHARGE

The trustees were not pleased with the progress of the First District A&M School after its first year-and-a-half. Around fifty students matriculated in the second full-year class. When Principal J. Walter Hendricks abruptly severed his ties with the school on November 3, 1909, enrollment had dropped to forty students.[1] Furthermore, the school had accumulated debts of $6,000. Creditors became uneasy, and some local merchants doubted the school could ever pay its past-due bills.[2]

Earlier that summer the board of trustees assumed control of fiscal affairs and farm operations. Sensing the school might collapse without vigorous leadership, they saw Hendricks' resignation as an opportunity to reshape the struggling school. They named as principal one of their own—Trustee Emmette Charles Jones Dickens. A newspaper editor and former Baptist minister from Vidalia, Dickens had helped organize the Union Baptist Institute (which became Brewton-Parker Institution in 1912) and once was president of its board of trustees.

A graduate of Mercer University, Dickens had earned an advanced degree in theology from the Southern Baptist Theological Seminary in Louisville, Kentucky. Board members had been impressed with his promotional articles and supportive editorials in newspapers he edited —the *Vidalia Advance* and the *Stillmore Leader*.[3] He had testified before the legislature in 1906, advocating the A&M school bill. The *Atlanta Georgian* generously praised him:

No venture he ever undertook failed, so it has come to be kind of a proverb that "Dickens" is synonymous with success. . . . Mr. Dickens is comparatively a young man yet, and his future is bright with prospects. He is a human dynamo of energy, and his fine executive ability, his learning, and his deep devotion to education and his high Christian character are a guarantee that the First District Agricultural School is going to be one of the very best of its kind in the state and country.[4]

Dickens, as an active board member, already knew the school had four basic weaknesses: poor funding, low enrollment, unattractive grounds, and limited support in the region. Even before Hendricks had removed his belongings, the new principal went to work with energy and enthusiasm. Local civic clubs and schools quickly became familiar with the tall, angular, energetic president. The town and campus buzzed with talk about this new leader who was bringing new life to the 'Culture.[5]

> " You have built and equipped the finest plant of any of the eleven district agricultural schools. The school should be the pride of Bulloch County. . . . The outlook for students for the spring term is, indeed, flattering. They will come to us from many counties, even beyond the limits of our district. "
>
> Emmette Charles Jones Dickens, *Statesboro News*, 30 December 1909

Students noticed two big changes: first, landscaping. Dickens wanted to transform the stump-laden front campus into an inviting entrance. After classes each day, the principal gathered the young men together and passed out shovels and pecan seedlings. Students dug up stumps and planted the young trees on both sides of the entrance near the administration building.

The second change thrilled the student body. The new principal immediately approved the addition of a new sport. Late in November 1909, students began practicing football. The 'Culture would be ready to face opponents by the beginning of the 1910 football season.[6]

While other school employees enjoyed time off for the Christmas holidays, the local press noted Principal Dickens and agriculturalist Otto Harper were "getting things in shape for the opening of the spring term on January 5th."[7] Dickens clearly had an appetite for hard work. He wanted to do more than salvage an academic year that had begun poorly. He was intent on quickly turning the school into "the pride of Bulloch County."[8]

In June 1910 the first graduates of First District A&M School received their diplomas: James Arthur Bunce, Clayton Hollingsworth, and Juanita Strickland. Bunce and Strickland were from Bulloch County, and Hollingsworth grew up near Dover in Screven County.[9] Bunce was the first to win the Edwards Medal for excellence, established in 1908.

Clearly the tide had turned. Within a year of Principal Hendricks' departure, First District A&M had grown from the smallest to the largest A&M school in the state. The Georgia Department of Education reported, "The total attendance of the eleven schools for the first complete year was 1,001. For this year the enrollment is between 1,200 and 1,300. The enrollment of the schools varies from about 45 to 180, the First District having the latter number."[10]

PUTTING A&M SCHOOL ON THE MAP

Principal Dickens welcomes William Jennings Bryan, June 1911

Front row, *left to right:* David Turner, Henry Olliff, Bird DeLoach, Wiley Williams, unknown, James R. Miller (not confirmed), William Jennings Bryan, J. A. Brannen, *behind, with umbrella*, E. C. J. Dickens, Gordon Blitch, Raymond Kennedy, Howell Cone, Sam Groover, and Julian J. E. Anderson. Back row: unknown, Sheldon Paschal, Brooks Simmons, Mrs. & Mr. Paschal (hotel operators), Edward Conyers Oliver, J. Ewell Brannen, *bottom step.*

On May 30, 1911 Dickens organized a barbecue and picnic to coincide with the second commencement. Using his political connections in Atlanta, he arranged to have Governor Hoke Smith speak. He knew that farmers, especially, were wild about the "down to earth" leader. Enthusiastic citizens turned out in droves, making the crowd one of the largest ever to assemble in Bulloch County.

The response amazed everyone, including Dickens. The *Statesboro News* estimated that three thousand people gathered for the graduation, followed by a meal and speech by Governor Smith.[11] Later, the principal spoke, and the crowd cheered when he reported "enrollment for the next term is nearing the 200 mark, and that with ample accommodation the number can be increased to 300." Listeners also clamored for a few words by the popular chairman of the board of trustees, J. Randolph Anderson.

Realizing the event symbolized far more than his words could express, Anderson eloquently reminded the audience the school really belonged to them.

Anderson had ordered extra passenger trains for the occasion. His Savannah and Statesboro Railroad overflowed early and late in the day, as passengers from coastal and southeast Georgia arrived and departed. The Central of Georgia's passenger cars also were packed to capacity. James R. Miller, editor of the *Statesboro News*, described what must have been a first-class traffic jam:

Every automobile in the city was pressed into service, and every livery team put to work. Regular runs were made to and from the city, [and] the road leading to the school and South Main Street out of town was almost impassable for several hours, owing to the congestion of the traffic in moving the great crowds.[12]

The principal created an aura of excitement when he hosted the popular Governor Hoke Smith. The same electricity swept through town twelve days later as he greeted William Jennings Bryan, "the great commoner" of Nebraska who thrice was the presidential candidate of the Democratic Party. Bryan was in Statesboro to speak, and Principal Dickens posed by his side in a group photograph at the Jaeckel Hotel. That evening Bryan delivered his spellbinding lecture, "The Prince of Peace." A year later he would become the secretary of state under U.S. President Woodrow Wilson.[13]

The school finally had turned the corner. Farmers realized the 'Culture deserved respect, and they began to send their teenagers there in record numbers. Winning over the doubters had not been easy. Yet Dickens could not for a moment enjoy his leadership triumph. Just around the corner awaited potential problems of major proportions.

When the trustees met in early June, Dickens showed them a large pile of applications for the fall term. At that point dozens could not be considered for one reason: lack of dormitory space and dining facilities. Furthermore, the dining hall—a small white building near the school farm—was painfully overcrowded.[14]

The choice was simple: either limit the enrollment or enlarge the facilities. A more conservative administration would have restricted admissions, but Anderson and Dickens acted on faith. The school must grow in spite of poor funding, they said. For the first time in its brief history, First District A&M's trustees decided to build for growth, while admitting they had no money to pay for it.

How to gain a fourth building for the campus—and without funding— was the question. The principal's answer was bold: build it for the cost of materials only. The school had a mechanical engineer on the faculty, Frank M. Rowan. Those farm-reared male teenagers in the student body already knew how to push shovels, swing hammers, and work with saws. Most had done this kind of hard work at home. Rowan, who served as architect, also assumed the roles of contractor and site foreman.

FRANK M. ROWAN
Supervisor of Anderson Dining Hall contruction

The story of Anderson Dining Hall

" I drew up the plans . . . We started to work with day labor, principally boys, under my supervision. The boys did all the excavating, made the window and door frames and put down all flooring and ceiling. We hired several masons and one carpenter, and I put in ten hours per day 'bossing.' This building was put up with the idea of plenty of room and cheapness uppermost in our minds. It has served very efficiently and has been a big asset to the institution when cost and other conditions are considered. "

Frank M. Rowan,
Statesboro News, 6 June 1911

THE FIRST ANDERSON HALL

For nearly fifty years Anderson Hall was like home—an inviting place to meet others, share meals, form friendships, and visit faculty and other students who lived upstairs. It symbolized what alumni often recalled with relish: the taste of home-cooked food, the comfort of friendships, and the sheer pleasure of a welcoming place. That is what "Old Anderson" meant to thousands of students from 1911 until the wrecking crew of progress demolished it in 1959.[15]

The generously gabled wooden and red-brick structure featured rambling porches on the second and third floors. The dining room and kitchen took up most of the first floor. The hall that students built quickly became their favorite building.

Prof. Rowan and Pres. Dickens are exceedingly busy gathering material and erecting a large two story brick building on the school campus, the lower floor to be used for a dining room and kitchen and is constructed so as to have a seating capacity of 250 people at the table at one time, the second story to be for the President's home and for a dormitory for quite a number of girls.

Statesboro News,
25 July 1911

"Anderson Hall and the original barn were built largely by the labor of the faculty and the students during the principalship of Mr. Dickens. Present day 'oldsters' in the area who were 'youngsters' in 'the old days' indulge in telling some 'tall tales' of their heroic efforts and achievements back in those pioneer times—house building, wood chopping, stump digging, tree planting, landscaping—much of which was done as a means of 'working off demerits.' They would have this generation believe that 'there were giants in those days.' We of this generation are caused to meditate upon the simplicity of life and the cheapness of labor—and to yearn for the simple life which we have not known and shall never know—except in imagination."

Marvin S. Pittman[16]

Tennis partners stand below the bell tower.

◄ The new dining hall, ca. 1912. ▲ A driveway connected Anderson to Sweetheart Circle.

▲ Anderson Dining Hall was located behind the Administration-Academic Building.

OLD BELL TOWER

A small tower in Anderson Hall, *top right,* attracted attention, because it held a bell that rang until 1940, when an electric bell replaced it. This relic of the early days of the A&M school originally was in a wooden bell tower near the Administration Building. Students rang it as one of their assigned daily tasks. In Anderson Dining Hall the bell assumed a place of dignity, and several generations of scholars grew accustomed to the deep tones that chimed the hours of the day.

In a well-crafted article in the *George-Anne* in 1941, Jimmy Jones described how he climbed into the tower and discovered the bell had been cast in 1889, the year of the Johnstown flood. He reminded readers of the significance of the old bell and called on the administration to restore it and use it as a tribute to the past:

Don't you know that its ringing would bring back cherished memories to the old, old grads at homecomings? Why not replace the rope and ring it before major ball games and other events?

Philadelphia has the famous old Liberty Bell that played so great a part in the birth of a nation, but G.T.C. has that historical old bell that dealt a hand in the birth of a famous institution.[17]

◄ Anderson dining hall in 1947 viewed from the southeast.

▲ Old Anderson Hall was a favorite place to "hang out" in 1948.

Chairman Anderson told trustees he would speak to the governor and explain how the state-supported school could gain a large new building for only the cost of materials, estimated at $4,000.[18] Governor Smith, who earlier had been enthusiastically received by the huge crowd on campus, encouraged the project. By the fall of 1911 the new dormitory and dining hall was ready. The materials and furnishings for this and two smaller buildings actually cost $7,500, but the new dormitory/dining hall was both a beauty and a bargain.

Finding the namesake for the first new building was easy. Trustees selected one who had been an advocate for the school since bidding day in 1906—the Honorable Jefferson Randolph Anderson. The chairman of the board of trustees had loyally and tirelessly supported the school, even while he practiced law in Savannah, served as president of the Savannah & Statesboro Railroad, and represented Chatham County ably in the state legislature.

Knowing the budget would be tight until the legislature provided funds for Anderson Hall and other projects, Dickens and Harper decided to turn the farm into a source of revenue. In 1911 student farmers produced corn, cotton, and dairy products that added nearly $6,000 to the school's treasury.[19]

Another innovation with Dickens' name attached was the annual catalog and bulletin. He prepared an attractive introduction to the school, its faculty, and courses for the year 1911–12. Several photographs illustrated the buildings and programs in agriculture and mechanics. Each year, until the 1920s, successive A&M publications improved upon earlier ones, both in content and layout.

The bulletin for 1913–14 features rare photographs, including a view of Anderson Hall with wraparound porches on the second and third levels. The pages also reflect well on the work of faculty with students, presenting views of classrooms and the entire graduating class of 1913. Realizing, perhaps, that the best advertisements for the school are its graduates, Dickens included a number of essays by alumni and current seniors. The following wrote generally well-crafted essays on the relevance of their education at the A&M school: George M. Futch, '11; Alex Futch, '12; Jessie Newton, '13; Jack Norman, '13; Nannie Thompson, '13; Sallie Thompson, '13; Doyle Dasher, '14; and Hattie Belle Delk, '14.

A member of the first graduating class of 1910, James Arthur Bunce returned to write "Three Years after Graduation." He recalled his senior essay on the topic "Why a country boy should stay on the farm." His own experience as a young farmer revealed the practical value of his education at

Annual catalog and bulletins

Principal Emmette Charles Jones Dickens published the first annual bulletins meant to introduce students to the school and faculty. Students and alumni also wrote essays chronicling their experiences at the institution.

First District A&M. He also noted how often he applied in the real world those lessons he learned in the classroom and laboratory. He concluded with advice to future farmers: "You have got to study your profession as the doctor does his. Our experience will be worth a great deal more to us after we have made a thorough study of the science of farming."[20]

Even though Principal Dickens enjoyed success in almost every endeavor, he could not pay off all the debts he inherited and incurred. The failure began with the state treasury, which habitually was tardy in sending the annual allotment of funds. At times the amount was less than promised. Understandably, some excellent faculty members left the school in search of more secure jobs. Professor Otto Harper, for example, had married Mary Cone, and the young couple could not begin a family without a reliable income. So he resigned in 1914 and took a job as an agricultural agent in Tattnall County.[21]

A devastating fire swept through some farm buildings on a cold February morning in 1914, destroying the sole means of transportation on campus—the horse-drawn omnibus. Although student enrollment continued to be strong, and the school had garnered an excellent reputation locally and regionally, Dickens struggled throughout the year to deal with the budget crisis. He approached foundations and individuals with little success. The population seemed obsessed with the specter of war in Europe. The national economy faltered.[22]

During the summer of 1914, the normally hale and hearty principal caught a bad cold and could not shake it off. He kept working relentlessly, even as his body grew weak. On October 3, 1914, he took the S&S to Savannah and called on the chairman of the trustees, J. Randolph Anderson. Anderson wrote later that day:

It is the first time I have seen him since early part of August, and he has been quite sick (ought to be still in bed I think) so of course I could do nothing but sit & talk or rather let him talk. I felt very sorry for him for he has a dreadful load on his shoulders in that school. He owes bills for it all about, & the State is behind in its remittances, so the poor man is being badgered and hounded with claims and is daily faced with suits and threats of suits till he is nearly crazy.[23]

Two months later Dickens, still beset with illness, decided to retire. Frank M. Rowan—faculty member and in-house architect/contractor—became principal, effective in January. Dickens had reason to have confidence in his friend and colleague during the past six years.

TRANSITION AND TRADITION

Just as the trustees did in the fall of 1909, when the school appeared hopelessly adrift, again in 1915 they acted as one. Trustee chairman J. Randolph Anderson decided to speak at graduation that spring.

Farming for revenue

Principal Dickens and Professor Harper, shown here in the agriculture laboratory, decided to use the school farm and students as a source of revenue for the school during tough economic times. The woman pictured is unknown.

First A&M bus destroyed

The omnibus that carried students to town burned in a fire in 1914 along with some farm buildings.

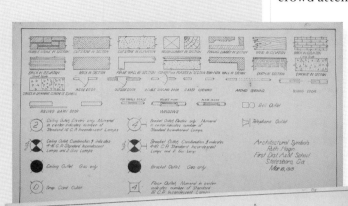

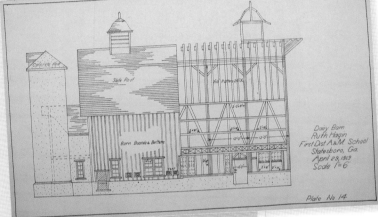

Student assignments

Drawing assignment, *above*, by Ruth Hagin, one of five Hagin sisters who attended the First District A&M School.

In the 1920s female students studied both sewing and costume design, *below*.

The stable and respected leader from Savannah would reassure students, faculty, and the community.

The joyful mood of commencement, however, did not sweep through the crowd attending graduation services in the spring of 1915. Students were still mourning a classmate who had succumbed to pneumonia earlier that spring. A local newspaper noted the event's significance. It was "the first student of the college who has died since its opening." Hughie Galbreath was his name. Six of his classmates traveled by train with the casket as pallbearers to Galbreath's home in Lyons, Georgia.[24] Somber, they returned to complete the term and take their exams.

Anderson used this moment to make a point he so often had made before. 'Culture Hill stood on solid democratic foundations, he said. He reminded the audience that Thomas Jefferson (his direct ancestor) was "probably the first man in this country to suggest a plan for the education of the people generally." Anderson told the audience of parents and students that a school such as this required more support by the state. He said he would urge the legislature to approve a new tax policy supporting public education.

Anderson concluded, "We must always bear in mind that we are not giving education to any individual for his own selfish benefit, but that education is given him by the States in order that he may grow up to be an enlightened and responsible citizen of a free country."[25] The chairman of the trustees had just reminded everyone what he and other trustees meant when they spoke of this as "the people's school."

Following Anderson's commencement address, local leaders made brief remarks, including school treasurer, Lonnie Brannen, and three representatives of local government: Robert Lee Moore, Greene Johnston, and Fred T. Lanier. They symbolized the community's commitment. Brannen paused and decided to give the students a few tips "on the subject of time and promptness in all matters social or business."[26] Again the community clearly made this point: Statesboro had an unshakable confidence in the school it created in 1906 and had nurtured ever since.

As he had done so often in the past, again Anderson asked Albert Deal to gather the deeds to the school property and bring them to Savannah. First, Anderson helped arrange a loan from the Sea Island Bank in 1915. Reflecting on this loan many years later when he was president of the bank, Charles Brooks McAllister wrote:

[T]here was a First District Agricultural and Mechanical school south of Statesboro on a sand ridge where you could not drive when the weather was dry. You would get stuck in the sand. The school was in financial trouble. It was about to close because they did not have the funds to continue operating, and the people of Statesboro were called upon for help and the Sea Island Bank made a loan for $12,000.00 to go along with what others put in to keep the school open. If the school had closed there is a possibility that the greatest institution we have in Statesboro . . . would not be in Statesboro today.[27]

The infusion of money allowed the school to survive for another year. But the solid local support for the school began to crack in the spring of 1916. The trustees, searching for more revenue, received state approval to sell the northeastern corner of the campus. It was then that some local business leaders began to express doubts about the survival of the A&M school. Their skepticism took the form of a proposal to use a portion of the campus for a new industry designed to serve the county's agricultural interests. It would be the largest meat-packing plant in the region. The trustees deliberated and made a decision that disappointed the businessmen:

The steering committee and special representatives selecting a site for the packing plant appeared before the Trustees of the First District A&M School at their annual meeting Monday [May 15] and presented an application for an option on the northeast corner of the school property which the state authorized them to sell. The Trustees after due deliberation decided that it was not desirable to open the land at present for manufacturing enterprises.[28]

A new editorial writer for the *Statesboro News*, Thomas D. Vanosten reacted with great relief. He also set forth a vision for the school:

The F.D.A.&M. School and the Bulloch Packing Plant Co. are as divergent in point of character as night and day. One is of the higher order of things learnedly, the other the lower order of things material. The school should be surrounded and approached only by that which is artistic, beautiful and refined. As a co-ed institution there is a moral side to the subject that should not be lost sight of. We hope some day to see a boulevard encircling the F.D.A.&M. grounds and a beautiful city thoroughfare leading to it. The packing plant is essentially commercial, and positively not refined in its necessary operation no matter to what degree the sanitary accomplishment may be carried out.

Meat-packing plant near campus rejected

On May 15, 1916, the board of trustees rejected a proposal to sell the northeast corner of the campus to businessmen who wanted to build a modern meat-packing plant there. Disappointed, the proposal's supporters later built the plant on what became Packinghouse Road.

Although their proposal was shortsighted, the businessmen assumed correctly the school was tottering on the edge of bankruptcy. In November 1916, Treasurer Lonnie Brannen wrote Anderson an urgent letter. Brannen reported that Albert Deal was preparing paperwork for yet another loan application.[29] Anderson arranged for the trustees to borrow $15,000 from

LIFE BEYOND THE CLASSROOM

The earliest gathering place for picnics and outings was called "Lovers' Hill." On Saturday afternoons, especially, boys and girls would carry a picnic basket filled with good things to eat and drink. They hiked about a mile northwest of the campus. Professors who were just a few years older than the students served as chaperones. Some students liked to slide down the sand hill. Others balanced on the railroad track, awaiting the Metter-to-Statesboro train that ran several times a day. Passengers would wave as they passed. Daytime was fun time. At night, however, only the brave dared visit this mournful ridge that most certainly was haunted. Here wandered the ghosts of thoughtless youth who, while seeking pleasure, mysteriously vanished at Lovers' Hill.

Images from the scrapbooks of Bertha Hagin & George Aull

Martha

Hikers at "Lovers' Hill"

Waiting for the train to pass by

Saturday afternoon at Lovers' Hill

Ruth Smith and Professor Aull

Senior boys, 1919-20

Senior girls, 1919-20

Chaperones also had fun. Left to right: Eva Baker (music), E. G. Cromartie (coach), Mary J. Whatley (education), and Miss King

Esten Graham Cromartie, football coach and agriculture professor

George H. Aull, military science professor

CULTURE vs AUGUSTA
Saturday, April 17th
Admission 35c

Known as the 'Culture, the football team attracted some outstanding players, such as, left to right, James Hagan, Mr. Morgan, and Charlie Gibson. Gibson, shown punting the football, *graduated in 1920 and enrolled at the Polytechnic Institute at Auburn, Alabama, where he became a valuable member of the proud War Eagles team.*

enrollment. The graduating class in 1919 had only fifteen students. Many male students had dropped out of school to join the Armed Forces in World War I.

A symbol of optimism came from a relative of a member of the first graduating class of 1910. Allen Hamilton Bunce, of Atlanta, created an award for the best student essay in Georgia history. It would perpetually honor his father, James Allen Bunce of Bulloch County. Over the years the award has done much more than honor students. It has served to stimulate scholarship, and several recipients have had distinguished academic careers. Recipients of Bunce awards include M. Edward Mitchell, Charlton Moseley, R. Frank Saunders, and Georgia Watson, all of whom received PhD degrees and returned here to teach.

Young women played an equal, if not dominant, role in shaping the collective memory of the institution. Unlike many southern colleges that began as male academies, this A&M school enrolled women from the start. Scrapbooks of Bertha Hagin ('20) and professor George Aull both reveal women playing sports, participating in literary events, and happily interacting with male students and faculty. Female students preserved what they also might have invented: the first school song. Hagin collected the earliest known expression of old school ties, an alma mater. The printed version ends with the word *anonymous*.

A student or students, perhaps, drafted the earliest available printed version of the song that celebrates the 'Culture. It contains some elements of the official alma mater that appeared in 1932. A printed copy of the song surfaced among the collected papers of Hagin. The page probably was an insert for a program marking a special occasion such as commencement. It is the only song in her collected papers, and it likely was printed in 1919 or 1920. However, it could have been written years earlier.

The lyrics of this early alma mater refer equally to both sexes, suggesting the words might have come from the pen of a female. Local students surely were familiar with another alma mater, sung by students at the University of Georgia in Athens; these lyrics chauvinistically lauded the "sons of Georgia rising."[40] By contrast, the A&M song pays tribute equally to "sons and daughters" and "lads and lass' of 'Culture."

The lyrics can be sung to the tune of the alma mater that the University of Georgia borrowed from Cornell University. This also happens to be the tune students sang at South Georgia Teachers College and, later, at Georgia Teachers College and Georgia Southern College.

By their nature alma maters relate a school to a place, as in Cornell University's opening line, "far above Cayuga's waters," the University of Georgia's "from the hills of Georgia's northland," or Vanderbilt University's "on the city's western border." This local emblem of old school loyalty provides a glimpse into the geography of memory: southern Georgia's bright landscape of cypress trees, Spanish moss, and the nearby sea.

First Alma Mater of the First District A&M School

Where the silver moss is hanging
   From the cypress tree,
There the lads and lasses of 'Culture
   Wave their banners free.

CHORUS
  Sons and daughters we will triumph,
   And with all our might,
  That the fame of dear old 'Culture
   E'er be in the light.

Where the waters slumber soundly,
   Deep within the vale,
There the trees of forest royal
   Shield us from the gale.

Where the ocean laps the shoreline,
   Where land meets the sea,
There the students of the 'Culture
   Fight for mastery.
          —Anonymous

Misbehaving in the 1920s

Left to right: Ansel Franklin (class of '26) with "Audio" Rushing, Pittman, and Anderson.

THE GIRLS OF A&M, GEORGIA NORMAL

From 1916 to 1929 girls wore uniforms and were expected to reflect the highest values both on and off campus. Huldah Cail, at the top of the pyramid, *right* (1929), loved gymnastics and promoted "modern dance, " á la Martha Graham. *Top far right*, Bertha Hagin, and, *bottom far right*, her friend. *Below*, Bertha's invoice for November and December 1919. The middle section recalls an outing of Bertha, *left*, and friends, *right*, at Mill Creek, where they secretly experimented with cigarettes. Meanwhile on campus, coeds visited each other at the dorm and played pick-up games of basketball nearby.

In the spring of 1920 the school completed its fourteenth year as an institution, twelve of which involved classroom instruction. Writing a report in January 1920, Principal Rowan was pleased students were reading *The Last of the Mohicans*, Shakespeare's *Merchant of Venice*, George Washington's *Farewell Address*, and *Old Testament* stories. Latin I and II were electives.

Compared with recent war years, when enrollment had declined, the number of students grew to 189. Students competed in football, basketball, tennis, baseball, and volleyball. The student body also participated in infantry drills, using eighty-three Springfield rifles.[41]

Alumni knew times were tough, and they pitched in their support. The library, always poorly funded, gained funds for new books after Rowan asked alumni "to give one dollar each with which to buy books, and most of them have responded promptly, giving more than was asked for. We carry practically all the best magazines, many of the daily newspapers of the State and practically all the county papers in the district."[42]

More than usual, local newspapers reported on A&M's achievements, both academic and athletic. The *Bulloch Times* noted with pride that women's basketball had become an extramural sport in February 1920. The headline affirmed the role of women in sports: "Farmettes Defeat Crack Savannah Team." Editor David Turner noted the significance of this event: "Until Saturday our girls had never entered any other than a practice contest."[43]

The editor also highlighted academic achievements. Whenever the forensic team competed, Turner usually wrote about it in detail, as he did when the local A&M competed against the Tenth District A&M debaters from Granite Hill in April. Turner bragged that in home-and-away debates, the team from Statesboro won both contests. Affirmative and negative teams included Wendell Crowe, Charlie Gibson, Lewis Gill, and Ethan Patterson.[44] During these years debaters squared off on such controversial topics as capital punishment, women's suffrage, and the future of cotton as a profitable crop.

That term the school sent its best students to compete in the state literary meet in Athens. The young men and women participated in literary, industrial, and track events. Turner's headline captured the community's pride in the result: "Statesboro Aggies Winners at Athens: 'Culture Lads and Lassies Make Impression—Win Nine Medals and Banner."[45]

By 1920 the school was no longer fledgling. It had become an established educational force in southeast Georgia.

Big men on campus

Wendell Crowe, *left*, practices the shot-put. Like Charlie Gibson, *right*. Crowe was an all-around athlete who competed throughout the year.

Early star athletes

The Farmettes basketball team in 1920 featured Ruth Smith, *right*.

Making the best of what you have

Candler Rogers sits at the steps of West Hall while repairing an old baseball, ca. 1923-25.

1920 A&M ring

Local citizens endowed awards

Clockwise from top left: Booth Medal in English, Bertha Hagin; General Excellence Medal for Boys, Barney Lee Kennedy; Grimes Excellence Medal for Girls, Ruth Hagin. Presented each year, the medals shown were presented in 1919.

Principal Rowan felt the time had come for him to begin a new career. Since he had come to town in that bleak January of 1908, much had changed about the school and himself.

Rowan had witnessed how the community relentlessly supported the school. Now he wanted to live and work in that community and continue to assist First District A&M as a private businessman. Since the town did not have a motor repair company, he began a new business, the Rowan Motor and Supply Company, a logical enterprise for a mechanical engineer. Later, he would return to academic life as a professor at the Georgia Institute of Technology in Atlanta. Looking back on his tenure, David Turner wrote that when Rowan began,

[T]he school was heavily in debt and without credit, but by good management has almost lifted this indebtedness. The school is in a flourishing condition today. The buildings have been overhauled and are being repainted, new laboratories have been installed, a new dairy barn has been built and equipped, much new machinery and farm stock has been bought and the farm has been brought to a high state of cultivation. . . . Mr. Rowan has worked tirelessly and faithfully to advance the best interests of the school, and has succeeded in a measure which is a pleasure to the friends of the school.[46]

The newspaper duly paid tribute to Rowan, who helped the school survive, with the aid of a strong board of trustees. Nevertheless, the school was not yet out of the financial danger zone.

OLD 'CULTURE AT THE CROSSROADS

When Ernest Victor Hollis replaced Principal Rowan, he became the first principal with a master's degree.[47] Hollis, a native of Mississippi, had graduated with a BS degree from Mississippi State College (later, Mississippi State University), where he also received a master's degree in agriculture. By the age of twenty-four he had earned a second master's degree in education at Columbia University Teachers College and recently had begun his doctoral studies.

The new principal took note of the school's current debts shortly after he arrived in the summer of 1920. Like his predecessors, he would wrestle with solutions. However, he was more successful than earlier principals in removing indebtedness. Looking back on his first years at the school from 1920 to 1923, Hollis wrote:

Through inadequate appropriations, poor collections, and inefficient management, the school had lost much of its prestige. For the most part those who had made it their first love had deserted it in despair; those who had trusted it financially still had the account on their books. Its credit was gone, the buildings and grounds were in rather dilapidated condition, and its clientele had begun to attend high school in the home community.[48]

Principal Hollis began to solve the budget crisis when he put it in perspective. The problem was not primarily a matter of money. The school needed to reexamine its mission. He said First District A&M School had stumbled because it had lost its focus. On the one hand it advertised itself as a general-purpose high school, but on the other hand the faculty was heavily weighted toward agricultural science and the domestic arts.

The new principal did not mention mechanical education in his first bulletin. In fact, Hollis deleted "Mechanical" from the school's name. For 1921–22, at least, the name on the cover was "The State Agricultural School: 1st District, Statesboro." His not-so-subtle changes—especially the deletion of mechanical education and the inclusion of teacher education—sent a signal to the region that the school in Statesboro was changing. (Apparently, state officials insisted that Hollis restore the statutory name of the institution, and he did so in the next bulletin.)[49]

In many ways the bulletin of 1920–21 revealed how Hollis approached his job, both as a leader and publicist. He presented a school calendar with designated holidays. He scheduled a new event to coincide with commencement—"Alumni Day." He featured a full-page photograph of a successful farmstead operated by an alumnus, Remer Lee Brannen II.

Other neat illustrations in the catalog show students and professors at work in the classroom and the field. Female students appear in the required uniforms, the Butterick pattern #1432 for blue skirts, #1420 for white shirt waists, and #2481 for middies (sailor blouses). They also wore regulation black lace-up shoes and knee-length stockings.[50] A student who wore the uniform described it in some detail in her later years. Ada Lou (Rowe) Waters recalled in 1952, "In the early days of the college, the girls wore uniforms, blue and white. Skirts were measured and kept near the floor."[51]

The catalog for the previous year noted "boys are required to wear overalls while working on the farm and olive drab woolen army uniforms at all other times except Monday. Monday is the only day a student is allowed to wear a civilian suit." The uniform included a shirt, pants, hat, hat cord, and "leggins."[52]

Student life, according to the principal, included appealing activities, such as literary societies, the dramatic club, and sports (football, baseball, and basketball). Students participated in Hi-Y, a branch of the YMCA and YWCA.

The senior class published a newspaper for the student body in 1921. Hollis described it as "a monthly paper devoted to school and student interests. It has proved a very effective means of acquainting students with the value of newspaper work and making them more thorough in English."[53] The name of the paper was the 'Culture Bulldog.

Uniforms for different occasions
True Watson of Metter, *top left*, in her gym suit. Males wore military uniforms, *right*, from 1916 to 1920. While off campus, females did not have to wear middie blouses with blue ties, *bottom*.

FROM 'CULTURE TO COLLEGE

ANGUS NESBIT GROVENSTEIN
Grovenstein was a state legislator from Effingham County and served on the executive committee of the A&M school's board of trustees.

After being on 'Culture Hill for a year, Hollis called for radical changes. In his first annual report he wrote that after "more than ten years of blind trials and error experiment," the time had come to focus on three activities: agriculture for boys, homemaking for girls, and teacher education classes for both.[54]

Why would Hollis emphasize teacher training classes for both male and female students? He said he had observed communities in the region organizing high schools at a rapid pace, and the future of any boarding high school was tenuous.

What southeast Georgia really needed, he said, was a college. So he began to speak to legislators about changing the mission of the A&M school. Soon, he met with key leaders in the county and region, and he began to sell them on his new idea. He recalled, especially, Bulloch County's Harvey Brannen, Howell Cone, George Peter Donaldson, Francis Hunter, Samuel Wister Lewis, John E. McCroan, John C. Parrish, and David Turner.

Others who deserved notice included progressive members of earlier executive committees of the trustees from neighboring counties: John D. Clark of Darien, C. S. Grice of Claxton, Angus Nesbit Grovenstein of Guyton, and Leonard Rountree of Graymont-Summit, Georgia.

The new principal from Columbia University tended to act first and, if necessary, apologize later. It was the style of a young man who sensed the school could not survive unless the trustees radically revised its mission.

1923 faculty

Ernest V. Hollis with the First District A&M School faculty of 1923. Front row, *left to right:* Inez Rudy, Lila Blitch, Janice Jones, Elizabeth Bruce, Clara Leek DeLoach. Back row: Davis Nye Barron, President Hollis, Albert Quattlebaum, and Wyley M. Pope.

Howell Cone represented Bulloch County in the state legislature as a senator (1921–22, 1927–28) and as a representative (1929–31). He was a devoted friend and supporter of the First District A&M School and worked closely with school leaders in the twenties and early thirties. He also served on the board of trustees, providing legal counsel. A member of one of Bulloch County's pioneer families, Cone quickly warmed up to the youthful principal. Later, he would champion legislative action the young Hollis encouraged.

Cone once wrote a correspondent confidentially that the principal liked to initiate changes and then gauge the "reactions" of the trustees.[55] Perhaps Cone agreed the institution needed Hollis' brand of bold and imaginative leadership. The trustees apparently recognized in him the kind of energetic leader who could transform the school into a viable institution with a realistic chance of survival.

The people of the town and county knew the principal was more than an advocate for the school. They realized he also championed their own aspirations for the region. Trustees and businessmen, perhaps, did not always understand the radical implications of his message, but they certainly liked the messenger.

He worked closely with the county's legislative delegation to remove the school's debt. Previously the trustees had sought loans from banks in Savannah and Statesboro. Hollis, on the other hand, encouraged the local senator and representatives to obtain a special allocation in the state budget. The *Bulloch Times* applauded Hollis on January 15, 1922, noting the school "is now free from debt, due to the recent settlement of an outstanding mortgage of more than $6,000. . . . Through the instrumentality of our representatives in the last legislature—Senator Howell Cone and Representatives Harvey Brannen and J. C. [John C.] Parrish—an appropriation was procured to make settlement in full. . . . Now that the school no longer labors under the embarrassment of debt, further progressive strides are in prospect."

The *Savannah Morning News* also paid Hollis compliments on several of his innovations, including the formation of the first alumni association in 1921: "At the very beginning of his administration, Professor Hollis recognized that a sleeping giant for service to the institution was tied up in the usual influence and energy of the finished products of the school, and in consequence secured the organization of the graduates into an alumni association."

The *News* article took note of two alumni projects: erecting an attractive sign for the entrance in 1922 and recruiting potential students in their respective counties. Describing an alumni association banquet, the *News* referred to remarks by alumni Lewis Gill, Sara Ila Sowell, Bertha Hagin, and a recent graduate, Jim Hagin. Alumnus Gill, in South Georgia parlance, provoked proud laughter with these words: "It's a poor frog that won't brag on his own pond, and we've a good one."[56] Later this same organization would plan a new "memorial driveway" for the entrance to the school.[57]

Principal Hollis also knew that alumni followed 'Culture sports, especially football. When he appointed a new football coach in August 1923, the students and community could hardly contain themselves. His name was Mark Anthony. Nicknamed "the noblest Roman of them all," Anthony had been a football star at the University of Georgia. The six-foot tall veteran of World War I had been an outstanding guard for the gridiron Bulldogs. Anthony was coach for only one season, but he gave the team instant credibility and earned young Hollis the admiration of alumni and fans.[58]

SENATOR HOWELL CONE

" If Georgia is to keep pace with its neighboring states, if the stigma of illiteracy is to be removed, if Georgia is to retain, or regain, her position in the sisterhood of states, the vital place from which this progress must begin is in the training of her teachers for the public schools. Tax reform may be vitally important, highway development may be a necessary accompaniment, but the permanent prosperity of Georgia is bound up with the progress of her educational institutions. "

Howell Cone, "Reasons for State Normal at Statesboro," *Station G.N.S.* (15 December 1924)

ERNEST VICTOR HOLLIS JR.
The son of President Hollis uses a rake to clean up the front yard of Anderson Dining Hall in 1925.

A NEW MISSION, A NEW NAME

The big news in 1924 came early that year in a meeting of the trustees. Hollis made the boldest move ever contemplated by any principal. He told the trustees the school they had nurtured so long had served its purpose. Instead of calling for its closure, Hollis had another idea, to transform the agricultural school into a teachers college. The trustees approved his request to add teacher training classes beyond the high school level. He said the Georgia Department of Education supported the idea and would monitor the new curriculum.[59]

The final bulletin of the First District A&M School reveals how Hollis worked as an agent of change. At the end of the magazine-like bulletin, he included a final section entitled "RIGHT HERE—Before we go farther, let us explain a little." Hollis reviewed how the school had changed its mission:

It is extremely difficult while in the midst of a development program to publish a booklet that will truly represent the school. You doubtless know already of the plans to convert this school into a Teachers' College. Even before this book reaches you the Legislature will probably have had the bill before it and made some disposition of the matter. What that disposition will be we cannot tell at this time.

Taking risks, while using words of caution, Hollis noted that the trustees already had added a twelfth grade to the high school, "specializing in training teachers for rural school work."[60] His point was clear: the school would offer education classes for teachers and prospective teachers. Furthermore, the new classes would be above the high school level. Change was coming to the A&M school, he suggested, whether or not the legislature approved. (When he wrote this final section of the catalog, Senator Cone probably had told him the outlook at the capitol was favorable.)

Realizing the emotional impact of changing the institution's mission, Hollis paid a tribute to the past. He offered praise to Old 'Culture in the last official publication of the A&M school:

Every institution . . . has its 'spirit'. There is that something in the atmosphere of the place that cannot be pointed out to the ordinary faculties of men but . . . is just as definitely here as the buildings and trees. . . . It is this spirit that one means when one speaks of 'Old 'Culture.' This intangible something that grips the boy or girl who lives for a time upon "Culture Hill" that gives to them the ideals of justice, integrity, and service, and that holds them loyal to the school and all that it stands for in the years that follow their departure from the school. . . . 'Old 'Culture' is still here. It has just grown up a little more—become a little bigger—increased its range of service.[61]

Senator Wallace Kennedy of Metter and Senator James L. Gillis of Soperton introduced the senate bill that became law when Governor Clifford Walker signed it on August 18, 1924—eighteen years to the day after Governor Joseph M. Terrell had signed the original bill creating the system of A&M schools. Ernest V. Hollis, the fourth principal of the A&M

school, now became the first president of the Georgia Normal School, a junior college.

The news from the legislature traveled quickly to the town and campus on that Monday, August 18. The story reminded many citizens of the school's birthday in Savannah on a December Saturday back in 1906. In 1924, however, no train whistle beckoned the town to celebrate. The news came by telephone and telegram. David Turner's headline in the *Bulloch Times* was icing on a cake long in the making: "A&M School is made State Normal." [62]

Ernest V. Hollis' speeches and newspaper columns did not dwell on the unfairness of the state's higher education budget that long had neglected South Georgia. He diplomatically left this truth unspoken, but third parties were free to make this point. One who did just that was the respected editorial writer of the *Macon News,* W. T. Anderson.

The metropolitan daily newspaper zeroed in on the lack of funding for higher education in South Georgia: "Until a month ago, when the . . . acts passed by the recent session became law, there was, in the entire lower half of the state but one State-supported institution of higher education, one teaching-training institution, the Georgia State Woman's College." [63]

Hollis was quick to acknowledge local legislators who worked on behalf of the proposal: local representatives John C. Parrish and Harvey Brannen (son of the late Lonnie Brannen, the school's first treasurer) and a senator from Metter, Wallace Kennedy. (Kennedy had supported Bulloch County's bid for the school as a delegate to Savannah in 1906.)

The board of trustees surely recognized the irony of the grand development at the capitol. Now they had to borrow more money to hire college-level faculty and make plans for a larger student body. In October the trustees authorized Hollis to obtain a loan of $20,000. Two years later the trustees went to the same local and regional banks, raising the debt to $45,000 to pay for a new auditorium and other improvements. But unlike risky loans to a tottering A&M school, these mortgages were backed by the good faith and credit of the state of Georgia. [64]

If anyone earlier had doubts about the wisdom of Hollis' leadership, the events in Atlanta removed them. Even as newspapers applauded his leadership, he began a campaign among civic clubs to support the school. Samuel Wister Lewis called a meeting of the Ad Club, of which Hollis was a mainstay. Senator Howell Cone moderated the session that quickly became a tribute to the young college president. In one of his last public appearances, the elderly pillar of the business community and, reputedly, the county's wealthiest citizen, Rafe Simmons, stood and "gave voice to his endorsement of the school and the things for

> "The development of the college here has been my 'first love,' and no mother has been more fond of her baby . . . I have been very happy in my work at Statesboro and reasonably successful. I know of nothing that could induce me to voluntarily give up my work here except this opportunity to better prepare for a lifetime of service to teachers. "
>
> Ernest Victor Hollis,
> *Bulloch Times,* 24 June 1926

Campus improvements

The Alumni Association provided a new modern sign, *above,* for Georgia Normal School in 1925.

President Wells hired an architect to propose Normal School facilities, *below,* for the future, ca. 1926.

which it stands."[65] Until that moment the pragmatic Simmons had withheld his public endorsement of the school.

A common theme among local citizens was that, for the first time in the state's history, the huge section of southeast Georgia (roughly two-fifths of the state) now had a college to serve the young people as well as current and future teachers.[66]

Building on the momentum of the fall, Hollis began writing an occasional column for the *Bulloch Times*. He called it "Broadcasting for education: A two minutes talk."[67] The young president also was a favorite of the local woman's club. The treasurer, Jessie Averitt, mailed him a check in the amount of $100, reflecting the club's commitment to the new Georgia Normal School.[68] Local citizens opened their doors to the new "college faculty." Mrs. Inman Foy, for example, was hostess for a "semiannual reception" for old and new faculty. One such event, in December 1925, took place at the residence of Fred T. Lanier on Zetterower Avenue.[69]

Burrus Matthews, who held a master's degree from the George Peabody College for Teachers, became the school's first dean in 1925. Earlier, Matthews had been a professor at Mississippi Woman's College in Hattiesburg. Mrs. Jesse Outland Johnston of Statesboro taught "expression," and Malvina Trussell, a popular young teacher in Bulloch County schools, organized the science department and became its first faculty member.

The second summer school in June and July 1925 attracted three hundred teachers from twenty-one counties, approximately one hundred more than in 1924. Many of them enrolled in college courses for the first time in their careers. Some noticed advertisements that President Hollis published in regional newspapers. An effective ad in the *Bulloch Times* for August 6, 1925, begins with a question: "What is a college?" The answer, of course, is Georgia Normal School, with four large brick buildings, twelve new classrooms, and an auditorium to seat a thousand. Reflecting the confidence of the educational community, a teacher from Candler County, Lota Trapnell, published a glowing endorsement of the summer school.[70]

On November 20, 1925, the trustees approved the addition of third stories to East Hall and West Hall, increasing dormitory space by one-half. Within a few months President Hollis announced that the legislature had provided funds to build a large addition of two levels to the administration building. Rooms for classes and laboratories would occupy the ground floor. The second floor would be devoted to a large auditorium "with seating capacity for 1,000."[71]

Students applauded another change the young president introduced in 1925. He authorized

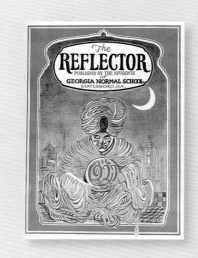

The school yearbook

The school yearbook, the *Reflector*, probably was named for a reflecting ball that rested on a pedestal near East Hall.

the first yearbook. Earlier, he had asked the community for suggestions for a name for a "new publication." He noted those that had been offered: "Whispering Pines, Pine Barks, and Station G. N. S."[72] Instead of these generic titles, however, the students and faculty agreed on the name of a unique object on campus. The book's title, the *Reflector*, appears to have originated with a reflecting globe on a pedestal near the southwest corner of East Hall. The globe was the subject of sketches and photographs in the early years of the publication, beginning with the academic year 1925–26.

Another change in the spring of 1926 brought an individual to the campus who arrived with a level of energy equal to that of the president. Hollis hired Guy Herbert Wells to replace Dean Matthews, who preferred teaching rather than administration; Hollis made Matthews head of the education department. Wells, recently the school superintendent of Eastman, Georgia, then was studying at George Peabody College for Teachers in Nashville, Tennessee. Wells had earned a master's degree at Columbia University Teachers College in 1925, his terminal degree. David Turner introduced the new dean to the community:

It is the universal testimonial of schoolmen in Georgia that Mr. Wells is one of the outstanding administrative officers in the state. He is eminently fitted by training and experience for the duties of a dean. . . . His work as superintendent of schools in Eastman won him a high place in the educational leadership of Georgia.[73]

President Hollis thought he was hiring a dean. Actually, he had just selected his successor. Within a month he learned that Columbia University had offered him a doctoral fellowship from the General Education Board of the Rockefeller Foundation. Hollis accepted.

SUCCEEDING WITHOUT OBVIOUS CONFLICT

President Hollis' decision to leave the campus and community disappointed students, faculty, and citizens. Trustees were fond of the young president, and they offered him a leave of absence, hoping he might return as "Dr. Hollis."[74] In the meantime Wells could serve as acting president. Hollis realized a temporary leader could not take measures required at this decisive time in the institution's history. Reluctantly, he decided to resign as president. He recommended Wells as his replacement.

Observers who regretted that Georgia Normal School had lost a skilled publicist soon recognized in Guy Wells a consummate master of promotion. David Turner observed Wells often and closely. Later, he would say Wells was "the best fitted man in the state of Georgia for building up a college." Turner wrote in the *Bulloch Times*:

There is something about Guy Wells that stamps him as a leader. If you try to walk down the street with him, you'll find he inadvertently walks two paces ahead of you; if you ride with him in his car, you'll find that he speeds where most drivers would feel

GUY HERBERT WELLS

ANNE WELLS

Anne Wells, daughter of Ruby Hammond Wells and President Guy Wells, was born in 1928. Students suggested the president should name her for the campus newspaper—*George-Anne*. From 1930 until 1934 she was a favorite mascot for campus clubs. After earning bachelor's degrees from the Georgia State College for Women and the University of North Carolina, she received a master's degree from Harvard University, and a law degree from Georgetown University. She married Harvard professor Lewis Branscomb. She was chairman of the Communications Law Division of the American Bar Association's Science and Technology Section. A distinguished attorney and author, she received an honorary doctorate from Notre Dame University in 1995. One of the first to use the term "information infrastructure," she wrote about the impact of digital communications upon modern society. Her book, *Who Owns Information?*, is a classic in the field.

Mission Statement, Georgia Normal College

" Georgia Normal by its organization, its correspondence courses and its co-educational features, hopes to meet a long felt need, not only to Southeast Georgia, but to the whole state. It is destined to become seen as the leading teacher's training institution in the state, and, in a few years, of the Southeast. "

Bulloch Times, 19 August 1926

Maud Moore Benson

Benson, a graduate of Wesleyan College, became the dietitian in 1922. She managed female students who worked in Anderson Dining Hall. Her son, Robert, attended the training school on campus.

their way cautiously; if you talk with him, you'll find that he frequently springs some subject that seems entirely remote, which indicates the speed with which his mind travels. All of which is to say that Guy Wells is not a man who stands still or even moves slowly; he is a man of action.[75]

Some who observed Wells at different times in his life noted he was "rough around the edges." A former student who knew and admired Mr. and Mrs. Wells in Milledgeville said there was "a sort of a real plainness about both of them, sort of like country, and fitting in, they couldn't fit into most situations."[76] Occasionally, the president displayed a crude sense of humor, even during academic proceedings. "Wells lacked polish," the historian of another college wrote of him. "Some of his humorous stories were indelicate and his grammar occasionally left something to be desired."[77]

While the man had great intellectual gifts, he never pursued the life of the mind: "I am not a scholar, but I am able to appreciate a person who is one," he said.[78] Yet throughout his life, observers tended to agree on one point: the man possessed unmistakable leadership qualities. Many administrators and faculty who worked with him over the years agreed he was an innovative and successful leader, as Turner pointed out. He easily identified with the region's large population of farmers. He not only knew their language but spoke it fluently. Wells had grown up on a farm in Carroll County, Georgia, and was the first member of his family to attend college. A president from a later era said Wells occasionally would sit on a bench at the courthouse square on Saturday afternoons and talk engagingly with farmers as they whittled sticks and chewed tobacco. They would tell the president, "Why, you're just as common as the rest of us!"[79]

Wells was fortunate to arrive at the institution shortly after the legislature had moved it to a higher level. He witnessed the first commencement exercise held in the new auditorium on June 7, 1926.[80] At that event he heard a former student extol Wells' twenty-nine-year-old predecessor, Hollis.

Carlton Purvis, president of the alumni association, presented a resolution praising the departing president for his "splendid success in raising the school from a preparatory institution to one of the foremost normal schools in the state."[81] Purvis encouraged all alumni to return to the commencement service in 1927 for their first annual meeting under the Wells administration.

At age thirty-four, Wells would assume responsibility immediately for running the third annual summer session for teachers. He witnessed how Hollis had organized a very popular summer session. Wells easily fell into the job, adding his personal touch. He divided the teachers into groups with such names as "Yellow Jackets," "Frogs," "Hornets," and "Crackers." After classes they played games and during morning assemblies presented programs. Each group tried to outdo the others. Teachers responded favorably and vocally. They found the new president "down to earth."

Knowing fall was approaching, Wells wanted to boost the enrollment for his first year. Throughout the summer, he spoke often at churches, schools, and civic clubs. He urged teachers in the summer session to encourage their students and relatives to attend Georgia Normal. He printed and circulated widely an ambitious mission. Written by Wells and approved by the trustees, the statement focused on improving the image of the institution both in the state and in the Southeast.

Among the many advantages Guy Wells possessed was his predecessor's record of involvement in the community. At the time Hollis had been preparing the A&M school to become a teachers college, he worked closely with the local board of education. Using a familiar model for schools of education, Hollis wanted Georgia Normal School to have a public school on campus. It would be affiliated with the department of education. Thereby future teachers could observe effective teaching methods.

Before Hollis left Statesboro, the local superintendent of schools had arranged to shift some local school districts in order to place an existing school on the campus. Bulloch County Superintendent of Schools B. R. Olliff had supported Hollis' efforts to offer summer classes for teachers, and he often used his columns to brag on the classes at Georgia Normal. While there is no way to determine who initiated the plan to fund the school jointly, the idea had Hollis' name written all over it. Olliff informed parents and children of the new district in August.

Sunnyside school district served the southeastern part of Statesboro and contiguous communities in Bulloch County. The district had three schools: Sunnyside, Warnock, and Jimps. Some students who had attended the old Sunnyside School would relocate to either Warnock or Jimps. Those who lived near the college could walk to the relocated Sunnyside School, now on the campus of Georgia Normal School. Workmen had moved the school and rebuilt it on the campus, placing it about one hundred feet north of East Hall. It was ready to open on November 15, 1926.

Funding for the Sunnyside School came from both Georgia Normal School and the Bulloch County Board of Education. Thus began a partnership that would continue until 1998. Students in the new Sunnyside district enjoyed the privilege of attending school on campus. The education department benefited by using the facility to provide laboratory experiences for both teachers and learners. Eventually, Sunnyside School became the "Training School" and, finally, the "Laboratory School," a name it carried later to newer buildings on campus. Beginning in 1926 and continuing for most of the twentieth century, the school provided classes for students from kindergarten through high school.

By the time classes began in the fall of 1926, President Wells had raised the profile of the college through his summer recruiting tour of southeast Georgia. He also had introduced a way to boost enrollment: correspondence

Sunnyside School

The old Sunnyside School, *top*, was moved and remodeled, *above*, in 1926.

" Beginning Monday morning, Nov. 15th [1926], the Normal School will open on its campus the Sunnyside model school. The school will include grades for the first seven, and is to be as near as possible what its name implies, a model school for the teaching of the children in Sunnyside district. . . . The old Sunnyside building has been moved and remodeled on the campus. It is now the latest word in a model plant for a school of its kind. . . . Several teachers will have charge of this school and these, under the supervision of a highly paid principal and all under supervision of the education department of the Normal School. Nothing but the best teaching will be permitted, for the first requisite of a model school is ideal teaching. . . . The patrons and public are cordially invited to be present the first morning for the opening exercises. "

Guy H. Wells
Bulloch Times, 11 November 1926

ERNEST ANDERSON

Dean Anderson in 1927 became the first administrator or faculty member to die while working for the institution.

courses. The director of off-campus learning, J. M. Phagan, also was head of the math department.

Wells found a way to increase annual enrollment by reorganizing the academic year into the quarter system. He told the trustees the new system had proven successful at the University of Chicago and the George Peabody College for Teachers in Nashville, Tennessee. This new schedule would enable public school teachers to enroll for classes in the spring quarter when many rural schools normally closed.[82]

The man President Wells selected to replace himself as dean was a popular principal at Emanuel County Institute (ECI) in Graymont-Summit (later, Twin City). Ernest Anderson had known those members of the student body who had attended his school. The popular principal attracted dozens of ECI graduates to Georgia Normal.

During his first few months in office, Anderson approved a new publication for the campus. The earliest issues appeared as mimeographed copies, with a hand-printed masthead and typewritten text. Published by the freshman class, it went by the name of the *George-Anne*. The first official issue appeared on April 12, 1927.

Campus historians disagree about whether the *George-Anne* was, in fact, the first campus newspaper. Hollis referred to an unnamed student newspaper in 1921. A feature article of 1985 by Alyson Bennett suggests the original name of the newspaper was "*Station G.N.S.*" and was published in 1924. Bennett reported that *Station G.N.S.* later gave way to the *George-Anne*.[83]

Hazel Dunlap was editor, and she was assisted by eight associate editors: Grace Bailey, Burman Bowen, Melba Dekle, Frank DeLoach, Julia Hargrove, Myrle Hutchison, Evia Dell Kea, and Dorris Lindsey. Mary Brinson typed the master copy, and Hilda Tubb, head of the English department, advised the new student publication. Very few copies of student publications exist prior to the April 12 edition of the *George-Anne*.

Student voices

In 1932 editor Ralph Stephens, advised by English professor Robert Donaldson, introduced the new campus newspaper, *The George-Anne*. It replaced earlier versions published under the names the *'Culture Bulldog*, *Station G.N.S*, and the *George-Anne*.

Another announcement by the dean dampened the enthusiasm of some male students. He called for an end to the initiation of freshman boys, nicknamed "rats."[84] For several years previously the upperclassmen had required freshmen to run the "belt line" periodically during their first semester.[85] Anderson called this practice "hazing," and he demanded that upperclassmen end it. (Initiation rites, known as "Rat Court," reappeared a year later and did not end until the late 1960s.)

During the spring of 1927, Dean Anderson attended the annual meeting of the Georgia Education Association in Macon. While making a speech to an assembly of the Parent Teacher Association, he became seriously ill and died two days later at a hospital in Macon. This was the first faculty member or administrator to die while serving the institution, and students took the loss personally. Not since the death of student Hughie Galbreath in 1915 had such a mood of somber reflection enveloped 'Culture Hill.[86]

In the spring Wells announced that he had found a replacement for Anderson. This man, he said, shared Dean Anderson's amiable ways and compassionate approach to life. His name was Zach Suddath Henderson, the man who had replaced Wells as superintendent of schools in Eastman, Georgia, in 1926. Henderson was enrolled in classes in the master's of education program at Columbia University. The new dean would join the faculty and staff in September.

The fourth annual summer school for teachers enrolled around 450, the largest number since Hollis began the program in 1924. The local newspaper lamented that, even after finding lodging for teachers at homes in town and completely filling the Statesboro Sanitarium, President Wells reluctantly turned away more than one hundred applicants.[87]

Wells organized this session into groups to encourage friendly competition, both academically and on the athletic field: "Blue Devils," "Cyclones," "Lindbergers," and "Campus Cats." Each group selected a faculty advisor and elected its own officers.

Burrus Matthews compiled a statistical report on teachers enrolled in Georgia Normal's summer program. Of 426 teachers who completed the classes, only 64 previously had taken even one course at a college or normal school. His report, published in the *George-Anne* on July 18, 1927, shows that public school teachers then were poorly prepared. Most of the teachers that summer completed at Georgia Normal their first academic courses beyond high school. The majority would return to one-room schoolhouses with fresh enthusiasm and new ideas for guiding the children under their care for another school year.

Teachers, feeling the pressure of cramped lodging and overcrowded classrooms, wrote an open letter to the Georgia legislature. Taking an initiative the president must have approved, they wrote their senators and representatives the following message:

Two genders, one "Georgian"— the "George-Anne"

The origin of the name of the campus newspaper since 1927 has piqued the curiosity of many freshmen and new members of the faculty and staff. Earliest issues of the newspaper did not discuss its peculiar name. Until October 31, 1932 the paper was simply *George-Anne*. With that issue, however, "the" appeared in the title, and it has stayed there ever since. The earliest explanation of the origin of the paper's name appeared in 1932:

"In the dim and distant past a movement was started on the campus to publish a school paper. There was much discussion, pro and con, about a suitable title for the publication. Such names as *High-Flyer*, *Times*, *Blue and White*, etc. were suggested, but none of them seemed to meet the approval of the student body. Finally someone had an 'idea.' It was suggested that due to the co-educational nature of the school, the paper should have a name representing both sexes on campus. It was also suggested that, as the school was in Georgia, supported by the people of Georgia and most of the students Georgians, the paper should have a name pertaining to Georgia. It was found that the word Georgian could be divided into two names—George-Anne. Hence, the paper was named George for the men and Anne for the women—*George-Anne*."

George-Anne, 31 October 1932

The George-Anne's advisor

In 1928 Statesboro native Robert Donaldson joined the faculty as an instructor of English and journalism. He also advised the student newspaper, the *George-Anne*, beginning in 1932, and functioned as a public relations director.

Teachers take field trip to the Bland Farm in June 1927

"At the home of Mr. and Mrs. Dan Bland we had the privilege of going through their yards and orchards. In the yard we found many beautiful flowers, shrubs and plants, many of which seemed new to us who know so little of the real beauty of nature. Many of the plants that seemed new to us came from our nearby swamps and branches, we were told. We learned the botanical name for some of these plants and saw that by careful transplanting and good care that anyone could be able to have beautiful surroundings at very little expense . . . .

After our visit through the yards and orchards, we were allowed through their lovely little home. Here we found all modern conveniences. In every room different articles of furniture have been built-in. Mr. Bland has built and installed a radio. Such a trip makes one think of Fairy Land. "

George-Anne, 29 June 1927

Botanical Garden, 1927

In 1927 the main road south was the old Pembroke road (later called Georgia Avenue). Then, Dan Bland's farm faced west. Later, Dan, *right*, and wife, Catherine, moved their home to face the new Pembroke Highway, Ga. 67. Today the restored Bland cottage is the headquarters of the Georgia Southern Botanical Garden.

Georgia Normal is young; we are not asking for the whole world. But we do need some things, and the legislature of the State should look our way. There are four women students to the room this summer; there are not enough recitation rooms to accommodate the classes; there are not enough chairs for the students to sit in; there is not room in the dining hall to serve the whole group; there are one hundred teachers in town, who would rather stay on the campus; the library room is too small, and there are not enough books. The legislature should look this way this summer. The friends of the school are acquainting the assembly with these facts. . . . The legislature does not meet again until 1929. Do something now.[88]

Guy Wells understood the political significance of the teachers' appeals to the legislature. Lawmakers were accustomed to receiving requests for funding from presidents and boards of trustees. But when highly respected members of their communities—teachers—made the approach, the senators and representatives would listen. That is what Wells believed, and he was right.

The legislature that met in the summer of 1927 looked at the new normal college in Statesboro and noticed its accumulated debt of $45,000. They paid that debt in full. Then they increased the operating fund by 50 percent, raising the annual appropriation to $60,000.

In just one year Wells had taken a relatively new normal college and turned it into an institution that earned legislative respect. To the surprise and relief of the board of trustees, the specter of debt no longer overshadowed 'Culture Hill.

When students returned to the campus to begin fall quarter in September 1927, President Wells hosted a reception, and each student received a warm welcome from the president himself and two others—the chairman of the board of trustees, John E. McCroan, and Senator Howell Cone. The general public recognized the significance of Cone's work in the recent session of the legislature.

Cone long had supported the Old 'Culture, both as citizen and lawmaker. Time and circumstance brought together the college president and the attorney. The relationship was fortuitous, especially for Wells. Howell Cone grew up in the Ivanhoe community, a descendant of a Revolutionary War hero, William Cone.[89] During most of Wells' eight years at the college, Cone lived and practiced law in Bulloch County.

Cone had been impressed with Wells' predecessor, Ernest Hollis. He acknowledged the young president's intellect and courage. As a senator he provided Hollis with guidance, especially helping him convert the A&M school into a junior college.

Cone admired Hollis. He liked Wells—genuinely. Cone probably identified with the homespun style of the president. Perhaps he realized he was in a position to help the relatively young man realize his potential as a leader. He became Wells' mentor in all things political. Cone reciprocated and often asked for Wells' advice and assistance. Until parted by death, the two nurtured their relationship through correspondence and frequent visits.

Howell Cone suggested Wells would be successful politically if he learned to express clearly his beliefs and if he learned to understand how others respond to his actions.[90] Cone believed these concepts were more useful than confrontation and struggle. Throughout his career, Wells put into practice these standards of conduct. On several occasions in later years, he reviewed them with his mentor. Cone and Wells developed a private metaphor for these standards. They called it "walking through the fodder."

Later in President Wells' career, when a governor injected politics into the university system, Cone wrote him: "I suppose you are now walking through the fodder." When Cone had reason to worry about his own career with the U. S. Office of Customs, Wells reminded him that "you know you have the reputation of being able to walk through a fodder field without rustling a blade."[91]

The fodder metaphor stems from agile farmers and hunters who know how to walk through rows of corn without rustling the long leaves. When the leaves are ready to be harvested or "pulled," the edges are razor-sharp and swiftly can cut one's skin. In other words, a wise person knows how to make progress (or avoid danger) without attracting attention and suffering pain. Wells' career in Statesboro reflects that he took to heart his mentor's lessons.

Wells understood what people wanted for Georgia Normal School, which was for it to become a four-year college. He said teachers in the region could not obtain a baccalaureate degree from a public college without having to drive two or three hundred miles. He alluded to the geographical unfairness of Georgia's system of higher education.

How did President Wells go about pursuing his objective? First, he tried not to "rustle the fodder." He encouraged teachers to make the case about cramped quarters and inadequate facilities on campus. He gave information to key editorial writers throughout the state. He was aware of a talented local journalist, Robert Donaldson, and in 1928 Wells asked him to teach English and journalism. Donaldson also became Georgia Normal's first public relations officer. Legislators in Atlanta, Macon, and Savannah soon were reading articles in their hometown newspapers about the college in Statesboro.

The president convinced students and faculty they were capable of performing at a higher level. Toward that end, he conducted affairs of the college at a higher level. For example, he invited nationally recognized speakers to address the student body and interested citizens.

Campus humor, 1926

"What do you slick your hair down with?"

"Crisco."

"Why?"

"Because I don't have to get any haircuts."

"How's that?"

"Because, Crisco's shortening."

Reflector, 1926

Note: Proctor and Gamble introduced Crisco®, made from cottonseed oil, in 1911.

He focused on upgrading the appearance of the buildings and grounds.

Often in assembly meetings the president said students should be treated as responsible adults. Both faculty and students should have access to the same information he possessed. He preferred to have students and faculty join him in making decisions about the future of the college.[92]

The first issue of the *George-Anne* reported that Wells had called for a form of student government: students should be accountable for enforcing classroom discipline and determining punishment for those who violate rules. He also enlisted students in improving the appearance of the campus. (One student recalled President Wells telling her to pick up trash whenever she saw it, because she "had the power" to make Georgia Normal "a prettier place."[93]) The campus newspaper endorsed the president's ideas: "Student participation gives a better name to the school."[94]

Momentum also helped the cause. From 1927 through 1929 the summer sessions for teachers expanded to the point that newspapers throughout the state took notice of four teachers sharing small rooms in the girls dormitory and of male teachers living in tents on the campus. Yet teachers returned, summer after summer, adding courses to their transcripts, while enjoying the Guy Wells brand of campus life—picnics, watermelon cuttings, songfests, and inspiring lectures. At least once each term the president recited his favorite poem, "If" by Rudyard Kipling, whose last stanza Wells delivered with great feeling:

> *If you can talk with crowds and keep your virtue,*
> *Or walk with kings—nor lose the common touch,*
> *If neither foes nor loving friends can hurt you;*
> *If all men count with you, but none too much,*
> *If you can fill the unforgiving minute*
> *With sixty seconds' worth of distance run,*
> *Yours is the Earth and everything that's in it,*
> *And—which is more—you'll be a Man, my son!*

A member of the audience in the summer of 1927, H. C. Justus, published a clever poem describing summer school and reminding the readers of the college president:

> *If you can keep the pace and keep it steady,*
> *Digest whatever's fed to you, and so*
> *If you can stay six weeks at Georgia Normal*

Football players—friends for life

Wearing simple leather helmets and light pads, the boys from 'Culture had the reputation for administering punishing blows on the field. Afterward, they remained friends for life, and some of the heartiest supporters at homecoming games on Thanksgiving once wore proudly the dark blue jerseys of dear old 'Culture.

Classroom humor

Miss Hester Newton: "In what battle was General Custer killed?"

Brown: "His last one."

George-Anne, 3 December 1928

And stand the gaff, and have a little fun,
Of all the schools of education formal.
This is the one for you—I think—my son! [95]

For two years Wells communicated his vision to opinion leaders in the state, beginning with rural teachers in south Georgia and ending with Governor Lamartine Hardman, whom he invited to campus on at least two occasions, in 1927 and 1929, during Hardman's tenure as governor (1927–31).

Wells led students to believe they were at a college equal to any four-year institution in Georgia. He invited national representatives of the YWCA and YMCA to organize chapters, knowing these organizations were popular at major universities.

Even the Georgia Normal football team, led by Delmas Rushing and Loy Waters, began to defeat stronger opponents. In 1929 the "Blue Tide" won the South Georgia Conference championship. The Oglethorpe and Stephens literary societies attracted dozens of members, including football players. The auditorium became the site of lyceums with speakers from such well-known universities as Harvard. A Faculty Club met twice each month for stimulating programs and discussions, including refreshments and/or a meal. On May 4, 1928, the old "field days" and "spring festivals" from A&M days gave way to an elaborate celebration, May Day, complete with a queen, her court of honor, and an impressive pageant featuring a maypole.

Finally, Wells transformed the physical appearance of the campus by planting dogwood trees and crepe myrtles. He smoothed the lawn and planted "carpet grass." A remodeled Anderson Hall, with the addition of a third floor, provided more housing for students and married faculty. The long-range campus plan, circulated in newspapers and campus publications, clearly depicted the ambitions of the Wells administration.

Seeking to give 'Culture Hill a new identity, Wells asked the U. S. Postmaster to establish an official post office on the campus. On August 10, 1928, he received this official notice: "The post office department, on recommendation of Senator Walter F. George, has ordered a post office established at the Georgia Normal School, Statesboro. Guy Herbert Wells was named as postmaster. The name of the post office will be 'Studentsboro.'" Realizing the name did not have that "collegiate" sound, Wells asked for a name change, and within a month it was approved: "Collegeboro." [96]

In just three short years, Georgia Normal School had assumed the appearance of a stable academic institution, one with a tangible past and a promising future. All that was left was the big move to the status of a four-year college. By ingeniously arranging the schedule of course offerings, the faculty in fact offered a handful of students enough hours to qualify for a baccalaureate degree. The board of trustees had authorized this move, anticipating a successful bill to rename the college in the 1929 General Assembly that met in July and August.

Social life, 1920s

In 1964 a seasoned teacher named Ada Lou Rowe, from Claxton, enrolled in summer school. She recalled being among the first students to receive a bachelor's degree after the institution became a four-year college in 1929. She summarized student life in the late 1920s in a newspaper interview:

• Social life consisted largely of vespers held in the auditorium, followed by literary and organizational meetings. Literary societies provided the main social activity on the campus. Rowe was a member of the Whistler Art Club and the Oglethorpe Literary Society, and served as president and vice president of the Dramatics Club.

• Boys could eat with girls in the dining hall but could not walk them to the dormitory.

• The road running straight to the administration building was the boundary, and girls could not cross it from the east, and boys could not cross it from the west.

"It All Started in 1925,"
Bulloch Herald, 14 July 1964

Bill Number 379, General Assembly of Georgia, 1929

"An Act changing the name of the Georgia Normal School, etc."

Section I—Be it enacted by the General Assembly of Georgia, and it is hereby enacted by the authority of the same, that from and after the passage of this Act, the Act approved August 18, 1924, establishing the Georgia Normal School at Statesboro, be and the same is hereby amended by striking from the caption of the said Act the words "Georgia Normal School" and substitution therefore the words "South Georgia Teachers College."

Students and faculty welcome Governor Hardman on May 15, 1929. Albert Deal stands on the far right.

Felix C. Williams of the sixteenth district and Andrew J. Bird of the forty-ninth district on July 25 introduced a bill to change the name from Georgia Normal College to South Georgia Teachers College. (Bird was involved in the sensational fight with trustee James R. Miller in 1909.) The legislature approved the change, and Governor Hardman, a familiar face in Collegeboro, signed the bill into law on August 24, 1929.

Because a group of students had already completed the required number of hours, the first graduating class was already in place. Before the ink from Governor Hardman's signature had dried, so to speak, South Georgia Teachers College passed out baccalaureate degrees to the following who actually had earned their degrees in June: Luniel Bell of Waynesboro; Zulieme Lane of Collegeboro; Ada Lou Rowe of Claxton; Dorothy Thomas of Jacksonville, Florida; and Earle Wood of Statesboro.[97]

To demonstrate immediately the strength of the institution, President Wells announced in mid-November 1929 that the once struggling college had ended the fiscal year with a surplus of $12,000. Coming a few weeks after the "Black Tuesday" on Wall Street, it was, perhaps, the first good economic news journalists had received that month. The *Columbus Ledger* applauded the achievement: "Due publicity should be given the accomplishments of the South Georgia Teachers College. It has set a mark for other state institutions."[98]

If anyone doubted that Guy Wells' ability to keep up with the ambitious pace of his predecessor, those doubts surely evaporated on that bright day, August 24, 1929—the day for which many supporters of the 'Culture had worked so hard.

The stumps and clutter that Professor Rowan found so depressing in 1908 were a distant memory. The debts that vexed Principal Dickens from 1909 until 1915 now were merely artifacts—pieces of paper marked "paid" in the vault of the treasurer's office.

South Georgia now had its very own four-year college. Its home was Collegeboro, located just south of Statesboro. South Georgia Teachers College had arrived, and it stood proudly on a gentle hill of ever-increasing beauty.

Nine years of ceaseless activity by Principal/President Hollis and President Wells now seemed justified. On a personal level, the current president had experienced something that eludes many leaders: a triumphal success without obvious conflict. He was making progress "walking through the fodder."

LAMARTINE HARDMAN
Hardman became the oldest elected governor of Georgia when he took office in 1927 at the age of seventy-one. He served until 1931. Known for his businesslike approach, he complimented President Guy Wells on his surplus budgets.

TEACHERS
COLLEGE

Teachers College
1929-1934

1929 – Rookie coach Crook Smith leads Blue Tide to 5–2 record and conference football championship. (12/13)

1930 – Legislature passes bill to phase out A&M schools. (1/29)

1930 – Huldah Cail, student from Screven County, promotes modern dance classes for females. (2/1)

1930 – Asa Wall, star of 1927 GNS baseball team, signs with Buffalo in the International League. (5/1)

1930 – Professor Lucy Gage of Peabody College is first female commencement speaker. (6/5)

1930 – *George-Anne* reviews W. E. B. DuBois' "Dark Water Credo of 1925." (6/20)

1930 – Sir Arthur Conan Doyle, novelist who created Sherlock Holmes, dies. (7/7)

1930 – Soccer remains popular on campus, but team competes less often during football season. (11/7)

1930 – Former star Delmas Rushing returns to support football team at Thanksgiving.

1930 – American author Sinclair Lewis wins the Nobel Prize for Literature. (12/10)

1931 – Board of Trustees declares blue and white uniforms for female students are optional. (3/3)

1931 – College glee club organizes first regional tour. (3/5)

1931 – Students excavate dirt and pour cement for new swimming pool. (3/31)

1931 – The Empire State Building in New York City, the world's most famous skyscraper, opens its doors. (5/1)

1931 – SGTC receives four-year rating from American Association of Teachers Colleges. (6/1)

1931 – Legislature abolishes six A&M schools and creates Board of Regents. (7/30)

1931 – Thomas Edison, owner of 1,093 patents, dies. (10/18)

1931 – Board of Trustees, ending twenty-five years of service, turns over control of SGTC to the Board of Regents. (12/17)

1931 – Third stories added to East Hall and West Hall at a cost of $16,362. (12/28).

1932 – Basketball team's nickname is "Teachers." (1/14)

1932 – Amelia Earhart completes first solo flight across the Atlantic by a woman. (5/21)

1932 – Acclaimed adventurer and author Richard Halliburton thrills SGTC audience with tales of around-the-world travels. (10/27, 28)

1932 – Franklin D. Roosevelt wins the U.S. presidential election. (11/8)

1932 – Four tennis courts are completed between the new Alumni Building and the lake. (11/14)

1932 – President Wells announces to faculty the state reduced university system's budget by 14 percent. (12/5)

1932 – County Commissioner R. J. Kennedy arranges for chain-gang laborers to repair campus roads and complete other projects. (12/5)

1933 – Campus celebrates state's bicentennial projects by planting trees and building fountains with stones from historic buildings. (1/19)

1933 – Adolf Hitler is appointed chancellor of Germany. (1/30)

1933 – English instructor Fielding Russell introduces art of boxing to campus. (2/27)

1933 – African American employees include Vandy, Wesley, and Melrose. (3/1-3/30)

1933 – SGTC athletic teams complete a sweep of conference titles in baseball, football, and basketball. (3/6)

1933 – Students present pageant, "Removal of the Cherokee Indians," at bicentennial event in Savannah. (3/20)

1933 – Former Teachers College star, Lefty Wilson, is dazzling in debut for Toronto Maple Leafs professional baseball team. (4/3)

1933 – *George-Anne* announces a campus concert by Cab Calloway and address by Mahatma Gandhi, inaugurating a tradition of April Fools' Day editions. (4/3)

1933 – SGTC operates community cannery for local gardeners and farmers who wish to preserve foods scientifically. (6/1)

1933 – Regents replace semester system with quarter system, making it easier for students to transfer credit hours. (9/7)

1933 – Women's Athletic Association is formed; Helen Olliff is president, Mary Margaret Blitch is vice president. (10/3)

1933 – George Washington Carver is first African American to present a major address at SGTC. (10/31)

1933 – Twenty-first Amendment to the U.S. Constitution repeals Eighteenth "prohibition" Amendment. (12/5)

1934 – Faculty member Alvin Singley is first to make hole-in-one on new campus golf course. (4/9)

1934 – Guy Wells is promoted to the presidency of Georgia State College for Women. He is replaced by Marvin Pittman of Michigan State Normal College. (4/19)

1934 – *Reflector* not published for 1934-35, due to economic hard times. (5/1)

DEFINING THE ROLE

The "roaring twenties" described the life and times of the college but not of Bulloch County. The American economy might have appeared promising, but local conditions were not encouraging. The boll weevil decimated the once-lucrative cotton market in the 1920s.

In other parts of the nation, farmers left the field and found jobs in manufacturing plants. Statesboro, however, had no manufacturers of any size. Owners of a large cottonseed oil mill tried to succeed locally, but by 1920 they had failed miserably. The big meat-packing plant on Packinghouse Road also failed, bringing financial ruin to local investors. Trustees of the A&M school could be thankful they had rejected the company's request in 1916 to build the huge plant on the edge of the campus.

The economic depression began early in Bulloch County. 'Culture Hill, however, kept in step with the national mood. During the latter part of the twenties, President Guy Wells maintained the momentum young President Ernest Hollis had begun. Wells became a symbol of a "new breed" of college presidents in Georgia. He seemed to know how to increase enrollments, improve facilities, and generate publicity. Amazingly, he managed to accrue budget surpluses rather than deficits.

Governors, senators, and state politicians came to Statesboro regularly to participate in meetings on topics of current interest. Nationally known authorities gave stimulating lectures, and Wells always invited the community to attend.

Educator William Heard Kilpatrick, who popularized philosopher John Dewey's "progressive education," spoke at commencement in 1929. Wells had studied under Kilpatrick at Columbia University. During the next decade, the popular professor from Columbia University became a familiar name and face on the campus. Audiences warmed up to Kilpatrick when Wells told them the scholar was a native Georgian, who earlier had taught at Wells' alma mater, Mercer University.[1]

Wells hosted major educational conferences. On November 11, 1929, the *Savannah Morning News* described a keynote address by an educator from the state teachers college in Michigan. The *News* reported: "Dr. M. S. Pittman . . . for one hour and fifteen minutes charmed the twelve hundred teachers who had crowded the auditorium to hear this authority on rural education. . . . He talked frankly to the teachers, giving them pointers that could be carried home and put into use." That speaker was Marvin S. Pittman, whose name later would become a familiar one locally and statewide.

The fall of 1929 also marked the beginning of a new era in athletics. Wells hired a new football coach and athletic director—Byron Lambert Smith,

WILLIAM HEARD KILPATRICK

A native of White Plains, Ga., Professor Kilpatrick taught Guy Wells at Columbia University. Kilpatrick popularized "progressive education" movement advanced by the philosopher John Dewey. Kilpatrick visited and spoke in Collegeboro from the 1920s through the 1950s.

Faculty and staff, 1925–1931

1925 – Marian Pate Johnson, Expression

1925 – Viola Perry, Mathematics and Registrar

1925 – Malvina Trussell, Natural Science

1926 – Dr. John Whiteside, College Physician

1927 – Carrie Clay Law, English

1927 – Joseph E. Carruth, Education

1927 – Robert Donaldson, Journalism

1928 – Hester Newton, Georgia History & Social Science

1929 – Esther Barnes, Music

1929 – Mae Michael, Secretary to the President

1929 – Marie Wood, Supervising Teacher

1929 – Byron L. Smith, Physical Education

1930 – Mamie Veazey, Dean of Women

1930 – W. S. Hanner, Science

1931 – Ruth Bolton, Home Economics

1931 – Robert L. Winburn, Comptroller

"A Calendar of Progress of Georgia Teachers College," *Georgia Teachers College Alumni Quarterly* 3, no. 4 (1952)

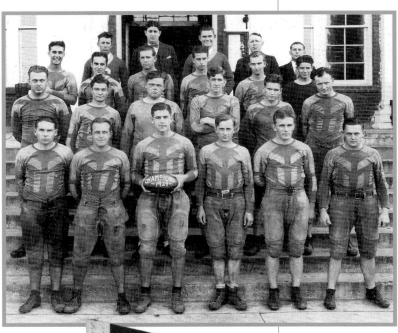

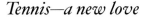

Tennis—a new love

"The tennis court is now in condition to play, and a number of teachers have expressed themselves as wanting to play this fascinating game."

George-Anne, 2 May 1927

nicknamed Crook. People who read the sports columns recognized his name instantly. Both Crook and his brother, nicknamed Phoney, had been star athletes at Mercer when the Baptist college was a powerhouse in football. Phoney was one of Mercer's greatest running backs. Crook was great all around: All-Southern Conference end three times and all-conference in three sports, the first four-letter man in Mercer's history, and holder of a record number of letters in sports—thirteen.[2]

Sports historians sometimes have misinterpreted his nickname. Although he was frugal to a fault, he was never dishonest. The nickname stems from a physical trait. He had a "crooked" or "low shoulder," the result, perhaps, of a football injury.[3]

Like President Wells, Crook Smith approached people in a down-to-earth manner. He quickly made friends both on and off campus. Athletes loved him. Chester Williams, who played for Coach Crook, entered South Georgia Teachers College (SGTC) in 1931. Williams recalled, "He was just a nice fellow. He never cursed, but always said, 'golly bum.'"[4] During his first season as football coach, in 1929, the "nice fellow" coached his team to finish first in the conference.

Zach Henderson, a friendly man like Smith, settled into the job he began in 1927—dean of the college. He took time off in 1928 to complete his master's degree in education at Columbia University.

The dean's wife, Marjorie Henderson, quickly became involved in the musical life of the campus, playing for vespers and directing the vespers choir. The petite woman lugged an accordion onstage and led students in familiar songs. The entertaining Mrs. Henderson occasionally played the piano while standing with her back to the keyboard, somehow reaching the right notes behind her. A student described her performances in rhyming lines:

> Her voice is like a mocking bird.
> There's never a time when it can't be heard.
> She plays and can sing
> And do most anything.[5]

Student life at SGTC was not unlike that of a community high school. Perhaps the mood carried over from A&M days. Professors typically lived on campus, and students knew them personally. Young people experienced a special camaraderie they long would remember. That most students held campus jobs further bonded them to the college and to each other.

"I wish each one would study, play, sing, laugh, joke and do all of the other worthwhile things needed to live the best life."[6] This statement by Dean Henderson in 1930 mirrors his personal and practical interpretation of education. The dean's approach to education was not of the "progressive" school, as John Dewey defined it. Rather, Henderson believed an educated person should be "well rounded." Neither academic pursuits nor social activities should dominate the life of an educated person, particularly one who plans to teach children.

During the early days of the Great Depression, when students had trouble paying tuition, President Wells seemed to find ways to keep them in school. Chester Williams echoed many alumni who recalled the president would locate a job on or off campus that would provide enough income to pay the fee of $14 per month for tuition and room and board.[7] Stella Vanlandingham from Wrightsville, Georgia, earned her fare by working in the library.[8]

Students tended to look on Wells as a father figure, albeit a liberated one. He took personal interest in them, even as he enforced the rules. He treated them with respect and encouraged them to be independent thinkers. He joked with students, remembering nicknames and repeating humorous events in their lives.

If for example, David Turner, the editor of the *Bulloch Times* were making a speech for the college in a nearby town, Wells would give his car keys to a student, inviting him to drive "Uncle Dave" to and from the event.[9] Williams recalled playing chauffeur to several well-known individuals, including a new power in state politics, Eugene Talmadge. Students whose parents did not own automobiles felt honored to earn the president's trust.

Running a student-centered college seemed natural for Guy Wells. After he became president he made clear his views that students should be responsible for resolving issues that arose from life outside the classroom.

Four months after the institution became SGTC, he announced the first student government. The officers were: President LaFiece Collins, junior; Vice President Waldo Pafford, senior; and Secretary Lillian Rocker, junior. Class representatives were Lester Newton, senior; Joyce Gardner, senior; Talmadge Roberts, junior; Elmo Mallard, sophomore; Kathleen Harmon, sophomore; Annie Ruth Moore, sophomore; and Boyd Boswell, freshman.

On many occasions the campus newspaper noted the student body had high regard for the president who seemed at ease around them: "He is widely known throughout several states and has perhaps done more toward furthering this school than any other person connected with it. His spirit of friendliness and good cheer is so evident that it permeates the lives of all with whom he comes in contact."[10] When he returned from a seminar at George Peabody Teachers College, the students welcomed him with "many applauses and yells." The campus newspaper continued: "We were glad to welcome our President after so long an absence."[11]

Students were not alone in their appreciation of the president. The community also lavished praise on him during his years at the college. The common refrain around town was that he cared as much about Statesboro

Dean Zach Henderson of Gillsville married Marjorie Clark of Eastman in 1927. They were the parents of Gene, Mary, and Ann.

The first museum—1929

The earliest reference to the Anderson Museum appears in the *George-Anne* for June 29, 1929. Its name honored the original chairman of the board of trustees, J. Randolph Anderson. Located in cabinets in the Administration Building, the museum moved in 1933 to the old Sunnyside School Building. When the new Training School opened in 1934, the museum gained new quarters—a room dedicated to the growing collections.

"The museum contains a rare and complete exhibit of birds typical of this section numbering over four hundred. Among the historic relics of importance are a lamp used during the first days of Mercer, limb from the famous John Wesley Oak at St. Simons Island, a window decoration from the renowned Richard Malcolm Johnston school, and rare potteries and stones from various sections of the state.... [Mr.] DeLoach, who is in charge of the museum, stated that it is for purely educational purposes and the public should feel free to come at all times. He urged that anyone who could contribute to the museum do so."

George-Anne, 2 October 1933

State historian verifies campus trees

"This is to certify that I accompanied President Guy H. Wells and Miss Caro Lane, of South Georgia Teachers College, on a trip to the John Wesley Oak and the Sidney Lanier Oak. I testify that they got a large quantity of acorns from the original trees which they were to plant on the campus of the college at Statesboro. I also testify to their possession of a large quantity of acorns which they gathered from the Oglethorpe Oak, located at Darien. . .and the tree that owns itself in Athens have been planted for this purpose. While gathering these acorns, plantings were also secured to be used in the college grounds."

Lucian Lamar Knight
Bulloch Times, 27 April 1933

as he did the college. He joined a committee to develop a community-wide landscaping plan. They applied for financial support from the Better Homes Campaign, organized by Herbert Hoover, Secretary of the U. S. Department of Commerce. The campaign in Washington formally recognized Statesboro's committee, naming Guy Wells as committee chairman.[12]

While the Great Depression robbed the community of federal funds for beautification, Wells pushed on. He visited his friends in Ivanhoe, including the Cones, searching for wild crepe myrtle and dogwood. Martha Cone Benson, recalled seeing Wells at her father's (Clisby Cone) farm, often wearing work clothes and carrying a shovel. She said her father liked Wells, because the president "didn't mind getting his hands dirty."[13]

Wells and coworkers removed native plants during their dormant season and, with the help of the garden club, replanted them to make a green border for Statesboro's streets. At the end of April 1930 he wrote a letter to local citizens, reminding them to water the plants and not to disturb the roots: "I am sure all of the city wishes to see our town grow as beautiful as possible, and that all will cooperate to help save all the trees possible."[14]

Young Jack Nelson Averitt attended a woman's club committee meeting as a guest pianist around 1931. He stayed for the program and heard Wells give an enthusiastic talk on beautification. "He gave clear instructions on how to help a transplanted tree thrive: Tie a ribbon on the northernmost limb. Then dig up the tree with its root system. Transplant the tree with the ribbon pointing north, so the tree will face the sun in its usual manner." Averitt recalled seeing Wells supervise the planting of dogwood trees, beginning on both sides of the drive leading to the campus, extending north on South Main Street toward downtown.[15]

Wells had a deep interest in horticulture, especially native plants. He took pride in campus landscaping projects. During the state's bicentennial year, 1933, the *Bulloch Times* reported a typical Wells story. Wells used historic trees to lend a sense of history to the relatively young campus:

Trees have been planted on the campus taken up from the most famous trees on the Georgia coast. First of all is the Oglethorpe Oak at Darien, under which General Oglethorpe camped in 1733. The college has secured a number of small trees that sprouted from acorns that fell from the limbs of the tree. Likewise they have secured trees from under the John Wesley Oak and the Sidney Lanier Oak at Brunswick. Along with the small trees, several thousand acorns from the trees have been secured to plant in the nursery. In a few years the college hopes to be able to offer [trees] to any school, church, club, or individual, for a small price.[16]

Quoting a campus visitor, Wells told the student body why the tree project was important: "No institution can be truly great until it is rooted in the fine tradition of the past." [17]

When Wells crafted his mission statement, he spoke of the college's destiny "to become seen." He wanted to improve the image of what only recently had been a junior college. Planting historic trees was a start. But the buildings on top of Culture Hill did not yet resemble a campus.

In 1927 Wells had hired an architect to develop a campus plan, keeping in mind the projected growth of the student body. The result was Wells' vision of an orderly arrangement of buildings, based on an enlarged circle, with landscaping. The architect planned a compact and traditional college on the crown of 'Culture Hill, without considering the possibility the campus would gain acreage over the years. Wells kept the sketch in his office as long as he was president, and he proudly showed it to visitors.

State support for building projects dried up during the early 1930s. Wells reluctantly postponed his long-term plan and settled for something more realistic—remodeling existing buildings and adding new buildings on a pay-as-you-go basis. Begun in the early 1930s as low-cost emergency measures, these projects provided needed space, improved student life, and enhanced the appearance of the campus.

Student survey reveals top twelve abuses of grammar on campus

- I seen
- can't hardly
- sure did
- she ain't
- can I go?
- she done it
- they was
- he don't
- ain't got
- I was mad
- he run
- sho''tis

George-Anne, 26 May 1930

BEYOND TEMPORARY SOLUTIONS

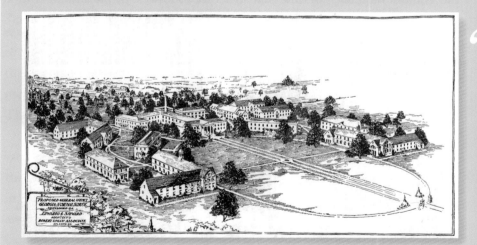

Campus of the future

"Architects who are experts on college planning have been employed to sketch a plan for the buildings which will be created on our campus within the next hundred years. This may seem a long time, but we must remember that we are going to grow slowly and surely: and for the sake of the future Georgia Normal we cannot afford to make any mistake in the arrangement of the buildings which will impede the work of the future students of our Alma Mater or hinder their progress in any way. It takes Time, Vision, and Faith to make a school."

George-Anne, 1 October 1927

Students living in tents

"Savannahians who visited Statesboro yesterday were . . . surprised to find more than six hundred students in attendance upon the summer session of this institution which is the only college in the First Congressional District. The dormitories are filled; every building near the college is filled; houses have been rented in Statesboro and more than a hundred students walk the mile to the college each day from the town. Tents are erected on the campus and scores of young men are camping in them and attending classes. . . . The college at Statesboro needs two dormitories—one for girls and one for the boys."

Savannah Morning News, reprinted in *Bulloch Times*, 16 July 1931

Byron and Martha Dyer

Byron Dyer, a special farm agent for Bulloch County, lived alone on the top floor of West Hall in 1932. A year later he married Martha Evans, a graduate of the University of Georgia. Both had earned master's degrees. The couple lived down the hall from the Fielding Russell family. President Wells depended on Dyer for advice about the college farm and campus landscaping. Dyer taught some classes and served as a scoutmaster. Mrs. Dyer, an athlete, coached women's basketball and soccer. She taught swimming and folk dance. The Dyers helped Hester Newton plan the Georgia bicentennial pageant in 1933, and they were active in social and athletic events on campus for several years.

"This . . . promises to be a thrilling time for all basketball enthusiasts on the campus. Mrs. [Byron] Dyer is acting as coach and the girls practice from four to six each afternoon. The clubs, societies and sororities also are practicing and have planned a tournament to begin January 25th."

George-Anne, 15 January 1934

and faculty Joseph Carruth in education, Hester Newton in history, Carrie Law Clay and Fielding Russell in English, and Malvina Trussell and William S. Hanner in science. The administration, guided by the faculty, applied for accreditation by the American Association of Teachers Colleges.

Later, Wells reported success: "In 1931 the college was admitted to a four-year rating by the American Association of Teachers Colleges; credits are now recognized by most of the Georgia colleges."[24] Immediately Wells began a campaign for the ultimate recognition—accreditation by the Southern Association of Colleges and Secondary Schools.

Wells knew the college needed to gain approval from its peers statewide. So he ran for the presidency of the Georgia Association of Educators (GEA). He won, and he spent several days each month traveling to schools throughout the state, gently reminding superintendents and principals that SGTC was, in fact, the only dedicated college for teachers in Georgia. He said he was proud to be president of "Teachers College."

On April 15, 1932, Wells claimed a role both for himself and his college. He demonstrated he was more than a politician at the helm of a teachers college. In his presidential address to the statewide meeting of the GEA in Macon, he made a case for the relevance of public education. No doubt his mentor at Columbia, William Heard Kilpatrick, was pleased.

Georgia lost its leadership in education to North Carolina, Wells said, because local schools no longer produced thinkers and speakers like Alexander Stephens, Robert Toombs, or Howell Cobb. If students understood literature and history as well as these men did, Wells observed, Georgia once again could be a light to the South and the nation. What the state needed was an educational reformation, not unlike the protestant reformation of the sixteenth century. He laced his speech with quotations by Martin Luther, St. Paul, Horace Mann, Thomas Jefferson, James Madison, and John Adams. On that day Wells, president of the "Teachers College," grew in stature as an educational leader.[25]

Accreditation at the collegiate level required library resources adequate for the student body and academic program. The library in the Administration Building was inadequate. Holdings consisted largely of books that generous citizens had donated, and some of the volumes had been in the high school library since 1908. The annual report for 1924 noted the collection comprised a thousand volumes. During Wells' first year as president, he made the library one of his special projects.

By 1927 the heavily used room in the Administration Building simply would not serve the growing student body, particularly during the spring and summer months, when teachers flooded the campus. "The library is so much in demand that additional rooms have been turned over for the accommodation of the students," reported the *George-Anne.*

While the extra rooms solved seating problems in the library, the president had not yet solved a more serious shortcoming: a woefully

VICTORY IS NOT ENOUGH

"From the viewpoint of this humble chronicler, there are many things in life more important as character builders, that makes for better preparation in life's battles, than victory. Victory is always sweet, but victory without sportsmanship, loyalty, and courage is not worthwhile."

Coach Crook, *George-Anne*, 28 November 1932

BYRON LAMBERT "CROOK" SMITH

Smith coached several championship teams in football, basketball, baseball, and track from 1929 to 1941.

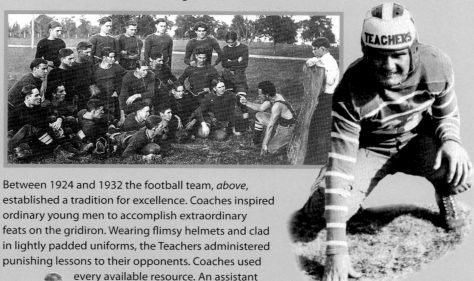

Between 1924 and 1932 the football team, *above*, established a tradition for excellence. Coaches inspired ordinary young men to accomplish extraordinary feats on the gridiron. Wearing flimsy helmets and clad in lightly padded uniforms, the Teachers administered punishing lessons to their opponents. Coaches used every available resource. An assistant held a crude slate chalkboard upon which the coach diagramed plays for the "single wing" system.

Joe Lambright ('38), *above right*, demonstrates the proper stance and protective gear. Later, he became editor of the *Savannah Morning News*. Jake Hines ('35), *far right*, compiled records as a swift halfback in football, a great hitting and fielding second baseman in baseball, and a leading scorer in basketball. Coach Smith called Hines "the greatest athlete in the history of the college." Earl "Coonie" Riggs ('37), *left*, excelled in football. Morgan Blake, sportswriter for the *Atlanta Journal* wrote of Riggs, "Old number 5 is one of the greatest centers we have seen."

Conference champions, 1931

First row, *left to right:* George Hagin, Jack Thompson, J. D. Fields, Clyde Greenway, Edward Jones. Second, *left to right:* Ray Bell, Oscar Joiner, B. C. Olliff, Bobbie Sasser, Elton Sanders, James Carruth (manager). Third, *left to right*: Coach Smith, President Wells

"In every success there are certain characteristics, certain policies that one must follow. . . . The teams as a whole were composed of young men of high character—men who had courage, conviction and manhood to stand up for the manly and fair and square thing. To this type of athlete, I attribute our success."

Coach Crook, *George-Anne*, 29 May 1933

Tobacco warehouse basketball

"The Blue Tide of the Georgia Normal School will officially open their schedule Friday night with South Georgia Junior College of Douglas at the Statesboro tobacco warehouse. . . . As a preliminary to the game Friday night with Douglas, there will be a girls' game beginning at 7:30."

Bulloch Times, 13 December 1928

During tobacco season (August–October), area farmers sold their tobacco in huge warehouses, located in Statesboro on College Street. Between November and March, the enclosed space was suitable for basketball. Georgia Normal and SGTC practiced and played here until the Alumni Gymnasium was completed in 1932.

Lyman Hall College?

A student survey revealed "Lyman Hall" was not the top choice. Hall was one of three Georgians to sign the Declaration of Independence. A patriot who attended the first Constitutional Convention, Abraham Baldwin, received the most votes.

Baldwin	198
Lyman Hall	89
SGTC	22
Walton	8
Lanier	5
Ga. Teachers College	4
Empire College	4
Stephens	3
Wells College	2
Wellington Institute	2

Bulloch Times, 27 February 1933

inadequate collection of books. He discussed the matter with many individuals, including the local historian of Bulloch County, Mrs. Julian Lane. She urged Wells to contact the state historian, Lucian Lamar Knight, with whom she had worked closely in 1931–32 while planning Georgia's bicentennial celebration.[26]

The president who sat at the courthouse on Saturdays shooting the breeze with farmers just as easily discussed books and historic trees with the scholarly Knight. On February 13, 1933, the *George-Anne* broke the good news: Georgia's esteemed state historian was donating his personal library to SGTC. The paper noted a casual remark of Wells to Knight: if he "would make a donation of his library the question of the book supply for the college would be solved."

Wells promised the historian the collection would be known as "the Lucian Lamar Knight Historical Library." The college's only obligation was to transport the books from Brunswick, where they were stored in the home of W. H. Harris.[27]

The Knight collection gave the college something it needed: scholarly books and recognition as an academic institution. Locals assumed, with good reason, that any college or university in the state would have been honored to receive the impressive Knight collection of three thousand volumes, many of which contained autographs of authors. One volume, a dictionary of languages, bore an imprint of 1564—just over one hundred years after Gutenberg produced the first book on his invention, the printing press.

At a time when banks failed and people struggled to keep body and soul together, the story of success out at Collegeboro inspired confidence in the future. During the dark days of the depression, the merchants in town learned to count on business generated by faculty, staff, and students. According to the *Bulloch Times* on September 27, 1933, the fall enrollment of "458 . . . is the highest mark attained by the college for a regular term since its creation almost twenty years ago [*sic*]. . . . During the summer sessions there has been as many as six hundred enrolled." In the summer of 1934, that number expanded to 765.[28]

The community might have been amused by news from the university system's Board of Regents. According to the *Bulloch Times*, the regents had requested that the legislature rename many of the state's colleges, because the public so easily confused their names and locations. For SGTC, the *George-Anne* suggested "Lyman Hall College."

David Turner of the *Times* weighed in by noting the college, just twenty-seven years old, already had used three different names. "Let it be hoped that it will eventually be given a permanent name. There are yet people in this community who know it by its first name and refer to it as the 'Culture.[29]

Had President Wells been given a choice, he would have chosen a name that contained the words "teachers" and "college," for that was his heart's desire—to establish SGTC as THE teachers college for Georgia. Ultimately the regents' proposal failed to win support in the legislature, and all colleges retained their given names.

ENHANCING STUDENT LIFE

When President Wells walked from the Administration Building to the dairy in 1931, his path led through several acres of unimproved property. On his way to the big barn, he would step down a gently sloping hill that led to a small wetland or swamp. In his mind's eye, he saw in this space three developments: a swimming pool, an amphitheatre on the hillside, and a lake at the base. Over a period of three years, he completed these projects that improved the southern side of the campus.

First came the swimming pool. He shared his idea with students during an assembly. They were enthusiastic. Early in the spring of 1931 the student body endorsed the president's plan for building a large, modern outdoor swimming pool. Each male student pledged to devote three days of free labor.

Students removed dirt, laid foundations and drains, mixed and poured concrete, and planted grass and shrubs on the edge of the pool. The *Reflector* described the progress: "It was a pleasant sight to see those boys working like a nest of huge ants, for the work was so cheerfully given, it amounted to play."[30]

The second improvement on the south side would reshape the campus forever: the lake. College students had neither the time nor the equipment to remove the soil and build a crescent-shaped dam of some two hundred feet in length. The president called on a longtime friend of the college, one who had been a delegate in Savannah in 1906—Raymond Jimmerson Kennedy. The dentist was by this time a county commissioner. Turner told the story of the lake in the *Bulloch Times* on July 14, 1932:

Through certain satisfactory exchanges . . . a group from the chain gang gave several days assistance in the building of a dam for the body of water. Hardly a month ago the lake site was dry ground, but today there is water to a depth of six feet at the deepest point. Small boats play upon the surface, and "Lake Wells" has jumped into popularity.

For July 11, 1932, when the college and town overflowed with summer-term teachers, students Oscar Joiner and Ralph Stephens planned a dedication ceremony. They focused the event on their president. The English professor, Carrie Law Clay, read Wells' favorite poem, Rudyard Kipling's "If."

First diver

"In March, a proud and happy student body gathered around the pool for its formal dedication. Kathryn Brett had been chosen to make the first dive which proved to be a beautiful swan dive. She was immediately followed by many others who felt the double pleasure in the first swim. This day will always linger in the memory, enriched with a touch of love and appreciation for the happy association of group work."

Reflector, 1931

Alma Mater, South Georgia Teachers College (1932)

Down among the murmuring pine trees,
Where old nature smiles,
Old T. C. holds up a standard,
Known for miles and miles.

CHORUS

Lift the chorus, Speed it onward,
Ne'er her standard fail,
Hail to thee our Alma Mater,
Hail T. C., All Hail.

From the blue and broad Atlantic,
Balmy breezes blow,
Wafting far old T. C.'s spirit
May she ever grow.

On that day she probably emphasized these lines, knowing the huge crowd would recognize in them the values of their president:

> *If you can talk with crowds and keep your virtue,*
> *Or walk with kings—nor lose the common touch,*

The students knew a speaker who appreciated the president's "common touch." They invited Howell Cone. These two, who had "walked through the fodder" together, recognized the moment for what it was—one of the happiest in Wells' career in Statesboro.

The program that afternoon reserved a time for the singing of a new song—an alma mater, the first one to appear in print since the "lads and lass' of Culture" version from A&M days.[31] The new school song substituted "murmuring pine trees" for "cypress," "standard" for "banners," and "broad Atlantic" for "the ocean." Students even incorporated the motto of Statesboro's chamber of commerce, "where nature smiles."

Borrowing similar images and words from the earlier alma mater of the A&M school, the students' new lyrics worked well with the earlier melody. Beginning with spring commencement on June 5, 1933, the alma mater became a standard part of the printed program at future commencements. Programs from the 1920s through 1932 included only class songs and hymns.

The year 1933 gave the student body an opportunity to gain statewide recognition in the state's bicentennial celebration held in Savannah. Guided by Hester Newton, a history professor, students planned a pageant devoted to a controversial theme, the removal of the Cherokee Indians from Georgia.

Newton easily rounded up faculty and staff to help direct some 150 college students—Caro Lane, Ruth Bolton, and Robert Winburn, as well as the new county special farm agent, Byron Dyer, and his wife. At the time Dyer advised the school farm superintendent and assisted Coach Crook Smith, and Mrs. Dyer was a physical education instructor.[32] During May Day ceremonies in 1933, the students repeated their spectacular performance on campus.

A portion of the May Day pageant took place near Lake Wells. At that time the lake had been enhanced. Work crews earlier that spring erected a stage near the base of the hill behind the Administration Building. Students sat on benches and on the lawn. In June 1933 the campus newspaper reported on this improvement: "The outdoor stage which is located on the shores of Lake Wells has also been equipped with lights. This will now take the effect of an amphitheatre." This outdoor assembly would become a central part of campus for nearly thirty years.[33]

The final improvement to Lake Wells came by way of France. Mae Michael, the secretary to Wells, was sister of Moina—the person who originated the poppy as a symbol to honor veterans of World War I. While the "poppy lady" traveled in Europe, Mae asked her to take cuttings from the Bonaparte willow that provided shade for the original grave of Napoleon.

Moina brought the willow cuttings back to Mae, who sought the horticultural advice of her green-thumbed boss. The new plants quickly took root along the banks of the new lake.[34] For decades those weeping willows and their offspring provided a delicate green border for Lake Wells.

At first, no one seemed concerned that the creation of Lake Wells caused the swamp below it to grow larger. They noticed it, however, during the summer months when mosquitoes swarmed the south side of the campus. After enduring a year of irritating episodes near the lake, students nicknamed the swamp below Lake Wells "mosquito breeder." Students created a new line for the alma mater: "Down among the murmuring pine trees, where old nature smells."

Making merry in May

On May 1, 1928, Georgia Normal School began a custom that continued for nearly thirty years— the celebration of May Day. As early as 1913, the A&M school sponsored a springtime athletic festival. After 1928 athletic events preceded the crowning of the queen of May in the afternoon. Daisy Fields, *top photo*, seated on her throne, was the first May queen. Eloise Smith Nessmith (indicated by arrow), a member of the court, provided the photograph.

After the creation of the lake in 1932, the May Day festival took place on the green between the amphitheatre and the lake. The queen of May and her court watched as student dancers platted long ribbons around three poles with skill and grace. The community joined the student body for this unique celebration brought to the campus by President Guy Wells. The celebration at the right took place on May 3, 1935.

"As a result of Friday's ballots, Louise Quantock, senior, will reign as queen over the May Day festivities of South Georgia Teachers College, May 3rd. Margaret Owens, also a senior, was chosen maid of honor. . . . The May Day festival, which will be held in the afternoon of May 3rd, will take the nature of an open air pageant, with Oriental and interpretive dances by different groups. The center of the program will be the May Pole dance."

George-Anne, 8 April 1935

Carver comes to Collegeboro

"A crowd which taxed the auditorium to its capacity, including many persons from all over the county and even from adjoining counties, heard Dr. George Carver, noted colored scientist. . . . The distinguished educator, member of the faculty of Tuskegee Institute, Alabama, came from Savannah and was accompanied by Prof. Hubert, head of the industrial college there. . . . For more than an hour the noted educator held his audience spellbound as he discussed the lowly peanut, and presented more than four score samples of products which he has evolved from it at his laboratory in Tuskegee. . . . Dr. Carver returned to Savannah immediately after his address to the student body at the college."

Bulloch Times, 2 November 1933

Top, *George Washington Carver, scientist, in the Tuskegee Institute laboratory.*

Bottom, *Guy Wells, George W. Carver, and Benjamin Hubert*

On Tuesday, October 31, 1933, Wells stood before a crowd estimated at fifteen hundred, took a deep breath, and began "walking through the fodder." The moment arrived—the first African American to deliver a major address at the institution sat on the stage.

Wells did not introduce Professor Carver. Rather, he presented the locally esteemed black principal, William James, who brought to the stage a choir of young people from his Statesboro High and Industrial School. The singers, conducted by Julia Anderson, thrilled the crowd with beautiful hymns. Then Wells welcomed his colleague from the university system, President Hubert, who, in turn, introduced Carver.

The occasion carried the risk of controversy, as Wells realized. But he was confident no one could take exception to Carver's modest demeanor and inspiring message. Some in the audience expected repercussions. Fleming D. Roach, an alumnus, in 2005 vividly recalled the impact of that moment:

Back then people did not give the black man any respect, as you know. So some people were surprised when Carver came there. It was a big thing. The auditorium was packed. Nothing bad happened. In fact, the students held onto his every word. He kept that group on the edge of their seats with his talk. And when it was over, people jumped up, clapping. They rushed the stage and wanted to meet him and talk with him.[43]

On that last day of October in 1933, SGTC grew in importance. So did the image of Guy Wells as an educational leader. Members of the audience by the score wrote letters of appreciation and admiration to Carver at his Tuskegee address.

A member of the Board of Regents of the University System of Georgia, Samuel Hill Morgan, drove to the event from nearby Effingham County. He returned to his office and put some official regents' stationery on his desk. He wrote by hand a letter on November 9, 1933. to "Hon. Geo. Washington Carver, Tuskegee Institute, Tuskegee, Alabama."

He began the letter, "My Dear Sir." The regent praised Carver's "wonderful exposition of what can be done with God's help and a clear creative brain. You put me to shame, because I've had a better chance in life than you did." He ended with a request for a copy of a poem Carver had read, saying his daughter wanted it.[44]

Wells eventually did write Carver personally, but in the early 1930s he asked President Hubert to communicate his requests. During the winter of 1934, the two planned to invite Carver to return that year. Hubert wrote Carver:

Dr. Wells asked me write you at once and make arrangements with you for a tour during the Fall term of the school year. He would like to have you come to Savannah first, then to Statesboro to South Georgia Teachers College and from there to Milledgeville. . . . Dr. Wells wants to travel over the state with you. He says he would just like to be in your presence so as to be inspired by your personality. He feels that it would be a great treat to the youth of Georgia to have you speak to them.[45]

After Carver indicated he would try to return, Hubert replied, "I am writing Dr. Guy Wells today and sending him your letter. I am sure that he will be pleased to know there is a possibility of getting you back here next year."[46] The plan did not materialize, because an illness prevented Carver from returning to south Georgia in 1934.

Carver's visit was the opening Wells wanted. He hoped to quietly challenge and ultimately change a long tradition of racial inequality and injustice. He found an ally in Benjamin Hubert. The two presidents realized Morgan had experienced in Carver's message the universal power of knowledge that transcends race. Wells found in Hubert an exemplary educator who also knew something about "walking through the fodder."

PROMOTED FROM PARADISE

When Guy Wells invited George Washington Carver to return, he looked forward to traveling with him throughout Georgia. He did not know what lay in store for him in Atlanta. During the April meeting of the Board of Regents, the inevitable happened: Wells was promoted. He became president of Georgia State College for Women in Milledgeville, a college almost three times the size of SGTC.

Samuel Hill Morgan, of the Board of Regents, believed Wells should move up in the ranks of the University System of Georgia. He had seen Wells create a four-year college out of a combination junior college and high school. Morgan time and again observed that Wells had the "right touch." Wells could make a proverbial silk purse from the scrawniest sow's ear. During a time of national pessimism, Morgan believed, Wells brought hope not only to the college in Statesboro but to the entire university system.[47]

He was president during the worst economic depression in the nation's history. The state budget simply had no resources available to fulfill Wells' vision of the campus. So he did what he could: he renovated, enlarged, landscaped, and used local resources to make the campus resemble a first-class institution. He thought he was creating his future academic home.

Did Wells want this "promotion" to an historic college for women? Would he be comfortable in a more refined environment? Was he a good match for Milledgeville? The answer to all three questions, according to Wells, was "no". He made this clear to the students and community; he did not want to move from his Collegeboro. In a letter to Morgan in 1935, he reminded him the new job was one he "shrank from, hoping to be permitted to stay in Statesboro."[48]

The local Milledgeville newspaper candidly acknowledged that Wells did not want the promotion: " He had preferred to remain there but was transferred to the local college here by the regents of the University System. . . . Dr. Wells was transferred here from the Statesboro college by the regents, over his protest, he preferring to remain where he had labored for the past eight years."[49]

When the Statesboro Chamber of Commerce met in April to make plans for his farewell party in June, the newspaper reported: "Sentiments of the

Regents transfer Wells and hire new president

"Upon motion of Regent Morgan, seconded by Regent Ault, and unanimously adopted: 'That Guy H. Wells be elected president of the Georgia State College for Women, Milledgeville for the Scholastic Year 1934 -35. . . .

"Motion by Regent Beaver, seconded by Regent Dunwody, and adopted:

"That the nomination of M. S. Pittman as President of the South Georgia Teachers College at Statesboro be approved."

Minutes of the Board of Regents, University System of Georgia, 11 April 1934

very deepest regret at his departure were expressed and tears came to the eyes of the members as Mr. Wells declared his regret at the necessity of his removal to another field."[50]

The final party at Collegeboro for President Wells unfolded atypically on an afternoon during the last week of May. Town and gown had organized a big campus farewell picnic for him and his family. Many tables laden with food and drink bordered the edge of Lake Wells. Several who attended the occasion recalled a huge rainfall that afternoon. Students quickly shifted the arrangements to the gymnasium, where regents, newspaper editors, clergy, professors, and students paid tribute. Newelle DeLoach sang "Listen to the Mockingbird" and Irene Enocks recited the poem everyone associated with Wells, Kipling's "If."[51]

The students led the way through their recently perfected alma mater. A tearful "Auld Lang Syne" bonded everyone with Wells, with each other, and with the institution.

Before he left for Milledgeville, Wells had set into motion the application for accreditation by the Southern Association of Colleges and Secondary Schools. Now a four-year teachers' college, the institution yet had miles to travel before it arrived. At least the institution was on the right course. The tears at farewell were genuine, and both faculty and students deeply regretted their president's departure.

In 1937 three-fourths of the student body had enrolled since 1934, and they did not know Guy Wells. The editor of the *George-Anne* introduced the former president to a new generation of students. The newspaper proposed naming a dormitory for him, "a man who did much to further the high ideals and purposes which the college stands for."[52]

The proposal, written during lean economic times, did not produce a Wells Hall. In 2006 the only memorial to Wells exists in campus folklore. The name of the smaller, unmarked body of water on campus, old timers say, is Lake Wells. Only a few have heard the story of those Bonaparte willows the president cultivated from shoots gathered in France by Moina Michael.

Although the name "Wells" does not appear on the official list of campus names, he left an identifiable legacy. In ways peculiar to his own creative personality and intellect, Wells moved the college forward. He put SGTC on the state map. Few Georgians who read newspapers in 1934 had not heard of the college in south Georgia dedicated to training future teachers.

Guy Wells invited Hoy Taylor to join him as dean at Milledgeville. Wells considered Taylor the ablest administrator and faculty member on the Collegeboro campus. Taylor came to SGTC in 1932 as a temporary

A metaphor of leadership— "walking through the fodder"

Howell Cone and Guy Wells invented a metaphor to describe Wells as a leader. While living in Bulloch County, Wells learned to "walk through the fodder without rustling a blade." Fodder is what the leaves of cornstalks become when they wither during late summer. Farmers gather the sharp-edged leaves and use them to make food for livestock. To walk quietly through a cornfield takes much skill. Cone helped Wells become a master. He learned to make progress without causing a negative reaction.

replacement for Dean Zach Henderson, who was attending graduate school. After Henderson returned, Taylor taught social science. Taylor had great personal gifts as well as a keen intellect, according to those who knew him at both colleges.[53]

Although Wells regretted, perhaps resented, his promotion, outside observers were not surprised. William Heard Kilpatrick of Columbia University and other educators assumed this talented leader was destined for greater tasks. Kilpatrick once speculated Wells would become chancellor of the state university system.[54]

Wells' departure left a vacuum at the college. Who else could possibly duplicate his unique style of leadership? Who else could relate one-on-one with farmers, bankers, journalists, and businessmen? Who else could aggressively seek recognition in a genuinely self-effacing manner? Who else could possibly gain such affection from students, and maintain the admiration of most faculty?

This common/extraordinary, progressive/conservative, humble/assertive man was uniquely Guy Herbert Wells. He knew he owed much of his personal growth to the people of Statesboro who so quickly had accepted him and his family. After all, it was here he learned a lesson that served him well—how to "walk through the fodder without rustling a blade."

Over the years he and his family returned again and again, renewing friendships. He retired some twenty years after he left Statesboro. Having recently lost his wife, Ruby, to cancer, he chose to return to Statesboro and buy a home. The former president remarried and became a familiar face around town and a recognizable voice on campus, even as he traveled around the nation and world. He called Statesboro his home until his death on July 15, 1965.

The legacy of this energetic man from 1926 through 1934 is more than the sum total of his achievements during hard economic times. Truly, he took pride in every shrub, tree, fountain, renovation, project, and program as well as each additional student. At the drop of a hat, he would gladly speak about all of the above (often claiming credit). More than these achievements, however, he embodied a passionate conviction that learning and living are inseparable.

Wells was the first president to embrace the local culture and attempt to move it forward both educationally and morally. This quality undoubtedly is what Kilpatrick admired in his former pupil. Wells was an excellent example of the educator-as-community-leader.

Wells used the presidency to influence his community and state. An educator should lead people toward both knowledge and compassion, Wells believed. Some would say the approach of Wells is *sui generis*. Others, however, would agree with Wells' mentor, Kilpatrick: Guy Herbert Wells was an excellent model for anyone who aspires to leadership in higher education.[55]

Guy and Ruby Wells with two-year-old Anne at their small home on campus in 1930.

Final farewell

"Before the utterance of his first words there was ample evidence of sadness on the part of the retiring president and his associates. Members of the faculty who sat with him on the stage for the final farewell controlled their emotions with difficulty. Throughout the audience young men and women—students of the college and members of the faculty—were in tears. . . . It was not a time for weakness, yet it was a tense moment when the retiring president arose to say the words which were to mark the termination of connection with the school. His face was flushed and his eyes betrayed the sadness which he sought to conceal. His voice broke, but he recovered himself and laughed—laughed like President Wells has laughed during the nine years he has been responsible for the progress of South Georgia Teachers College."

Bulloch Times, 5 July 1934

TEACHERS COLLEGE
1934-1941

1934 – President Marvin Pittman introduces "leisure arts" to teachers in summer school, encouraging amateur singers, dancers, and musicians. (7/26)

1934 – Upon the death of President Paul von Hindenburg, Germany's Nazi Party elevates Adolf Hitler from chancellor to führer. (8/2)

1934 – Jane Franseth introduces innovative program of rural school supervision funded by the Rockefeller Foundation's General Education Fund. (9/30)

1935 – College begins annual springtime "Georgia Progress Days," a two-day event focusing on topics of interest to Georgia and the nation. (3/8)

1935 – The Administration Building now wears a remodeled roof. (10/1)

1935 – Black Sunday , the worst day of several years of dust storms in West that killed crops and displaced thousands of families. (4/14)

1935 – A government-funded mattress factory south of the alumni gymnasium provides jobs for the unemployed. (3/1)

1935 – College moves cottages for black employees near the dining hall south of the corner of Forest Drive and Georgia Avenue. (6/1)

1936 – George V, king of England, dies, and his son succeeds him as Edward VIII. (1/20)

1936 – Health cottage expands service once rendered in dormitories. (10/30)

1936 – American athlete Jesse Owens wins four gold medals in track at the Olympic Games in Berlin, Germany. (8/3-8/9)

1936 – New industrial arts curriculum influences high schools to add shop classes statewide. (9/30)

1936 – Chancellor Steadman Vincent Sanford dedicates Sanford Hall in the spring. (12/10)

1936 – Franklin D. Roosevelt is reelected as U.S. president. (11/2)

1936 – Southern Association of Colleges and Secondary Schools accredits TC. (12/12)

1937 – TC organizes faculty professionally according to systemwide standards. Positions are classified by academic qualifications. (9/30)

1937 – The Hindenburg, a German airship, crashes in the United States, killing thirty-five. (5/6)

1938 – Students enjoy Sunday night "dates" in renovated East and West halls, featuring large foyers and parlors. (9/1)

1938 – Southern Naval Stores sells college 26.5 acres of land between Georgia Ave. and Highway 67; Marvin Pittman purchases adjoining 65.5 acres. (7/20)

1938 – Orson Welles spreads panic with his fictional radio program about aliens from Mars invading New Jersey. (10/30)

1938 – The college dedicates library, laboratory school, and girl's dormitory (Lewis Hall), funded by the state and the Rosenwald Fund. (12/7)

1939 – Pittmans buy plantation-style home near the college on Highway 301. (4/18)

1939 – Board of Regents changes college name from South Georgia Teacers College to Georgia Teachers College. (8/1)

1939 – Britain and France declare war on Germany, beginning World War II. (9/3)

1939 – Teachers football team twice defeats the University of Havana at Collegeboro (10/14) and at Havana, Cuba. (12/9).

1939 – The films The Wizard of Oz (6/6) and Gone With the Wind are released. (12/15).

1940 – Franklin D. Roosevelt is reelected for a third term as U.S. president. (11/4)

1940 – The most popular major among students is social science. (11/20)

1940 – The first aviation students to fly solo are Tom Vandiver, Knapp Boddiford, Floyd Wardlow, Pete Parrish, Jones Lane, and A. J. Bowen. (12/2)

1940 – American Jazz Age author of The Great Gatsby, F. Scott Fitzgerald dies. (12/21)

1941 – Students protest the firing of President Marvin Pittman by refusing to attend classes and marching in an impromptu parade in downtown Statesboro. (6/5)

THE DREAM, THE DRAMA

SETTING THE SOUTHERN STAGE

He was the first leader of the institution with prior administrative experience in a college, the first to hold the PhD degree, and the first to have a national reputation as an educator. When the Board of Regents named Marvin Summers Pittman to the presidency on April 11, 1934, they sent a message: The time had come for South Georgia Teachers College to move to a higher level.

Many on the faculty and staff recalled his powerful message in 1929, when he spoke to a receptive audience of 1,200 educators and local citizens. He talked plainly and forcefully about how America's schools could fulfill their mission as democratic institutions. By 1933 he had carried this message to more than thirty states. Joseph Enoch Carruth, a faculty member who had attended Millsaps College with Pittman, rejoiced in the regents' decision.[1]

Born and reared in Mississippi, Pittman owned credentials as a southerner. Yet some local citizens regarded the new president as an "outsider." A few forever called him a "Yankee," based on his thirteen years in Michigan, preceded by six years of graduate studies in Oregon and New York. Most citizens, however, realized how fortunate the college was to have this highly regarded and innovative leader at the helm.

Those most surprised by Pittman's new job lived in Ypsilanti, Michigan. As director of rural education and teacher training at Michigan State Normal College, he had proven himself an imaginative leader and successful school consolidator. With the help of local civic clubs, Pittman convinced thirteen rural school districts to vote to dissolve their schools (some historic) and build a huge school for more than six hundred students.[2]

He was active in civic life—the president of the Ypsilanti Chamber of Commerce, an officer in the Rotary Club, and a board member of a local bank. Earlier he had completed a report on the system of education in Cuba, and he had planned to apply his concept of teacher training in an international setting. Called Eastern Michigan University since 1959, Michigan State Normal College was established in 1849 at Ypsilanti—the first teacher-training college west of the Appalachian Mountains. Pittman thrived at this historic and influential teachers college.

Pittman's departure from Michigan also left a political void. The *Detroit Free Press* observed that Pittman was an anomaly—an educator in a Republican State "who dared be a Democrat." He was elected temporary chairman and keynote speaker for the 1928 Michigan Democratic

MARVIN SUMMERS PITTMAN

The first president who had earned a PhD, Pittman wrote several books and consulted with international educational organizations before moving to Statesboro in 1934. He typed much of his correspondence on his portable Corona® typewriter, *below.*

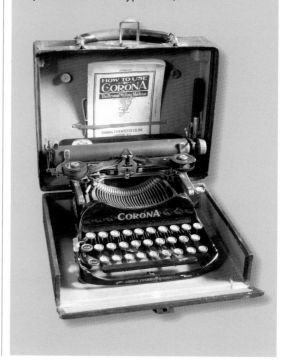

CHESTER McARTHUR DESTLER

Pittman wrote Chancellor Philip Weltner that Destler "is the type of a man we wish to have in our institution—physically vigorous, morally clean, intellectually well-trained and alert, clear-sighted in his social outlook and generous in his contribution to the community of which he is a part. He will add intellectual strength and professional dignity to our institution." Destler lived at 11 Woodrow Avenue.

Marvin Pittman, letter to Philip Weltner, 22 May 1934. Papers of Chester McArthur Destler.

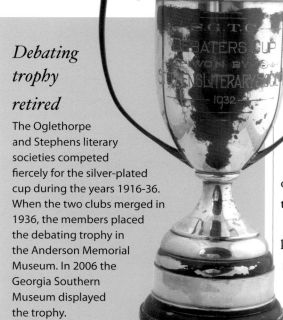

Debating trophy retired

The Oglethorpe and Stephens literary societies competed fiercely for the silver-plated cup during the years 1916-36. When the two clubs merged in 1936, the members placed the debating trophy in the Anderson Memorial Museum. In 2006 the Georgia Southern Museum displayed the trophy.

Convention. He ran unsuccessfully for state superintendent of instruction. He was a popular leader of Democrats. Powerful forces in Ypsilanti, Detroit, and Ann Arbor declared their support for Pittman early in 1934, when he announced he would challenge U. S. senator Arthur Vandenberg.[3]

The *Ann Arbor Tribune* wrote: "He is an excellent example of the educated man in politics, of good citizenship in action. Georgia's gain is great, Michigan's loss is greater."[4] Pittman's early interest in politics was rooted in his family history. Two of his Mississippi relatives, Key Pittman and Thomas P. Gore, then were members of the U.S. Congress. Senator Pittman served Nevada from 1913 until his death in 1940, and Senator Gore (grandfather of author Gore Vidal), Oklahoma's "blind senator," served from 1931 until 1936. Had Marvin Pittman remained active in Michigan politics, his political fortunes might have improved with President Franklin Roosevelt at the head of the Democratic ticket.

Another Democrat in Michigan who knew Pittman well was on the faculty of Albion College in eastern Michigan. Chester "Chet" McArthur Destler, who had earned a PhD, had studied with southern historian Avery Craven at the University of Chicago. After his college roommate, William Duren, introduced him to the winsome sister of his girlfriend from Louisiana, Destler's interest in the South became personal.

Pittman asked this native of Cincinnati, Ohio, to accept a faculty appointment at Collegeboro. Destler accepted. He considered Pittman a thoroughgoing intellectual who could inspire others to action.

In early May 1934, Pittman invited Chet Destler to visit him in Ypsilanti, just sixty miles from Albion. At age fifty-two, the president-elect spent a Saturday planning a new administration with a twenty-nine-year-old historian.[5] Pittman said scholars could do more than teach students; they could influence the region's population and, perhaps, improve the quality of the students' lives.

Destler described Pittman's plans for SGTC as "the most interesting experiment in higher education in the South."[6] In partnership with a visionary president, Destler chose to work in a part of America that was awakening from educational slumber. Neither man seemed concerned that students there scored poorly on standardized tests. Rather, they were driven by a mutual desire to demonstrate that a state teachers college in the Deep South could unleash the region's human potential.

Destler accepted this offer to "do good," personally, in a part of America known for poor schools and substandard living conditions. As a professor he could also "do well," financially, during economic hard times.[7]

The academic landscape at Collegeboro was not particularly promising. An alumnus, Julian Stanley ('38), recalled, "In 1934, SGTC freshmen ranked fourth from the bottom on a college admissions test among 300 colleges. . . Swarthmore College was No. 1." [8] President Guy Wells had submitted an application for accreditation to the Southern Association of Colleges and Secondary Schools. Pittman realized he would have to update the document, answer questions, and host reviewers. Accreditation was a big step forward and by no means guaranteed.

The leading member of the faculty—the only one to hold the PhD, Hoy Taylor, was Guy Wells' choice as dean for the college at Milledgeville. Joseph Carruth, age fifty-three, was scheduled to receive his doctorate at George Peabody College for Teachers, after a number of years of part-time study. Pittman asked him to continue as head of the education department and to direct the senior division.

Under the Board of Regents' systemwide curriculum plan, SGTC offered courses through two divisions—junior and senior. The junior division, throughout the university system, shared the same general curriculum. Social studies classes, for example, required a common text and workbook. Pittman promised Destler, then an assistant professor of history at Albion, the rank of full professor, the chairmanship of social studies, and the directorship of the junior division at SGTC.

Destler and Carruth would work with Dean Zach Henderson, who managed student life and academic affairs in the manner of a high school principal, which he had been before coming to the college. Henderson had been taking graduate courses, part-time, at George Peabody College for Teachers and at Columbia University.

Pittman proposed for Destler an initial salary comparable to full professors in the university system. In time young Chet Destler reputedly became the highest-paid member of the faculty and staff, second only to President Pittman.[9]

During the spring of 1934, Pittman zeroed in on that small college atop a sand ridge south of Statesboro, Georgia. That would be the stage upon which he earnestly played the greatest role of his life. For the next seven years he performed creatively and energetically.

Many locals were wary of the "outsider" president. They were relieved when they heard him make his first informal talk at the college at the end of June. The occasion was a joint reception for the arriving Pittmans and the departing Wells:

During the years I have been away . . . my heart has yearned for the homeland. Living in another section, I felt that I was not of it. And as for my family, when Mrs. Pittman prayed each night, she always closed with these words, 'O lord, take me to heaven when I die, but take me back South before then.'[10]

A member of the audience that evening, Robert John Henderson DeLoach (called "John" or "R. J. H."), was not swayed by those words. A loyal friend of Guy Wells, DeLoach initially was not pleased with Pittman's appointment. Not only had Pittman lived away from the South for the past twenty years, he also spoke in the crisp, quick manner of a Midwesterner.

First Teachers College student to win national academic competition

Harvin Mulkey, a student from Pompano Beach, Florida, fell under the influence of Professor Chet Destler in 1934. He was among a large number of history students who eventually attended graduate school. Mulkey, in particular, seemed destined for serious research. Destler encouraged him to enter a national essay contest sponsored by the American Bar Association on "How and to What Extent the Rights and Liberties of the Individual are Protected Under the Constitution." Competing against students from well-known colleges and universities, Mulkey won first prize. Destler arranged for him to present his paper to groups in Statesboro and Savannah.

Mulkey was pursuing a PhD at the University of North Carolina when he informed Destler the *Journal of Negro Education* would publish one of his essays. He had used in part information provided by Destler and a friend, Knapp Boddiford. The subject was the future role of the Negro in the South. Unfortunately, he did not continue his scholarly career. Mulkey was among five alumni who died defending the nation during World War II.

The Cost of Ignorance
by Marvin Pittman

" No nation can afford ignorance, because ignorance is a nation's largest and most unbearable tax.

Ignorance permits mud holes where there should be pavements, hovels where there should be health and happiness.

Ignorance tolerates nakedness where there should be broadcloth, hunger where food should abound, and paupers begging for pennies where plenty could be the portion of all.

Ignorance degrades. Enlightenment uplifts.

Ignorance hates. Enlightenment loves.

Ignorance wastes. Enlightenment creates and conserves.

Ignorance is man's greatest destroyer. Enlightenment is his only salvation.

Enlightenment and opportunity may both be had for a price. "

Pittman wrote these words and attached them to an unpublished review of educational facilities in Cuba, 1932. Department of Archives and Records Management, Georgia Southern University

Traveling in good company

In the 1920s R. J. H. DeLoach, *seated below*, belonged to the Vagabond Club, whose members included, *left to right*, Thomas Edison, Harvey Firestone Jr., John Burroughs, Henry Ford, and Harvey Firestone Sr.

DeLoach believed the new president would not "fit in" with locals who were accustomed to the folksy ways of his predecessor.

Within a few months DeLoach's suspicions about the new president returned. The sixty-one-year-old DeLoach had been teaching in the social science department, even though his academic training was in agricultural science. He had expected to be named chairman of the department.[11] He objected to Pittman's selection of Destler, a man half his age.

A student in 1934–35 recalled DeLoach's contempt for Destler. "Dr. Destler went in and said, 'Doctor, have you prepared your lecture?' Well, DeLoach—he didn't have a real doctor's degree—says, 'You little whipper-snapper! I'm old enough to be your daddy!' It just set him on fire. He never did like that Destler, either."[12] DeLoach spoke openly of his dismay that the college had been "run over by Yankees." He meant not only Destler and Pittman but also other faculty, including an education professor from Michigan, Jane Franseth.[13]

DeLoach was well-connected, well-traveled, and well-read. Around 1908 he became friends with the famous American naturalist John Burroughs, who later invited DeLoach to travel with him and his customary companions, Henry Ford, Thomas Edison, and Harvey Firestone.[14] DeLoach traveled more frequently after 1917, when he took a job with the Armour Company of Chicago.

DeLoach was an avid book collector, and his personal library reputedly was the best in town. He produced a handsome book in 1912, *Rambles with John Burroughs*. DeLoach wrote original commentary on Walt Whitman and on his relationship with Burroughs, including sixteen photographs he took of Burroughs. DeLoach was a founder and early president of the Georgia Ornithological Society. He keenly observed nature, and his retreat, "Beechwood," in a remote section of Bulloch County, was a naturalist's haven. Although he had earned only a master's degree, many people called him "Dr. DeLoach," perhaps, in deference to his experience and age.

After DeLoach joined the faculty of SGTC around 1932, he settled into a large Victorian home at 319 Savannah Avenue. When Henry Ford traveled to his Richmond Hill plantation, he occasionally stopped at that address in Statesboro. Neighbors said they saw a new Ford automobile parked in DeLoach's garage after his friend from Detroit visited.

DeLoach identified with the Lost Cause sentiments of many southerners who kept alive romantic visions of the slavery days, before the Civil War, or War Between the States. He placed his hopes for vindication on the shoulders of the popular Eugene Talmadge, who, during the summer of 1934 won reelection as governor in a landslide. Talmadge became a vocal opponent of U.S. president Franklin Roosevelt's New Deal and governed Georgia in the manner of a dictator. Talmadge also inflamed uneducated Georgians with racist rhetoric. Destler regarded the governor as a temporary disgrace; DeLoach saw him as an emblem of hope.

The college president, on the other hand, withheld comment about the chief executive of the state. Pittman invited the governor to speak at his first commencement in June. Governor Talmadge honored President Pittman's invitation. The governor told the graduates they were educated if they had learned "common sense." He concluded, "This institution right here at Statesboro . . . is a good enough place for anybody to finish an education."[15]

SCRIPT AND CAST

As president, Marvin Pittman revealed himself as a pragmatist. He held progressive ideas about race, religion, and social justice. However, he took a neutral and nonpartisan stance in his public comments about these issues.[16] Pittman devoted his attention to a practical issue—providing resources for teachers and students.

From the very start, Pittman applied what he firmly believed as a progressive educator. At Columbia, guided by William Heard Kilpatrick, Pittman had studied the philosopher John Dewey. Like Kilpatrick, Pittman believed the schools of the nineteenth century were inadequate.

The modern classroom should focus upon the learner: how one learns deeply influences what one learns. Pittman shared Kilpatrick's view that progressive educators should not abandon traditional subjects.[17] An indicator of the educator's reputation appears in the South Georgia Teachers College faculty minutes for October 31, 1938, when faculty voted to name the new laboratory school in Kilpatrick's honor. Because he was then living, the naming was postponed.

Within a decade progressive education's ideology so permeated the campus that an editorial writer for the *George-Anne* could explain the concept to entering students:

Probably the best summary of progressive education . . . is compiled in three words: observation, experimentation, and individualism. Essentially that is the scientific method. . . . Progressive education does not accept the rigid disciplinary rules of learning that we once held so unquestionable. Let the student be his own guide. Let his inclinations be the criteria that lead him.[18]

More than an educational philosopher, Marvin Pittman was an administrator. He focused attention on creating environments in which progressive educators could teach. Yet Pittman regarded himself not as progressive education's interpreter but as its enabler. For example, he advocated consolidating small schools, because supervisors could monitor progress, observe classrooms, and provide assistance to teachers.

The last confederate veteran
R. J. H. DeLoach unfurls a Confederate flag on April 26, 1937, honoring William Jasper Brown, Bulloch County's last surviving Confederate veteran.

WILLIAM DEAL

In 1934 he became the first band director at South Georgia Teachers College. His father was Albert Deal.

Local AAUW discusses racial inequality

" The December meeting of the local chapter of the American Association of University Women will be held next Tuesday evening [December 8] in the yellow cottage on the Teachers College campus. The subject for the evening is, 'Where the Color Line Leads Georgia.'

Mrs. C. W. Smith, chairman of the program committee, has announced the following program:

Introductory remarks: Mrs. Chester Destler

Panel discussion, 'Inequality of Opportunity'

'Our Alleged Biological Differences,' Miss Malvina Trussell

'Our Double Standard,' Miss Helen Dunlap

'Our Inequality of Recreational Facilities,' Miss Eleanor Ray

'Our Modes of Legal Injustice,' Miss Hester Newton

'Accomplishments of Outstanding Negroes Despite Unfavorable Conditions,' Miss Louise DeLoach

General discussion, 'How Can We Work to Balance the Equation?' "

Bulloch Times, 3 December 1936

He had learned the importance of supervision during his master's degree studies at the University of Oregon. He successfully applied a zone system of supervision in South Dakota in 1919 before joining the faculty at Michigan State Normal. He would introduce the concept to Georgia. In northern Bulloch County, the school board consolidated schools at Clito, Eureka, and Dry Pond, forming Cliponreka School. Pittman pleased them by assigning a zone teacher for the school.

Marie Wood was the "critic teacher," a role model for future teachers, at the Sunnyside School. When Pittman learned she sang and played the guitar, he suggested she teach her students to do the same.[19] Soon she was offering students individualized music lessons after school.

The summer session for teachers already had begun when Pittman arrived. In a very short time, he suggested teachers learn the "leisure arts" by doing them: "Students who had never seen a violin, those who had never touched a cornet, and other instruments, rendered numbers on the various instruments. Those who could hardly carry a tune were taught to sing in groups. . . . [tap] dancing was taught many, and other forms of leisure arts."[20]

The president demonstrated his commitment to music immediately by hiring William Deal as the college's first band director. The son of Albert Deal, one of the school's earliest supporters, Deal had directed a band in Alabama. He and the president mounted a drive for instruments.

The student body buzzed with excitement at the formal convocation to open the new academic year. Two hundred new students showed up for classes, pushing the enrollment to five hundred for the first time. Right away they noticed how the president involved students in the program. James Cherry, J. D. Purvis, Hassie McElveen, George Carter, Grace Cromley, and Frank Quattlebaum spoke about campus organizations and school spirit.

Within a month the faculty and student body had discussed and voted on a representative form of student government. The *George-Anne* applauded it as a "new deal." The editor was pleased to hear the new president speak these words: "We want the wisest administration . . . and I suggest the students carry on the affairs . . . as they affect the student life of the college."[21]

Students flocked to the classes of Chet Destler. He and his wife, Katharine, were active members of the local Presbyterian church. The bright and personable Katharine was popular among students and faculty, whom she often entertained.

As a local leader and state officer of the American Association of University Women, Mrs. Destler planned relevant and sometimes provocative programs on race relations and international affairs.[22] Her credentials as a woman of the South made it easier for her to moderate these discussions.[23] The soft-spoken Katharine both blended and bonded with members of the community.

The *Bulloch Herald* organized a series of articles about leading local citizens. Early choices for the honor were Marvin Pittman and Chet Destler. The selection of a professor for this local recognition probably surprised some faculty, like R. J. H. DeLoach, a native of Bulloch County. The article underscored how much citizens valued his leadership:

In every community there are a few men and women who, when asked to do something, can be depended upon doing it and doing it well. And these are always the community's busiest people. Our "Man of the Week" this week is one such person. It pleases us to present Dr. Chester McArthur Destler, Professor of History of the Georgia Teachers' College, as our "Man of the Week."

Widely published in highly regarded academic journals, he is senior editor of "Studies in Social Progress" for the University System of Georgia. Current research [topics include] . . . Henry Demarest Lloyd, an influential American liberal of the late nineteenth century.

Locally, Dr. Destler is one of the founders of the Bulloch County Library, and the Bulloch County Hospital Services Association was based to a large degree upon the results of his findings in communities similar to Bulloch county.[24]

Pittman expressed his appreciation and affection to his friend Chet Destler in handwritten notes at different times:

I sincerely hope that you are enjoying the South and liking your position. The outward evidences are all good and all of the reactions to you are most favorable. I wish you to know that I appreciate the way in which you are taking your place in both the college and the community.[25]

One of the greatest kindnesses I ever did Georgia was to bring you to it. You have made a splendid contribution and I shall always be proud of what you have done.[26]

In early 1935 Pittman traveled to Nashville, Tennessee, to present a brief program. He took with him William Deal and the new band. Together they appeared on radio station WSM—known locally as the home station of the Grand Ole Opry.[27] Southeast Georgia blushed with pride.

The president probably mentioned to the big WSM listening audience a new series on education with statewide significance. He called it "Georgia Progress Days." The very name struck a responsive note. For the first time in its history, the college was playing a role in the larger arena of public discussion.

President Pittman was committed, first, to the people of a largely rural state. Before worrying about how to pronounce properly the French words *beaux-arts*, Pittman believed south Georgians first should appreciate the arts of everyday life. So the president began with leisure arts during the summer session of 1934. In the fall he introduced industrial or manual arts.

He found a young, energetic, recent PhD graduate from Ohio State University. His name was Hoyt Hobson London. Pittman thought London practiced "a correct modern philosophy of education." The president gave him the ground floor of the alumni building, underneath the gym. Young London put together simple machines, using scrap parts. He taught future teachers how to guide young people through a "modern shop," equipped with basic tools—drills, lathes, saws, and other woodworking equipment.

Pittman organized Teachers College into seven divisions in 1934-1935

1. Arts and Industrial Education
2. Languages
3. Libraries and Library Science
4. Natural and Exact Sciences
5. Social Sciences
6. Physical Education
7. Professional Education

Herty returns after thirty-four years

Charles Holmes Herty, *left,* returned in 1935 to the site of his experiments of 1901. The college honored the internationally known chemist by dedicating the Herty Pines and unveiling a plaque. *Standing right:* are Mrs. M. E. Judd, President Pittman, and Regent Samuel Hill Morgan. Writing for the *George-Anne,* Mary Margaret Blitch noted the pine on which Herty hung his first cup "is still alive, tall, and stately."

George Anne, 6 May 1935

Pittman speaks on practical education

"Every boy and girl likes to 'make things.' Any man who has not made things feels as if all his fingers are thumbs. A good course in what we call general shop will give a boy or girl a sense of mastery which every individual should have. He will be able to fix a doorbell or an electric light, re-bottom a chair or solder a hole in a dishpan, make a bookrack or a reading table, fashion a card case of leather or a metal belt buckle. We feel that every child in the state should have the privilege of learning how to do these things. For that reason we are preparing teachers who can give such instruction."

Marvin Pittman, *Bulloch Times*, 17 August 1939

In the 1930s males often were department heads, and females held teaching and management jobs.

ESTHER BARNES

RUTH BOLTON

ELIZABETH DONOVAN

SOPHIE JOHNSON

GENERIA HONEYCUTT

MAMIE JO JONES

CARO LANE

HOYT LONDON

HESTER NEWTON

THOMAS STROUP

MALVINA TRUSSELL

MAMIE VEAZEY

Years later Pittman wrote:

Because of the vision and work of Dr. London and his worthy successors and their students, that modern shop has grown into a more excellent one. It compared favorably with the best in the nation. Industrial Arts has now become in Georgia one of the fundamentals in Georgia schools, and Industrial Education is accepted in the large fraternity of general education as an equal.[28]

Educators realized the significance of London's work at SGTC, and he became a popular speaker at educational conferences. Soon Mississippi State University offered him a significant raise and better equipment to build a program there. Afterward he moved to the University of Missouri, where as department head he led the university to attain preeminence in the field of industrial education.[29]

Before the Pittman administration began, faculty focused attention almost exclusively on teaching, in the manner of high school teachers. The presence of an influential scholar in the president's office encouraged faculty to reinvent themselves. Hester Newton, a historian, began to publish scholarly articles in the *Georgia Historical Quarterly* and signed up for graduate classes at Duke University; Malvina Trussell, already enrolled in the PhD program at Cornell University, regularly took summers off to travel to Ithaca, New York, to continue her course work in biology at Cornell.

A number of women on the faculty rose to prominence during the mid-1930s, and the community, especially, took note of their achievements. Caro Lane, the dynamic director of physical education for women since 1931, caught the attention of professionals in the Southern Physical Education Association.

In 1936 Louisiana State University invited Lane to join their physical education department, and her career continued to blossom there. Lane had organized the SGTC Women's Athletic Association and advocated health services for students.

When she left, students hosted a reception downtown at the Tea Pot Grill on East Main Street.[30] There they gave testimonials about her various acts of personal kindness and financial assistance. Decades after this event, alumnus J. D. Purvis credited his success to Lane, who advised him and paid for his food and lodging during the Great Depression. He called her his "fairy godmother," who always inspired him to succeed.[31]

Elizabeth Donovan, also an educator from Michigan, introduced Pittman's zone supervision program in south Georgia so well that the State Department of Education hired her to do the same for the rest of Georgia. Other faculty and staff of the 1930s recalled often by students were housemothers Sophie Johnson (dean of men) and Mamie Veazey (dean of women).

Three made an immediate impact after they began their work in 1937: Marjorie Guardia (English), Ruth Bolton (home economics), and Hassie McElveen (library). Students quickly latched onto Guardia, who always scored high in the "popular teacher" contests. She also made her place in history by recording accurately and reading aloud precisely the minutes of faculty meetings.

Another woman who endeared herself to the community managed to land a *Bulloch Herald* feature story in what normally was called "Man of the Week." The article begins:

Our "Woman of the Week" is Miss Jane. . . . Her services to the children of Bulloch County, the parents, teachers, and to the communities, are innumerable. She is kind of heart, with an understanding feeling toward all, regardless of race or color.[32]

The article makes clear that she had been involved in Pittman's zone supervision program for rural schools in Michigan and continued the program in Georgia: "She initiated the zone plan of supervision in Wheeler and Treutlen Counties . . . in Evans, Liberty, and Bryan Counties . . . and in Bulloch County where she has served for four years." Jane Franseth, the article notes, published essays on school supervision in national journals.

Altogether the series spotlighted thirty-eight individuals in this series; four of them were employees of SGTC—Marvin Pittman, Chester Destler, Zach Henderson, and Jane Franseth. Pittman, Destler, and Franseth all moved to Statesboro from Michigan.

Another member of the faculty who contributed to scholarship in the 1930s was Thomas Stroup, who held the PhD. Like Destler, Stroup was an outstanding professor who represented SGTC as a speaker and panelist at academic meetings. He published articles on English literature in national and international journals, while collecting folklore in southeast Georgia.

Stroup commanded respect among his professional peers. Yet he also found time to direct plays and present book reviews for campus literary societies and civic clubs. Local readers especially recalled his review of Margaret Mitchell's *Gone With the Wind*.

A young instructor in the English department found encouragement in Stroup's example. Fielding Russell, a popular teacher since arriving in 1931 had received his master's degree at the University of Georgia. He began a long journey toward a PhD, which he doggedly pursued to completion in November 1947.[33]

For the most part, faculty members devoted themselves to teaching, because they did not begin their careers at the college with scholarly aspirations. The few who did found it easy to fit into the new systemwide ranking system instituted in 1937.[34] The university system set uniform standards for promotion for all faculties. For example, full professors at South Georgia Teachers College received the same pay as full professors at the University of Georgia.

Once the system took effect, some local faculty found they had been reduced in rank and salary, because they did not meet systemwide performance requirements. Two who held their positions were Professors

Jane Franseth, national leader in education

Jane Franseth moved to Georgia from Ionia, Michigan, in 1934. After she was fired, she easily found another job, though she regretted deeply her treatment by the governor. She carried her program of teacher supervision to Clinch and Fulton counties before becoming director of the Program of Education of School Supervisors at the University of Georgia. In 1950 she earned her doctorate at the University of Chicago. Later, she became a specialist in the U.S. Office of Education. She was president of the Association for Supervision and Curriculum Development from 1958 to 1959. She published widely, and her book, *Supervision as Leadership*, is regarded as a classic.

Blue Tide, Little Store

"The 'Blue Tide' is the nucleus for the students during the week. It serves as a post office and as a supply center. Also the 'Tide' provides recreation, music, newspapers, refreshments, a hangout and bulletin board news.

"Originally the 'Little Store' was a section of the dining hall. It was a new small cove, next to a barber shop, that functioned to give students a very limited choice of refreshments. After remaining camped for seven years, the 'Blue Tide' was constructed in 1935. From the establishment of the 'Blue Tide,' '. . .its functions have been similar to those of today.'

"The first students to work in the 'Blue Tide' were Waldo Pafford and Hubert Dewberry. Today Pafford is superintendent of the 'Bradwell Institute' located in Hinesville. Dewberry holds the position of director of plant and business operations for the University of Georgia. Students have always done the work in the 'Blue Tide.'"

"Blue Tide Remains Popular TC Hub,"
George-Anne, 9 October 1953

MARJORIE GUARDIA

The popular English professor served as secretary to the faculty in the 1930s and 1940s.

Faculty minutes, November 6, 1939

" By way of 'offering orchids,' the President commended Miss McElveen's newspaper article concerning libraries, and referred to the good account in 'Nation's Schools' of Miss Franseth's work. Other items mentioned in this category were: Dr. Destler's broadcast over WSB; Dr. DeLoach's initiation into the highest order of Masons; the election of Dr. DeLoach to the presidency of the Ornithological Society of Georgia; a paper read by Mr. Thompson before the Ornithological Society; and many other praiseful remarks about faculty members made by students in conferences with Dr. Pittman. "

Marjorie Guardia, Secretary to the Faculty

Stroup and Destler. Indeed, Destler was given several leadership roles in the social science curriculum committee appointed by the Board of Regents. Stroup also held committee assignments in the system.

Now well underway, Pittman's program for change in Georgia's educational system complemented the national recovery programs of President Franklin Roosevelt. He sought funds from the Federal Emergency Relief Act (FERA) and the Works Progress Administration (WPA). His first FERA project came three months after he arrived—a network for training teachers and, for a brief time, a small mattress factory on campus. The factory, south of the alumni gymnasium, provided jobs for twenty formerly unemployed citizens. For more than three months workers produced up to three dozen mattresses a week. After the factory closed, the college used the building for storage.[35]

Between 1933 and 1940 WPA projects revitalized the local economy and helped the college grow. In 1937 the local press noted the importance of recently approved federal funding to improve the campus: "[A] total of $195,000 [was] granted by WPA for additional buildings on campus. . . . Patrons and friends of the college are much pleased over the distinct progress which it is making."[36] This amount did not include earlier projects funded by the WPA.

Federal relief funds through the WPA changed the face of SGTC. The WPA supported in part the construction of two new residence halls (Lewis and Sanford), the Rosenwald Library, phase one of a new laboratory school, new football and baseball fields, six tennis courts, improvements to the golf course, an enlargement of Anderson Dining Hall, a health cottage, a central water system, as well as smaller construction and landscaping projects.

SPOTLIGHT ON PROGRESS

In the 1930s H. L. Mencken's *American Mercury* lampooned the state's social and cultural status. Mencken caustically wrote that Georgia was the worst part of a region virtually devoid of the fine arts. Condescendingly, he called the region "the Sahara of the bozart." Mencken wrote, "Virginia is the best of the South today, and Georgia is perhaps the worst. The one is simply senile; the other is crass, gross, vulgar and obnoxious. Between lies a vast plain of mediocrity, stupidity, lethargy, almost of dead silence."[37]

Marvin Pittman, southerner by birth and choice, would never agree with Mencken's snobbish diatribe. Yet he realized the region, after experiencing the catastrophe of the Civil War, had not recovered. Most of the South, especially the rural South, had fallen well behind mainstream America. Before coming to Georgia Pittman and Destler planned to develop a cadre of enlightened teachers who could bring about change. That is what the "experiment" at South Georgia Teachers College was all about.

Pittman built on the new optimism by organizing an annual series called Georgia Progress Days. He mailed letters to school superintendents, journalists, lawmakers, ministers, and local elected officials. The first event on March 22-23, 1935, introduced Georgia's educators to the concept of supervision by zones. It was a new plan, and presenters made plain how easily the program could be initiated statewide. Elizabeth Donovan of the education faculty demonstrated Pittman's innovative version of teacher support and enhancement.

The president involved SGTC faculty, students, and alumni, including elementary school teacher Bertha Hagin, an A&M graduate who continued to take college classes each summer. Others on the program included faculty from the University of Georgia, former president Guy Wells, and chancellor of the university system, Philip Weltner.[38]

During the next six years, the annual Georgia Progress Days programs broadened in scope and significance. The following year guest speakers from Emory and Vanderbilt universities joined the new chancellor, Steadman Vincent Sanford, in an exploration of the role of fine arts in public education.

President Pittman asked Chet Destler to plan the program for 1937. By this time Destler had become well known among southern historians and sociologists. He planned a program of national significance and received funding from the Rosenwald Fund.[39]

Destler drew upon his professional contacts and tapped as his main speaker W. T. Couch of the University of North Carolina. Destler proposed the topic "Whither Georgia—Poverty or Abundance?" Couch was a progressive southern editor and thinker deeply concerned about the plight of black citizens in the South. He organized projects in black history and folklore as southern director of the federal writers project of the Works Progress Administration.

Panelists included officials from the state health department, the state college of agriculture, a leader in industry, a scientist, a journalist, and an educator. Destler's program ended on Saturday evening with a pageant featuring the children of Bulloch County's schools, "Georgia's Achievements and Her Problems."[40]

There would be future programs of consequence from 1938 until 1941, but none as bold as this one. Newspapers on the campus and in the region carried no negative editorials or letters of disagreement. It was just another "outstanding" program "out at the college." A positive outcome of the panel was a forward-looking conclusion: rural Georgians needed a form of affordable health insurance.

Destler saw health insurance as a local issue and dealt with it accordingly. During the next year he discussed the idea with local doctors and county officials, people he knew well. In 1938 he requested assistance of the American Hospital Association and organized discussions with the physicians and board of the new Bulloch County Hospital on Grady Street. Eventually

Mattress factory funded by FERA

President Pittman applied for several federal grants during the Great Depression. From 1934 to 1935 the factory provided employment for out-of-work citizens. When the factory closed, the college used the building for storage space.

" Every person in this section should attend this Georgia Progress program and listen and take a part in the working out of a plan for a better Georgia. . . .

"The program was planned and based on the reports of the Citizens' Fact-Finding Movement and will be directed by Dr. C. M. Destler, of the Georgia Teachers College, who with a keen insight into the problems of Georgia . . . he has challenged the most stimulating minds in the State to lead the discussions. The challenge extends to every straight-thinking person in the State. "

Bulloch Herald, 18 April 1940

Campus humorist
Dippy Dutch debuts

❝ Advice to the lovelorn, hints on gardening, rumors concerning the weather, politics in Novaschmozkapop, and the latest recipes. ❞

In 1937 readers of the *George-Anne* looked forward to weekly installments of a humorous column by student William Gesmon Neville Jr. Neville wrote under two pseudonyms: Dippy Dutch—a not-yet-educated student—and Slats Seagram. He also wrote semi-straight stories as an editorial staff writer for the *George-Anne* and the *Reflector*.

"Air Flow Taxi:

Dew to the fack that the air-flow taxi was demolished last sat. pm, when it run into the back of miss viola perry's v8, it is now forced to discontinue its valuable free taxi service to its meny passingers and customers.

The former and present oner, gesmon neville, phT, estimates that hit will take approx. c25 for haywire and c25 for tire patches too put the air flow taxi back on the job. He is afeared to say how much hit will cost to flicks miss perry's v8."

Describing a band tour in which he participated, Neville wrote about a stressful stay in Sycamore, Georgia, after which the tour ended at Climax:

"To begin with, the powers-that-be had chosen twenty peaceful, innercent, corntented towns in South Georgia and we invaded the same with much blaring of horns, beating of drums, and making of speeches much to the amazement and amusement of the populace. The object of the tour was to promote the interest of music, etc.

"The members of the band were niftily decked out from head to feet respectively in blue and white. . . . We escaped from Sycamore with our lives and our hostesses' embroidered guest towels and played the next night in Climax."

*George-Anne, 15 February 1937, 13 March 1937, 29 March 1940

the hospital named Destler to its advisory board and endorsed a plan of low-cost health insurance for residents of the county.[41] (The plan began successfully, and many local citizens participated. However, it dissolved during World War II and did not resume afterward.)

Georgia Progress Days became a powerful educational force statewide. Pittman involved the historian as much as possible. Again in 1940 he asked Destler to plan the program. The Board of Regents had appointed Destler to the statewide Citizens Fact Finding Committee, composed of leading businessmen, educators, and concerned citizens. Destler planned a forum to explore the committee's report.

Destler used good judgment in planning the event. He involved well-known and highly regarded local citizens to serve as panelists, including Harry Aiken, C. M. Coalson (a pastor), and Maude Brannen Edge, an articulate and well-educated native of Statesboro. The final discussion on Saturday was "Planning a Better Georgia," featuring O. C. Aderhold, president of the University of Georgia. Others involved in arranging the program were Malvina Trussell, Hester Newton, Ivan Hostetler, Marian Groover, Mr. and Mrs. Pete Donaldson, and Dean and Mrs. Zach Henderson.

The topics explored in detail some of Georgia's critical social and economic problems. The local newspaper regarded the topics of great importance: "Three problems will be studied, including 'Increasing our Wealth and Income', 'Improving our Human Resources' and 'Constructing an Adequate Government.' For each problem a goal has been set with ways of achieving it. Suggestions will be made as to what we can do about each problem."[42]

DEVELOPING CHARACTER:
STUDENT LIFE IN HARD TIMES

Most of the students had this in common: they were poor. They knew they were fortunate even to be enrolled in college, when most young people stayed at home to help their parents make ends meet. For the decade of the 1930s, less than a dozen brought cars to campus. Fleming Roach said he owned the only car on campus in 1934. Mary Thomas Perry King recalled only two student cars in 1939, driven by Curtis Lane and the Christie brothers. Gesmon Neville at times operated a borderline vehicle, the "Air Flow Taxi."

Stella Vanlandingham attended the college during the transition from Wells to Pittman. She recalled most students considered President Pittman more student-oriented than his predecessor, whom she considered more political. She recalled many occasions when the president would prepare breakfast for groups of students, cooking the meal himself over a campfire in the college forest. She said these were the most delightful moments of her college career.[43]

College life in the 1930s was not unlike that of a typical Georgia high school. The main difference was the absence of parents. The faculty and staff took the place of parents (*in loco parentis*). Males and females had little opportunity for private encounters.

Dormitory mothers and the dean enforced the line separating East and West halls. Occasionally students crossed the line and returned unscathed. They shared delicious tales of life on the "other side." Once caught, however, violators typically suffered the ultimate punishment: they were "shipped." Chester Williams recalled the daughter of a prominent physician who was sent home in the early 1930s, never to return, because she permitted some members of the football team to visit her room. The football players also were "shipped."[44]

To compensate for their lack of social interaction, students organized clubs. Some had Greek letters in their names, lending a collegiate image, but all clubs were strictly local and required only modest dues. These clubs gave students an opportunity to form friendships and enjoy campus life outside the classroom.

Dean Henderson since the late 1920s had approved requests for "supervised play," as long as "play" was part of a larger program. He made sure events were amply chaperoned. Students cleverly organized teas (followed by dancing), receptions (followed by dancing), and promenades or semi-private walks by couples (followed by dancing).

The greatest social gift to young women and men in the 1930s was President Pittman's "leisure arts" program. He declared that dance was a "leisure art" *par excellence*. Unfortunately, most students had never attended a social dance.

Genario Honeycutt "Honey" Bowen, instructor of physical education, offered the first dancing classes in 1936. The response literally overwhelmed her—almost one third of the student body showed up for lessons. The *George-Anne* reported on February 15, 1937, that some 150 freshly minted dancers were ready for their first official ballroom dance in the alumni gymnasium.

Six organizations served the cause of the performing arts in the 1930s: Glee Club, Vesper Choir, the thirty-four-piece College Band, and Little Symphony of sixteen instruments. The Music Club included both musicians and music boosters.

The Dramatics Club produced several plays each year. During the 1938-39 academic year, campus thespians created a new organization. The Masquers, using a student-crafted logo of comic/tragic masks, presented plays on campus for more than forty years. Mamie Josephine Jones, the first director of Masquers, led the troupe in a memorable production of Thornton Wilder's *Our Town* just one year after the play opened on Broadway.

Academic and religious clubs provided a forum for discussions. The Stephens and Oglethorpe Literary Societies originally were debating clubs. Each organized in 1916, and the two clubs merged in 1936. The English

> ❝*I did not consider that dating.*
>
> Really, you did not have dates on campus. It was virtually impossible for a boy to have any contact with a girl. You couldn't hold hands. Boys could never cross the road leading to East Hall. Once a week, if you were an upper classman, you could go to the parlor where other boys and girls would be sitting. Then you could sit there and talk, as the housemother walked around, checking on everything. I tried it a time or two, but I did not consider that dating, so I just gave up. ❞
>
> Fleming D. Roach,
> interview with author,
> 10 January 2006

Humor: The making of a career

"It seems that when George was very young his father tried a little experiment on him to determine what career he would follow when he was older. So he placed a Bible, a five-dollar bill, and a big drink of whiskey on a table and waited for George to come into the room. He figured that if George picked up the Bible he would be a preacher; if he picked up the money, he would be a banker; and if he picked up the liquor, he would be a drunkard. Well, George finally came in and drank the whiskey, put the money in his pocket, and walked out with the Bible under his arm. So the old man decided then and there that he was going to be a politician."

George-Anne, 1 February 1937

Rules relaxed for seniors in 1935

"The administration recently granted privileges, including dates in the lobby of the auditorium on Sunday nights, one date a week in Little Parlor, selection of May Queen from Senior Class each year, spending two week ends off campus each month, having Sunday dinner at hotels and restaurants in Statesboro twice a month (12:30 - 2:30 p.m.), attending [the] 7 p.m. movie twice a month in town, pending approval in advance by dean of women."

George-Anne, 28 October 1935

Full dance card

Iota Pi Nu fraternity existed for one purpose: to provide such social occasions as dances, banquets, and proms. The downtown Jaeckel Hotel was a perfect site, because the restaurant served a fine meal and provided a dance floor as well.

John King of Jeff Davis County and Mary Thomas Perry of Screven County met at SGTC, became sweethearts, and later married.

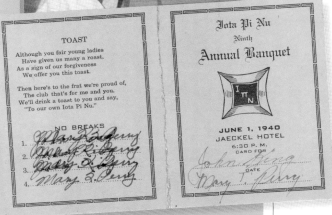

Club, sponsored by Marjorie Guardia in the 1930s and 1940s, hosted book reviews of contemporary works, led by faculty and students. The science club, organized by Malvina Trussell in 1926, presented and discussed popular scientific experiments.

With the help of the Carnegie Endowment for Peace, Chet Destler organized a local chapter of the International Relations Club. Quickly the club became the most active on campus. To review the club's agendas is to observe the rise of totalitarianism in Europe.

THE LARGER STAGE

Historians and social scientists in the university system held President Marvin Pittman and historian Chet Destler in high regard. They elected Destler chairman of the social science curriculum committee and editor of the standard textbook used throughout the university system.

After a particularly stimulating meeting of the social science committee, an official of the American Council of Education, Fred Sturges Beers, wrote Destler:

Your insight and your analytical powers are among the most promising for making an entity of the University System rather than the induced dream that it now is. . . . You have the respect of everyone who knows you; and since your report on the library situation, you have earned yourself a very considerable amount of admiration.[45]

Pittman and Destler in the late 1930s together shared the task of representing the college in the larger world of ideas. Judson Clements Ward Jr., teaching in the summer session of 1940, expressed these sentiments in a letter to Destler, who was teaching during the summer at Tulane University: "With you gone, it seems to me that most of our scholarly forces are gone. Plenty of people appreciate this quality whether you hear it frequently enough or not."[46]

There were competent, sometimes excellent, faculty members in place. For example, Wendell Smiley represented the college well among professional librarians and was elected president of the Georgia Library Association in 1941. Ronald Neil could sing, speak, and conduct the chorus and band, much to the public's pleasure. Jane Franseth published articles in national education journals and spoke effectively on school administration. Other than Pittman and Destler, however, no one else could represent the college as confidently in academic circles or in the public arena. In the state and nation, they projected an image of the college as an educational force.

Destler once confided to Pittman he sometimes felt lonely, because relatively few faculty members were interested in pursuing intellectual conversations:

There is something about our good-natured, friendly campus and faculty that seems to paralyze interest in completing advanced study even among those whose rank and responsibilities should make them most anxious to push ahead. The decline in the intellectual tone of the faculty as we have lost PhD's in the past several years has been quite marked and it has been a source of keen personal regret.[47]

Twice the Board of Regents called on Destler to speak for the university system on statewide broadcasts on Atlanta radio station WSB, "the Voice of the South." In his first broadcast, aired in early November 1939, he discussed "A Program for Agricultural Regeneration in Georgia."

Destler urged state leaders not to depend upon government assistance or outside capital. Rather, farmers and businessmen should work together to diversify and expand the state's farm production.

The engaging speaker demonstrated to listeners throughout the state that Teachers College in Statesboro had faculty who could discuss practical issues facing most Georgians. In short, the college was becoming the relevant institution that Pittman had planned from the start.

In 1941 the Board of Regents asked Destler to be the spokesman for the statewide Fact Finding Committee—the theme of Georgia Progress Days for 1940. Instead of making a speech, Destler chose to be interviewed. Using conversational language, he applauded the state's positive accomplishments, while recognizing obvious shortcomings. Again he said the state must learn to exploit its rich human and natural resources.

Destler Interviewed on WSB, March 22, 1941

WSB: [What can be done?]

Destler: *It is high time that Georgia and her neighbors follow the example set by Washington and set up funds of their own to help tenants up the ladder to ownership.*

WSB: [If we cannot rely on the government at Washington to solve our problems, upon whom must we depend?]

Destler: *Upon ourselves, and upon our own wealth and resources, with what help we can get from our neighbors and the federal government.*

WSB: [What is holding back progress?]

Destler: *I suppose we are handicapped more than in any other way by the conservatism of many influential citizens who refuse to depart from their traditional way of doing things to join in the work of building the civilization and prosperity of the South.*[48]

At 319 Savannah Avenue in Statesboro, a sixty-eight-year-old man sat near his radio. The companion of John Burroughs, the friend of Edison, Ford, and Firestone, probably listened and was not pleased. What irritated R. J. H. DeLoach was the very existence of the Fact Finding Committee. He called it the "Fault Finding Committee," complaining that Destler and others should focus on what was "right" about Georgia.[49]

Freshmen beware, ca. 1935

"Everyone is expected to contribute to a fund being asked to buy a new canopy for the sun dial."

George-Anne, 23 September 1935

Rat days end with flag rush

"The Freshmen are now upperclassmen, or rather they aren't rats anymore. After having duly and completely captured the banner in the Freshman-Sophomore Rush on Thanksgiving, they are at last free from any Rat Court. From now henceforth, no Freshman, to the great grief of several upper-class boys, may be called upon to make up beds, clean rooms, or run errands. Much as we hate to admit it, the rats have at last become human beings who may think, act, and talk at least like college students."

George-Anne, 27 May 1937

As recently as the 1980s, student organizations continued the flag rush tradition. In the 1930s, this event ended the ritual of initiation at Thanksgiving, assuming freshmen rats captured the sophomore flag. If they failed to capure it, intiation continued until the Christmas vacation.

Rats: The female species, ca. 1934

"Fay Foy was accused of not getting hot at the joint dance, so she was sentenced to sit on the radiator and strike matches until she reached the desired temperature...."

"After the formal charges, there was open criticism of freshman behavior by several upperclassmen and more penalties were inflicted.

"Finally, the rats were entertained by an eventful journey through the belt line."

George-Anne, 17 December 1934

Veteran teachers among TC graduates in 1941

Several public schools in Southeast Georgia bear the names of teachers who graduated in the class of 1941. All of them completed their degrees by taking classes from June-August, while teaching school children from September-May. Left to right are Irma Cox Spiers, Savannah; Sallie Zetterower, Statesboro; J. C. Cato, Ellabelle; Maxie Alderman, Savannah, Sam P. Jones, Adrian; Mattie Lively, Statesboro. Miss Lively began her teaching career in 1900-1901 at the Statesboro Academy.

The fourth name

On September 1, 1939, an influential legislator, L. Lamar Wiggins ('40), approached the Board of Regents and gave good reasons to amend the name of the college by dropping the word "South." This was the fourth name of an institution that began just thirty-three years earlier. Since 1935 President Pittman preferred to call it "Teachers College," which continued to be popular until the Board of Regents authorized a new name, Georgia Teachers College, in 1939.

DeLoach disagreed with Destler about the South. What the region needed most, he felt, was a renewed appreciation of southern tradition. Destler urged Georgians to reach beyond the past. DeLoach wanted to recover the past. Not only was Destler, a historian, unqualified to talk about agriculture, DeLoach lamented, he was not even a native Georgian.

DeLoach had spoken to friends and students about why he objected to "outsiders" like Pittman and Destler. He later would write down the opinions he had held since that day in 1934 when the people from Michigan came to town:

One of the great difficulties in our higher educational ranks is the transfer of educators from one section to another of our country and then trying to impose new doctrines in sections where people are not ready for them and are not going to tolerate them. . . .

Another fatal mistake teachers make is to get training in sections other than their own in the formative period of their lives, and then bring back home with them these contrary doctrines. In such cases if they have good judgment, they will sponsor political and social ideals promoted by the home folks, and help to change by slow degrees those ideals, or return to the place of their training.

Public education is supposed to render continuous service, and in its continuity cannot take a chance on trying to make changes to suit individual college teachers or presidents for or against political administrations.[50]

DeLoach genuinely believed "teachers" like Chet Destler and "presidents" like Marvin Pittman should be barred from employment in Georgia's colleges or universities. Even native Georgians should not be permitted to teach in their home state if they held points of view contrary to the majority.

Even though he resented Destler's appearance on statewide radio, DeLoach had reason to be pleased on that March evening in 1941. The highest authority had told him to wait until May. Then Pittman's stage would be cleared, and the spotlight would shift from the cast of characters DeLoach so despised.

DeLoach took comfort knowing the score would be settled in May. Talmadge would finally pay back the ghost of William Tecumseh Sherman for that humiliating march through Georgia in 1864. DeLoach could hardly wait to hear the governor's message: Georgians would control the university system, not intellectuals from northern states who held "foreign" values. DeLoach's reasoning was provincial and intellectually indefensible, of course, but it struck a responsive chord in the mind of his regular correspondent and good friend, Governor Eugene Talmadge.

THUNDER FROM A CLEAR SKY

Eugene Talmadge won the Georgia Democratic primary in September 1940. His key leader in Bulloch County, William Hubert Crouse, should have been pleased. Talmadge had just won the popular vote in Bulloch County for the first time in his long and successful career in state politics. Crouse, an influential Primitive Baptist preacher, was disappointed, nevertheless, because the majority of voters in the county's largest precinct, Statesboro (the 1209th), had voted for Talmadge's opponent.

The reason Statesboro voted against Talmadge, Crouse believed, was that Marvin Pittman had organized an anti-Talmadge campaign among the "college crowd." A faculty member and close friend, R. J. H. DeLoach, had told him so. Furthermore, Crouse accused Pittman of removing Talmadge's campaign poster during a political rally in Statesboro near the end of the campaign.

Guy Wells and Howell Cone discussed the Crouse-DeLoach disinformation machine four months before Talmadge was inaugurated. They knew that Rufus Lester Cone, the town's mayor, not Pittman, had removed the poster. They also knew Pittman was out of town on the day of the rally.[51] (The two Cones were not related.)

Wells and Cone corresponded often about the impending crisis from the fall of 1940 until the spring of 1941. They agreed the charges of DeLoach and Crouse against Pittman were malicious. They knew Pittman had been in the hospital on election day and did not even cast his vote. Wells and Cone urged Pittman to meet with Talmadge's supporters in town and let them know he had not been involved.

During the same period of time, Crouse, whom Talmadge had rewarded with an important patronage job, amplified DeLoach's rumors. Crouse was among a handful of local partisans who never had accepted "that man from Michigan." Another Talmadge supporter in the community of Denmark, Carlos Eustis Stapleton, also believed Pittman came across as an aristocrat unwilling to do politics the "Bulloch County way."

Some did not like his curbside manner downtown. Sometimes he took jokes personally and demanded an apology. Guy Wells wrote: "He is . . . always rubbing people the wrong way with his brutal frankness. I respect him for his honesty and am willing to overlook his shortcomings, which some others are not willing to do."[52]

Pittman, of course, had not learned Cone's art of "fodder walking," which seemed to work for Wells. Both correspondents agreed that Pittman could be a "blunderbuss." Had he been more of a "team player," they agreed, he might have quelled the DeLoaches and the Crouses.[53] In spite of behind-the-scenes work on Pittman's behalf by Talmadge's local friends, William Gesmon Neville Sr. (father of student Gesmon Neville) and Homer Cling Parker, the moment of truth arrived at the end of the Board of Regents regular meeting on Friday, May 30, 1941.

The radio listener at 319 Savannah Avenue must have smiled as he heard the news bulletin from the capitol on WSB: the Board of Regents had voted not to extend a contract to Marvin Pittman as president of Georgia Teachers College. DeLoach also knew Pittman would be the first of several "outsiders" to leave the college. Their names would be released later.

"Dr. Destler spoke [at Armstrong College] on 'Propaganda and the War.' He reviewed the development of propaganda from the time of the Crusades, when Western Europe was aroused to a war of vengeance and imperialistic aggression in the Orient.

"Dr. Destler is one of the state's ablest speakers. His direct method of addressing a group completely commands his listeners' attention. One cannot say that he 'makes a speech.' He just 'converses' with the group he may be addressing."

Bulloch Herald, 8 February 1940

Graduate of 1938 recalled academic life

Julian Stanley, class of '38, who later earned a doctorate at Harvard and achieved fame as a professor at Johns Hopkins University, recalled GTC during the late 1930s:

Even in those depression days SGTC had a few well-qualified instructors. . . . Most of the instructors seemed more steeped in education courses than in subject matter. . . . SGTC did not seem to value academic scholarship greatly, either.

The greatest teacher on campus then was Chester McArthur Destler, PhD from the University of Chicago. I took 'History of the Far East' from him. Inspiring!

Julian Stanley, letter to Marvin Goss, 3 November 2004

Dr. Pittman Says He Will Answer All Questions Asked

"I will answer any questions that the board of regents wish to ask me," Dr. Marvin S. Pittman told The Herald Tuesday morning.

Dr. Pittman stated that he will be present at the public hearing to be held in Atlanta Monday morning of next week before the board of regents to answer any questions arising from the charges made by Gov. Eugene Talmadge precipating in the board of regents' refusal to reappoint Dr. Pittman president of the Georgia Teachers college.

It was learned here Tuesday morning that a motorcade which is expected to be made up of more than one hundred persons from this section will leave the court house square Monday morning about 5 o'clock to go to Atlanta to attend the hearing. The meeting is scheduled for 10 o'clock at the state capitol.

It is said that the motorcade will be made up of representatives of the chamber of commerce, the Rotary club, the Lions club, the junior chamber of commerce, the Womans' club, the Business Girls' club, the county council of the P.-T. A., the various P.-T. A. organizations, lawyers, doctors and farmers.

The motorcade is described as a spontaneous demonstration of representative people of this section who wish to acquaint the board of regents with the true picture of the situation and to show the appreciation which this section has for Dr. Pittman and the work he is doing at the college.

Bulloch Herald, 12 June 1941

Not everyone in Statesboro shared DeLoach's sense of relief. The editor of the *Bulloch Times*, David Turner, reacted with utter disbelief. For the next edition of the newspaper, he composed this headline:

"Friends endorse head of college—Refute charges Dr. Pittman unfitted for position held here for past seven years." The article followed:

Like a clap of thunder from a clear sky there was heard the announcement over radio last Friday evening, following the meeting of the Board of Regents of the University System, that Dr. Marvin S. Pittman, president of Georgia Teachers College for the past seven years, had failed reelection because of charges made at the meeting of the board by Governor Talmadge that evening that he (Dr. Pittman) was unacceptable because of "having taken a too enthusiastic part in partisan politics," and that "he just don't fit in the community at Statesboro."[54]

On July 14 Governor Talmadge and the Board of Regents conducted a so-called trial and dismissed Pittman by a vote of ten to five. No one seemed to know exactly why the regents took this action. At this heated hearing, no regent mentioned the two original charges against Pittman.

A former faculty member and friend of Pittman, Jake Ward, was present that day. He was on the history faculty in 1939-40 and later became GTC president. He recalled his friend's hour on the stand: "Pittman couldn't give a good account of himself. They would just use this Talmadge technique to call him down. Dr. Pittman would talk about needing books in the library for the students to get all kinds of views, but they wouldn't listen to that. The governor had a great habit of slapping the desk."

As Ward recalled the hearings, "There was no way Dr. Pittman could have been cleared." Ten regents had made binding commitments to the governor, and the moderator, Regent Sandy Beaver, had made public his allegiance to Talmadge.[55]

At the July hearing regents did not charge Pittman with political activism or incompatibility with the community. They found him guilty of using college staff and equipment to improve his farm near the college. He was also criticized for entertaining faculty from the all-black Tuskegee Institute and circulating books in the library that advocated interracial cooperation. Like Tuskegee Institute, Georgia Teachers College had used grants from the Rosenwald Fund to support rural teachers and build a library.

Pittman organized an impressive defense by Statesboro attorney William Gesmon Neville. Elder J. Walter Hendricks, the first principal of the A&M school, served as a character witness. Fifty citizens from Bulloch County earlier had volunteered to travel to Atlanta to testify for Pittman. The group included ministers, lawyers, bankers, and farmers, but the regents told Pittman his friends in the community could not speak at the July hearing.

On the surface the choice of Neville made good sense. He was a loyal ally of Talmadge, and the defense hoped Neville would be able to persuade Talmadge to keep Pittman at the school. On the other hand, Neville was not a close friend of Pittman. Yet he did his best under the circumstances.

The charge that Pittman had used college labor on his farm was misleading. Pittman pointed out he had assigned the profits of his farmland to the college. He produced an agreement for the arrangement, approved previously by the Board of Regents.

Pittman did not deny faculty from Tuskegee had visited the school and acknowledged support of the Rosenwald Fund. He noted that Harvey Van Buren, a local black physician, had hosted the visitors from Tuskegee. He did not have to remind the regents they had approved Rosenwald Fund grants to a number of colleges in the university system.

Neville emphasized the potential impact of Pittman's removal on the community. He reminded his hearers of a fundamental truth about GTC. Old Culture on that sand ridge south of Statesboro had been and always would be "the people's school."

With his best melodic courtroom voice, the able Neville ended his remarks by echoing the words of Daniel Webster, who defended Dartmouth College before the U. S. Supreme Court in 1819: "She may be small, but there are those who love her."[56]

At the end of the hearing that day, two men on trial lost their jobs in the university system: Marvin Pittman and Walter Cocking, the dean of education at the University of Georgia. Vice Chancellor Curtis Dixon also was fired, as Chancellor Sanford had requested. The firings, and many to follow, would thereafter be remembered as a turning point in the University System of Georgia.

Regent Ormonde Hunter, a member of J. Randolph Anderson's old law firm in Savannah, was among five who voted to retain Pittman. Hunter told the Savannah Kiwanis Club, "The whole proceeding took on the aspect of a New England witch hunt in our early history, or perhaps one of the mock trials of the Spanish Inquisition. . . . To say that I was mortified is putting it lightly. I am ashamed to be on a board which deliberately crucified the reputation and future of two apparently honorable gentlemen."[57]

A TIME TO BROOD

Pittman cleaned out his office promptly. He packed the photographs and boxed his correspondence. Then he began jotting down notes on several pieces of paper. Later these notes appeared in the local newspaper: "Total number of college buildings doubled . . . New furnishings throughout all resident halls . . . Carnegie music set and library . . . complete equipment and uniforms for band . . . Constructed ten tennis courts." When secretary Mae Michael typed the notes, she used three pages.

In one column he showed university system support declining from nearly $59,000 in 1934-35 to under $47,000 in 1940-41. During this time the

WILLIAM GESMON NEVILLE SR.

The Statesboro attorney, a supporter of Governor Talmadge, defended Marvin Pittman at his trial in the Capitol on July 14, 1941. He invoked the oratory of Daniel Webster who defended Dartmouth College before the U.S. Supreme Court in 1819.

THE CRISIS OF 1941:
LOCAL AND STATE POLITICS

Guy Wells on the role of DeLoach

GUY WELLS

"It seems to be a political scrap by Talmadge henchmen and John DeLoach, which is about as dangerous as nitroglycerin and gunpowder. If we can keep the fuse from being lighted, we may save the situation. I think it is very desirable for [Fred] Lanier and some of these men to go to Atlanta and see Talmadge as quickly as possible. I think I found that some of the Talmadge group are on both sides in this matter."

Guy H. Wells, letter to Howell Cone, 16 May 1941

HOWELL CONE

"The burden of the argument is that Pittman is a 'Yankee,' and that he brings none but Yankee teachers to the college; that he, DeLoach, is a native, understands the people, and should be in a position of leadership to lead the people into 'The Promised Land.' I granted for the sake of the argument that perhaps Pittman has brought too many Northerners to the college, but that he is an honest, able man, and should not be moved at this time."

Guy H. Wells, letter to Howell Cone, 23 May 1941

DeLoach could not confirm Tuskegee faculty luncheon

R. J. H. DELOACH

"The prosecution, conducted by James S. Peters, recently appointed regent, then brought up the question of a visit of a delegation from Tuskegee Institute, a Negro institution, had made to the college here in 1938. It was charged that the delegation had spent most of three days at Statesboro and that the visiting Negroes had eaten on the campus with white teachers but a later witness [R. J. H. DeLoach] said that he would not swear that he saw the blacks and whites eating together."

Bulloch Times, 17 July 1941

The role of the Board of Regents

"Chairman Sandy Beaver . . . on Monday, July 7, came as the messenger of Governor Talmadge, to ask me to resign and to indicate if I did not he would either 'smear' me or refuse to give me a hearing."

Marvin Pittman, interview with M. C. Huntley, SACS Report, November 1941

MARVIN PITTMAN

The community responds

"Local organizations—Chamber of Commerce, Junior Chamber of Commerce, Rotary Club and Lions Club—have formally adopted strong resolutions of endorsement of Dr. Pittman's administration; the pastors of every church in Statesboro have written to the regents their words of appreciation; the county PTA in session Saturday adopted a resolution of endorsement."

Bulloch Times, 12 June 1941

Ormonde Hunter

Although Governor Eugene Talmadge appointed him to the Board of Regents, Ormonde Hunter felt compelled to rise in defense of Marvin Pittman and Walter Cocking at the capitol tribunal of July 14, 1941. When he returned to his home in Savannah, he told a civic club the governor had "deliberately crucified the reputation and future" of Marvin Pittman. Later, the governor removed Hunter from the board.

National media reviews Pittman case

"Last week, in a packed hall in the Capitol, the Board of Regents held a hearing. The Governor, himself a regent, was there, munching his lunch and prompting his fellow board members. Regent James S. Peters waved a copy of *Brown America*, a book by the Rosenwald Fund's President Edwin Rogers Embree, charged it preached Negro-white equality. Cried he: 'Negroes will ride in the same railroad cars, sit in the same schools, go to the same lavatories as white men.'

"'They won't do it,' shouted Talmadge. . . .

"Said Talmadge to Peters: 'Hit the chair and holler.' Peters hit, hollered. Cried Talmadge: 'Tell 'em about the niggers from Tuskegee visitin' the college [Georgia Teachers] at Statesboro.' Peters related that Negroes had munched sandwiches on the campus with whites. . . . Educators, North and South, lost no time in rebuking Talmadge."

"Lynching in Georgia," *Time*, 28 July 1941

Scenes from the trial of July 14, 1941

Clockwise from top right: Governor Eugene Talmadge, a spellbinding orator who campaigned on a platform of white supremacy, presided at the dramatic hearing in the capitol; Attorney Hatton Lovejoy pleads for justice, as Marvin Pittman, *left*, and Walter Cocking, *right*, listen intently; Chairman of the Board of Regents Sandy Beaver counted the ballots: ten regents voted to fire Pittman and Cocking, and five voted to retain them.

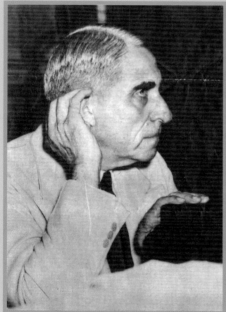

Students demonstrate downtown

At the end of the 1941 spring quarter, many students remained on campus after taking final exams. They wrote letters, circulated petitions, and conducted demonstrations on Main Street in Statesboro. The photograph, *left*, appeared in a *George-Anne* retrospective on February 8, 1943.

TEACHERS COLLEGE
1941-1948

1941 – Regents replace President Marvin Pittman with Albert Martin Gates, former president of Brewton-Parker Institute. Gates fires five faculty members. (7/24)

1941 – Student government passes new hazing rules for "rats."

1941 – University System of Georgia loses accreditation. (12)

1941 – Japan attacks Pearl Harbor, killing 2,335 Americans, causing the United States to enter World War II. (12/7)

1942 – College suspends intercollegiate sports. (1/19)

1942 – College discontinues Georgia Progress Days. (2/2)

1942 – Nazi and SS leaders meet at the Wannsee Conference in Berlin to coordinate the "Final Solution," an attempt to exterminate the Jewish population of Europe. (1/20)

1942 – Marvin Pittman accepts job as director of instruction at Louisiana State Teachers College. (2/9)

1942 – President Gates fires Mae Michael, longtime presidential secretary, citing her "disloyalty." (3/16)

1942 – Chancellor plans to convert college into a trade school. (7/7)

1942 – Police arrest Talmadge aide for using tear gas against students at Statesboro rally. (7/28)

1942 – Coconut Grove nightclub in Boston burns, killing more than 400 people. (11/28)

1942 – Ellis Arnall defeats Eugene Talmadge in gubernatorial election. (9/9)

1943 – Marvin Pittman resumes presidency of Teachers College. (2/5)

1943 – College becomes base for STAR unit, a screening program for army officers. (9/1)

1944 – Spring quarter enrollment drops to 130 students. (4/3)

1944 – Air force pilot James Arthur Bunce Jr., who attended the Laboratory School and Teachers College, is awarded Distinguished Flying Cross.

1945 – President Franklin D. Roosevelt dies in Warm Springs, Georgia, and Vice President Harry Truman becomes U.S. president. (4/12)

1945 – After the death of Chancellor Steadman Sanford, *Bulloch Times* recommends either Guy Wells or Marvin Pittman as successor. (10/4)

1945 – Germany surrenders unconditionally to the Allies. (5/7)

1945 – Marvin Pittman Jr. is released as German prisoner of war. (5/10)

1945 – U.S. B-29 bombers drop the atomic bomb on Hiroshima and Nagasaki, Japan, killing more than 130,000 civilians. (8)

1945 – Japan surrenders to the Allies and World War II officially ends. (9/2)

1946 – Soldiers come home, baby boom begins.

1946 – United Nations General Assembly meets for the first time at St. James' Palace in London. (1)

1946 – *George-Anne* notes Abraham Lincoln's birthday (2/12) and criticizes Georgia legislature for proposing "whites only" primary. (2/17)

1946 – College makes apartments from fourteen barracks for ex-soldiers and families. (3/21)

1946 – Gubernatorial candidate James Carmichael wins popular vote but loses electoral vote to Eugene Talmadge. (9/9)

1946 – Marvin Pittman seeks job with U. S. War Department. (11)

1947 – Regents accept Marvin Pittman's resignation and name Judson Clememts Ward Jr. as president, effective 9/1. Dean Zach Henderson is acting president. (2/20)

1947 – President Ward announces record enrollment of 650 and introduces popular policies. (9/18)

1947 – Regents criticize Chancellor Paty for appointing Jake Ward as President. (12)

1948 – Regents inform President Ward he will become assistant chancellor and will be replaced by Zach Henderson. (1)

PERFORMANCE POSTPONED

COPING WITH CONSEQUENCES

During the fall of 1941 Marvin Pittman realized, perhaps for the first time, how many friends he had in Statesboro. Because several regents told him they would try to overturn the board's decision of July 14, he stayed at home, unemployed, for the next seven months.

Pittman agreed to speak on educational, not political, topics. Invitations poured in from civic clubs throughout Georgia. He formed a local book club, taught his Sunday school class, and occasionally filled the pulpit at the Methodist church. Statesboro Rotarians welcomed him to the club he organized.[1]

Editor David Turner of the *Bulloch Times* wrote upbeat columns about the former president. Those who read only the *Bulloch Herald* found no supportive editorials. The *Herald* in 1941 served the interests of local Eugene Talmadge supporters who considered Turner's *Times* biased.[2]

The *Herald*, unsurprisingly, warmly greeted Pittman's replacement, Albert Martin Gates. For twenty years he had been president of Brewton-Parker Institute, a Baptist junior college in Mount Vernon, Georgia. Governor Talmadge, Board of Regents chairman Sandy Beaver, and Chancellor Steadman Sanford recommended and approved the appointment. The *Herald* wrote of Gates:

His moral stamina, high nobility of character, and deep devotion to his work bodes well for the future of that institution. This newspaper bespeaks the full and fine cooperation of the school faculty and of the community as a whole with this man whose genuineness and ability are a guarantee of success for the college.[3]

The faculty hoped the announcement of Pittman's successor would end the sense of uncertainty. Dean Zach Henderson met with the president and said, "I am impressed with the insight Dr. Gates has into the matter of our problems and believe that he will be able to carry on our program."[4]

Faculty, however, grew uneasy during August after Gates fired five of their colleagues: Chester Destler, Donald Doane, Jane Franseth, Leslie Johnson, and Mamie Veazey. A number of others retired, resigned, or decided to walk away. By mid-September, according to Chester Destler, "Some sixteen changes were made in the faculty and staff."[5]

Before the gubernatorial contest between Ellis Arnall and Eugene Talmadge reached fever pitch, Pittman moved to Louisiana State Teachers College at Natchitoches, Louisiana, in February 1942 to become director of instruction. The headline in the *Bulloch Times* read, "Pittman Takes Temporary Job." Locals assumed he would return to lead the college in 1943, if Attorney General Ellis Arnall somehow could defeat Governor Talmadge.

MAE MICHAEL

From 1929 until 1953, Miss Michael served as secretary to five presidents. President Gates fired her in 1942, because he believed she was disloyal.

The Michael Mentality

In the fall of 1931, during the economic depression, President Guy Wells notified faculty members the Board of Regents had cut their salaries by fifteen percent. He avoided enforcing the reduction until March of 1932, when the college treasury had only enough money to pay current bills. At a meeting where some voiced their complaints, Mae Michael advised the faculty, "instead of talking hard times and depression, we should go on living serenely and cheerfully with that innate dignity and self-respect which forbid us to show any feeling except that of optimism."

Minutes of the Faculty Meeting
9 March 1932

Hester Newton, a loyal colleague of Destler's and a friend of his wife, Katharine, wrote them several letters during 1942 at their Elmira, New York, address. She brought them up to date about departed faculty. Others, including Sophie Johnson, dean of men, searched for positions elsewhere. The faculty "fence sitters" who were "still swaying first one way and then the other" dismayed Newton who was fiercely loyal to President Pittman.[6]

Some professors, concerned about their economic future, might have vacillated, but the student council stood firmly as one. The council organized a vigorous campaign to restore the former president; President John Dunn and executive committee chairman William "Tiny" Henderson (unrelated to Dean Henderson) led the effort. They drafted a petition and circulated it at the annual meeting of the Georgia Education Association, obtaining hundreds of signatures.

The council wrote alumni a well-crafted letter, making clear their objective: "On the campus we want Dr. Pittman reinstated. Mr. Gates has tried and failed. No one else could have succeeded in his shoes." The letter brought home the enormous impact of the political purge:

It would break your heart if you could come and see. We've been harder hit than any of the other colleges. Enrollment cut from 550 to 318, a drop of more than 200, no college band, no interest in athletics, no pep, no college spirit, one dormitory almost vacant and the other only partly filled, resentment in the heart of everyone, faculty members and students alike. The leprous hand of politics has had a blighting effect on the whole institution.[7]

The loss of accreditation also took its toll throughout the university system. Accredited colleges in the nation would not recognize course credits and degrees authorized by the University System of Georgia. All units of the system suffered, but Georgia Teachers College, stripped of its visionary president and leading faculty, suffered most. The rough hand of political force virtually crippled the school.

The enrollment eventually shrank by 70 percent to 130. Eventually, some faculty, including Fielding Russell, did not have enough registrants to hold classes. Students were shocked when they found the popular English instructor behind the lectern in their history class. After school he joined other faculty and worked on the grounds crew.

On Monday morning, March 16, 1942, President Gates finally did what he believed he should have done months earlier: He called his secretary, Mae Michael, into his office and fired her. He had grown weary of hearing secondhand comments about Michael's loyalty to Pittman and reports of her correspondence with those Gates fired earlier. The president probably did not realize the secretary to Guy Wells and Marvin Pittman was a campus icon and a highly regarded citizen.

Most Georgians knew about the work of Michael's sister, Moina, "the poppy lady," who memorialized veterans. The news of Michael's plight spread quickly. Alumni who recalled her rehearsed sternness and spontaneous humor were heartbroken.[8] The affront aroused even the *Bulloch Herald*, and its editors for the first time took note of college "problems."

The *Herald* suggested citizens had accepted the departure of Pittman and others as permanent. However, the firing of Mae Michael refreshed sad memories and reopened old wounds. The editors also invoked local pride, the spirit of 1906:

Previous fires had died down to only smoldering embers and only time was needed to completely put them out. . . . And now Miss Mae Michael . . . She was fired it is said because of "disloyalty to the college and the president." . . . And so a brand new fire has been built under the College which belongs to the people of Statesboro and Bulloch County.

THE CHANCELLOR'S PROPOSAL

At this moment of institutional weakness, Chancellor Sanford discussed his new proposal for Teachers College with some legislators, college presidents, and regents. After he talked with the President Guy Wells at Georgia State College for Women, Wells wrote Howell Cone, "I had a long talk with Chancellor Sanford a few days ago, and I was very much worried over the tone of his conversation."

The chancellor proposed moving the struggling college elsewhere, perhaps to Savannah, and converting the Collegeboro campus into a technical school. The prospect deeply concerned Wells: "I have no sympathy with this idea. I think the function of the college was well thought out by those who wrote the bill creating the institution, and I see no reason for trying a new field when it has succeeded so admirably in teacher-training." Wells said he understood Sanford "has been commissioned to go to Statesboro soon and 'straighten out things' before the Regents approve the personnel for next year."[9]

Eight years earlier Cone had moved from Bulloch County to Savannah to begin a long tenure as U.S. Collector of Customs at the port. Yet Cone defended old TC with remarkable vigor. First, he tried to dissuade the chancellor during his visit to Savannah. Sensing Sanford was determined to close the college, Cone drafted a two-page document with six points and mailed it to him, forwarding a carbon copy to Wells. Cone sketched the history of the college and its gradual transformation into a first-class teachers college. Then Cone made his strongest point:

The college at Statesboro was and is located in the largest territory in the State without a denominational or State institution of college grade. Its future was well thought out, and the fact that its growth was greater than any of the branches of the University is proof of the fact that it was, until its administration was interfered with, performing its right mission.[10]

Cone urged the Chancellor not to drive the final nail in the coffin of a once-vital and proud academic institution.

Reclassification." The "fast track" program for screening potential officers began during the fall of 1943 and continued for almost a year.

The army provided funds for renovating Anderson Dining Hall.

SENATE APPROVES FIFTEEN REGENTS

Marion Smith, Atlanta, To Serve As Chairman

Following the reorganization of the Board of Regents under a bill passed by the 1943 General Assembly, Governor Ellis Arnall promptly appointed a new Board of Regents who were confirmed by the State Senate.

The new members and the terms for which they were appointed follow:

J. L. Renfroe, Bulloch county, representing the First congressional district, to serve until January 1, 1948.

Ed Jerger, Thomas county, representing the Second district, until January 1, 1947.

George Woodruff, Muscogee county, representing the Third district, serving until January 1, 1944.

C. J. Smith, Coweta county, representing the Fourth district, until January 1, 1949.

Rutherford L. Ellis, Fulton county, representing the Fifth district, until January 1, 1947.

Miller S. Bell, Baldwin county, representing the Sixth district, until January 1, 1950.

Roy Emmett, Polk county, representing the Seventh district, until January 1, 1945.

Prince Gilbert, Glynn county, representing the Eighth district, until

DR. MARVIN S. PITTMAN

TEACHERS COLLEGE RESTORED TO FULL ACCREDITED STATUS

Membership In Southern Association Reinstated As Of September 1, 1942, The Date Schools Were Suspended

Noted Educator Returns to Former Post as Head of Teachers College

Dr. Marvin S. Pittman, who for seven years served as president of Georgia Teachers College and was fired in July, 1941, by a "stacked" Board of Regents on false political charges, returns today as executive head of the college after an absence of eighteen months. The reinstatement of Dr. Pittman was one of the first actions taken by the new constitutional Board of Regents at their first meeting last month.

Pittman, since leaving Teachers College, has been serving as Director of Instruction at Louisiana State College at Natchitoches, La., where he did his first college teaching.

'Charm,' Masquers' Winter Production

Dramatic Presentation Is Comedy; Complete Cast Has Been Selected

"That elusive, intangible, indefinable something that you cannot put your fingers on." The Masquers guarantee that you will know the answer to this mysterious riddle if you see their next stage production, "Charm," a comedy in three acts. The play is scheduled for presentation on February 25th.

The action of the play is laid in a small American town in pre-war days. The plot of the production revolves around the troubles of an average family who has a young daughter loved by two men. Their exploits

Bastile Trial Day

Along with Dr. Cocking, of the University of Georgia, Pittman was tried at a "mock trial" on July 12, 1941, by a Board of Regents who had already received a typed verdict from former Governor Talmadge before the trial began. After Pittman left the college on September 1, 1941, and was succeeded by Dr. A. M. Gates, who had been president of the college at Mount vernon. Gates relinquished his position last week by order of Regents, and at the same time the board named Dr. Pittman to succeed Gates.

Rehires Michael

Miss Mae Michael, who served under three presidents as secretary, was rehired last week by Dr. Pittman as

"Back to the top with Pittman"

"In a short period of time enrollment has dropped from over 500 in 1936 to a total of 141 this quarter. The faculty, which was once one of the best in the University System, has been depleted to such an extent that there remains little resemblance to that of which we were so proud."

The enrollment dropped to 130 during the spring of 1943, according to an article of April 3, 1944.

George-Anne, 8 February 1943.

East Hall, normally the girls dormitory, became home of the STAR unit. Soldiers and staff lodged in East Hall, displacing more than a hundred women, who moved into the traditionally all-male West Hall. (Because of the sharp decline in female students during war years, the college closed the other dormitory for women, Lewis Hall.) Sophie Johnson recalled moving the population of male college students, numbering around thirty, to the upstairs apartments of the dining hall and another building nearby.[24]

During the academic year 1943-44, more than five hundred soldiers called TC home. They stayed at Collegeboro for relatively short periods of up to one month, as they completed screening and training before receiving their new assignments. The permanent staff consisted of nine officers and eleven enlisted men.

Using income from the STAR unit, the college spent $12,500 to acquire one hundred acres of land, known as the Johnson farm.[25] The campus expanded to nearly four hundred acres.

The predominantly female student body welcomed the young soldiers, although they had few opportunities to interact with them. By October, the male-to-female ratio stood at three-to-one. The female students applauded this advantageous arrangement. Officers warned soldiers about the imaginary line running north from the administration building to the flagpole. They called it the "Maginot Line," meaning "impenetrable" (from a series of fortifications developed by French defense minister André Maginot, after World War I).

Soldiers playfully presented Mamie Veazey a certificate, naming her "Ladder Girl of 1944." A student recalled the story: One evening the housemother noticed a ladder leading to a second-floor window. Immediately, she pushed it to the ground. No one could determine who put the ladder in place. Thereafter, soldiers referred to the housemother as "Ladder Girl."[26]

Each Saturday night the STAR unit and female students bedazzled each other in the Alumni Gymnasium. The spectacular evenings began after Dean Zach Henderson determined that supervised dancing would benefit both students and soldiers. On alternating weekends, soldiers and students competed to present the "best dance yet."

A regular column in the *George-Anne*, called "STAR Gazin'," kept both soldiers and students informed about social events, concerts, and dances. Soldiers included former faculty of Ivy League universities as well as professional musicians. They gave lectures and concerts in the college auditorium. The Statesboro Music Club sponsored a holiday musical in December, featuring local talent and professionals stationed in the STAR program.

Students worried about their friends who fought in the war. Classmates received letters from Europe and the South Pacific and shared them with students and faculty. Occasionally national media noted heroics of TC alumni, such as Charlie Paine of Waycross. The former star athlete and excellent student appeared in a feature story in *Look* magazine, entitled "Forty Against One." A journalist described how Lieutenant Paine "brought a Boeing Fighting Fortress through one of the great fights of the war."[27]

Five alumni of TC died defending the nation: Leroy Cowart Jr. and Roland Warnock, both of Statesboro; Charles H. Browne, Brunswick; Hardy Lee Pilkington, Manchester; and Harvin D. Mulkey, Pompano, Florida. At the war's end, the college dedicated a plaque honoring their service.[28]

As the nation planned for peace in 1945, Pittman thought conditions were ideal for a new beginning at TC. The chancellor, experiencing poor health, was in his seventy-fourth year and probably would retire soon. Pittman, at sixty-two, was well into what he considered his last decade of public service, and he was ready to realize his dream. He hoped to fulfill his ambition of making TC the intellectual center for public education in Georgia.

Pittman believed he needed an individual to lead the faculty by example—a person of solid intellect, proven will, and boundless energy. Together they could restore the momentum the college enjoyed in the late 1930s.

The president turned his thoughts to Connecticut College in New London, where Destler served as head of the department of history. Pittman began his letter, "I wonder if you and your family are not tired of the frigid North and aren't ready to come to a good country to live and labor. We really do need you and want you; we need you now."[29]

Destler replied that he and Katharine both would enjoy "the opportunity to renew our friendship with the Pittmans, and . . . we would like to help you put the college back where it was before Talmadge's raid in '41." Yet, Destler acknowledged, his salary in Connecticut was considerably higher than he

CHARLES PAINE

Charles J. Paine of Waycross was a senior when he enlisted in the Air Force. A member of the football and track teams, Paine also participated in the chorus, debate team, and several clubs. *Look* magazine on January 12, 1943, featured him in a heavily illustrated article entitled: "Charlie Paine– One Against Forty." Forty German planes fired 200 bullets into Paine's Boeing Flying Fortress. Paine miraculously piloted his aircraft, minus two engines, instruments, landing gear, rudder, and stabilizer. Somehow he eluded enemy aircraft as his crew fought back. He guided the severely crippled bomber back home, skidding to a stop on the runway. Look described the courageous and quick-thinking Paine as a true World War II hero.

The drive in front of the Administration Building was known as the Maginot Line during STAR occupation.

When STARs fell on Collegeboro

From September 1943 until May 1944, the U.S. Army operated a Specialized Training Assignment Reclassification (STAR) unit on campus. Draftees who had scored well on standardized tests underwent further screening and instruction, prior to moving to their permanent assignments. The typical STAR member spent from three to five weeks on campus. What did the STAR unit mean to the campus? In a word, survival. Supported by government funding, the college ended the 1943-44 academic year with hope.

MAJOR LEON WHITTIER

STAR *members in local newspapers*

Name	Title or Previous Position
Maj. Leon A. Whittier	.Commandant
Capt. William Lorimer III	Acting Commandant
Capt. Ralph H. Lyon	Staff, College Professor
Lt. Norman A. Arbaiza	Staff
Lt. John B. Depot	Staff
Lt. Sam Miguel	Staff
M. Sgt. Saul Miller	Staff
Pvt. Lockard	Inspector Department of Labor
Pvt. Noah Lipton	New York lawyer
Pvt. Herman Mattehi	Boston lawyer
Pvt. Frank W. O. Jones	Rhodes Scholar & Yale U. Faculty
Pvt. Tyborowski	Professional Musician
Pvt. Stefan Freid	Professional Musician
Pvt. Malcolm Holmes	Entertainer, Musician
Pvt. Eugene Kurtz	Professional Musician
Pvt. Chris Schenkel	Radio Announcer, Princeton U. Student

NOTES*
by STAR GAZERS

"The astronomy class of Teachers College is doing excellent work. Yes, indeed, they go out every night whether rain, sleet, snow, ice, dew, frost, or shine, to add to the variety of astronomy.

"A few of these interesting speculations may be seen in the east of West Hall almost every night (regardless of weather cocks). The sparkle of the 'well-pressed khaki' draws crowds of Sinatra-swooners and never do these friends part until a silver or gold bar separates them. (Four-star generals are also included in this group.)"

— ••• —

"We just got in from a luscious dance! Of course all the STARS were there and did we get a rush! . . .

"Tonight at 10 o'clock, all the STARS and the college students gathered under the flag and had a combined 'Evening Watch' service. It was so impressive. We all had lumps in our throats, when at the end of the program 'Taps' sounded out over the silent campus. . . .

"Lunch was certainly unusual, though. We had a 'mock banquet.' A group of soldiers came marching in, after we had been seated at our tables, tied dainty white aprons around their GI waists, and proceeded to serve us in the grandest of style—they thought! Anyway, we felt like King Arthur of the Round Table, while splitting our sides laughing at the soldiers' antics. What a cute bunch of STARS we have on the campus! . . .

"Today was chapel day and the program was the best yet. The STARS put on a 'variety show' for us. They certainly have a lot of talent in that unit."

— ••• —

"On the campus we have seen the coming and going of the STARS, we have seen boys leave for various branches of the service, we have seen students and faculty members doing labors that certainly they would not have been doing in ordinary times. We have seen the president of the college up at four o'clock in the morning attending to the milking; we have seen college professors working on the campus. Students have made sacrifices, they have been loyal throughout the year."

*George-Anne, 17 January 1944, 22 May 1944.
Jerry Hamilton and other students contributed to the notes gathered in this section.

When girls ran the George-Anne

Because of wartime conservation programs, the campus newspaper went to press only once a month during 1943-44. During the year the army drafted editor Dan Chambliss and associate editor Hubert Callaway. For the first time in its history, women totally controlled the college press. An editorial in the April 3, 1944, edition noted the situation:

"The women are carrying on and the *George-Anne*, despite shortages, decreases in enrollment, hopes to not only continue throughout this school year, but for the years to come." Names of staff members who led the newspaper through wartime appeared on the editorial page:

Associate Editor . . . . . Adell Callaway
Business Manager . . . . Beverly Edwards
Business Manager . . . . Pruella Cromartie

Reporters:
Ruth Exley	Claire Floyd
Betty Bird Foy	Doris Greer
Betty Jones	Beth Stanfield
Hazel Wildes	

Reluctant farewell

My dear Chet:

I have your letter of April 2; while I am naturally disappointed, I nevertheless recognize the logic of all you say and perhaps the wisdom of your decision, but I should like to find somewhere another 28-year-old C. M. Destler that we could start with to build our program. You did some grand service for Teachers College for which we shall always be grateful. . . .

Sincerely yours,

Marvin

would earn in Georgia. He ended his letter by recommending a friend with a PhD from Harvard.

After mailing his noncommittal response, Destler and his wife talked about resuming the life and work they had loved in Statesboro. Realizing they might regret not pursuing the matter, Destler sent Pittman a telegram, asking for additional time to think about the offer.

Encouraged, Pittman put his heart on the line: "I feel that Georgia needs you, and that you can make a distinct contribution to the State and to this section of the country." [30] Destler noted potential jealousy by Zach Henderson, dean since 1927, who would be earning less than Destler. His chief concern, however, was whether he could be dismissed again for political reasons. [31]

Pittman acknowledged, with regret, that there were no safeguards against future tyranny. He philosophized, "If a Talmadge or one of his type were to become governor, there is no guarantee against such action. Those are some of the hazards of human existence." [32] Destler found that hazard too great a risk. He did not return to the college and town he so dearly loved. Within a few months he moved his family to New Haven, Connecticut, where he became a visiting professor in the department of history at Yale University.

The reason Destler did not resume the "greatest experiment in education in the South" was not complicated. He simply refused to subject himself or his family to another abrupt dislocation and cycle of grief. Pittman could not have realized the depths of Destler's suffering and loneliness in September 1941.

The final letter Pittman wrote Destler reflects how deeply the president regretted the history professor's decision. Pittman acknowledged the contributions of his young friend whose path through life once merged with his. [33]

RELUCTANT DEPARTURE

Campus life at TC recovered its prewar vitality in 1946, as more than two hundred veterans pushed the enrollment to more than six hundred. New faculty brought with them a sense of confidence and stability. The campus and community bonded with the president when Pittman's son, Marvin Jr., returned from his year of captivity in a German prisoner-of-war camp.

Ralph McGill had predicted Pittman would "build the college to the heights of scholastic repute it previously enjoyed." The president, however, would not fulfill the prophecy. He could not put together a faculty and staff like those who with energy and enthusiasm worked with him in the 1930s.

While the college bustled with a record number of new students in 1946, a ghost of 1941 preoccupied the president. The Talmadge wing of the

Democratic Party revived itself and ran a spectacularly successful campaign. Since Governor Arnall could not succeed himself by law, the Democratic primary featured two former governors, E. D. Rivers and Eugene Talmadge.

A newcomer to statewide politics, the progressive James Carmichael entered the contest. The president trusted positive reports by former TC faculty member Jake Ward, who had been Carmichael's roommate at Emory University.

Although Carmichael won the popular vote, Talmadge captured the majority of county-unit votes and claimed victory on June 17, 1946. Now the president himself faced one of those "hazards of human existence." The issue was not merely a philosophical discussion with Chet Destler.

After pondering the implications of Talmadge's comeback, Pittman decided to follow the lead of Destler. He refused to play the role of target in yet another political battle. He might withstand the abuse, but his wife, Anna Terrell Pittman, could not. The purge of 1941, as their friends knew, had affected her profoundly.[34] Ultimately, the college could suffer once again, and he would not accept that risk. He set in motion his retirement plans.

In September 1946, knowing Talmadge would be the next governor, the president resigned as superintendent of the Methodist Sunday school. Then he applied to the U.S. War Department for a position as an educational consultant. After receiving assurances he would get an assignment, Pittman informed Chancellor Raymond Paty he wanted to retire early. (Paty had succeeded Sanford, who died in 1945.) The Board of Regents already had reelected Pittman president for the 1947-48 year, so they rescinded their decision.[35] He decided to end his career as president less than four years after he returned from his "Talmadge sabbatical."

With mixed emotions Pittman heard the shocking news on December 20, 1946. Governor-elect Talmadge had died after a brief illness. The political equation changed overnight. Pittman, bound by his earlier decision, did not cancel his plans.

As Pittman began his premature retirement in 1947, his colleague of 1934 also was entering a new phase of his life. At the age of forty-three, Chet Destler began a long struggle that would consume most of his remaining years. He entered a dark tunnel of mental illness that few physicians then knew how to treat. He endured treatments that enabled him to resume productive activity, even a brief stint on the faculty at Cornell University.[36] But he would never again be that Chet Destler who, with colleague Marvin Pittman, planned and built something of great value—an academic institution many Georgians knew and admired as Teachers College.

Pittman suffered a fate he did not deserve. He gave the best years of his life pursuing a dream that brought change and hope, not only to rural Georgia but also to the state at large.

Pittman survived but did not triumph. He defined his life by his career at TC. Here he etched a legacy both in dreams realized and in dreams unfulfilled.

JACKIE ANDERSON STRANGE

Jackie Strange ('47) was named as Deputy Postmaster General on January 9, 1985. After Strange had a successful career as a regional postmaster, Postmaster General Paul N. Carlin named her to the post. Alumna Strange made history as the first female Deputy Postmaster General in United States history.

JUDSON CLEMENTS WARD JR.

Judson Clements Ward Jr. the fifth president of Georgia Teachers College formerly taught at TC and West Point Military Academy. Later he became dean and vice president at Emory University.

P̲ittman believed no one currently serving on the faculty and staff should succeed him. He wanted someone who shared his dream of TC. He needed an intellectual with personal skills, a leader who could continue the tradition, build a new stage, and resume the great drama. He consulted with Chancellor Paty, and they agreed that one person, especially, would make an outstanding president: Judson Ward. The man everyone knew as Jake Ward had won many friends on campus and in the community when he taught history in 1939-40.

Ward, a Phi Beta Kappa graduate of Emory with bachelor's and master's degrees, was completing his PhD dissertation and could not move to Statesboro until September 1947. Pittman's assignment with the U.S. War Department began in February. The chancellor asked Dean Henderson to preside until Ward arrived during the summer, depending on the advice of Pittman. The local newspapers anticipated the arrival of the thirty-five-year-old president and his new bride, twenty-one-year-old Susan.

Having lived in the community for an academic year and a summer, Ward had left a favorable impression. As president, the unpretentious Ward made friends in civic clubs, where he spoke in an entertaining and down-to-earth manner. Most who recalled him from his earlier years agreed on one point: he was a "mixer," exactly what they wanted in a college president.

In 1940–41 Ward had taught at Birmingham Southern College, where Raymond Paty was president. While writing his doctoral dissertation on southern history at the University of North Carolina, he served in the army and was a member of the history faculty at West Point Military Academy. He had been "Dr." Ward only briefly when he became president of TC.

Statesboro welcomed warmly President Ward: "I was well received in the community, joining the Rotary Club for Monday noon meetings and making speeches here and there. I had been an active member of the Baptist Church during my year as a teacher. . . . Charles Jackson, the Methodist preacher and a longtime acquaintance, had me speak at his church several times."[37]

Under the direction of Dean Henderson for seven months, the campus seemed to be standing still, awaiting the arrival of Pittman's replacement. The student body saw in the thirty-five-year-old Ward a leader capable of restoring the college to its glory days of the late 1930s. The editor of the *George-Anne* wrote, "Within a relatively short span of three weeks there is to be seen a tremendous difference in the attitude and spirit prevailing on the campus."[38]

The editor wrote about the immediate impact of Ward on the campus newspaper. Student editors of the *George-Anne* believed the previous administration had not fully entrusted them with gathering news and making editorial judgments. Ward told the editor he disapproved of censorship: "The masthead says this is a student newspaper. The students will run it.

I'll be glad to help in any way I can, but don't come to me to have anything censored. Print anything you see fit as long as it is the truth."[39]

Ward found the cost of a full-blown inauguration excessive, considering the college's limited budget. Rather than the traditional occasion, featuring a processional of visiting delegates from academic institutions, he planned a local inaugural program for the campus auditorium. His choice of a speaker, Governor Melvin E. Thompson, made sense to him and the community. Also an alumnus of Emory, Thompson had been elected lieutenant governor in 1946 and became governor earlier in 1947.

Within four months of his inauguration, Ward saw his presidency begin to unravel. His plight was unrelated to his leadership on campus and in the community, which was superlative. The difficulty originated on the ground floor of the capitol in Atlanta.

Ward became a pawn in a contest between members of the Board of Regents and Chancellor Paty. The issue was the chancellor's leadership, not Ward's. The inauguration appearance of Governor Thompson, an Emory alumnus, did not please some politicians in the state. Sandy Beaver, still chairman of the Board of Regents, might have considered the choice unfortunate.

Ward's friendship with Talmadge's opponent in the recent election, also James Carmichael, did not help his cause. The president's college roommate was too liberal for the version of Georgia espoused by some of the regents. Some longtime regents began to express concerns about Paty's independence. They preferred the style of the late Chancellor Sanford, who carefully attended to political matters.

Regents questioned the chancellor's decisions on other matters. They suggested Paty's management was flawed, as he revealed in his "premature" selection of Ward. Some regents believed TC did not need another Marvin Pittman, but Paty had accepted without question Pittman's nomination of Ward. Regents who considered Ward an outsider did not realize he possessed leadership qualities.

His recent inaugural was still a pleasant memory when Ward lost control of his presidency. Paty, a newcomer to Georgia's political system, had learned a lesson. Jake Ward became an example. After the Christmas break, Paty called Ward to Atlanta and told him the details: He would become assistant chancellor, replacing temporarily Vice Chancellor Hollis Edens, who eventually became president of Duke University.[40]

Seven issues in seven months

1. Reinstate Football?
"There was pressure to resume intercollegiate football, which had been abandoned during World War II. At that time the college used only a pasture with a few wooden bleachers for a football field. Coach Crook Smith had departed. Resumption of such a program required money. Pressure was put on me from the community. At Rotary meetings I heard many pleas for the resumption of football. I was saved by the arrival of Coach J. B. Scearce, whose emphasis was on basketball, and he was so successful with that sport that pressure for football died down."

2. Leaky Roofs
"I learned a lesson about leaky roofs. The Marvin Pittman Library building had a flat roof. Architects must think flat roofs are more aesthetic, but we never could get the leaks stopped in the roof of the library building while I was president."

3. Locating a New Building
"I secured a small building for GTC, with the help of former president E. V. Hollis, who had a high position in the U.S. Office of Education. The question was its location on campus. The chairman of the Industrial Arts Department to be housed in the building wanted it in a very prominent place, and unfortunately for me, former President Pittman, who had refrained from interference, sided with him. I thought the space should be reserved for some more important permanent building."

4. The Cracked Boiler
"The question was whether to try to braise or seal the crack or buy a boiler used for steam heating the buildings. With finances as tight as they were, the decision was to try to seal the crack. For several weeks all attempts to seal failed as the crack reappeared ahead of the sealant. As I recall, a new boiler had finally to be bought and installed."

5. Dangerous Wiring
"I had heard about the bad wiring in East Hall. I went over there and put my hand on the fuse box. It was hot. In place of fuses, somebody had put pieces of copper pipe in the fuse box. I went home that night and I could hardly sleep. There were a hundred women living in that dormitory and the fuses were nothing but pieces of copper pipe!"

6. The Farm and Dairy
"I meant to impress on the people in Statesboro that we were an educational institution. The farm and the dairy were big distractions. I wanted to immediately get rid of the farm and the dairy, but I did not accomplish that before I left. We would have been better off with a business manager, not a farm superintendent."

7. Knowing Where to Shop
"After the inaugural program, I went into town to buy a bottle of rum for Sue and me to celebrate the end of a strenuous but pleasant day. The next morning Bill Bowen, longtime friend and owner of a furniture store, warned me never to go to the liquor store again. He said that if we wanted anything to come into his furniture store and someone there would do the shopping for us."

Judson Clements Ward Jr., interview with the author, 25 June 2003

"I left Atlanta perplexed and downhearted," Ward said. He realized he could not continue as president, because he was "out of the loop." The Emory and UNC man, like the Oregon and Columbia man who preceded him, had a basic flaw; he was not a "good old Georgia boy," at least in the eyes of some regents. University system officials acted arbitrarily once again, but this time they made sure the victim was not left hanging. They "promoted" him to the chancellor's office.[41]

He served as assistant chancellor until autumn—long enough to realize the office at the capitol was inherently political. Regents responded to public opinion, he learned, and they made demands on the chancellor. Some major controversies had little or nothing to do with the academic mission of the university system.

Ward became aware of a running feud between a longtime regent and Chancellor Paty: "I later heard that at the most recent meeting of the Regents, General Sandy Beaver, head of the Riverside Academy at Gainesville and Dr. Paty had almost come to blows over something." Ward concluded, "I was lucky to get out of there after a few months."[42] Emory University, his alma mater, invited him to become dean.

The president who served TC only seven months—the shortest tenure in the institution's history—became the administrator with the longest tenure in the history of Emory University. In December 1948, Ward began a career that continued into the year 2006, as undergraduate dean, executive vice

BASKETBALL IN 1947-1948

1948 Varsity Squad

Front row, left to right: J. B. Scearce, C. Wireman, F. Bagley, T. Dykes, Jerry Conner, M. Conner, Jimmy Conner, H. Reeves, M. Greene. Back row: J. Murphy, B. Carter, C. Adams, G. Lindsey, G. Eanes, L.D. Bowen, M. Prosser, W. Whaley, C. Hill.

Left, fans packed the Alumni Gym to see the Professors begin a new era in basketball.

president, and alumni dean. During this time, Emory attained elite status among American universities.

While adjusting to his rewarding work at Emory, Ward found himself returning to Bulloch County on numerous occasions. He spoke at high school graduations, annual civic club dinners, and college functions. He also visited numerous friends on campus and in the community. He regularly met with his mentor and friend Marvin Pittman.

Ward never told his many friends in Statesboro the whole story, because they could do nothing to change the outcome. He did not want to leave his new job so quickly, but he had no choice other than to honor the request of his superior, whom he admired. He had a job, at least, but not the one he wanted—the presidency of Georgia Teachers College.

President and Mrs. Ward, dining with Governor Melvin E. Thompson at Anderson Dining Hall after Ward's installation on September 30, 1947.

The Scearce era begins

J. B. Scearce completed his master's degree at Eastern Kentucky College and began a new era in Teachers College athletics in 1947. Earlier he had learned how to lead players to reach their potential at North Georgia College, Norman Park Junior College, and Cumberland College in Kentucky.

Scearce's "Teachers" hit the hardwood of Alumni Gym in great form on December 12. Still early in the season, the team shellacked Piedmont College, 63-24. In its December 15, 1947 issue the *George-Anne* was impressed: "Every combination Coach Scearce put on the court performed like a well-oiled engine, and balls poured through the Teachers' basket. . . . They all scored but 'Lard' Green [the trainer]."

The team that began a great era in basketball included holdovers from 1956—Jimmy Conner, Mitchell Conner, Jerry Conner, Walker "Bo" Whaley, George Eanes, Frank Bagley, and Marvin "Rhed" Prosser. Newcomers included Tom Dykes, Carlton "Bulldog" Adams, George Lindsey, Charlie Wireman, and Herb Reeves.

Marvin "Rhed" Prosser

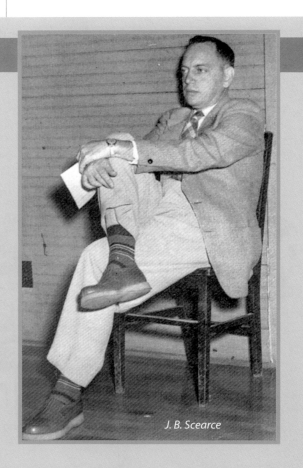

J. B. Scearce

TEACHERS COLLEGE
1948-1958

1948 – The USA and the USSR officially recognize Israel as a nation. (5/17)

1948 – Piedmont College awards new TC president, Zach Henderson, honorary doctorate. (5/31)

1948 – U.S. Armed Services desegregate. (7/26)

1948 – Frogs from Lake Wells sing on new recording by Cornell University naturalist, Arthur Allen. (9/20)

1949 – Margaret Mitchell, author of *Gone With the Wind*, dies. (8/16)

1950 – Hester Newton takes history students on twentieth annual tour of historic sites in coastal Georgia. (4/30)

1950 – Largest June graduating class in history, 115, includes 58 veterans. (5/27)

1950 – Korean War begins as North Korea's troops invade South Korea. (6/24)

1950 – Albin H. Eber of Germany is first foreign student to receive degree. (8/30)

1951 – *I Love Lucy* show debuts on U.S. television. (10/15)

1952 – Radio announcer Alan Freed popularizes the term *rock 'n' roll* in America. (4/30)

1952 – Graduating seniors participate in seventeenth annual Lantern Walk on the circle. (6/4)

1952 – United States reports 57,628 cases of polio, mostly among children. (12/30)

1953 – J. D. Park, head of the division of education, tells Rotary Club a TC graduate program would help region. (3/7)

1953 – Edmund Hillary and Tenzing Norgay reach the summit of Mount Everest. (5/29)

1953 – Alfred Kinsey publishes his report on female sexuality. (9/14)

1954 – The U.S. Supreme Court rules segregation unlawful in *Brown v. Board of Education*. (5/17)

1954 – Former President Guy Wells, a Statesboro resident, is executive secretary of the Committee on Interracial Cooperation. (10/20)

1955 – Auditorium named to honor the late J. E. McCroan, former trustee chair. (1/30)

1955 – Basketball team sets thirty new records, including double-figure scoring by Chester Webb (All-American), Doug Corry, Don Wallen, Bo Warren, and Garland Campbell. (3/10)

1955 – Nobel Prize–winning physicist Albert Einstein dies. (4/18)

1956 – Minta Tyre of Alma, becomes the three-thousandth degree recipient at TC. (8/17)

1957 – Professor Parrish Blitch and sophomore Ric Mandes star in Columbia University film on *U.S. v. Darby Lumber*. (2/7)

1957 – USSR successfully launches into orbit the first man-made satellite known as Sputnik I. (10/4)

1958 – Elvis Presley, a draftee, is inducted into the U.S. Army for a two-year stint. (3/24)

1958 – Unis Abdullah, a student from Baghdad, Iraq, introduces Islam to *George-Anne* readers. (4/4)

1958 – Senator Richard B. Russell, brother of faculty member Fielding Russell, speaks to TC graduates. (6/2)

1958 – Congress authorizes National Aeronautics and Space Administration (NASA). (7/29)

1958 – New nine-hole golf course on northeast campus replaces old course. (10/9)

CHAPTER EIGHT

THE FINAL DECADE

THE DEAN BECOMES PRESIDENT

Sandy Beaver announced to the Board of Regents on February 11, 1948, that Zach Suddath Henderson would replace Judson Clements Ward Jr. as president of Georgia Teachers College.[1] "The chancellor has seen fit to rearrange the personnel," said President Ward. Correcting what they considered an oversight by the former President Marvin Pittman and Chancellor Raymond Paty, the Board of Regents awarded Dean Henderson the presidency.

The regents made a point, and they underscored it: the Pittman era was over. The protégé of the former president, Jake Ward, would work in the chancellor's office in Atlanta, not at Teachers College in Statesboro. Before his departure, President Ward reminded the community that both he and Dean Henderson were employees of the University System of Georgia. They served at the pleasure of the Board of Regents. The press spun the news positively: "Statesboro's loss is Georgia's gain."

Without prompting, local residents figured out the transition: the regents appreciated loyalty as much as predictability. Zach Henderson would be a stabilizing influence, a manager who would not rock the boat. He had a record of loyal service dating from 1927. Most citizens were aware of his support and encouragement of President Albert Martin Gates during the difficult years, 1941-43. Some observers regarded his action as selfless and charitable.

While local newspapers lamented the departure of the "ideal president," they congratulated Henderson, a familiar face at the college for the past twenty-one years.[2] Standing tall at six feet, four inches, Henderson was a solid citizen: "We've known 'Dean' a long time. We've worked with him as a Rotarian, in Scouting, in civic affairs, in college affairs. . . . There's something substantial about the new president of the college. Not just his physical stature. It's just something," wrote the editor of the *Bulloch Herald*.[3]

During the spring and summer months, Henderson experienced the smoothest presidential transition in the history of the college. He had worked in the same building for twenty-one years. Virtually all institutional policies and precedents came into play while he had been an administrator. He needed no orientation.

The decade following Henderson's elevation to the presidency proved to be one of the fastest growing in history. Large numbers of veterans, supported by the GI bill, moved to Collegeboro between 1946 and 1950, restoring the enrollment to earlier levels and beyond.

ZACH SUDDATH HENDERSON

On April 1, 1948, Henderson became president after serving for twenty-one years as dean. He was president until June 30, 1968, the longest tenure of any president in college history.

BILL SARRATT

The editor of the *George-Anne* criticized inflexible attitudes about race and racial segregation in 1948.

DAN BIGGERS

The *Who's Who* graduate of 1952 combined a career of teaching and administration, mostly at Berry College, with his avocation—performing. He appeared in more than one hundred films and television dramas, including a six-year stint as Dr. Frank Robb in *In the Heat of the Night*. A native of Toccoa, Biggers credited TC's Masquers and director, Dorothy Stewart, with preparing him for his highly successful career in film, television, and theater.

vice president and program chair, citing a technicality at the election held the previous school year.[26]

Some readers were outraged that Sarratt had introduced the figure of Jesus into the discussion of race. One student concluded that the actress, Skinner, was at fault for accepting the invitation originally and for not "respecting the inner feelings of her audience." The writer defended the practice of discrimination: "Racial segregation is a workable thing in the South with the conditions as they now are . . . Georgia might even be considered progressive in that we do not discriminate against any other race or nationality except the Negro. This 'discrimination' is open and above board."[27]

The stance of the newspaper on social issues depended largely on its editors. Race and politics seemed to disappear until 1953. Then, editor Remer Tyson heard Governor Herman Talmadge say he would abolish public schools before he would allow them to be integrated. Tyson responded by criticizing the governor's spiteful proposal. He concluded, "Shall we let race prejudice control our decision or shall we try to extend our great freedoms to all? The decision is ours; which road shall we take?"[28]

The *George-Anne* printed an editorial immediately after the U.S. Supreme Court handed down its long-awaited decision in 1954. In *Brown v. Board of Education,* the court ruled that racial segregation "violates the 14th amendment to the U.S. Constitution, which guarantees all citizens equal protection of the laws." Editor Tyson concluded succinctly, "The fact is apparent that segregation will be abolished," without indicating his own preference.

The next week Tyson printed a response from three students who resented what they interpreted as the newspaper's pro-integration stance. The authors wrote, "If we accept these Negroes into our schools now, they will slowly but surely seep into our living rooms. . . . [T]here is no outcome for the white race except to deteriorate socially, spiritually, and morally, if segregation is not upheld."[29]

Race relations in Georgia did not improve immediately as a result of the Supreme Court decision of 1954. The following year the state attempted to deprive black citizens of equal opportunities when the governor recommended and the legislature approved a law that would divert public funds into private schools that practiced segregation.

TC students, like most Americans, often disagreed about race and social policy. Those on both sides of these great issues, however, had one thing in common: they all loved Sophie Johnson's right hand man, Mose Bass. Bass, who was black, drew no distinction between integrationists and segregationists.

A former student who earned a PhD in history, Charlton Moseley, sought to gather information about Bass in the 1990s. Moseley attended twelve years of public schooling in the Marvin Pittman Laboratory School on campus, and he remained at TC for his undergraduate education. After Moseley retired as

THE NIFTY FIFTIES

"Going into that senior year (1953), I, a major film fan, noted that 20th Century Fox was using Cinemascope, making the movies appear on a much wider screen than was used earlier. The Rosenbergs lost their appeals and were executed. A young revolutionary lawyer named Fidel Castro launched an unsuccessful attack against Cuba's armed forces. Senator Joseph McCarthy accused President Truman of heading a Communist administration. Winston Churchill received the Nobel Prize. Joe DiMaggio married Marilyn Monroe. . . . *Catcher in the Rye* was just catching on. As far as I can remember, none of my professors strayed off into discussion of current fiction."

Robert Latimer "Bubbles" Hurst ('54)

"We didn't have a football team in my era. Baseball and basketball were our teams, and we cheered them on with gusto. Swimming was a small outdoor pool behind the Administration Building. A tennis court next to the pool was always in use. Three of my friends and I claimed a court at 5 a.m., played an hour, ate breakfast, then went to class. . . .

"In Lewis Hall a favorite thing to do was to gather around the piano in the parlor and sing. We found many opportunities to visit in rooms, thus forming lifetime friendships.

In the early 1950s students gathered in the Blue Tide's "Little Store" to hear popular ballads and big band music on the jukebox. A few years later the place shook with the rhythm of rock 'n' roll.

In 1997 the "TC Girls" renewed fifties' friendships at the Windsor Hotel in Americus, Georgia. *Seated, left to right:* Anne Trice Middleton, Dottie Aycock Kergan, Bettye Lewis Mitchell. *Standing, left to right:* Allene Timmerman Haugabook, Maxine Corbitt Wilson, Gay Kimbrough Dull, and Marjorie Weatherford Hern. They wore scarves presented by Bill Golden, GSU Foundation President.

"So how did we survive the 'Dark Ages'? I guess it's because a close community of people in an atmosphere of friendliness surrounded us. Now we remember that bond as we meet over fifty years later as the 'TC Girls.'"

Gay Kimbrough Dull ('51)

"I remember hitchhiking to and from uptown Statesboro and thinking nothing about being afraid. . . . Having to walk behind the buildings to the cafeteria on Saturday because we were wearing pants. . . . Signing out whenever we went anywhere (other than class), and having to go before house council if you were late coming back from a date. . . . Classes were small enough that every professor knew all of the students' names. Mr. Moye even associated me with my aunts that had gone there in the '30s."

Betty Watson Spaid ('58)

"I remember that Sunday's dinner was special—always fried chicken and strawberry shortcake for dessert. But when you arrived at the appointed hour for Sunday's supper, you were handed a sack lunch from one or two fellow students. We soon learned not to get the brown sack and go into town to the Dairy Queen for a charcoal grilled hamburger."

Sandra Tindol ('59), gave her friend, Sandra Wiggins ('58), a "call down" for the offense of not making her bed. After accumulating a number of "call downs," a student's extracurricular activity could be restricted.

Hitchhiking—a coed's quick way to town.

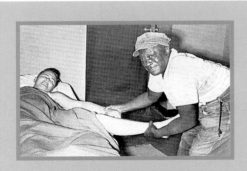

Approved & awakened by Mose Bass

Male students knew and loved Mose Bass, the five-foot-tall janitor, counselor, and friend. He retired after thirty-eight years of service in 1967.

During his early years, he milked twenty cows by hand every day at the college dairy. He became a campus icon after Sophie Johnson asked him to serve as the janitor for Sanford Hall in 1947. Later, he followed her to Cone Hall. Many students shared their burdens with Bass, who offered both consolation and advice.

Grateful students showed their appreciation in an unusual way. They searched campus bulletin boards for new announcements, upon which they wrote: "Approved by Mose Bass." The inscription made the piece of paper official. The student body dedicated the *Reflector* to him in 1955.

He voluntarily awakened students who overslept. Alumni recalled his musical "Get up, baby!" and his firm nudge of the sleeper's shoulder. Don King, a student leader in the 1950s, said he never forgot the time he invited his father to spend the night in his room in Sanford Hall:

"About 6:45 the next morning, Mose comes into my room and jumps on the top of my Dad, shaking him by the shoulders, thinking it was me, yelling 'Get up, baby! Get up, baby!' Those big white eyes nearly scared my Dad to death."

Don King ('55)

MOSE BASS
1929 – 1967
CUSTODIAN, HOUSING

from The Builders of the University Terrace

professor of history at Georgia Southern, he wanted to document the career of Mose Bass so that his name would appear on the Builders of the University memorial. He reviewed newspapers and found no published obituaries for Bass or his wife, Cassie. Even in the 1970s, few local newspapers printed obituaries of black citizens.

After visiting several rural cemeteries, Moseley finally found the grave markers for the Basses. Bass died in 1970, just three years after he retired, and his wife followed him within a few years. Moseley also learned that, for most of his career at the college, Bass lived in a residence provided rent-free by Dan and Catherine Bland. His modest home and small farm stood on the southeast corner of Lanier Drive and Georgia Avenue.[30]

Since the 1920s the YMCA, YWCA, and other student religious groups had supported interracial cooperation. In 1954, on the heels of the historic Supreme Court decision, the Methodist Student Movement (MSM) in Georgia decided to integrate its annual statewide meeting. The MSM could find no local white church to sponsor an integrated meeting. White colleges also declined. Clark College (today known as Clark Atlanta University), a black institution in Atlanta, invited the student organization to meet there.

Cathy Holt, Cherrell Williams, and Betty Altman (sister of China Altman) planned to represent TC at the meeting at Clark College. "President Zach Henderson called us into his office and told us that he had a telegram from Governor Talmadge threatening us with being expelled if the Methodist Student Movement meeting at Clark College got any publicity."[31]

The TC coeds attended the integrated meeting on November 4-7, 1954, without incident. "I remember feeling very excited to get to meet some black students. I do remember that one girl from TC couldn't go with us because her parents forbade it. She was always sad when we would talk about the experience," Cathy Holt Norton recalled.[32]

The *George-Anne* took a strong stand in support of former president Guy Wells, who had endorsed integration as a democratic and Christian policy. The Board of Regents promptly revoked Wells' president emeritus status (at Georgia State College for Women), and the State Board of Education recommended that his pension be removed.

This attack on a former TC president called forth an impassioned response by Carlton Humphrey of Milledgeville, the editor/columnist of the *George-Anne*:

The Governor of Georgia offered free tuition to a leader of the Alabama riot against Autherine Lucy. The people complained, accepted the whim, and forgot. . . .

Last week a former GTC president, Dr. Guy H. Wells, fell out of the administration's graces because he held a view of segregation that didn't correspond to the official belief.

As a result of his plunge from the heights, this gentleman has been stripped of his title of President Emeritus of GSCW, and his retirement fund is threatened. . . .

If this infringement upon the right of free speech goes unchallenged, if this threat becomes a reality, fear will reign in Georgia. . . . No individual will be able to express

When China Found Her Place

"When I heard in 1951 that black college students had invited white students for a weekend at Paine College in Augusta to talk about the racial situation, I determined to go, though I was broke, and the administration said I'd be expelled. My friend, Mary Flanders (Collins), gave me $25 from her father for my bus fare and expenses (one of the magnificent gifts of my lifetime).

"At the bus station in Augusta, I climbed into the lone cab and gave the address. The white driver gruffly refused and made me get out. I started walking in the direction he told me—'It's along there.' As the skies grew dark, a white woman stopped and asked if I needed help. I could see she was scared when I told her where I was going. 'That's all right, I can walk,' I said. But she opened the door and took me to the gates, then drove off hurriedly.

"I found a teacher involved in the conference. He said, 'Well, it's supper, and you'd better go get something to eat, because there won't be anything else. There are no stores around here.' He took my small suitcase and pointed the way.

"I hadn't yet realized I was the only white person there for Friday night. (A few white students and adults drove from other colleges on Saturday.) As I walked through the double doors of the central dining hall, I saw two long rows of family-style tables and an ocean of black faces. The room became instantly hushed, as if astonishment were transformed into silence. Supper had begun, and I could see no empty seats.

I kept on walking as softly as I could down the center aisle.

"When I found and sat down in an empty chair, the students at the table were as if frozen in place. I looked down and saw the white heavy plate in front of me was turned upside down—in its center a faint blue word said: 'China.' I gestured toward it, looked up and said into the silence: 'Maybe I'm supposed to be here, because that's my name on the bottom of the plate.'

"Intakes of breath—'oh. . .what did you say. . .oh. . .that's your name?' Suddenly we were all talking and I told them why I had come. They passed me chicken-and-dumplings, beans, salad, beets—a bounty like manna. Every word they shared seemed like gold to me. There was more to come, because I stayed both nights in the room of a Paine coed, and we talked for hours.

"On Sunday afternoon the president of Morehouse College, who had been the main speaker for the conference, kindly drove me to the bus station. The tall and eloquent man with silver hair, Dr. Benjamin Mays, said to me, 'I feel so sorry for you white children who want so hard to do something about the way it is. You might have a harder time than we do.'

"I wasn't expelled. This life-enhancing weekend has enriched all the days of my life."

China Altman ('54)

Top, front row, third from left: China Altman ('54) stands next to Dr. Benjamin Mays, president of Morehouse College in Atlanta, noted educator, and civil rights pioneer, at Paine College in Augusta, 1951.

Above, Yvonne Jones (Jeffords), Dan Biggers, China Altman, and Anne Higginbotham (Timmerman) on the steps of a side entrance to East Hall.

Below, China Altman, journalist, in the 1970s.

At TC China found the world

China Altman, born in Waycross, Georgia, was one of the first women reporters hired by United Press International. She worked as a journalist for many years in Boston, London, Rome, Budapest, and Greece for UPI, *Life, Time, People,* and environmental publications. She hosted a TV series on WGBH-Boston, and was the first woman on the East Coast to have her own call-in talk show simulcast on 50,000-watt radio stations WRKO/WROR-Boston. In 1969 she directed a national inquiry into campus uprisings for the U.S. Senate. In the 1980s she founded the Office for the Arts at the Massachusetts Institute of Technology. She is a lifelong activist for the equality of women and people of color, has been a national spokesperson for runaway and abused children, and works as an animal activist.

CARLTON HUMPHREY

Editor of the *George-Anne* in 1956, Humphrey defended former President Guy Wells after the Board of Regents revoked his emeritus status, specifically because he criticized segregation and advocated interracial cooperation.

Sweethearts return to the circle

Curtis Lane ('40) of Statesboro first dated Billie Turner ('42) of Millen at TC on July 26, 1939. Turner was May Queen in 1942. After completing dental school, Lane served as a World War II dentist. The couple became husband and wife in 1943. In 2006 the longtime residents of Statesboro revisited the place where they found each other, the "Sweetheart Campus."

his beliefs unless they comply to the letter with those of the state officials. Freedom will be a thing of the past.[33]

The reference to Autherine Lucy carried implications for TC. A mob led by Leonard Wilson prevented Lucy from attending the University of Alabama.[34] The rioters almost lynched her. Wilson was barred from attending the university. Both Governor Marvin Griffin and senatorial candidate Herman Talmadge invited Wilson to attend, tuition-free, one of Georgia's public colleges, perhaps TC. Wilson came to Georgia and campaigned on behalf of Talmadge, a candidate for the U.S. Senate.

Editorial writer Ellen Blizzard commented, "No Marvin, we don't want him here. He has no place in Georgia, no place in our colleges, certainly no place at Georgia Teachers College."[35] Not surprisingly, her column provoked a guest editorialist's rebuttal the following week.

At the time of Humphrey's and Blizzard's opinion columns in 1956, the Montgomery bus boycott, begun by Rosa Parks, was in its fourth month. During the autumn of that year, the Supreme Court ruled the city of Montgomery's seating plan for buses violated the Fourteenth Amendment.

Humphrey and Blizzard took moderate positions, and some of their fellow students regarded them as radical. History happened to be on the side of these young journalists and also on the side of Parks and former TC president Wells.

VETERANS ENRICH CAMPUS LIFE

Between 1946 and 1956 the enrollment of the college grew for one reason: the GI bill provided college tuition and expenses for veterans of World War II. These widely traveled and somewhat sophisticated young men contributed to the campus in many ways, both intellectually and socially.

John "Bud" Stone of Wrens, Georgia, had been a student before he entered the U.S. Army. When he returned, he was older, wiser, and experienced. He said veterans presented a challenge to professors who were accustomed to docile students. Sometimes veterans felt obliged to correct what they considered misinformation by professors and the authors of textbooks. Veterans also peppered their conversation with expressions some professors found objectionable.[36]

Veterans were accustomed to leading an unhampered lifestyle. Many of the former servicemen previously had frequented clubs for officers and enlisted men. Occasionally they enjoyed drinking beer and shooting the breeze with their buddies in the clubs. They continued this practice at the local American Legion post located near the campus. Two traditions clashed, and older veterans did not easily give up their GI privileges.

Some GIs drank beer. TC students, on the other hand, were not allowed to consume alcoholic beverages.

George Rogers, a geographer and historian, served as faculty advisor to the Veterans Club. He and his wife, Betty, believed veterans were entitled to enjoy a meal at the local American Legion post. At first President Henderson would not permit veterans to meet at the post. Rogers assured him he and Betty would chaperone closely these meetings in a section of the club outside the bar. Thus veterans who dated coeds could enjoy a meal with members of the club and return to campus. Afterward, married veterans and their wives could go into the bar room.

Rogers, also a veteran, valued the contributions of veterans to campus life in the fifties and sixties:

These young combat veterans received a special kind of respect from the other students, and the veterans tried to give something back to the college. Each year they decided on a special project. One year they proposed the planting of a tree on the front campus in memory of fallen comrades. Some wanted to have everyone there at the planting and, at the end, we would form ranks, come to attention and have someone play "Taps."[37]

THE LITTLEST PROF

James Boyd Scearce came to Teachers College for two reasons: to teach health and physical education and to coach basketball. Many students who were not athletes reported he was the best instructor on campus. He earned his salary by teaching. He gained his reputation in his unpaid job—coaching a basketball team called the Professors.

Marvin Pittman had contacted him about a job in 1946, but he retired before Scearce responded. In 1947 "the coach" moved up the ladder and accepted a job at TC after successfully coaching at a high school in Kentucky and at two small colleges in Georgia, Norman Park and North Georgia.

Scearce began teaching and coaching at TC as Jake Ward launched his brief career as president. Then locals called on Ward, lobbying him to resume football. Once basketball season began in the fall, however, no one even whispered the word "football." Scearce was a smashing success.

The coach taught spectators a ball game requires "a real ball, a round ball."[38] The Alumni Gymnasium could not hold the crowds clamoring to see Scearce's nonscholarship team compile an 18-3 record during his first season. In the spring he put on his cleats and coached the baseball team to a respectable record.

After his former student at Norman Park Junior College, J. I. Clements, joined his department, Scearce invited his younger colleague to manage TC's diamond business. Scearce needed time to fill his other role as head of the division of health and physical education.

The story that began with Clements recapitulates Horatio Alger at his best. At TC Clements would push the rags-to-riches plot to fairytale proportions in the 1960s. But the fifties belonged to Scearce and his hardwood Horatios.

JAMES BOYD SCEARCE

"The little fellow with Phil Rizzuto's size, Eddie Cantor's eyes, George Gobel's hair and Charlie McCarthy's vocal chords whistled a group of young men. . .at Collegeboro.

'Men,' he said in his hoarse tones while he held up a large round object, 'this is a basketball.'"

Furman Bisher, "The Littlest Prof,"
Atlanta Constitution, 8 November 1955

CHESTER WEBB

The State of Georgia's first All-American basketball player.

The Sweetheart Campus

Hope flares high

And lives awhile, but soon must die;

Confused young loves their lives must chart,

With broken hearts—with broken hearts.

Edith Carpenter
George-Anne, 10 February 1951

Juanita Freeman and Travis Doss, front, *and Ralph Turner and Sandy Martin,* back, *enjoying the Starlight Ball.*

Still together, still friends

"I met Travis Doss in Dr. Tully Pennington's science class. He took us on a walking field trip to point out the fauna and flora, but we were more interested in studying each other. Ralph asked Sandy Martin and Travis asked me to go to the Starlight Ball with them. . . . Ralph and Sandy were married in 1957. Travis and I married in 1959. Both couples are still together and are the best of friends."

Juanita Freeman Doss ('58)

The best year the school ever experienced in basketball came three years after he moved to Collegeboro in 1950. The team won its conference game against the State Teachers College of Troy, Alabama, 112-36. Going into the national National Association of Intercollegiate Athletics tournament, the team had 27 wins and 2 losses.

While the team did not advance to the finals that year, it raised the eyebrows of sportswriters all over the country, including Furman Bisher of the *Atlanta Constitution* who wrote that the "Littlest Prof" was one of the best coaches in the nation.[39]

Some of the great moments of the 1960s involved games with well-known major colleges in the Southeast. The crucial game came in 1952, when the Professors went to the Gator Bowl basketball tournament in Jacksonville, Florida. The team had not gone toe-to-toe against the University of Georgia Bulldogs since 1934, when Crook Smith coached the team to a stunning 34-22 upset.

At the '52 Gator Bowl Scearce's team faced a nationally ranked "big school" team, led by the talented Zippy Morocco. At the end of the evening the Professors had taught the Bulldogs an obedience lesson by a score of 85-57, stunning fans who had driven all the way to Jacksonville from Athens.

Most South Georgians savored the Little Prof's victories over Georgia, Georgia Tech, Florida, and Florida State in the 1950s. But that game of December 29, 1952, lingers in the memory of all loyal fans. The *Savannah Morning News* sportswriter captured the occasion for posterity:

It was a great team victory. Five players hit double numbers in the scoring, and Jim Harley held Georgia's celebrated Zippy Morocco to but 11 points for the night. . . . They had a 36-point advantage right after the final period started and then Scearce, confident of the triumph he wanted so badly, started using his reserves.

Jim Hutto, a demon under the basket, was leading scorer for the night with 20 points. He was followed by Harley, with 16, Captain Boney Phillips with 14, and Horace Belflower and Jimmy Tudor with 11 each.[40]

After this momentous occasion, local boosters insisted that TC build a gymnasium and enable more than two thousand fans to enjoy Professors basketball. In 1955 the team occupied its new quarters, later called Hanner Gym, honoring W. S. Hanner, science professor and athletic committee chairman.

Athletes were enthusiastic about playing for Coach Scearce. Scotty Perkins of Williamsburg, Kentucky, had heard about Scearce's excellent coaching at the high school level in his home state. He played for the Professors for two years before entering military service during the Korean War. Perkins, who averaged 590 points in each of his two years, reflected on the qualities of his coach:

I'm not sure he knew what I could do. Really, he was not one to go into a high school and pick out the really great players just by looking. But once he saw players together on the court, he could see what needed to be done. He could figure out how to get the best out of them. He didn't believe in controlled plays that move slowly. He wanted us to run all out. That's what we did. I'm telling you, it was something.[41]

Basketball fans in the 1950s would agree with Coach Scearce's assessment that the best basketball player he ever coached was a native of Elberton, Georgia, Chester Webb.[42] During his career he scored 2,540 points and twice was named to the All-American team of the NAIA in 1955 and 1956. He was the first All-American basketball player in any division in the state of Georgia.[43] Webb had an opportunity to play professional basketball, but he returned to Elbert County and enjoyed a career as a public school administrator. Webb said Scearce was not a typical "player's coach":

He did not try to get players to be his friends, really. He wanted to put us in a position where we could make the scoring plays. Everybody learned where to be and how to get there. Once you got there, you knew what you had to do. . . . Fast break, yes! He liked to turn us loose.

He was a good teacher in the classroom. He knew how to get the information across. On the basketball court, he felt that if he had the right player in the right position, things would take care of themselves, and they usually did. He did not do a whole lot of teaching about basketball per se.

The players liked to play for him. We were a team, and we knew we had the student body and Statesboro behind us. That was something, to see the gym packed with great fans for almost every home game.[44]

THE SWEETHEART CAMPUS

Born during the Great Depression, they were children during World War II. They arrived in Collegeboro at the dawn of a new age—the age of optimism. Leaving home, they folded and packed inside their luggage a pattern for their lives. They desired earnestly to emulate the role models they knew and respected back home. They wanted to become teachers.

Most students also brought with them a vague mental outline of a physical reality, a person of similar age but of opposite sex. This most desirable somebody lived in their post-puberty dreams. They searched for someone to call *sweetheart*. Juliet Oliver ('51) recalled the lower end of the circle provided enough seclusion to carry on an intimate conversation with an upperclassman, E. Mills Tarver ('50), whom she married.

The nickname for TC in the thirties and forties came from the landscape itself. Students called it *the sweetheart campus*. The heart-shaped formation of main campus vanished as new buildings required an expanded entrance. Gradually students began referring to the front part of the campus as *Sweetheart Circle*. On this beautiful green space some young lovers joyfully united here forever. Others, alas, parted in sorrow, in the words of poet Edith Carpenter.

The Blue Tide, like Sweetheart Circle, linked students with the past. The very name of the clapboard structure carried a sense of tradition. It was the short-lived nickname of Georgia Normal School's football team in the late 1920s.

The beauty revue

A modest announcement appeared in the local newspaper on November 7, 1946: "A beauty revue will be presented at the Georgia Teachers College tonight at 8 o'clock, staged and directed by Jack Averitt of Statesboro."

The first revue was a smashing hit. In the early years local citizens vied with students for tickets to sold-out performances. The first accompanist was Earluth Epting, a harpist of the music faculty. The famous beauty expert, Helena Rubenstein, selected six beauties as finalists and the winner, Margaret Dean Howard, was presented in February of 1947.

COMING!

FOURTH ANNUAL BEAUTY REVUE
Teachers College—February 2, 8:15 p.m.

Beauty Revue Winners, 1947–1958

1947 - Margaret Dean Howard
1948 - Jean Hodges
1949 - Betty Fuller
1950 - Lonadine Morgan
1951 - Jo Starr
1952 - Bettye Hendrix
1953 - Yvonne Jones
1954 - Shirley Hanson
1955 - Diana Bair
1956 - Janice Mayers
1957 - Sis Heys
1958 - Kerstin Pihl (native of Sweden)

Jo Starr was crowned "Miss TC of 1951" at the fifth annual beauty revue.

The Blue Tide, the Little Store, the Post Office

"The 'Tide' provides recreation, music, newspapers, refreshments, a hangout and bulletin board news.

"Originally the 'Little Store' was a section of the dining hall. It was a new small cove, next to a barbershop, that functioned to give students a very limited choice of refreshments.

"After remaining cramped for seven years, the 'Blue Tide' was constructed in 1935. . . . The first students to work in the 'Blue Tide' were Waldo Pafford and Hubert Dewberry. Today Pafford is superintendent of the 'Bradwell Institute' located in Hinesville. Dewberry holds the position of director of plant and business operations for the University System of Georgia. Students have always done the work in the 'Blue Tide.'"

George-Anne, 9 October 1953

The white rectangular building east of Anderson Dining Hall beckoned students daily. There they picked up their mail and spoke with Z. L. Strange, postmaster, or his daughter-in-law, the winsome Jackie Strange. The campus poet laureate in 1946, Albert Howard, memorialized the postmaster in a song, *Home, Home of the Strange*, which borrowed the melody from *Home on the Range*.[45]

> O give me a home
> Where the postal cards roam,
> Where the stamps and the envelopes lay,
> Where they always wail,
> 'Sorry, no mail,
> Cause your box rent was due yesterday.'

Students dropped by the Blue Tide to get their mail, and they hung around to socialize. At the Little Store they bought books, Cokes, peanuts, crackers, candy bars, and (starting in October 1954) Chase & Sanborn coffee at five cents a cup. Conversation began with the shop manager, Margie Jones, and flowed over the lush sounds of sentimental top tunes. Music played at the drop of a nickel in the nickelodeon. Also known as a "jukebox," the three-by-five-foot gargantuan prototype of the iPod® richly amplified the tunes of the day.

Columnist Robert "Bubbles" Hurst reported to *George-Anne* readers in 1952 that students particularly enjoyed Johnny Ray's *The Little White Cloud That Cried*, and Nat King Cole's *Unforgettable*. In 1955 seniors grew sentimental in the little store as they joined in with The Four Lads:

> When other nights and other days
> May find us gone our separate ways
> We will have these moments to remember

Students celebrated their college years less sentimentally in the late 1950s. By the spring of 1958, the lilting harmonies of vocal groups had all but disappeared from the music menu. Bold new sounds flowed from the jukebox and shook the walls. It was new, rhythmical, and sensual music. They called it *rock 'n' roll*.

Almost any time of day or early evening, the jukebox captivated the collective student body and soul. Bill Haley, Little Richard, Elvis, and dozens of other artists were commonplace names among students, but virtually unknown among faculty.

The chairman of the music division, Ronald Neil, assured readers of the *George-Anne* in 1958 that rock 'n' roll was not here to stay.[46] A poll among faculty obtained these responses: Ela Johnson, Clark Knowlton, and Dan Hooley found the music harmless. Donald Hackett and Jack Averitt were not impressed. Averitt said, "Distractions like rock 'n' roll cheapen the musical medium." Fielding Russell comically concluded, "It makes an old man dizzy."[47]

That vibrating vanguard of cultural change—the Little Store—quickly grew quiet in 1958. The very building where students collected mail and caught up with friends fell to a wrecking crew that cut the structure into two small sections and hauled it away. A similar fate awaited the historic Anderson Dining Hall, located thirty yards away. Construction crews began clearing the way for a real student union and dining hall.

The year 1958 brought with it a series of programs on the history of the institution, focusing on fifty years of teaching that began on February 5, 1908, two years after the school was organized. Professor Jack Averitt organized a program of lectures, publications, and campus events, recalling the institution's pilgrimage from First District A&M School to Georgia Normal School to South Georgia Teachers College.[48] Perhaps no one anticipated Georgia Teachers College soon would wear yet another name.

Signs and Sighs of Change

By 1958 students could kiss in the semi-privacy of a dorm parlor without fear of being expelled from college. According to custom, kissers should be engaged or the-next-thing-to-it (indicated by the boy's class ring on the girl's left hand, third finger).

In February 1958, the college celebrated the fiftieth anniversary of the institution's first day of classes in 1908.

In 1959 the new F. I. Williams Student Center and Dining Hall replaced the old Blue Tide.

In the 1950s coeds had a favorite spot to sunbathe—the lawn behind Lewis Hall, protected from public view by a tall hedge row.

Students began making their own music, singing such somber ballads as Hang Down Your Head Tom Dooley.

In 1959 the college began a new classroom building named for the chemist Charles H. Herty.

GEORGIA SOUTHERN
COLLEGE

Georgia Southern College
1959-1968

1959 – Rock 'n' roll musician Buddy Holly dies in a plane crash. (2/3)

1959 – *Atlanta Journal* names Chester Curry Georgia College Player of the Year, and Atlanta Tip-Off Club selects Whitey Verstraete Most Valuable College Player. (3/5)

1959 – East Hall house director, Mrs. J. B. Johnson, reports 912 crinoline petticoats hanging on pipes, doors, "and almost any place they can be hung." (5/8)

1959 – Hawaii becomes the fiftieth state. (8/21)

1959 – College issues first traffic fines, ranging from $2 to $5 for parking without permit or in a visitor's spot. (12/7)

1959 – Board of Regents change name from Georgia Teachers College to Georgia Southern College. (12/9)

1960 – *George-Anne* announces winner in contest for a new college nickname: Ralph Swords, a business major, won $10 for submitting "Eagles." (1/15)

1960 – Everett Williams, Statesboro pharmacist, is appointed to Board of Regents. (3/17)

1960 – Russians shoot down U-2 spy plane piloted by U. S. pilot Gary Powers, causing diplomatic crisis. (5/1)

1960 – Herty Building is ready for occupancy by divisions of business, home economics, and science. (5/19)

1960 – Joe Axelson, college public relations director and sports director of local radio station WWNS, is elected to Honors Council of the Prep Sports Hall of Fame. (8/18)

1960 – President Zach Henderson estimates $2 million in local economic impact of college on business community. (9/22)

1960 – Doris Fuchs (Brause), a gymnast in three Olympics, trains at GSC with Coach Pat Yeager.

1961 – East Germany closes border with West Berlin; construction begins on the Berlin Wall. (8/13)

1961 – Biology professor Gordon P. DeWolf is first faculty member with PhD from England's Cambridge University. (9/15)

1961 – Board of Regents approves first MA degree, in history, and first language BA degree, in French. (11/15)

1962 – Baseball team wins first national title for Eagles in NAIA championship, sweeping Portland State in four games. (6/9)

1963 – Board of Regents provides college with first $1 million budget. (9/26)

1963 – U.S. President John F. Kennedy is assassinated in Dallas, Texas; Vice President Lyndon Johnson becomes president. (11/22)

1964 – The Beatles appear in U.S. on The Ed Sullivan Show. (2/7)

1964 – Delta Pi Alpha gives college a four-foot statue of the Georgia Southern Eagle as a mascot. (11/19)

1965 – Former President Guy Wells praises early President E. V. Hollis and Controller Robert Winburn, urging college officials to name buildings in their honor. (2/11)

1965 – The Rolling Stones perform first college concert in U.S. at Hanner Gymnasium before an unimpressed audience. (5/4)

1966 – Walt Disney, filmmaker and creator of Mickey Mouse, dies at age sixty-five. (12/15)

1966 – New Weis Theatre, with more than five hundred seats, opens for business at corner of Georgia Ave. and Lanier Rd. (12/25)

1967 – Nathan Byrd is first full-time director of new Baptist Student Center. (6/1)

1967 – Administration finally permits national Greek organizations on campus. (6/12)

1967 – Mose Bass retires as custodian after thirty-eight years of service. (6/30)

1968 – College charters Kappa Alpha as first national Greek social fraternity. (3/31)

1968 – Martin Luther King Jr. is assassinated in Memphis, Tennessee. (4/4)

1968 – Zach Henderson retires, and John Eidson becomes new president. (6/30)

CHAPTER 9

FROM PROFESSORS TO EAGLES

A WINNING TRADITION

Without an obvious lobbying effort on behalf of Teachers College, the Board of Regents authorized a new name, Georgia Southern College, at its December meeting in 1959. The *George-Anne* announced the news in its December 14 issue, noting the change would take place "immediately." The article quoted President Zach Henderson, who said the reason for the change was that the college had broadened its mission five years earlier by offering non-teaching bachelor of arts and bachelor of science degrees. Henderson reassured readers, however, that the major emphasis of the college would remain "teacher education."

The name change would open the door to a broader and more diverse faculty and student body. Regrettably, however, it also would close the door on one of the twentieth century's most familiar names in the small college arena—the Professors. Respected by opponents and worshipped by local fans, the Professors exemplified excellence on both the basketball court and the baseball field.

The basketball team began the 1958-59 season at Alexander Memorial Coliseum in Atlanta. Coach Whack Hyder's Georgia Tech team was strong and eventually appeared in the National Collegiate Athletic Association (NCAA) national tournament. But on that first day of December, Tech fell to the small college National Association of Intercollegiate Athletics (NAIA) team from Statesboro. TC's Whitey Verstraete was "good enough to be on any team in the Southeastern Conference," Hyder said. Verstraete's court leadership and Chester Curry's twenty-three points sealed the 72-64 win over the Yellow Jackets.[1]

Students overflowed their section in Hanner Gymnasium for the season's home opener on December 3, 1959, against the University of Georgia. The crowd, as expected, looked professorial. Men wore jackets and ties; women donned skirts and sweaters. They were, after all, tomorrow's teachers, scholars, principals, and superintendents.

Coach J. B. Scearce confidently led his Professors onto the court that evening. The future mentors of the nation's youth cheered. They stood, clapped, and voiced their support throughout the evening. That night the men in blue out-hustled their red-clad opponents coached by Red Lawson. The Profs once again taught the Bulldogs a lesson they would long remember.

Original Hall of Fame

During halftime of the homecoming basketball game on Saturday evening, February 7, 1959, Teachers College honored its first athletic Hall of Fame. The chairman of the selection committee, Charles B. McAllister, announced the inaugural inductees:

Byron L. "Crook" Smith
    Coach, athletic director (1929–41)

Chester Webb
    First basketball All-American

Jake Smith
    Outstanding basketball player in the 1930s

J. C. "Jake" Hines
    Best all-around athlete in college history

Hollis Ray Powell
    Best baseball player

Frank "Sonny" Clements
    Outstanding in baseball and basketball

Earl "Cooney" Riggs
    Lineman and best football player

Wade "Scotty" Perkins
    Early basketball star under J. B. Scearce

Howard "Bo" Warren
    Basketball and baseball star

George-Anne, 13 February 1959

ANTICIPATING GROWTH

Female athletes could earn letters in intramural sports in the 1960s, above. The Women's Inrtramural Association represented the interests of female athletes.

In the fall of 1960, President Henderson sat down with Dean Paul Carroll and began planning for the future. The official enrollment that year was 1,262 students. Men slightly outnumbered women by 636 to 626. Since 1940, the student population had doubled. Most of the growth had occurred in the late 1950s.

Anticipating future needs for the next ten years, the president and the dean gambled.[7] The Board of Regents office projected continued expansion of the second-fastest-growing institution in the state.[8] They predicted the student body would reach 2,800 by the fall of 1970.

During the next decade, the outlook changed annually. In 1962 the president increased the projection for 1970 to 3,500. When some 3,000 students enrolled for the fall of 1965, the president raised the projection for 1970 to 7,500.[9] For the record, 5,719 officially enrolled in 1970. The college did not register more than 7,500 students until the 1980s. Nevertheless, the president's ambitious projections influenced the Board of Regents to authorize a series of important buildings, enabling campus facilities to catch up with the surge in enrollment.

Roy Powell and Richard Joseph "Ric" Mandes wrote glowing feature stories about the growth of Georgia Southern, and newspapers in Georgia shared them with their readers. Regularly the public relations office generated articles with photographs about new buildings at GSC. The "people's campus" prospered.

On the heels of the new student union and dining hall, more construction followed. The Frank I. Williams Student Center was named for the father of Everett Williams, who was a member of the Board of Regents. In the fall of 1960, students began learning in the new Herty building, named for the chemist Charles Holmes Herty; the divisions of science, business, and home economics moved there. The face of the new campus included a lawn and garden where Anderson dining hall had stood since 1912. The space surrounded by the Administration Building, Williams Center, and the Herty building became a beauty spot and remained so in the twenty-first century.

Smaller buildings fell to demolition or moving crews. The Blue Tide, the science building (the old Sunnyside School), and the chemistry building quickly faded from the landscape. Small homes and apartments along Georgia Avenue and nearby streets also vanished.

New buildings literally reconfigured the campus. A wave of construction swept the campus in the 1960s. The first structure to appear, the home management building, served the home economics department, led by Betty Lane. Home economics majors used the 3,400-square-foot facility as a laboratory. The state-of-the-art facility introduced the work of local architect Edwin C. Eckles. Later, he would design a number of new buildings for the campus, reflecting a contemporary style of architecture.

For the most part, names of buildings in the 1960s paid tribute to popular faculty, administrators, and trustees. Veazey Hall, a dormitory for women, was completed in 1961 and honored Mamie Veazey, longtime dean of women. Simultaneously, construction began on a west wing to Lewis Hall for fifty additional coeds. A new building for arts and industry bore the name of Joseph Enoch Carruth, formerly head of the division of education.

In 1963 two new dormitories appeared, Hendricks for women and Brannen for men. Hendricks honored the founding principal of the First District A&M School, J. Walter Hendricks. The men's dormitory memorialized Statesboro native Harvey Brannen, a legislator who led the effort in 1929 to elevate the Georgia Normal School from a junior to a senior college. In May 1963 the regents approved a major annex for the cramped Rosenwald Library.

Buford Knight in 1963 announced he was building Lanier Hall for forty men and Buford Hall for eighty women (complete with maid service). For the first time in the institution's history, a private developer erected buildings near the campus, designed exclusively for college use. Later, Knight built a shopping center adjacent to the campus, as well as a restaurant named the Varsity, featuring a big color television and "piped-in music and radio."[10] Knight sold the southeast corner of Georgia Avenue and Lanier Road to Albert Weis of Savannah, who built there a state-of-the-art movie theater.

In 1963 the youngest governor in the nation, thirty-seven-year-old Carl Sanders, took office at the capitol in Atlanta. During his administration the college benefited from his progressive leadership. Because his wife was a native of Statesboro, as well as a former student and *George-Anne* staffer, local citizens assumed Governor Sanders tended to favor Georgia Southern. President Henderson would have argued, however, the remarkable progress of the institution simply attracted the governor's support.

While visiting a Rotary Club meeting on March 2, 1964, the moderator welcomed the governor, who stood up and spoke for three minutes. He wanted Statesboro to know he had approved six new buildings for Georgia Southern: dormitories for men and women, a fine arts building, a science building, a dining hall, and an addition to the physical education building.[11]

Local legislators, Senator Jones Lane and Representative Paul Nessmith, played a major role in obtaining state funding. In October the local newspaper listed their achievements under the capitol dome:

Now under construction on the 380 acre campus are a classroom building and a library annex. A fine arts building, a dormitory to house 250 men, a dormitory to house 550 women and one for 1,150 women, a gymnasium addition and an additional student center building and dining hall are the next to go up. Construction on a new girls' dormitory is to begin in about 90 days.[12]

Governor Sanders returned to the campus on October 30, 1966, to dedicate three new dormitories—Dorman Hall on Chandler Road and Olliff and Winburn halls on Georgia Avenue. Dorman and Olliff recognized two

New names for streets in 1963

The Student Congress recommended and the administration approved permanent names for seven streets in February. One of them, Congress Street, in front of the Carruth Building, no longer exists. Six are well-known names in the twenty-first century:

Forest Drive
Georgia Drive
Herty Drive
Lake Drive
Pittman Drive
Southern Drive

George-Anne, 28 February 1963

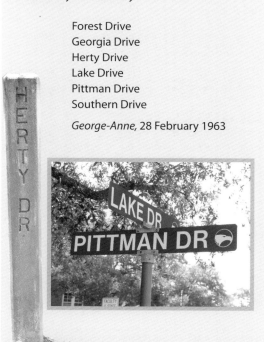

The medium was food, but the message was change

On some campuses in the 1960s, students protested racial segregation, war, intolerance, and injustice. At Georgia Southern those topics played out on the pages of the *George-Anne*. The pressing issue was student life. Some students said they had more freedom at home than they enjoyed on campus. Instead of marching or boycotting classes, the student body chose to make a mess in the cafeteria.

It happened on Saturday and Sunday, May 6-7, 1967. Students overturned trays and left litter in the dining hall. Those who returned to campus on Sunday heard about the previous day's affair. That evening, according to the *George-Anne* on May 12, 1967, students engaged in a more serious demonstration: "a mass exchange of mayonnaise, bread, canned ham, ice, cups, plates, etc."

Student Congress president James Stapleton convened a meeting and heard more than fifty student grievances. Later that week the newly elected president of the Student Congress, Larry Duncan, convened a meeting of a "committee of 13" with President Henderson, who agreed to seek social fraternities, relax women's dress regulations, and open the library on Sunday afternoons and evenings. Students were satisfied and ended their brief episode of culinary misbehavior.

Greek organizations in 1968

Sororities in Spring/Fall of 1968
- Alpha Delta Pi
- Alpha Xi Delta
- Delta Zeta
- Kappa Delta
- Phi Mu
- Zeta Tau Alpha

Fraternities in Spring/Fall of 1968
- Alpha Tau Omega
- Chi Sigma
- Delta Chi
- Delta Tau Delta
- Kappa Alpha
- Kappa Sigma
- Phi Delta Theta
- Pi Kappa Phi
- Sigma Nu
- Sigma Phi Epsilon
- Sigma Pi
- Tau Epsilon Phi
- Tau Kappa Epsilon

leading citizens of Statesboro, Charles P. Olliff and Alfred Dorman. The other dormitory paid tribute to the long-time comptroller at the college, Robert L. Winburn, as former President Guy Wells had recommended.

Sanders and honored family members walked across the street from the dormitory and dedicated the Blanche Landrum Dining Hall in memory of the dietitian who died in 1938 after six years of service. (She was the mother of an influential congressman from north Georgia, Phil Landrum.)

Later, the group walked north on Georgia Avenue to honor the family of Jesse Ponita Foy at the official opening of the Foy Fine Arts Building. Betty Bird Foy, a daughter and one-time staffer for the *George-Anne*, was the wife of Governor Sanders. Finally, the party walked to the corner of Georgia Avenue and Herty Drive, where they broke ground for the new field house next to Hanner gym.

The unprecedented series of five dedications and a major ground-breaking—all on one Sunday afternoon—made a lasting impression on the community. The college clearly was making progress toward the goal of building a campus sufficient for a larger student body. Once again, south Georgia blushed with pride.

President Zach Henderson knew a growing enrollment could be counter-productive. Professors needed classrooms equipped for larger numbers of learners, as well as more office space. Seeking a quick solution, the president asked the Board of Regents to fund a temporary building in 1967.

At a cost of $200,000, the metal blue building provided virtually instant classrooms and office space. Believing the building would be gone within a few years, college officials called it the "temporary building." After ten years, it appeared on campus maps as the "Blue Building." The building had completed thirty-seven years of service when workmen demolished the square structure in 2004 to make way for a major addition to the library.

The division of science received a major boost when the regents authorized successively in 1967 and 1968 a new biology building and a project called "phase two of the science building." The final big building project of the 1960s was announced on April 18, 1968: a new education building facing the lower lake. It would connect physically to the laboratory school where education students regularly served as observers and teaching assistants.

The state of Georgia, through the Board of Regents of the University System of Georgia, oversaw the physical plant and paid salaries. President Henderson realized, however, the time had come to gather funds to support the college in other areas. Other colleges and universities in the state and nation had developed foundations. He talked with local businessmen about organizing the Georgia Southern College Foundation. When Henderson explained that the National Defense Loan program required matching funds, locals responded and began organizing a committee.

Albert M. Deal was president; Everett Williams, vice president; Don Coleman, secretary; and William Dewberry, treasurer. William A.

Bowen led the 1962-63 fund drive. Members of the first foundation board included Francis Allen, Sidney Boswell, Don Coleman, Albert M. Deal, William Dewberry, Bill Fordham, Zach Henderson, Ric Mandes, and Harry Zalumas. Avant Edenfield, William Ference, and Ray Hendrix represented local civic clubs.

Ike Minkovitz and Tiny Hill chaired the downtown Statesboro effort in November 1962, hoping to resolve "many of the problems facing GSC: maintaining top personnel, supporting a student finance program, and starting an effective building program." [13]

At first fundraising campaigns focused exclusively on matching funds for NDEA loans and grants: "The Georgia Southern College Foundation can obtain about $294,000 in Federal funds, provided it can come up with $33,000, and will make available to the Foundation a total of $327,000 to help . . . needy, qualified college students to attend Georgia Southern College." [14] The ten-to-one match encouraged both businesses and citizens to support college fund-raisers.

STUDENT LIFE IN THE SIXTIES

At the beginning of the 1967-68 academic year, students once again petitioned the Dean of Students, Ralph Tyson, and President Henderson with a familiar request to permit nationally affiliated Greek organizations.

Kent Dykes, president of the Student Congress in 1967-68, recalled factors involved in the renewed effort. "All this started with the 'food riot' of spring quarter 1967. This was a time of campus unrest throughout the country and I guess this was the GSC equivalent of rebellion." [15]

In view of the volatile environment and the president's impending retirement, "a group of students went to President Henderson," Dykes recalled, "and asked for social fraternities and sororities and, to our surprise, he said, 'OK.' I am sure he did not want any more unrest before he retired."

The first Greek colony on campus, Alpha Tau Omega, appeared in November 1967, according to Dykes. By the spring of 1968, "there were probably seventeen fraternity and sorority colonies on campus at various stages of maturity. Greek organizations were chartered by their individual national organizations." [16]

During the spring of 1968 the campus and community grew accustomed to seeing Greek letters on clothing and automobile windshields. Citizens responded favorably to the change, primarily because the new organizations became involved in community projects. In April the chapter of Tau Kappa Epsilon painted the community building at the Fair Road recreation park. The chapter president, Buddy Clay from Savannah, pointed out "'fraternity

First Jewish student organization

Jewish students attended the college throughout its history, but until 1966 they did not have a place to assemble on a regular basis. Founded during the winter quarter of 1966, the Jewish Student Organization provided opportunities for Jewish students to meet and discuss academic, social, and religious topics.

Seated, left to right: *Allan Pollard; Steve Myers, Vice President; Claire Halpern, Treasurer; Ron Baruch, President; Charlet Lind, Secretary; Dr. Robert Boxer, Advisor.* Standing, left to right: *Martha Haimovitz; Marilyn Rosenberg, Religious Chairman; Jerry Michaels; Sandord Nichosson; Robert Stein; Janet Fox; Irene Cohen.* (Not pictured: *Dr. Nathaniel Shecter, Advisor.*)

First chartered social fraternity

"The first national social fraternity was chartered at Georgia Southern College this weekend. Formal installation services were held on the GSC campus Saturday and Sunday [March 30-31, 1968] for the Chartering of the Kappa Alpha Fraternity. . . . The fraternity's first president is Mike Long, senior political science major from Warner Robins.

"Special guests for the occasion were president-elect of Georgia Southern, Dr. John O. Eidson, and dean-elect, Dr. Pope A. Duncan."

Bulloch Herald, 4 April 1968

First college gig for Stones

The first and only chapter of a make-shift service fraternity, Sigma Epsilon Chi (spelled "S-E-X" in English), sponsored numerous popular musical groups on campus. On May 4, 1965, the fraternity made history as it hosted an upstart band from the U.K. Known as the Rolling Stones, featuring Mick Jagger, *above*, the group was rough around the edges and somewhat inebriated. Later, the Stones matured into the world-class entertainers some GSC fans thought they might become.

spirit' is more than competition for athletic or homecoming trophies."[17]

The addition of national social organizations enhanced campus entertainment. Fortunately for non-Greeks, the student government continued the tradition of encouraging visiting performers.

In the early 1960s, a faculty committee selected entertainers and artists to perform on campus. Faculty representatives to this committee in 1962 included Jack Broucek (chairman), Frieda Gernant, Ric Mandes, Robert Overstreet, Fred Wallace, and David Ward. For the initial year, the committee approved appearances by journalist Drew Pearson, a mind reader named Polgar, and a young actor, Hal Holbrook, who was beginning to perform impersonations of Mark Twain.[18]

Students at GSC in the sixties and seventies somehow managed to secure nationally known musical groups. Male students formed a local fraternity, Sigma Epsilon Chi, for the purpose of bringing popular musical groups to the campus. In 1965 Jimmy Hilliard was responsible for the first collegiate appearance in the United States of a motley band of singers from the United Kingdom known as the Rolling Stones.

Mick Jagger and company performed in a sold-out Hanner gym. On that particular night, witnesses said, the band appeared tired and unkempt, as well as intoxicated. Most of the audience seemed to prefer the warm-up group, the Bushmen. Nevertheless, GSC students took pride in that historic appearance by a band that came into its own after a dubious collegiate beginning in Statesboro.[19]

In the sixties and seventies students were responsible for booking an amazing lineup of popular musicians: the Lettermen, the Four Preps, John Tillotson and the Dovells, the Chad Mitchell Trio, Ike and Tina Turner, Otis Redding, the Platters, the Tams, the Kingston Trio, Dionne Warwick, Simon and Garfunkel, and Stevie Wonder. Later, they added other major acts, such as REO Speedwagon, Fleetwood Mac, Jimmy Buffet, B. B. King, and Lynyrd Skynyrd.[20]

In the early 1960s the great tradition of campus dances continued in the old alumni gym. "Right after supper on Wednesday," the student government sponsored a "Mat Dance" (short for "Matinee Dance"), according to Barbara Hale Davidson ('66). These informal dances brought together males and females who simply enjoyed the fun of dancing to prerecorded popular music.

Campus musical groups and Masquers also contributed to the cultural explosion on campus in the 1960s with Leonard Bernstein's *West Side Story* and other cutting-edge productions. In 1967 music division chairman Ronald Neil commissioned Halsey Stevens of the University of Southern California to compose music for the dedication of the Foy Recital Hall. Stevens called the work for timpani, chorus, and organ *Te Deum*. The student chorus, known as the Southern Singers, prepared the piece throughout the fall and performed it at the opening in early November.[21]

The new Foy art gallery featured an illustrated art lecture by Sheldon Nodelman, professor of art history at Yale University. The art department presented an exhibition of four "nationally acclaimed artists," including Jimmie Y. Buie, Helen Gerardia, Ralph N. Hurst, and George I. Parrish Jr. Parrish began his public career as an artist and illustrator while a staffer at the *George-Anne* around 1950.

RETHINKING RATS AND RITUALS

Since the 1920s, students had begun college life as "Rats." In the earliest days, upperclassmen subjected freshmen to humiliating rites of initiation throughout the year.[22] In the 1930s the hazing ended at the Thanksgiving football game. From September through November, upperclassmen without warning could haul freshmen out of bed and conduct impromptu sessions of rat court.

Male rats usually participated in at least one involuntary parade around Sweetheart Circle, clad only in their underwear. They also ran a gauntlet of belt-wielding upperclassmen. The college permitted upperclassmen to escort all male and female rats downtown for the annual parade of freshmen on Main Street. Rats, wearing mismatched clothing, carried silly signs. Males fell to the pavement when upperclassmen yelled "air raid!" Females recited the rat poem in unison. Shoppers and merchants enjoyed the ragtag entertainment.

In 1940 the tradition continued virtually unchanged, according to the *George-Anne:* "Our 'Rat Court' was held on Friday night with the Honorable Judge Vandiver presiding. After a lot of quizzing and seat warmings [belt line] we were sent through the lake to think things over and to cool off. At one o'clock (or a little after) we were allowed to hit the hay. Oh, boy! What a relief!"[23]

In addition to college-approved hazing of freshmen, some clubs added their own requirements. Harold Tillman, a student from Tattnall County, underwent an initiation that almost cost him his life in May 1943. His superiors blindfolded him and drove him to a remote farm in northern Bulloch County. Unfamiliar with the territory, he spent the night in a vehicle parked there.

When Tillman sought directions the next morning, the farm's owner, Bennie Hendrix, fired a shotgun at the defenseless young man, staggering him. Although he held his hands over his head and pleaded, the farmer shot him a second time, leaving him severely wounded and bleeding. Thanks to a neighbor's intervention and excellent emergency care at the hospital, Tillman survived. Campus clubs immediately halted this form of hazing.[24]

'THE PLATTERS' TO APPEAR IN CONCERT
Group Will Climax 'Spring Swing' Week In Hanner Gym On May 8

Let the good times roll

"In 1965, 'Spring Swing Week' sponsored by the Student Activities Committee brought the Drifters and the Platters to Statesboro. The Drifters songs include 'Save the Last Dance for Me' and 'Under the Boardwalk.' The Platters golden hits were 'Only You,' 'Twilight Time,' and 'The Great Pretender.'"

George-Anne, 23 April 1965

LOOKOUT, HERE COMES THE BARBER!
Actually it isn't that bad, and these long, shaggy haired guys represent one of Britain's top three vocal groups. The Rollingstones, sponsored by Sigma Epsilon Chi fraternity, will appear on campus May 4, for a concert in the W. S. Hanner Building.

George-Anne, 23 April 1965

College-community orchestra

"The idea of the community-college orchestra was originated by Dr. Fred K. Grumley and Mrs. William McKenney. A call went out to musicians in Statesboro and Bulloch County and music students at the college. The orchestra was organized and held its first rehearsal on October 11, 1965.

"Mrs. William McKenney was named director and Dr. Grumley was named associate director. . . .

"Mrs. McKenney, the director, states that as of right now 'we have a string symphony,' but explained that in time other instruments of the orchestra will be added until they have a full symphony.

"The orchestra is now rehearsing each Monday night from 7:30 until 9 o'clock in the Georgia Southern College music building."

Bulloch Herald, 11 November 1965

The Otis Redding Show, sponsored by Delta Pi Alpha, a service organization, took place Wednesday, October 27, at the Farmer's Tobacco Warehouse (No.1) on Highway 301 North. Redding and his band of thirteen instruments peformed along with Mona Lisa and Speedo Sims. Redding, a native of Macon, began his career by singing with Johnny Jenkins and the Pine Toppers.

By the 1950s upperclassmen knew the rules by heart: Freshmen wore their clothes inside out and backward. Men wore mismatched clothing during the day and occasionally paraded around campus in their underclothes at night. Women wore skirts upside down. They began the day by braiding their hair into thirteen pig tales. They used lipstick to write the word rat on their brows.

Women mastered the art of ascending steps backward and bowing to all upperclassmen and teachers. They had to obey ridiculous orders from upperclassmen. Each freshman wore a necklace of string that dangled an onion beneath their chins. Rats collected autographs of twenty upperclassmen on the shell of a raw egg. The *George-Anne* provided details:

Freshmen girls were ready, on command, to assume an awkward balance position on one foot and quote a poem, "I am a Lowly Freshman," and the men were required to fall flat on their faces at an "Air Raid" warning shout from an upperclassman. In addition they were called on to perform certain special acts such as kissing their teachers, going into dance routines, and singing love songs. Many of these were done riotously in classes.

A "Rat Parade" from the G.T.C. campus to downtown Statesboro was a feature of the afternoon activities, but the traditional "Rat Court" was the highlight of the day. . . . Completing the initiation was the "tug-of-war." The freshmen were victors and the program ended with the traditional removal of the rat cap.[25]

On November 6, 1957, an assistant professor of English, Frederick Keefer, looked outside the window of the administration building and noticed a manikin hanging in the oak tree near the edge of Sweetheart Circle. Although the face on the object bore little resemblance to his, the sign was unmistakable: "Mr. Keefer."[26] The figure might have been used earlier, when students hung Coach J. B. Scearce and Professor George Rogers in effigy on an issue unrelated to rat activities.[27]

Keefer realized his earlier criticism of rat traditions had irritated the student body. He said the lengthy initiation period should be reduced. He called for ending the embarrassing parade of freshman boys at night, as well as a long list of humiliating and time-consuming activities. These events distracted students from studying, Keefer pointed out in the *George-Anne*.[28]

Keefer might have stimulated discussion among faculty and students in the mid-1950s, but rat customs continued to prevail. By the mid-1960s, however, initiation consumed only a few weeks at the beginning of the quarter. Freshmen still wore their blue-and-white hats, commonly called "rat caps."

The freshman class of 1966 unknowingly made history when it experienced the last Rat Week. Frances Worden Wood recalled participating in a "required march" to an open field for an unknown reason. Yet some of her fellow freshmen refused to march.[29] In 1967 GSC initiated entering freshman merely by requiring them to wear the official blue-and-white "rat cap" during orientation.

Nostalgic in 1967 about those long, lost rituals, the *George-Anne* editor Elaine Thomas wrote, "Upperclassmen recall the days when they were afraid to leave their dorms without rat hats. And they recall the one day, Rat Day, when they were subjected to all sorts of tricks and commands dreamed up by devious upperclassmen. . . . Rat day is a tradition which should not be abandoned; it is a tradition which should be improved and maintained."[30] The editor argued in vain. In the fall of 1968, recently chartered fraternities and sororities began conducting initiation rituals of their own.

HOW THE DOORS OPENED

When the 1964-65 academic year began, the student body resembled the first class of 1908: all were Caucasian. A major transition occurred after Christmas 1964, and few actually realized its historic importance at the time. Georgia Southern College admitted its first African American student.

John Bradley taught music and directed the marching and concert bands at Statesboro's all-black William James High School. He wanted to complete requirements for a T-5 (master's level) teaching certificate. He decided to apply for admission at the nearest four-year college. It happened to be located on the other side of town from his school. He signed up for a graduate-level education course offered in the evenings. Over the next year he would complete three education classes and a music class in applied trumpet.

As he walked to the gymnasium to register, he noticed serpentine lines of students, moving slowly. Suddenly a smiling, tall man warmly greeted Bradley and, in a matter of minutes, escorted him through the registration process. "It took ten minutes, at the most," Bradley recalled. Quietly and swiftly Bradley became the first African American student to enroll at Georgia Southern College.[31]

President Henderson personally supervised the integration of the college, and no one demonstrated disapproval. The *George-Anne* failed to record this historic event. Of course, Bradley had not sought confrontation. He merely wanted to gain a higher-level teaching certificate.

Bradley said his education professors generally ignored him and did not encourage him to participate in class discussions. Bradley wanted to impress a professor in his leadership class who assigned "outside" papers. He diligently gathered research, typed his papers, and asked an English teacher to review them for grammar and style. Other members of the class turned in papers written by hand on notebook paper. They received As and Bs, compared to Bradley's Cs. "I never knew why I deserved a C. There was no comment, just a C, maybe a C plus. But I did pass the leadership course with a C plus. All of my other grades were B or better."[32]

Fellow students did not actively snub Bradley. "If being overlooked means being accepted, then I was accepted," he said. "Yes, I heard the *n-word* directed at me from a distance." One day, however, a student invited him to attend a meeting of intellectuals interested in Jean Paul Sartre and other existential writers. He became a regular participant and looked forward to

Poem for Female Rats

I am a lowly freshman,
I have no poise nor grace.
I must respect the upper class
To show I know my place.
My place is very low, indeed,
I am a humble soul.
I crawl around like a centipede,
When I should crawl in a hole.
I am a lowly freshman,
I have no sense of knowledge.
To learn respect and discipline
Is why I came to college.

Punishments for failure to learn poem: (1) Bite onion; (2) Clean rooms of upperclassmen; (3) Run errands.

George-Anne, 13 October 1951

African American firsts

First Student:
John Bradley, Statesboro, Winter 1965

First Graduate (transfer):
Catherine Davis, Statesboro, Spring 1968

First Graduate (four year):
Jessie Zeigler, Statesboro, Spring 1969

First Scholarship Athlete:
Roger Moore (basketball), Savannah, 1967

First Candidate for Miss Georgia Southern:
Carolyn Milton, Sylvania, 1969

First Miss Georgia Southern:
Ericka Brayboy, 2003

First Homecoming Queen:
Yolanda Epps, 1982

First Homecoming King:
Carlton Dickerson, 1994

BRADLEY   DAVIS   ZEIGLER

MOORE   MILTON   BRAYBOY

EPPS   DICKERSON

the philosophical discussions. "I enjoyed talking with students and professors in the Existentialist Club. It was one of my favorite things there. I learned a lot, and I hope I contributed something."[33]

During the fall quarter of 1965, according to the registrar's records, six black students attended the college as undergraduates: Clavelia Love Brinson, Arlene Marie Daughtry, Ulysee Moseley, Shirley Anne Woodall, and Jessie Zeigler. A native of Statesboro, Catherine Davis transferred as an entering sophomore from Paine College in Augusta. Three years later Davis, a sociology major, received the first bachelor's degree awarded to an African American in the history of the institution.

Some professors refused to acknowledge the presence of black students and did not call on them to speak in class. Davis, who grew up in Statesboro's Butler Housing Project, recalled two professors who immediately accepted her without reference to her skin color. One was a teacher in the division of languages, Billy R. Thompson. The other, Harris Mobley, prepared her for a career in social work. "Dr. Mobley taught most of my major courses in sociology. He was such a good teacher and so thoughtful. He cared about and inspired me."[34]

White students sometimes ignored the obvious newcomers in the late 1960s, and black students sought friendship wherever they could find it. The black coeds found each other. "Our favorite meeting spot was in an alcove near the entrance to the gym. We all were day students. We would meet there and talk about everything, including the new basketball players, Roger Moore from Savannah's Beach High School and that cute guy, Gene Brown."[35] During the following years, black students were few in number. In 1969 they accounted for just 74 students at a college with 5,178 enrolled.

One advantage of belonging to a campus minority group, Jessie Zeigler said, was a heightened sense of camaraderie. Zeigler, also a graduate of William James High, enjoyed her close friendships. She majored in home economics and found her department head, Betty Lane, to be most cordial and helpful. Part of Zeigler's curriculum required her to spend one quarter in the home management house. Her roommate was a white student, Carla Holt. In 2002 they became reacquainted and have corresponded in recent years. Zeigler was among the first black students to live on campus. (She and other minority students previously had lived at home or in apartments in Statesboro.) In 1969 Zeigler was the first black student who entered as a freshman to graduate from the college.[36] Ulysee Mosely graduated three months later.

Clavelia "Sherry" Brinson grew up on Baldwin Street on the northwest side of Statesboro, some two and a half miles from the college. She walked to and from GSC each day. As she passed near the housing project on Johnson Street, she recalled vowing "never to live in the project and never to accept welfare." Brinson found the upperclassmen both tolerant and sympathetic, the opposite of some of her teachers. Early in the quarter two professors, she recalled, expressed their displeasure over her presence. One professor "took pleasure in embarrassing me," she said, but students after class gave "comfort and support."[37]

As a physical education major, she took dancing classes with Reba Barnes in the Skate 'R Bowl on Highway 301 near the campus. When the time came for couples to dance, no one chose to dance with Brinson. Sensing her predicament, Professor Barnes said, "Clavelia and I will demonstrate this dance. Please observe." Brinson said Barnes brought "sweetness and light" into her life.

Physical education majors participated in annual meetings, usually held on Jekyll Island. Brinson's friend, Frances Worden, encouraged her to attend, and Brinson rode with a group of white coeds. When they stopped for a meal at a roadside restaurant, the manager told them his firm did not serve integrated groups. He insulted all the students. They continued their trip until they found a friendlier place.

Brinson made satisfactory or better grades in all of her classes except one—English. She realized she had deeply ingrained speech patterns and deficiencies in grammar. After flunking freshman English four times in classes taught by different professors, she concluded she needed to find a professor who was sympathetic and would help her understand her weaknesses.

She summoned her courage and approached the college president. He listened to her and reviewed her academic record. Then he called an English professor and asked her to permit Brinson to enroll in her class. However, the president asked if he might grade her essays. The professor agreed. On her fifth attempt at freshman composition, Brinson passed with a grade of C, certified by President Zach Henderson, who read and discussed each writing assignment with her. She remembered this act of compassion throughout her long and distinguished career as a teacher and public school administrator in Florida.[38]

Carolyn Milton, a native of Sylvania, entered the college in 1966. She recalled painful moments when some professors did not acknowledge her presence. Some students refused to speak to her. There were no threats, but the rudeness was palpable. "That first year was rough, but after the deaths of Robert Kennedy and Martin Luther King, people began to accept us as equals."[39]

Milton joined the Humanities Club, sponsored by Billy R. Thompson, one of her favorite professors. Campus rules allowed clubs to submit candidates for entry into the campus beauty pageant. The Humanities Club made history by sponsoring Carolyn Milton as the first black contestant in the Miss Georgia Southern pageant in 1969. For her talent piece she chose to recite Shakespeare's memorable scene of the sleepwalking Lady Macbeth. She did not win, but the audience in McCroan Auditorium accepted her as a legitimate contestant.[40]

Looking back on her age of firsts, some thirty-six years later, Milton said some students were kind, and some professors treated her with "dignity and

BETTY LANE
Head of the home economics division, Betty Lane organized the home management house to provide hands-on experiences in household leadership and consumer affairs. She was the sister of State Representative Jones Lane, who worked diligently to support Georgia Southern in the legislature.

Beginning in 1965, African American students joined the Georgia Southern journey toward knowledge and self-realization. They became brothers and sisters of all who went before them—the boys and girls of the 'Culture, the collegians of the Blue Tide, the Teachers, the Professors, and forever, the Eagles.

Number 25

Roger Moore was the first black athlete to receive a scholarship in the University System.

Reflector, 1968

Remembering their contributions

When he left Georgia Southern on his "Talmadge sabbatical" in 1941, Marvin Pittman paid tribute to black employees, calling them by their first names: Melrose, the custodian; Joe, the garbage man; Wesley, the carpenter; Mose, the dairyman; Dave, the cook.

Eliza Clark, who began working as a custodian in the early 1950s, was the daughter of Melrose Mincey. Clark recalled the last names of Mose Bass, Stella Clouden, Doney Jones, Herbalene Jones, and Genorn Fields, all employees in the thirties and forties.

Melrose Mincey, top, *worked in Anderson Hall and the administration building.*

Children of African American employees, above, *including those of Mrs. Mincey, around 1940.*

respect." She concluded, "I still enjoyed my time at Georgia Southern and I still support the university in all its endeavors."[41]

One graduate and six undergraduate students broke the color barrier in 1965. In truth, African Americans had been a quiet presence on campus since 1906. They were the carpenters, cooks, custodians, waiters, farm hands, groundskeepers, and day laborers.

The girls who gathered in Hanner gym each day found support in two elderly custodians who had worked many years on the campus, Everlina Murray and Roosevelt Jones. In the administration building they chatted with the friendly Eliza Clark, daughter of Melrose Mincey, who began working as a custodian in the same building in the 1930s. They also shared their concerns with three women who prepared food and worked in the snack bar at the Williams Center—Lois McRae, Mattie Parker, and Mary Parrish.[42]

Since black students could not find lodging on campus in 1965, they lived in town. Everlina Murray invited Ulysee Mosley of Albany, to stay at her home, and the others either lived at home or with friends and relatives.

During 1965, the first year of integration on campus, legendary basketball coach J. B. Scearce asked the athletic committee for permission to recruit two or more black basketball players. He had located a pair of athletes who could move Georgia Southern up a notch. Even though he had kept President Henderson informed of his successful recruiting efforts, the president finally told him in the spring of 1966 that the chancellor, George Simpson, thought an integrated basketball team was not a good idea.[43] Scearce ended his efforts to recruit the pair.

During the 1966–67 season, the players Scearce had released from consideration performed spectacularly as freshmen players at Marquette University and Northwestern University—major NCAA Division I teams. When he reminded the president he had virtually signed them to play at GSC, Scearce said the president replied, "Well, go ahead."[44]

Roger Moore, an outstanding player at Beach High in Savannah, joined the team in the fall of 1967 and became an instant success, coached by Frank Radovich.[45] The color barrier not only collapsed but vanished. After the NCAA accepted the Eagles as a Division I competitor in 1968, the team continued to be a powerful force on the basketball court.

Virtually unnoticed, Coach Scearce claimed, was GSC's leadership. In 1967 Roger Moore was the first black athlete to receive a basketball scholarship in the University System of Georgia.

The local transition to inclusion lacks the tension and drama connected with the University of Georgia, where Charlayne Hunter and Hamilton Holmes enrolled in 1961. When James Meredith requested admission at the University of Mississippi in 1962, tragic stories flowed from the quaint town of Oxford.

The transition from inequality to inclusion at Georgia Southern is a long one, dating to President Guy Wells in the early 1930s. While the institution's faculty and presidents led the discussion originally, leaders in the 1950s tended to follow regional trends. Who kept the provocative discussion going? Students. Back issues of the *George-Anne* make clear that young people had learned to ask hard questions and to question easy answers.

Periodically, editorialists and opinion columnists rose up and challenged the customary way of thinking about race. The U.S. Supreme Court in 1954 settled the matter of where black students could learn in America. Both before and after that decision, students debated each other and shifted their opinions radically. When John Bradley finally enrolled at GSC in 1965, equal opportunity was an idea whose time had come on the campus.

Seven black students on campus accounted for a fraction of 1 percent of the student body in the fall of 1965. In 2005 minorities composed almost one-fourth of the enrollment at the university. Inclusion became a presidential priority in the 1980s, and it remains at that level in the twenty-first century.

RETIREMENT AND RENEWAL

From 1927 until 1968 he climbed the same steps, walked the same halls, and stood behind the same lectern on the auditorium stage. The tall man at age sixty-six still had a bounce in his step, still sliced watermelons with authority, still spoke his wisdom with a gentle accent.

President Henderson told the student body he wanted to spend his time observing construction projects rather than lobbying for them. The Board of Regents had approved six major buildings for completion between 1969 and 1970: the New Field House attached to Hanner Gymnasium with seating for 5,500, the Biology Building, the Physics Building, the Education Classroom Building, the New Warehouse, and the New Dormitory for Women.

Compared with the teachers college Henderson had led in 1948, Georgia Southern College was remarkably different. Not only had the student body grown sevenfold, it had begun to resemble in color the youth of America. Professors generally were better prepared, and more than 40 percent had earned doctoral degrees.[46] The community's historic support of the institution now had a name: the Georgia Southern Foundation.

When Henderson announced his retirement in the fall of 1967, Dean Paul Carroll followed suit. Since 1948 the two administrators had worked together during an unprecedented era of growth. Most students, faculty, and local supporters agreed on one point: the leadership team had positioned the college for another move forward.

The Board of Regents on November 9, 1967, recognized their achievements by appointing a well-known and experienced academic leader to succeed Henderson, John Olin Eidson, dean of the Franklin College of Arts and Sciences at the University of Georgia. Pope Alexander Duncan, the president of South Georgia College, a junior college, became GSC's first vice president, at Eidson's request.

"President Henderson, Master Slicer"

"When Dr. Henderson became president of GSC in 1948 he initiated twice-a-week watermelon cuttings during summer school. On Tuesdays and Thursdays between morning classes, the students can—if they like watermelons—drop by, dig in and spit seeds at the campus melon slicing [*above*]. The affair continues from about the last week in June into August, watermelon crop willing. . . . The president's performance on a Georgia melon has been compared to that of a surgeon doing brain surgery. Dr. Henderson modestly explains, 'It's all in the wrist.'"

Bob Harrell, *Atlanta Constitution*, 11 November 1967

Zach and Marjorie begin retirement

In May 1968 alumni and friends presented Zach and Marjorie Henderson a color television set for their new home, located less than a mile from the college. The Henderson family lived on the campus for forty-one years. As the college changed its name three times, they observed enormous improvements and growth.

Under Henderson's watchful eye

Hundreds of tons of beams to be hoisted, oceans of cement to be poured, thousands of nails to be hammered: President Emeritus Henderson could watch the building projects with undivided attention.

A Time for Growth, 1948 to 1968

	1948	1968
Number of graduates:	32	542
Enrollment:	723	4,405
Degree programs:	1	15
Buildings:	8	35

For thirty-one years Eidson had been an English professor and dean. He had established a reputation as a scholar, editor of the *Georgia Review*, and researcher in the field of nineteenth-century British literature. He specialized in the life and works of Alfred, Lord Tennyson. His long tenure at the university in Athens gave Eidson insight into the structure of academic institutions.

Henderson shared the headlines with his successor during his last six months in office. As the spring quarter ended, however, he enjoyed an outpouring of appreciation from the campus and community. The culminating event, a dinner and tribute, on May 22, featured the Governor Lester Maddox, and University System Chancellor George L. Simpson Jr. Students, faculty, alumni, and local citizens all praised the retiring Henderson and Carroll.

The former president kept his word during the next decade. He watched with interest the completion of construction projects he had advocated. He visited the campus often, talking with faculty and staff. He also enjoyed slicing the first watermelon each summer underneath the spreading oaks near Lake Wells.

Some ten years after Henderson retired, Professor T. Ray Shurbutt began preparing a history of the first seventy-five years of the institution, entitled *Georgia Southern: Seventy-Five Years of Progress and Service*. He often commented about information gained from his enjoyable conversations with Henderson, who must have been pleased with the book's publication in 1982. He died three years later, on January 6, 1985, and was buried in Statesboro's Eastside Cemetery.

An alumnus, Carl Hodges ('34), the first executive secretary of the Georgia Association of Educators, followed his alma mater closely through the years. As a student Hodges knew Zach Henderson as his dean. When Henderson in 1965 was elected president of the Georgia Education Association (later GAE), Hodges worked with him. He also took note of the president's devoted lay ministry in the Methodist Church. Hodges concluded:

It was my observation that, for many years, Georgia Teachers College (or Georgia Southern) and Zach Henderson were almost synonymous terms. He was viewed widely as a man of admirable values, great integrity, a champion of public education, and a friend of teachers. His personal qualities, I think, accrued to the institution.[47]

The institution did not forget. In 1985 at a homecoming gathering in the Conference Center, alumni and college officials attended a brunch and dedication ceremony on October 26. On that occasion, President Dale Lick officially named the largest building on campus the Zach S. Henderson Library.[48] In 2004 the library began a major addition and renovation, nearly doubling the size of the facility named in honor of that big man, President Zach Henderson.

LIFE AT SOUTHERN STARTS WITH A LINE AND ENDS WITH A LINE

FRESHMEN RATS line up to register, make new friends.

SOPHOMORES burn midnight oil, depend on Mose Bass to wake them. They discover the Line at the Candler/Bulloch County border.

JUNIORS continue to develop their social skills, including dancing, panty raids and dorm pranks.

SENIORS hang out at the Union, visit the Health Cottage and line up to receive their diplomas.

Reflector, 1965

GEORGIA SOUTHERN COLLEGE
1968-1977

1968 – John Olin Eidson, former Arts and Science Dean at the University of Georgia becomes seventh president. (7/1)

1968 – Pope Alexander Duncan, former President of South Georgia College, is named vice president, the first in the history of the institution. (7/1)

1968 – President Eidson announces plan to phase out academic divisions and create a School of Arts and Sciences, a School of Education, and a Graduate School, effective on July 1, 1969. (10/10)

1968 – College announces record enrollment of 4,669 students . (10/17)

1968 – Republican Richard Milhouse Nixon defeats Democrat Hubert Humphrey and third party candidate George Wallace in presidential election. (11/5)

1969 – College opens graduate centers at Hunter Air Force Base in Savannah and Fort Stewart Army Base in Hinesville. (1/9)

1969 – Vietnam peace talks begin as number of U.S. troops increases to record level of nearly 550,000. (1/18)

1969 – Nicholas W. Quick, English professor at Arkansas State University, is named the first dean of the School of Arts and Sciences. (3/13)

1969 – First inaugural convocation in the institution's history for the inauguration of President John Olin Eidson.

1969 – Sports announcer Chris Schenkel awards GSC golfer Pat Lane from Sylvania the first Shenkel Golf Scholarship. (4/11)

1969 – Apollo crew member, Neil Armstrong, becomes first man to step onto the moon, accompanied by U.S. Apollo crew member, Edwin E. Aldrin. (7/20)

1970 – Eagle gymnasts easily defeat Universities of Georgia and Florida. (1/29, 2/5)

1969 – Psychology, math, and recreation added to graduate program. (9/18)

1970 – Joe Frazier defeats Jimmy Ellis to become World Heavyweight Boxing Champion. (2/16)

1970 – President Eidson announces four new buildings: Newton, Family Life Center, Physics-Math, and Library. (5/7)

1970 – College begins first community fund-raising drive, "Spirit of Southern." (8/1)

1970 – New dormitory for girls honors former dean of men Sophie Johnson. (9/17)

1971 – Bulloch Herald endorses effort to make college a university. (1/4)

1971 – Twenty-sixth Amendment lowers voting age from 21 to 18. (7/1)

1971 – John O. Eidson named as vice chancellor, effective 9/1, and Pope A. Duncan becomes president on 9/8.

1971 – Twenty-sixth Amendment to the U.S. Constitution ratified, lowering the voting age to eighteen. (7/1)

1972 – Thirty-eight black employees strike, protesting low wages and lack of black supervisors and professors. (3/24)

1972 – Pope Alexander Duncan inaugurated as eighth president. (4/5)

1972 – The Washington Post reports a burglary at the Democratic headquarters in the Watergate Hotel. (6/18)

1972 – Model U.N. Conference for public schools organized by Lane Van Tassell and others. (3/10)

1973 – "Day for Southern" replaces "Pull for Southern," and "Spirit of Southern" as the annual fundraising drive by the Georgia Southern Foundation. (9/1)

1974 – Naked males run across Sweetheart Circle, beginning a springtime of streaking. (3/6)

1974 – U.S. President Richard Nixon resigns; Gerald Ford is sworn in as president. (8/8)

1975 – Jack Stallings begins tenure of 24 years as coach of Eagle baseball. (9/1)

1976 – State of Georgia, for second straight year, fails to provide salary increases for faculty and staff. (9/1)

1976 – Democratic candidate Jimmy Carter, former Georgia Governor, wins U.S. Presidential election. (11/2)

1977 – Pope A. Duncan departs to accept presidency of Stetson University. (7/15)

1977 – Elvis Presley dies at age 42. (8/16)

CHAPTER 10

ORGANIZING FOR QUALITY

T he steady growth of the 1950s accelerated in the 1960s. In 1957 some 900 students attended Georgia Teachers College. A decade later, with almost 4,500 students, it ranked as one of the fastest-growing colleges in the South. The student population expanded rapidly, forcing both state and private developers to invest in new dormitories almost every year. Campus social life, on the other hand, evolved at a much slower pace.

Although bulging at the seams with students, the college seemed frozen in time, in spite of occasional rock concerts planned on campus by musical nonconformists. The freshman's neat Kodak Instamatic camera produced great snapshots, but the images seemed to belong in an old yearbook.

Female students lived under strict curfew, and they dressed conservatively. Kent Dykes, president of the Student Congress in 1967-68, recalled: "There were many rigid rules on campus regarding students and they [the administration] had no problem in expelling students for violations that would be inconsequential today." [1]

Pages from the yearbook, the *Reflector*, for 1967 could have appeared a decade earlier, with one exception: race. In 1966-1967, one dozen black students attended. Otherwise, remarkably few were the signs of change. In some ways the administration of President Henderson echoed an earlier age of innocence, not unlike the campus he found in 1927 when he became dean.

When the president announced his retirement in the fall of 1967, John Olin Eidson was dean of the Franklin College of Arts and Sciences at the University of Georgia. Chancellor George Simpson appointed a presidential selection advisory committee, and he recommended Eidson as a candidate. After reviewing Eidson's impressive résumé, the committee nominated the fifty-nine-year-old dean as the seventh president of the college. [2]

Chancellor Simpson recommended Eidson as Henderson's successor for a good reason. The chancellor believed the college needed to move into modern times, and Eidson presumably was the man to bring about a major shift in direction. Considering the size of the faculty, Eidson suggested the college could benefit by creating a new position of vice-president. Simpson at first refused, because he knew other four-year colleges soon would be asking for vice-presidents. Eidson pointed out Georgia Southern was larger and more academically diverse than her sister senior colleges. The chancellor reluctantly agreed to appoint a vice-president. He recommended an experienced university system administrator, Pope Alexander Duncan. At forty-eight, the former president of South Georgia College was eleven years younger than the new president.

PRESIDENT JOHN OLIN EIDSON

Formerly the Dean of Arts and Sciences at the University of Georgia, he served as president of Georgia Southern College from 1968-1971. The native of Johnston, South Carolina, earned the PhD in American literature at Duke University. Eidson, a Fulbright fellow and Tennyson scholar, was a faculty member and administrator at the University of Georgia from 1936–1968.

LEADING COUPLES

Left to right: Margaret Duncan, Perrin Eidson, President John O. Eidson, and Vice President Pope A. Duncan.

First official inauguration

Chancellor George Simpson encouraged President Eidson to plan an inauguration. Eidson's was the first formal inauguration ceremony in the history of the institution.

More than two hundred delegates and nearly three hundred special guests declared they would attend the event scheduled for April 2-3, 1969, including England's Sir Charles Tennyson, grandson of the poet Alfred, Lord Tennyson, subject of Eidson's recently published book.

The inaugural program listed an address by Senator Richard Brevard Russell, brother of GSC English professor, Fielding Russell. A technical problem with the airplane carrying the senator prevented his appearance. Instead, Governor Lester Maddox, *below*, delivered the inaugural address.

Eidson's barbecue strategy

"Mills Lane, the successful Atlanta banker, directed Callaway funds through the regents, providing two chairs for universities and one chair for colleges. Eidson quickly obtained Jim Oliver's chair in biology. Immediately he invited Lane to Statesboro. They had lunch at Vandy's Barbecue downtown. Eidson noticed his guest really enjoyed the meal.

"Lane told Eidson he was the first president in the system to thank him for a Callaway chair. Then he asked Eidson if he could pick up some barbecue to share with Mrs. Lane. Eidson bought the barbecue and stew and presented it to Lane who talked happily as they drove to the airport. At that moment Eidson asked the banker if the regents would regard Georgia Southern as a university-level institution and provide a second Callaway professorship. Lane replied: 'You've got it.'"

Ric Mandes, interview

Duncan, a Baptist minister and longtime professor of church history at Southeastern Theological Seminary, changed his career abruptly in 1963. He applied for the deanship of a new state junior college in Brunswick, Ga., beginning in January of 1964. After Duncan served briefly as dean, Chancellor Simpson asked him to fill the position of president of South Georgia College, a junior college in Douglas, Ga.

While at Douglas, Duncan said he realized the chancellor preferred presidents who precisely followed university system guidelines. He memorized the "rules and regulations and conformed to them in every detail." The chancellor never reprimanded Duncan for violating the rules; with confidence he recommended him as vice-president to John Eidson.[3]

The personable and easy-going Henderson had represented the college well. The former superintendent, scoutmaster, and Sunday school teacher compiled a long list of achievements to validate his approach. Eidson, on the other hand, brought to the presidency a different concept of institutional success: verifiable academic excellence.

President Eidson wanted to build on Henderson's foundation of good will. The college needed a solid academic structure familiar to institutions of higher learning, Eidson believed. Before Georgia Southern could function as an equal to the best colleges, however, the college needed to look the part.

Seven academic divisions served the college well in 1937 when 508 students enrolled in only one program, the Bachelor of Science degree in education. Divisions were adequate, even in 1957 when candidates for that degree numbered almost one thousand. By 1967 some 4,500 students pursued fifteen different programs of study. Meanwhile the administration had added only two new divisions: fine arts and business education.

Eidson realized the problem: divisions were inadequate for the variety of degree programs on the horizon. What Georgia Southern needed, he suggested, was a logical way to organize its academic structure. He employed a pattern he knew well at the University of Georgia—schools and departments.

Eidson proposed three schools, in addition to divisions of business, industrial arts, and physical education. First, a school of arts and sciences would include departments largely responsible for the core curriculum. Second, a school of education would consolidate the teacher education programs that, in some cases, academic departments still managed. Third, a graduate school would consolidate a growing number of post baccalaureate programs taught on the campus and in regional centers at Hinesville, Savannah, Brunswick, and Augusta.

Suddenly the college had three new deans: Jack Averitt, dean of the Graduate School; Starr Miller, dean of the School of Education; Nicholas W. Quick, dean of the School of Arts and Sciences. Averitt previously was chairman of the Division of Social Sciences, and Miller was chairman of the Division of Education. Quick moved to Georgia Southern from Arkansas State College, where he had been a professor of English.

President Eidson, a humanities scholar, believed the college needed to establish a tradition of academic excellence. He made a concerted effort to establish a chapter of Phi Beta Kappa. He was not successful, because Georgia Southern College did not qualify as a liberal arts institution. Instead, he received authorization for a Phi Beta Kappa Association for coastal Georgia, and he served as the founding president. Then he worked with faculty members to organize a local chapter of Phi Kappa Phi, the nation's oldest and largest academic honor society.[4]

When the highly regarded Hassie McElveen retired as librarian, Eidson sought an experienced librarian with academic credentials. He chose Richard Harwell, author of more than fifty books and monographs. At the time of his appointment, Harwell, a native Georgian, was head librarian at Smith College in Massachusetts. Harwell brought a familiar name to those who followed baseball. His brother, Ernie, was a major league announcer in Detroit.

Eidson contacted the Callaway Foundation through his friend, Mills B. Lane, a banker. In 1969 the president announced an alumnus of Georgia Teachers College, James H. Oliver Jr., '52, would be the first Callaway professor at Georgia Southern, beginning in 1970.[5] A distinguished biologist in the field of parasitology, Oliver later established here the Institute of Arthropodology and Parasitology, a center for research in the area of ticks and mites. Eventually the college added another Callaway professor in the field of business, Bernard Keys. Georgia Southern College's second Callaway Professorship surprised other four-year colleges that received only one.

A local savings and loan association, First Federal, funded a series of scholarly writings by graduate faculty, *The Marvin Pittman Studies*, edited by Graduate Dean Jack Averitt and Dean Emeritus Paul Carroll.

John Eidson looked upon each big spring commencement not as an event to be endured, but as a ceremony to cherish. After the deans had passed out all diplomas at commencement each spring, he reflected on Mortimer Adler's familiar saying: "The purpose of learning is growth, and our minds, unlike our bodies, can continue growing as long as we live." He used his own words, but before the happy graduates left Hanner Fieldhouse to celebrate, the gentlemanly president leaned over the lectern and reminded them, in professorial tones: "I encourage you to continue your education."

When he formed the division of continuing education in 1969, he was inspired by the approach of the Kellogg Foundation. He believed in lifetime learning, and he organized this new division, hoping to see residents of southeast Georgia participate in evening classes, conferences and educational events. Hilton T. Bonniwell initially directed the division of continuing education.[6]

Visitors to the president's office noticed on the wall the master copy of the institution's first modern organizational chart, designating clearly the lines of communication. Eidson saw information technology as another way to bring order and improve communication. He hired a computer specialist and statistician at the University of Georgia, Frederick Russell Helm, and he

JAMES HENRY OLIVER JR.

Director, Institute of Arthropodology and Parasitology and Fuller Callaway Professor, Department of Biology

President Eidson enjoyed the friendship of the banker, Mills B. Lane, who was an advisor to Fuller Callaway and the Callaway Foundation. Lane was instrumental in arranging for Georgia Southern University to host the first Callaway Professorship in the University System of Georgia. Oliver, an alumnus who received a BS degree in 1952, was a leader in student activities and served in the Student Congress. Before joining the faculty in 1970, Oliver had distinguished himself as a specialist in medical entomology and acarology and was a member of the faculty of the University of Georgia. Oliver led Georgia Southern's Institute of Arthropodology and Parasitology successfully and continued to head the program in 2006. The recipient of many awards internationally, Oliver served as president of the Entomological Society of America. He also was elected to membership in the American Association for the Advancement of Science.

Remembering an energetic Eidson

"On one special occasion the Olivers accompanied the Eidsons for a dinner sponsored by the Callaway Foundation in Atlanta. President Eidson, in his early sixties, worked in his office all morning. Then he drove all of us up in the afternoon and back at midnight. He was more alert than the rest of us on the drive home. I hate to admit it, but I kept dropping off to sleep. He enjoyed noting that and laughingly said I shouldn't work so hard."

James H. Oliver Jr.

Faculty Dames reveal secrets

Organized in the 1930s by Anna Pittman, the Faculty Dames Club provided social and service opportunities for wives of faculty members. In 1973 the organization published a cook book, *Secrets from Southern's Kitchens,* with a cover designed by Susan Oliver. The book included well-known recipes, such as English Professor Woody Powell's pecan pie, as well as historical notes, *below.*

```
        WOODY POWELL'S PECAN PIE

1 9¼ in. pie shell   1 c. white karo syrup
3 eggs               1/3 stick butter or oleo
½ c. white sugar     1 c. chopped pecans
1 t. vanilla

Beat eggs somewhat (not extensively) and add
sugar and Karo.  Heat liquid in double boiler
until ingredients are well blended (hot, but
not very hot).  Add butter or oleo and remove
from heat.  Allow liquid to cool.  Add vanilla.
Pour chopped nuts in pie shell and add cooled
liquid (filling).  Bake in a 300° oven for one
hour.

                         Dr. Woodrow Powell
```

```
Dr. Fielding Russell drove into Statesboro in a
Model T truck, with his lovely wife, Virginia,
sitting on a sofa in the back of the truck,
holding her first born in her arms and an umbrella
over her head, to ward off the rain.  This was
in 1932.
```

developed a department of computer services to serve administrative needs and to assist faculty with research projects. He connected Southern's IBM teleprocessing unit with an IBM 360/65 computer in Athens.[7]

Another important change concerned the role of faculty in governing the institution. Eidson appointed a committee to devise a plan for faculty involvement. Headed by Dean Jack Averitt, the committee developed a document, the "Faculty Statutes." For the first time in the institution's history, faculty became more than employees. The "Statutes" encouraged collegiality and provided guidelines for a senate of faculty, elected by their peers, and administrators. The faculty senate advised the administration on academic matters and issues related to faculty welfare.

A fortunate byproduct of these changes was the Academic Club, Inc., informally known as the Faculty Club. It began as a singles club around 1969, but in 1971 the club changed its name to include spouses and guests. Participants enjoyed the interdisciplinary conversation and collegiality. Club members collected dues for the purpose of building a permanent facility, and President Eidson was among the first to pay his dues. Members elected a president each year. In 1975-76, the club made history by electing two members as co-presidents: Sarah Savage and George Shriver. Savage arranged for the college food service to provide delicious meals for club members at a low cost.[8]

The Academic Club originally met in the back room of the House of Sirloin, formerly known as the Varsity. Later members purchased a building nearby. In 1992 the club sold the facility to Georgia Southern University. Eagle Village, a campus dormitory complex for 775 freshmen, opened in 2005, occupying what once was the site of a favorite meeting place for faculty and staff.

An older social organization for the wives of faculty, the Faculty Dames Club, continued to function in the 1970s much as Mrs. Marvin Pittman had organized it in 1939. The club published two cookbooks. The second, in 1973, reflected the diverse cuisine of an increasingly cosmopolitan faculty.

In 1986 the Dames voted to change the organization's name to Association of Georgia Southern Women, acknowledging its tradition of welcoming all female faculty and staff. In 2005, led by Carrie Mitchell, the AGSW sponsored one dozen interest groups and awarded a scholarship each year to a non-traditional female student attending the university.[9] The organization decided to dissolve in 2006. The Georgia Southern University Foundation managed the ongoing AGSW scholarship fund of $35,000.

RISING EXPECTATIONS

Within two years the Eidson administration had accomplished a major feat: the college that drifted into the late 1960s no longer existed. Reflecting upon the significance of President Eidson's sweeping changes, Leodel Coleman, editor of the *Bulloch Herald* in 1969, echoed the opinion of James Sharpe, president of the Georgia Southern

Alumni Association, who said "university status" was the next logical step for the institution.[10]

In 1970 the *Millen News* put the university issue on the table for regional discussion: "We cannot move forward on the feet of uneducated people. . . .We believe that Georgia Southern College will help us meet the challenge of the future, and we look forward to the day when they shall enjoy university status."[11]

Eight months after touting this regional support for university status, the *Bulloch Herald* seriously considered the implications of such a move: "We must begin now to move ahead with bold and imaginative planning. There must be more land for our new 'University,' improved transportation, more adequate fire protection, more water, expanded sanitation facilities, and more of just about everything"[12]

President Eidson did not conceal his attitude toward those who advocated upgrading the institution to a university. After reading Coleman's editorial, he wrote a letter to the editor, thanking him for the positive review of homecoming and approving the newspaper's endorsement of the college's academic evolution.

The chancellor, Eidson believed, favored the movement toward doctoral level courses at Georgia Southern. While he was still president of South Georgia College in 1968, Pope Duncan spoke with president-elect Eidson who "strongly implied that the chancellor had given assurance that once we had things properly organized, we could begin to offer the doctoral degree in education."[13] Eidson assigned the new graduate dean, Jack Averitt, the task of preparing a proposal for a doctoral program, and in 1970 the college submitted its first proposal for a doctorate in education.[14]

Speculation about the possibility of university status encouraged local businesses to support the Georgia Southern Foundation. Since 1962 fundraising volunteers annually had solicited funds to match the federal student loan program. Eidson thought the foundation needed a full-time administrator. In 1969 he appointed James Pollak as the director of a new office of development.

Pollak organized in 1970 the first major fund-raising drive in the history of the college, known as the *Spirit of Southern* campaign. Francis Allen, an alumnus and local attorney, was chairman. In the spring of 1971, Eidson appointed William Franklin to serve as head of fund raising. He would be responsible for developing an annual campaign for gifts to the college. Previously he had been assistant alumni director at the University of Georgia.[15]

When the president announced that the regents had authorized a fourth school, the School of Business, in the spring of 1971, the regional business community approved enthusiastically. At that time more than 1,000 students—815 undergraduate majors and some 200 graduate students—were enrolled in the division of business. Paul LaGrone, head of that division since 1962, became dean of the newest school on campus.

Doctoral proposal of 1970

A committee led by Graduate Dean Jack N. Averitt proposed the first doctoral program for Georgia Southern. The document contained a map demonstrating how the college served a region neglected by doctoral-level universities. The twice-submitted proposal did not receive formal consideration by the Board of Regents.

JAMES POLLAK

The first director of the Office of Development, James Pollak ('62), began the *Spirit of Southern* fund-raising event in 1970, later known as *Pull for Southern* and the *A Day for Southern*.

Conscience on campus

During the administration of President Eidson, professors and students actively voiced concerns about the Viet Nam war and other social issues. Signs of protest appeared in dorm rooms and on bulletin boards. A homecoming parade float in 1969, *below*, called attention to mounting casualties among United States soldiers in the war.

AWARENESS AND ACTIVISM

Fashion on Southern's campus in the early 1970s reflected trends of the 1960s in urban America. Male students and faculty sometimes were indistinguishable. Some men had shoulder-length hair and wore non-traditional clothing—leisure suits, brightly colored pants, tank tops, and Nehru jackets. A few mixed informal with formal, wearing blue jeans with sports jackets.

Females wore bellbottom pants, mini skirts, gypsy dresses, hot pants, and cool T-shirts. Some preferred more traditional skirts, sweaters, and blouses. A few wore ankle-length dresses familiar to their grandmothers. They clad their feet with clogs, earth shoes, sandals, boots, and platform shoes. Polyester and denim soared to popularity; cotton and wool waned.

Freedom in fashion signaled independence in intellect. Locally some students and professors began to think about political and social issues in an unconventional manner. Georgia Southern College joined the national dialogue about war and peace, justice and equality.

One year after the assassination of Martin Luther King, Jr., April 4, 1969, a number of faculty members and students joined hands with the Statesboro-Bulloch County NAACP. Together they participated in a memorial service at the Bulloch County Courthouse commemorating the life and work of Georgia's heralded civil rights spokesman. Robert Overstreet of the division of languages moderated the program, and Harris Mobley of the social science division spoke briefly, along with several ministers. The crowd of more than 275 persons included a large number of GSC students and faculty.[16]

The war in Vietnam also stimulated occasional forums and debates. Alumni had been answering the call of duty in Southeast Asia since the early 1960s. An article in the *Bulloch Herald* in 1964 brought sorrow to those who remembered alumnus, Charles Kelly: "The 1950 graduate of Georgia Southern College was killed last week when his helicopter was shot down by Communist guerillas in South Viet Nam. . . . Major Kelly taught school at Warm Springs for a short time before deciding to return to the army as a paratrooper, later becoming a helicopter pilot. He is a native of Sylvania." The headline noted Kelly was the 149th American to die since the war began.[17]

The war in Vietnam eventually claimed the lives of more than 54,000 Americans and more than three million Vietnamese and another two million residents of Laos and Cambodia. Public support for the U.S. war against North Vietnam sank to a new low in 1969. Each evening the television news programs juxtaposed the Asian battlefield with American campuses. Democratic Senator Eugene McCarthy and child-care author, Benjamin Spock, often rallied campus groups that opposed the war.

On October 15, 1969, from 1-5:30 p.m., hundreds of students and professors participated in a "teach-in" on Sweetheart Circle. Both pro-war and anti-war speakers presented their points of view. In the evening, more than three hundred students, faculty, and local citizens stood on the pavement of Southern Drive, forming a circle of light. Slowly the line of candle-bearers walked east on Herty Drive, turning right on Georgia Avenue and right on Chandler Road. Along the way less than one hundred supporters of the war heckled the walkers who arrived unharmed on the lawn of Trinity Episcopal Church. There they ended the peaceful protest by singing hymns and patriotic songs.

The peace vigil of 1969 coincided with thousands of vigils across America.[18] This event marked the first campus political demonstration since students organized a protest march against Governor Eugene Talmadge in 1941. Then they supported Governor Talmadge's victim, President Marvin Pittman. The Eidson administration appeared to understand the importance of permitting the "fair and balanced" teach-in, as well as the "anti-war" candlelight vigil. Students who participated that day learned lessons about freedom of speech and political responsibility.

On May 18, 1970, four hundred students and professors marched to the Administration Building and sat on the lawn of Sweetheart Circle, facing the office of the president. Many thought they were protesting against the government's brutal use of force against student protestors at Kent State

STUDENTS AIR GRIEVANCES

Above: Ric Muccia presents a list of student grievances, *right,* to President Eidson on May 18, 1970. Protestors sat on the lawn and Southern Drive in front of the Administration Building.

Below: Students and faculty members participated in a march and candlelight vigil, part of a nationwide protest of the war in Viet Nam, on October 15, 1969.

The following is the list of grievances presented to Dr. John O. Eidson:
"As a group of students interested in the betterment of Georgia Southern College we would like to see these following changes made:
1. "The compulsory housing rule for men and women students abolished.
2. "The compulsory purchase of meal tickets abolished. 3. "The sending of male student records to draft boards left to the discretion of the student.
4. "The abolition of the rule that does not permit students to see and hold their permanent (personel) record cards.
5. "The establishment of a draft counseling service for students.
6. "A counsel or committee set up of students and administrators to re-evaluate the spending (distribution) of student activity fees.
7. "A counsel set up for any possible discussion of grades. (The counsel to be made up of students and faculty.)
8. "A board set up to evaluate the relevancy of some courses (Health), and the addition of credited current events courses. (The board should consist of students, faculty, and administrators.)
9. "The hiring of black professors.
10. "The establishment of fraternity and sorority houses.
11. "The establishment of an unlimited cut system.
12. "The hiring of more qualified House mothers, and a proclamation declaring specifically their powers.
13. "A proclamation stating clearly the functions and powers of each administrator.
14. "The establishment of a time each week set aside for students and faculty to bring and discuss grievances directly to the college President without fear of reprisal.
15. "A proclamation stating our opposition to the present training of National Guardsmen brought on to college campuses for riot control be sent to the state government.
16. "The acceptance by the administration of the Action Committee as a recognized organization.
17. "The abolition of the rule that states that an individual may not sponsor a speaker or entertainment on campus.
18. "The abolition of regulations (hours, place of residence, sign-in and sign-out cards, weekend permit slips, etc.) with the exception of first quarter freshmen.
19. "The abolition of permission sheets.
20. "The establishment of inter-visitation between men's and women's dormitories.
21. "The decision of appropriate dress left to the discretion of the woman student.
22. "The abolition of the search-and-seizure clause in all dormitory leases.
23. "The abolition of room-check.
24. "In the event that the college does not accept the request for the abolition of these regulations, a set of regulations should be devised that is applicable to every dormitory."

The Nunnery

" Not all students wanted to live in 'open' dorms, so we worked out a choice system. Students could have different rules in different dorms and define their community. Residents could choose: 'we will have visitation' or 'we will not have visitation.'

"Winburn Hall was often referred to as the nunnery. That's where the nuns lived. No visitation in Winburn! In this kind of village, women preferred not to have men accidentally see them with curlers in their hair. But if they didn't mind risking this possibility, they could move into a dorm that was 'open' to visitors. Otherwise, stay in the nunnery at Winburn. "

Larry Davis, Director of Housing, 1972-1981

International Club, 1970-71

The organization of Americans and international students encouraged the exchange of ideas and social occasions. President Eidson endorsed cross-cultural experiences among students and faculty.

Front row: Vickie Gaulding, Alejandro Avila, LiLiana de La Guardia, Debbie Vanderenter and Tadessee Seifu. *Second row*: Marilyn Womack, Aristides Castillo, Chang Shuang-Chao and Margaret Boringer. Third row; Ginny Price, Linda Galostian, Mike Cornelius, Alton Bennett and Susanne Ramussen. *Back row*: Susan Miles, Mike Graham, Nancy Woodley and Stephen Bradley.

University. At the last minute, Ric Muccia, a freshman from Edison, New Jersey, circulated a list of grievances ranging from social regulations to the use of student records by military draft boards. An additional three hundred spectators arrived to observe the confrontation.

President Eidson emerged from his office and stood between the huge white columns on the front porch. Muccia presented him with a list of two-dozen proposed improvements. After reviewing the list, Eidson looked at the students and lifted his voice: "I am going to see that careful consideration is given to each one of these. . . . I'll see that it's done promptly." The students responded, a reporter noted, "with a solid round of applause."[19]

During the Eidson and Duncan administrations, the student government lobbied for less stringent rules governing student housing, curfews, and personal freedom. The administration responded favorably to student initiatives, and Deans Ralph Tyson, Ben Waller, and Virginia Boger, aided by Shelton Evans, mediated difficult issues. For example, students were surprised that Waller endorsed a proposal for allowing men to visit women's rooms, on a limited basis, for the purpose of studying and conversation. Before the policy became effective, however, Waller had to convince Duncan the policy was sound and would not encourage promiscuity.[20]

THE EIDSON APPROACH TO ATHLETICS AND CAMPUS LIFE

O bservers of John Eidson often remarked at how easily he shifted roles. The former university dean genuinely seemed to enjoy even the mundane chores of the presidency. The man who had spent a lifetime cloistered in the halls of ivy proved he could greet supporters downtown as well as cheer for the Eagles basketball team in the field house.

President Eidson and Athletic Director J. I. Clements worked together to move the college from the NAIA to the NCAA, an achievement they celebrated on October 12, 1968. In September of 1969, the two men helped Development Director Jim Pollak organize Big Blue, the first athletic boosters organization in college history. (Coach Scearce, alumnus John "Bud" Stone and others formed an athletic association in 1951, but it did not function as a community-based boosters group.) Eidson named Charles M. Robbins Jr. as president. One year after its formation, Big Blue raised more than $38,000.[21] Later Southern Boosters replaced Big Blue.

At first the institution competed at the college division of NCAA, but in 1971, the basketball team joined the university division. The era of big time competition began on December 1, 1971, when the Eagles visited the University of Arkansas Razorbacks. Even though sportswriters had picked

Arkansas to contend for the national championship that year, the Eagles were eager to prove they could play with the "big boys."

After building an eight-point lead to start the game, the Eagles played solid defense and ran the Razorbacks ragged. With seven and one-half minutes left in the game, the Eagles led 69-55. Johnny Mills and Charlie Gibbons were virtually unstoppable. Then, with two minutes remaining Gibbons fouled out. The Razorbacks pushed their way back into the game and, in the final seconds, pulled out a 93-91 victory over the upstart Eagles. Arkansas fans and players agreed they were lucky to eke out a win that night. Eagles fans grieved the loss but took pride in the team's spectacular performance.[22]

The president appeared both omnipresent and indefatigable. He would leave an afternoon faculty meeting and attend a reception for a retiree. Then he would take off his jacket, roll up his sleeves, and cheer on the Eagles at a basketball game that evening. He sat in the audience when guest lecturers visited. If the speaker happened to mention American or English literature, the president usually asked a probing question. He encouraged faculty members to send him copies of their recently published articles and books. He would read each work and usually respond with a telephone call or personal letter.

Perrin Eidson, the president's wife, loved to entertain guests. The couple frequently invited faculty and local residents into their home for a meal, followed by friendly discussions. The Eidsons welcomed, especially, international students. Seeking to enlarge and enhance this small segment of student life, President Eidson appointed Harris Mobley as the first foreign student advisor. Mobley organized receptions for international students. The Eidsons usually dropped by and chatted eagerly with those interesting young people.

Mobley, a professor of sociology and former foreign missionary, supported the president's effort to increase foreign student enrollment: "We started with about a dozen, and before long we had forty or fifty. Dr. Eidson insisted I go to seminars and national meetings of foreign student advisors, and he paid travel expenses out of the presidential budget." Mobley reported to the president.[23] In time international students increased from the dozens to the hundreds.

VICE CHANCELLOR EIDSON, PRESIDENT DUNCAN

At the July meeting of the Board of Regents in 1971, Chancellor Simpson recommended President Eidson as Vice-Chancellor. The move took President Eidson by surprise. Some faculty and staff thought the chancellor was easing the president into retirement. Another theory, unproven, suggested Eidson had been too zealous to advance Georgia Southern to the university level. More likely, the university system needed his talents in Atlanta. Whatever the reason for his elevation, the campus and community agreed he had put the college on track for a brighter future.

John O. Eidson Alumni House

John and Perrin Eidson were the second and last presidential couple to live in the president's residence on the corner of Herty Drive and Georgia Avenue.

On Friday, April 28, 1995, President Nicholas Henry and Vice President for Development, Perk Robins, conducted a ceremony to name the John O. Eidson Alumni House. President and Mrs. Eidson lived there from 1968 until 1971, after which it was remodeled and used as offices for development and university relations. In 2005, the estate of Mrs. Perrin Eidson augmented an earlier scholarship fund she had established, making $845,598 available to support annually eighty-four scholarships for honors students.

Eagle kidnapped, once again

"This past week the Eagle was confiscated from atop its perch facing U.S. 301. The theft of this austere aviary was first brought to our attention by a member of the *George-Anne* Editorial Board. The Board member was in the process of gathering information concerning how to make the entrances to our campus attractive."

George-Anne,
10 October 1969

Eidson demonstrated that a self-confessed "old fashioned academic" was capable of grappling with complex issues of change. He was far more than engaged in his tasks. In three short years he had given the college a major makeover. He implemented a solid structure, and it could be expanded. As Georgia Southern grew in the eighties and nineties, the schools he created became colleges, but his plan remained intact. John Olin Eidson, in three action-packed years, gave Georgia Southern a framework for progress.

Chancellor George Simpson met with Vice President Duncan before the regents had announced their decision to make President Eidson vice chancellor. Simpson told Duncan he wanted him to succeed Eidson as president.[24] He realized, of course, that Duncan's vice presidential role had enhanced his marketability as a presidential candidate.

Search committees at Augusta College and West Georgia College recently had considered Duncan as a potential president. A Baptist minister, Duncan was a viable candidate for presidential appointments at denominational colleges. During the summer of 1971, Meredith College in North Carolina, a woman's college, had placed Duncan on its list of presidential finalists.

The chancellor's advisory committee, headed by Clair Colvin, chairman of the Chemistry Department, favorably reviewed Duncan's performance as vice president. Committee members assumed he would serve as acting president while they reviewed other candidates during the fall of 1971. On September 8, the chancellor came to the campus and informed the committee Meredith College had made an offer that Duncan said he would accept or decline on that very day.

The committee met immediately and advised the chancellor Pope Duncan should be named the eighth president of Georgia Southern College. His family had planned to celebrate his birthday on the evening of September 8, 1971. They also celebrated his new position at the college.[25]

THE DUNCAN DISCIPLINE

President Duncan had been John Eidson's vice-president from 1968 until 1971. His major task was to follow through with projects they had planned, including the construction of a new library. The former dean of the School Arts and Sciences, Nicholas Quick, became vice president. The new team maintained the momentum of the Eidson administration—not a small task.

Representing the Georgia Humanities Council, formed in 1971, President Duncan encouraged faculty to apply for grants designed for the general public in the region. A number of professors of literature, history, and sociology conducted projects involving thousands of citizens in seminars, field trips, and group discussions.

A fellow member of the council, James W. Fanning, suggested Duncan should offer the campus as headquarters for the eastern district of the Cooperative Extension Service of the University of Georgia. This strategic move, Duncan believed, encouraged the Board of Regents to approve a continuing education center, because the new facility would support the extension service. The former vice president proved he knew how to move the college forward.

During Duncan's presidency, new academic leaders energized the students and faculty. Warren F. "Spike" Jones, an administrator at the University of Louisville, became dean of the School of Arts and Sciences in 1972. Known for his humor and intellectual breadth, Jones encouraged interdisciplinary projects and dialogue. He led a large, diverse, and productive faculty during the next two decades. Dean of the Business School, Paul LaGrone, who since 1962 had transformed the division of business into a school, resumed his successful career in the accounting classroom. Origen James, a professor of accounting, became dean and led the school through the final steps toward accreditation by the Association to Advance Collegiate Schools of Business.

Duncan brought a discipline to his work that paid dividends in the local community. With the help of Ric Mandes, director of public relations, he made time in his schedule for three kinds of activities under code names: *Community*, *Downtown*, and *At Random*. Secretary Kirbylene Stephens arranged the president's schedule accordingly.

Community referred to updates, "a quarterly campus visit by citizens from other towns and cities located near the campus. These people came in mid-morning; I talked to them for a while about the college. Then they were taken on tours . . . Finally I hosted a luncheon for them as a kind of follow-up during which they had opportunity to make comments and ask questions." [26]

Downtown simply reminded him to schedule an occasional morning for walking the streets of Statesboro and visiting merchants and offices. "We planned very carefully which businesses I would call upon, and I would spend a few minutes with the owner or manager talking about the college and making him realize that we felt that he was very important to the success of the college. I also hosted a monthly breakfast meeting with young community leaders and campus representatives." [27]

At Random referred to a practice of randomly selecting students who would meet with the president's administrative council. Duncan thought mainstream students could express concerns that elected student leaders overlooked.

Residents of southeast Georgia in the twenty-first century still marvel that the college hosted legendary comedian Bob Hope twice. President Duncan set into motion the appearances for two reasons: First, to give the college greater visibility in the state and region. Second, to raise funds for the Georgia Southern Foundation. He was successful on both counts.

PRESIDENT POPE ALEXANDER DUNCAN

President Duncan had been a Baptist minister and professor of theology until 1964, when he began a four-year career in junior colleges, serving as the first dean of Brunswick Junior College and President of South Georgia College. At Georgia Southern, his three years of service as vice president prepared him for his duties as president.

Bob Hope performs at Hanner

Telling a locally popular joke, Ric Mandes, *left*, warms up Bob Hope, *right*, before his performance on April 7, 1972. Athletic Director J. I. Clements, *center*, listens.

Bob Hope returned later to enthusiastic audiences in Hanner Fieldhouse. Both performances benefited the Georgia Southern College Foundation.

The world-famous comedian first visited in 1972, after Director of Alumni Development Gene Crawford made arrangements with Hope's agent.

A one-day fundraiser, A Day for Southern, *began as* Pull for Southern *in 1971, an idea of architect Edwin Eckles. In 1973 the Georgia Southern Foundation changed the name to* A Day for Southern. *Volunteers raised $15 thousand. On September 12, 2006, they collected $1.27 million.*

Why the president made the college two years older

Since the beginning, local college officials set the first day of classes as the beginning of college history – February 5, 1908. During the summer of 1971, president-elect Duncan asked the regents to change Georgia Southern's founding date to 1906.

Many faculty members remembered commemorating the year 1908 during the college's fiftieth anniversary in 1958. Class rings and diplomas all bore the mark of 1908. Nevertheless, President Duncan won the argument technically. The Regents approved the change, and he authorized a painter to change the date on highway signs. When upperclassmen arrived to start the fall quarter in 1971, they noticed their college had grown two years older overnight.

President Eidson initiated a fund-raising program in 1970, "Spirit of Southern." Then Everett Williams chaired the foundation and Francis Allen headed the campaign effort. One goal was to match the federal student loan program, but the effort had a larger meaning: to "move Georgia Southern forward and upward toward university status over the next few years." [28]

By 1973 the fundraiser went by the name of "A Day for Southern." After providing direct mail and local news stories about the impact of the college on the community, volunteers canvassed the county and campus for one day only, and assembled to review their total receipts. At the end of the day, in 1973, volunteers on campus and in the community had received donations and pledges amounting to nearly $15,000.

The Eidson-Duncan administration developed the college's public relations efforts. Director Ric Mandes hired a former *Reflector* editor, Gordon Turner, who had assisted with President Eidson's inauguration. Turner organized a professional publications program. Duncan wanted to generate more news, and he found funds for Ric Mandes to hire a writer. Claude Felton turned out excellent articles about the college for several years before taking a position at the University of Georgia, where he became the sports information director and associate director of athletics.

A TIME TO PLAY

During the fall semester of 1973, "streaking" swept across college campuses in America. The singer Ray Stevens gave listeners a hit record, "The Streak." The fad enlivened a variety of public events, including the nationally televised Academy Awards on April 2, 1974. That year, a naked man streaked behind co-host David Niven. About that time police arrested two streaking Memphis State football players, charging them with public indecency.

The normally quiet campus buzzed with anticipation, with everyone wondering what would happen if streakers descended upon Sweetheart Circle. Anxiety gripped the campus on a spring evening in 1974. On March 6 a large group of naked young men, with towels wrapped around their heads, romped across the front lawn of the campus. No one seemed alarmed that campus policemen did not pursue Southern's streakers. [29]

Both gratified and emboldened, the informal band of fleet-footed men gathered in a dormitory and plotted a future streak involving a larger number of streakers. Some female students sent word they were interested in participating in a rare, if not unique, coeducational streak. The moment of truth arrived on March 7, 1974.

An informant tipped off the campus police chief, Harold Howell. Instead of orchestrating a mass arrest, however, Chief Howell decided to let the young people enjoy themselves. He blocked off Georgia Avenue from

Chandler Road to Herty Drive and instructed officers to intervene only if the crowd became unruly.

The long-awaited event began at dusk on Georgia Avenue. Alumnus David Thompson rushed out of his dormitory to observe the huge throng of students in a state of watchfulness. They stood on the sidewalks and lawns from the Foy Fine Arts Building to Landrum Center.

"There were literally thousands of students spilling over into Georgia Avenue, and there was a corridor through the middle of the students. Streakers and people would pass through that corridor, moving from Chandler toward Herty. Some of them were running, some of them on bicycles, some of them in backs of trucks, some on motorcycles. All were naked. The streakers were mostly men, but there were some women. I recall one poor guy that fell off his bicycle. The crowd picked him up, cheered him, and sent him on his way."[30]

As the finale, four males and one female streaked up a ladder to the roof of Landrum Center and treated the spectators to a well-rehearsed chorus-line dance routine. The female danced in the center, and two males danced on each side of her, Thompson recalled. The crowds cheered, and campus policemen smiled.

This event ended the mass, coeducational streaking episode at Georgia Southern College. Later in 1974-75, lone streakers appeared infrequently at baseball and basketball games. Within a few years campus folklore kept alive the bizarre tales.

CONFRONTING CRISES, DEALING WITH DISAPPOINTMENTS

Duncan revealed his approach to administrative matters at Georgia Southern in his *Memoirs of a Peripatetic Educator*. He wrote the volume between 1987 and 1997, after he retired as president of Stetson University.

As president at GSC, Pope Duncan experienced a number of events as crises he tried to resolve in a positive manner. He recalled some division chairmen and staff members were incompetent, and he replaced them. He mentioned a faculty member who "lambasted" him, but later followed the president's advice productively. A labor organizer from "the North" sowed dissension among cafeteria employees. Duncan defused a potential crisis by meeting with the workers and dealing with their complaints.

Black workers found it difficult to provide for their families at an hourly wage of $1.75. They asked for $2.00. They also requested that experienced black employees be considered for supervisory positions. Another concern was the firing of a black employee named Junius Reed without due cause. The employees asked the college to hire at least one black professor. While

Charles "Cholly" Robbins believed the Pull for Southern *campaign should limit local college fundraising to one day each year. He suggested a new name,* A Day for Southern, *for the 1973 campaign. In 1975, chairman Robbins, left, presented President Duncan a check for a record $60,000 from local contributors.*

streak•ing

"the act or practice of running naked through a public place"

Webster's Third New International Dictionary, Unabridged, (2002) s.v. "streaking."

The Naked Truth: A President Remembers

"The first streaker we had was a young man who, in a state of undress, somehow got through the outfield fence during a baseball game and streaked across to the opposite fence and disappeared through it. The next I remember occurred when I was entertaining guests in the President's Dining Room in the Williams Center. We heard much noise in the hall, later to find that a streaker or streakers . . . had run through the building to the delight of many other students. The climax came one evening when I, fortunately, was in Atlanta for a meeting of the Advisory council the next day."

Pope A. Duncan,
Memoirs of a Peripatetic Educator, 207

Harold Howell,
director of public safety

Howell dealt thoughtfully with students during the days of teach-ins, demonstrations, and streaking. He had learned how to deal with crisis situations when he twice served as Sheriff of Bulloch County. He said he realized the fad quickly would vanish. He urged college officials not to overreact. On the night of March 7, 1974, Howell simply closed the campus to traffic and allowed the youth to streak "until they got it out of their system." Almost as quickly as it came to campus, streaking left and became a memory that made Harold Howell smile in his later years. He was director of public safety from 1965–1988.

the college did not reinstate Reed, it gave the workers a raise and pledged to hire supervisors and faculty without considering the applicant's race.

Duncan gave credit to the "great negotiating ability" of Vice President Nicholas Quick who "served him well." On both critical and routine matters, he acknowledged the tireless work of his able secretary, Kirbylene Stephens.[31] He also credited William Cook, who during the 1974-75 academic year, became the college's first director of administration and fiscal affairs, a position Duncan had hoped would be at the vice presidential level.

President Duncan confidently predicted that the college would continue the growth trend that began in the late 1950s. He popularized the slogan "7,500 by '75." He was disappointed when the enrollment for 1973-74 actually declined by 260 students to 5,921. The Board of Regents had authorized graduate studies at Armstrong State College and Augusta College, thereby shrinking Georgia Southern's pool of graduate students.

Actions by the chancellor's office and Board of Regents sometimes disappointed him. Chancellor Simpson asked Duncan to serve as chairman of a committee to consider "the possibility of testing all undergraduates in the University System at some point in their careers with a common instrument." Duncan reported his committee did not favor this approach, "believing it contained more problems than advantages."

WALKOUT, MORE DEMANDS

On March 24, 1972, while President Duncan was planning his inauguration, thirty-eight black employees walked off the job, leaving Landrum Dining Hall without a staff of cooks and custodians. The workers protested low wages ($1.75 per hour) and the firing of a fellow employee, Junius Reed. They asked for a raise of .25 cents an hour, a hearing for Mr. Reed, and a more positive attitude toward minorities. The college should hire at least one black faculty member and should recruit more black students, they maintained. The president, *standing in front,* assigned Vice President Nicholas Quick to negotiate a settlement, which he did.

Duncan honestly reported the committee's recommendation against this form of testing. "Obviously, our conclusion was not that which the Chancellor had wanted, and he proceeded to give us a dressing down, an attack primarily directed at me . . . At any rate, he ignored the recommendation of the committee and proceeded to have a rising junior test developed and implemented in the System." President Duncan wrote that, although he doubted the efficacy of the "rising junior" test, he believed it served a "useful political purpose."[32]

President Duncan also resisted the chancellor's plan to introduce remedial work or "special studies" designed to assist students who were unprepared academically for college life. He believed junior colleges could handle these students' needs more readily than senior colleges. Duncan believed the chancellor's program, "handed down from above," succeeded mainly in "padding of enrollments." With a sense of relief, he wrote in 1997: "it is being phased out of the senior University system units at this time."[33]

Perhaps the most difficult moment in his presidency came when he again had to notify the faculty that the State of Georgia would not provide faculty members with a salary increase in 1976-77. The previous year faculty members in the University System had filed a suit against the state for canceling raises. Faculty morale plummeted when the college reduced its operating budget, due to decreased funding. The cut came when the college had enrolled 6,252 students, the largest number in its history.

An issue continued to nag President Duncan throughout his presidency: the failure of the college to offer a doctorate in education. Both he and his predecessor, John Eidson, were convinced the chancellor had promised the doctorate. He recalled discussing the matter with the chancellor:

Toward the end of my tenure, I asked the Chancellor why he had never submitted our requests to the Board. The Chancellor's answer went something like this, 'Pope, had you rather have the proposal be alive or have it submitted, turned down, and dead?' Of course, I had to reply that I had rather have it alive. This confirmed a point of view that I had held for some time. . . . [The chancellor knew] he could not get such a proposal through the board. This was the only explanation for his having backtracked on what we all understood was a commitment to Dr. Eidson. . . .

This was not a surprising development when an examination of the individual regents' college experiences would show that a large majority of them attended a university level institution of the system. Thus the opposition, which would come to such a proposal from those institutions, would be of considerable influence upon these Regents.[34]

He recalled, especially, the reason the chancellor did not approve Duncan's request to name William Cook as vice president of fiscal affairs: "Pope, if I let you do that, I'll have to let all of the senior colleges do the same." Duncan reflected: "I never did buy that answer. . . . None of the other senior colleges, certainly, had the enrollment Georgia Southern had or the complexity of operation that Georgia Southern had." Duncan also learned the chancellor did not want to give him the title of vice president, but he did so reluctantly, "in a moment of weakness," because he respected John Eidson.[35]

CHARLES WESLEY BONDS
First African American faculty member

In 1972 Charles Bonds became an instructor in the Right to Read program, funded by a grant. After completing his service, Dean Starr Miller invited him to accept a faculty position in the School of Education. Encouraged by the dean, Bonds earned a doctoral degree at the University of Florida in 1979. Until his retirement in 1996, Bonds taught reading and other education classes. His wife, Lella Theresa Gantt Bonds, also earned her doctorate and taught in the Marvin Pittman Laboratory School and the School of Education. A community leader and author, Bonds won numerous elections to the Bulloch County Board of Education.

WILLIAM COOK
President Duncan appointed William "Bill" Cook as director of administration and fiscal affairs. In 1979 the position carried the title vice president for business and finance.

GEORGE COOK

President Duncan had worked with Athletics Director George Cook at South Georgia College. Following the death of J. I. Clements, Duncan hired Cook. The new A.D.'s first crisis was to find a replacement for the NCAA Coach of the Year, Ron Polk. Cook hired Jack Stallings, *below,* former coach at Florida State University, who firmly established Georgia Southern as a consistent winner of conference baseball titles.

JACK STALLINGS

Duncan believed Georgia Southern suffered, because the university system operated according to a hierarchical perception: at the top were the universities in Atlanta and Athens. The senior and junior colleges belonged to a lower category. This view, Duncan believed, failed to account for Georgia Southern's service to the region, its academic advancement, and its growing student body.[36]

President Duncan believed members of the Board of Regents were outstanding individuals with divided loyalties. On the one hand, they ably supported higher education statewide. On the other hand, he believed, they tended to protect the domains of their alma maters, typically universities in North Georgia. Because Georgia Southern alumni rarely became regents, Duncan argued, the system likely would not represent the college's best interests. (Marvin Pittman made this identical observation after he retired.)

In 1976-77, Pope Duncan regretted losing several outstanding coaches: Ron Polk, the baseball coach who in 1973 led the baseball team to a sixth place finish in the College World Series; J. E. Rowe, former Eagle star and an excellent basketball coach, resigned. Ron Roberts, who led the golf team to national rankings in Division I, moved to Wake Forest. The loss of Polk especially distressed Duncan, because he was the first Georgia Southern coach to be named "Coach of the Year" in Division I of the NCAA.

The college gained a new athletics director. George Cook replaced J. I. Clements who died during heart surgery on October 24, 1974. Duncan believed Cook had been an outstanding athletics director at South Georgia College. He also lauded Cook for being "the only person in athletics that I have ever known who could stay within a budget!"[37] Soon Cook hired the former coach at Florida State University, Jack Stallings, who helped Georgia Southern maintain its national reputation for excellence in baseball. In 2005 the Board of Regents authorized the naming of the baseball field in honor of Jack Stallings who coached the team from 1975 until 1999.

GREEK WEEK & DERBY DAYS

After national fraternities and sororities organized in 1968, members did more than stress community service and academic success. Young men and women created special moments for fun and games, called Greek Week and Derby Days.

These events featured athletic contests and comical events, such as greased pole climbing, *left;* games of tag, *right;* tricycle races, *middle right;* and tug-of-war tournaments, *far right.* Traditionally the losing tug team ended up in the campus lake.

Duncan's last year at Georgia Southern, 1976-77, in his words, was a "Year of Recovery." He and his wife Margaret hosted the artist Lamar Dodd, their friend of years past at the University of Georgia. He came to open an exhibit with Roxie Remley in a gallery of the renovated Rosenwald Library, one year after the new library opened.

Margaret Duncan had kept up her spirits by writing a column for the *Statesboro Herald*, and she also continued to write poems that eventually appeared in book form.[38] Their daughters, Mary Margaret, Laurie, and Kathy, all were involved in visual arts to varying degrees. Laurie already had married a local young man, Bill Kelly, son of Statesboro's musical legend, Emma Kelly.[39]

Furman University, a Baptist college in Greenville, South Carolina, had contacted Duncan about a presidential appointment in 1975, and he interviewed for the position. When the president of Stetson University accepted the presidency of Furman in 1976, a vacancy appeared at the school he had loved since he taught religious studies there in the late 1940s and early 1950s. He eagerly became a candidate for the position.

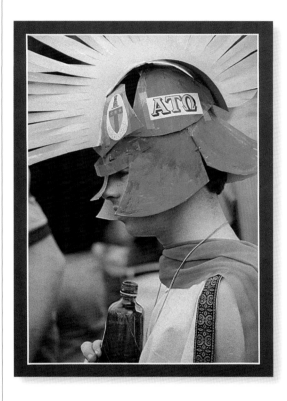

He accepted the presidency of Stetson University in DeLand, Florida, beginning in the fall of 1977. Pope Alexander Duncan ended his tenure at Georgia Southern College on July 15, 1977. The eighth president of Georgia Southern became the seventh president at Stetson, serving that institution until his retirement in 1987, when he became Chancellor—a position he held until 2002. As president and chancellor, he also was chief fundraiser. Within ten years he increased the endowment at Stetson from less than $6 million to nearly $100 million. Stetson published his memoirs in 2005, two years after his death on December 18, 2003. Three of the volume's twenty-six chapters deal with his nine years as vice president and president of Georgia Southern. He called this section of his book "The Good Years."

GEORGIA SOUTHERN COLLEGE
1977-1986

1978 – Recently appointed President Dale Lick tours campus and says he favors university status for GSC. (1/12)

1978 – On his first day at his new job, President Lick asks permission from the Board of Regents to begin a nursing program for undergraduates. (7/1)

1978 – Hal Averitt announces *A Day for Southern* raised $65,000. (9/18)

1978 – The last part of I-16 opens, completing the 165 mile interstate highway from Savannah to Macon. (9/22)

1978 – Noting the college had only one black faculty member, President Lick appoints sociologist Harris Mobley as affirmative action officer. (11/1)

1978 – Alumnus Darwin Humphrey, a.k.a. Don Harris of *NBC News*, is killed while reporting a congressional investigation of the Jim Jones cult in Guyana. (11/20)

1979 – Movie star John Wayne dies. (6/11)

1980 – President Lick appoints committee to study the feasibility of renewing football as an intercollegiate sport. (10/30)

1980 – Former Beatle John Lennon dies in New York City after being shot in front of his apartment complex. (12/8)

1981 – U.S. hostages are freed in Iran after 444 days of captivity; Ronald Reagan becomes president of the U.S. (1/20)

1981 – After failing by one vote to fire President Lick, the Board of Regents reprimands him for improperly advocating new programs. (6/9)

1981 – Erk Russell and President Lick hold press conference in Hanner Fieldhouse, announcing Russell's decision to become head football coach at Georgia Southern. (5/23)

1982 – World's first artificial heart given to American Barney Clark in an operation in Salt Lake City, Utah. (12/02)

1982 – Regent Erwin Friedman announces the Board of Regents had determined the State of Georgia did not need additional universities. (12/28)

1983 – Astronaut Sally Ride is first American woman to travel into space. (6/18)

1983 – Gordon Alston, GSC financial aid officer, is appointed first black member of the County Commission. (6/21)

1983 – Lech Walesa, Polish Solidarity leader, is awarded the Nobel Peace Prize. (10/05)

1984 – Tornado strikes Bulloch County, injuring twenty-eight people and damaging homes and stores, but campus escapes major damage. (5/3)

1984 – On September 29, 1984, the Georgia Southern Eagles played their first Division I-AA home game in Paulson Stadium, defeating Liberty College 48-11. Attendance was 12,097. (9/29)

1984 – Fourteen campus buildings have asbestos contamination removed. (2/1)

1984 – Ronald Reagan wins re-election in the presidential election. (11/06)

1985 – Zach Suddath Henderson who was dean (1927-1948) and president (1948–1968) dies in Statesboro. (1/6)

1985 – British musician Bob Geldof organizes Live Aid, featuring concerts in London and Philadelphia, raising funds for famine relief in Africa. (7/13)

1985 – Eagles win first NCAA I-AA national football championship, defeating Furman University 44-42 in Tacoma, Washington's Diamond Bowl. (12/21)

1985 – Rotary Foundation Summer Language Institute for international students completes tenth and final year at GSU, directed by Jack N. Averitt and faculty from the English department. A total of 1,510 students from nations across the globe studied here. (8/10)

1986 – Eagles repeat as NCAA I-AA national football champions, beating Arkansas State 48-21 at the Diamond Bowl in Tacoma, Washington. (12/20)

1986 – U.S. space shuttle Challenger explodes in the sky after take-off at Cape Canaveral, killing all seven crew members on board. (1/28)

1986 – Dale Lick appointed president of the University of Maine. Vice President Harry Carter is acting president. (9/1)

Toward a Regional University

THE WHOLE WATERMELON

The chancellor released the names of the presidential search committee on June 3, six weeks before President Duncan's departure. Leo Parrish, chairman of the management department, assembled the twenty-five members in the summer of 1977. He was unaware of the event's historical significance: Never before had the college conducted a national search for a president.

Since its inception in 1932, The Board of Regents had selected independently the presidents from Marvin Pittman through Zach Henderson. The chancellor used "advisory committees" to assist with the nominations of his preferred candidates: John Eidson and Pope Duncan. Both men lived up to the chancellor's expectations.

When the chancellor met for the first time with members of the committee, he brought no list of preferences. He said he wanted the committee to conduct a wide-open search. Newelle Anderson, representing the alumni, asked a question on everyone's mind: "Shouldn't we look for somebody with experience managing a university, since that is what Georgia Southern needs to become?"

Chancellor Simpson replied with unmistakable body language: he walked toward the exit door, telling the astonished committee he did not come to Statesboro to discuss university status. Then he suggested members could ask the Board of Regents to rule, once and for all, on this issue. Then they would know precisely the institution's future. Implying the move was fraught with grave risks, the chancellor said he could go back to Atlanta and await the committee's recommendation.[1]

Chairman Parrish urged the chancellor to remain in the room and allow the committee to begin its work. The chancellor returned to his chair and put the stub of a cigar into the corner of his mouth. Then someone asked him what kind of leader the committee should seek. The chancellor, chomping his cigar, responded with the watermelon story:

A man with a huge watermelon in the back of his pick-up truck told some good old boys at the country store: 'I'll bet you five dollars you can't eat this here watermelon.' When nobody accepted the wager, a small boy on a bicycle spoke up: 'I think I can, mister. Let me go home, first, and I'll come back and let you know.' The boy came back, ate the watermelon, rind and all, and collected the five dollars. As the man gave him the money, he asked the boy why he went back home, before he accepted the wager. The boy replied: 'We had one about that size at home, so I ate it, just to be sure I could do it.'[2]

DALE WESLEY LICK

At the age of twenty-seven, Lick earned his PhD in mathematics from the University of California. After three years as a professor and research consultant, based at the University of Tennessee, he began his administrative career. Drexel University invited him to move to Philadelphia to become head of the mathematics department. Soon he moved to Troy, New York, where he became vice-president of academic affairs at Russell Sage College.

His next move was southward: Norfolk, Virginia. At Old Dominion University, a doctoral level research institution, he served as Dean of Sciences and Health Professions. There he organized a set of health programs that professionals held in high regard.

NICHOLAS QUICK

Georgia Southern's first dean of the School of Arts and Sciences, Nicholas "Nick" Quick, succeeded Pope Duncan as vice president. Quick served as acting president for ten months between the administrations of Pope Duncan and Dale Lick.

CHARLES J. AUSTIN

Like President Lick, Vice President Austin had a background in mathematics and health science. He served Georgia Southern until 1982 when he became president of East Texas State University.

The chancellor summarized the moral of the story: "Find someone who can eat the whole watermelon." Committee members filed away the story as they began their work. Actually, two search committees worked simultaneously.

Uncertain about how the process would unfold, the chancellor formed a "shadow committee" of three regents to monitor the work of the twenty-five. The three reviewed reports and randomly picked up information about the committee's activities, both first and second hand. At times the chancellor's arrangement proved cumbersome, but the twenty-five operated quickly and efficiently.

Eventually the committee invited six highly qualified candidates to the campus, and several of them later found leadership positions at major universities. The Board of Regents appointed the candidate at the top of the search committee's list on January 11, 1978, less than six months after Pope Duncan vacated the office. His name was Dale Wesley Lick, a dean at Old Dominion University. The committee believed the forty-year-old native of Michigan would pass the chancellor's watermelon test.

UNLEASHING POTENTIAL

A scientist on the faculty at Old Dominion asked Lick why he would "go to a sleepy little college like Georgia Southern?" Lick told him he didn't see the college in Statesboro as "sleepy" at all. Lick said "I came down and looked at it, and what I saw was tremendous potential being bottled up and held back. If you can free it, lots of wonderful things can be done."

For twelve years as a young professional, Lick had developed a philosophy of education. By the time he arrived in Statesboro, he could speak off the cuff about something more important, his philosophy of life: "My core belief is a commitment to the worth and dignity of people." He said that fundamental concept "had become very personal to me—that all people have worth and we should treat them with dignity—young, old, black, white, handicap, non-handicap, whatever . . . We are not here to serve ourselves . . . but we are here to serve others and to enhance the quality of life."[3]

During his first visit to campus on January 12, 1978, he answered the question of the hour: "Yes," he said, "I think Georgia Southern should become a university." He would visit the campus and correspond with the college officials during the next six months, as he completed his assignment in Virginia. During the interim, Vice President Nicholas Quick served as acting president. The new president complimented Vice President Quick: "He made some hard decisions which saved me problems when I got here. . . . He was extremely sympathetic."[4]

Lick was both astonished and delighted to read the annual report for 1997-98 to Chancellor Simpson. Nicholas Quick reviewed the college's previous twelve months in four typewritten pages, double-spaced—an all-time record for brevity in a field known for verbosity.[5]

One new building had appeared—a new infirmary. Quick reminded the chancellor the continuing education center, approved by the Board of Regents, was desperately needed and should be built as soon as possible.

Another important development for the campus, Quick told the chancellor, was an innovative legal entity, a nonprofit 501 (c) 3 corporation, Southern Greek Housing Corporation. The governing authority consisted of representatives each fraternity, sorority and the college. The group acquired twenty seven acres of land adjoining the campus in 1977-78. The corporation restricted the property for large Greek houses. Members could solicit tax deductible donations that were intended for "academic portions" of the structures. Associate Dean of Students, James D. Orr was the first president of the Corporation.[6] In 2006 the property, known as Olympic Boulevard, was an attractive village of large and well-designed fraternity and sorority houses.

Quick, an English professor and lawyer, returned to the classroom and later practiced law. Lick found an able replacement that communicated well with faculty and proved proficient in curriculum planning: Charles J. Austin, who had an academic background in mathematics, health science, and social studies. Austin served as vice president for academic affairs until 1982.

As Lick spoke at civic clubs in southeastern Georgia, his audiences expressed overwhelming support for making Georgia Southern the state's first university in South Georgia. Lick then began to introduce his concept of a future Georgia Southern University. During question-and-answer sessions afterwards, "two questions always came up," Lick said, "nursing and football." Lick accepted these queries positively, and he answered in kind: "I'm working on both ideas, and I'll be back in touch."

The search committee knew Lick had been dean of a major component of a regional university. At the time, however, most members of the faculty did not realize the implications of Lick's regional vision.

Presidents Eidson and Duncan, as well as Vice President Quick, had studied and taught in liberal arts institutions. Naturally, they made decisions based on their experiences and assumptions. Furthermore, the largest number of faculty at Georgia Southern held appointments in the School of Arts and Sciences. They shared familiar, sometimes subjective, aspirations about the future of the college.

Lick realized the nature of the problem when he met with deans, directors, and department heads: "Some of my top people fought me on the regional university. They wanted to back off and become a liberal arts institution. But that didn't fit what I thought that region desperately needed. The people needed a regional university to serve their needs."[7]

President Lick officially began his career at Georgia Southern on July 1, 1978, with his wife, Marilyn, and four children. Their children, all school age, were Lynette, Kitty, Diana and Ron.

On September 15, 1978, he spoke to the faculty for the first time. Earnestly, honestly, and self-effacingly, he spoke. For two hours he spoke, and

Lick's story, King of the Jungle

"One day a lion ran through the jungle, feeling frisky. He came upon a monkey and asked: 'Who's the king of the jungle?' The frightened monkey replied, 'you are, sir.' Then the lion came upon a giraffe and asked, 'and who's the king of the jungle?' The skittish giraffe retreated and answered: 'you are, sir.' He continued his way through the jungle until he met an elephant. The lion looked up at the gray mass and growled: 'Who's the king of the jungle?' The elephant reached down with his trunk and slammed him into the ground. Before the lion could recover, the elephant again picked him up and slammed him into a tree. Then the groggy lion backed away, looking up at the elephant, saying: 'Look, just because you don't know the answer is no reason to get mad.'"

Dale W. Lick, Address to the Faculty,
15 September 1977

The Licks felt at home in Statesboro in 1977: left to right, *Kitty, Lynette, Ron, Marilyn, Dale, and Diana.*

Marilyn Lick and the sense of community

She always thought of herself as a cheerleader, a role she enjoyed in the Michigan high school where she met her husband, Dale. She was president of the Statesboro-Georgia Southern Symphony Association and was active in the Faculty Dames Club and other groups. On Sundays she and her husband led and ministered to church missions in Savannah and Augusta. *Below,* the Licks prepare a playing field for the first Family Fun Day in 1978.

A Tree at Christmas

Instead of sending Christmas cards to faculty and friends, the Licks planted a tree on campus, in consultation with the campus horticulturalist. The first tree planting took place in December of 1978, and the custom continues into the twenty-first century. The original tree at Christmas, a holly, stands near the Administration building, adjacent to the Builders of the University Terrace.

he did not ramble. He referred to the region's demographics, economics, and local traditions. He had been in town for ten weeks, but he reviewed issues as though he had lived in South Georgia for years.

Marvin Pittman and Guy Wells could have expressed those sentiments, perhaps more succinctly, but devoid of details. Lick, however, presented the faculty with "the whole watermelon." He communicated personally and with passion.

During this memorable maiden address, Lick introduced three specific initiatives he intended to pursue: increased faculty involvement, affirmative action, and a school of nursing.

The new president saw the issue of governance as "fundamentally a communications issue."[8] He told the assembled faculty a story they would hear often enough to commit to memory—"Who's the King of the Jungle?" He explained the moral of the story: "I will not know all the answers, and I hope you won't get mad. . . . It is very important that you do disagree with me. . . . But we need to work together with the same basic premises."[9]

Realizing the college foundation was in debt by $90,000, Dale Lick did what came naturally for him. He abandoned the traditional inaugural festivities and, with his wife, Marilyn, planned a picnic for faculty and staff, families included. The invitation appeared on green mimeograph paper:

Dale and Marilyn Lick

Cordially invite all faculty and staff members

And their families to the

Faculty/Staff Family Fall Frolics

Sunday, October 29, 1978

1:30 – 5:00 p.m.

Sports Complex

Activities for all ages • Goodies to eat • Haunted House

Organized and staffed by the Department of Recreation, the event drew a huge crowd. Members of the staff since the 1950s noted similarities to spring festivals at the old Teachers College. Men and women formed impromptu softball teams and played in games of three innings. Novices learned to toss horseshoes, play badminton and volley ball, and run three-legged races. At the end of the day, Marilyn Lick drew names for dozens of neat door prizes. The cost of the event was a fraction of an inauguration. The Licks instantly became symbols of a new kind of administration: down home, family-oriented, and sensibly frugal.[10] What the Licks thought would be a one-time event became a highly anticipated annual festival for several autumns.

Beginning his tenure with the GSC Foundation in debt, Lick dramatically expanded the *Day for Southern* local support program (from thousands to well over $1 million in 2006), implemented the college's first-ever major fundraising campaign, upgraded the development division, and organized a process for soliciting private support. Lick also personally encouraged faculty and staff to seek grants and contracts.

SEARCHING FOR THE ANSWER

The longest presidential address any faculty member could remember became the Lick administration's template. During the next eight years new academic programs, special projects, and athletic initiatives all began with assumptions about the "worth and dignity of people. Georgia Southern exists to serve people. Once we acknowledge this fact, our job becomes easier to visualize."

Lick emphasized he wanted a loyal faculty and staff. He said loyalty did not mean withholding personal judgment or blindly following presidential preferences. Colleagues should be loyal to the mission of the college—to serve people. Lick promised to respect each faculty member's commitment to his or her discipline. In general, observers reported, Lick lived up to his promise and tried to learn from those who honestly disagreed with him, and he "tended not to harbor grudges." [11]

Within a few months his management style revealed itself. He was hands-on and mind-on. He liked to communicate his vision personally, and he followed up his individual conversations with faculty and staff by writing afterthoughts on a pad he kept in his shirt pocket. These prescription-pad-sized notes reflected his thinking process. His cordial message typically included his response to an idea related to the recent conversation.

Lick realized he had a penchant for acting spontaneously and leading with passion. As a mathematician he knew that data ultimately rules the minds of those who make decisions. He observed an absence of data in the president's office. An academic advisory council reflected the collective wisdom of deans and a handful of faculty. The cordial council members made notoriously unrealistic projections about enrollment trends and needs of future students.

During his first year on the job, he began looking for presidential assistants who would focus on planning. Lick learned that a talented, young professor of management was considering leaving the college for another position. He realized Georgia Southern needed his expertise, so he asked the dean of the business school, Origen James, to discuss a new job with Harrison Sharpe Carter. Carter, nicknamed "Harry," used a statistical approach to management. In time he took charge of strategic planning.

Carter accepted and began methodically. He applied for and received a fellowship from the American Council on Education. For a year he worked as an understudy to President Lick, taking occasional trips to conferences at various institutions, including a pivotal seminar with the Rev. Theodore M. Hesburgh, President of Notre Dame. [12]

Searching for a symbol of excellence

Ben Dixon, director of Auxiliary Services, paid Pam N. Hagan of Winterville, Ga., $50 in 1974 for rights to use an image of the GSC Eagle for promotions and merchandise.

"© 1974 by Georgia Southern College."

In 1981 President Lick formed a committee to recommend a logo that could represent the larger aspirations of the college in a positive and dignified manner—Linda Smillie (chair), Steve Batson, Sharon Fell, Wendell Hagins, Hank Schomber, and John Parcels. Earlier Mr. Roy Parcels of Dixon & Parcels Associates, New York, had contacted President Lick, and the committee chose to hire the firm. The result was a circular eagle logo, incorporating traditional colors of blue and white with the accent color of gold. The fee, considered reasonable at $19,000, did not include payments to a patent and trademark attorney.

On April 7, 1982, Georgia Southern adopted the logo and established rules and fees for its use by vendors. However, Pam Hagan's cartoon eagle also continued to be used for informal purposes.

Along with the logo, Georgia Southern adopted a motto, *Academic Excellence* and a type face for both the motto and *Georgia Southern*.

MICAL WHITAKER

Mical Whitaker comes home

Mical Whitaker, a theatre director and producer from New York, happened to be visiting his ailing mother in Metter in 1981. Harris Mobley told the president about him. The president talked with Whitaker and asked: "Would you consider coming back home permanently and joining our faculty?"

The sudden offer took Mical by surprise. He had no academic abbreviations to attach to his name. As an undergraduate at Howard University he rose to the top quickly as a student and moved to New York for advanced study. He won awards for directing Ossie Davis and Ruby Dee and for directing plays on the New York stage, at Lincoln Center, and in the Black Theatre festival.

President Lick reassured him that successful theatrical experience was the equivalent of an academic degree. Whitaker could take additional courses, if necessary, Lick said. It was an easy sell, because he really wanted to live near his mother at that time in her life. Convincing the faculty was more difficult, and Lick eventually funded a new faculty position designed for the successful young director.

In 1981, Lick recalled, Mical Whitaker became the third black faculty member. And what did students think of Mical Whitaker? They flocked to his classes and helped him breathe new life into theatre at Georgia Southern. Professional actors and directors—his former students—joined faculty and friends who honored him at his retirement on April 23, 2005.

The college never before had pursued a viable plan for facilities. Carter and a strategic planning committee established criteria, based on growth trends of schools and departments, as well as the existing physical facility. The council's work influenced profoundly a document President Lick would present to the Board of Regents on November 11, 1980: "A Perspective on Higher Education in Georgia."

After Carter became vice president for academic affairs in early 1982, Owen Gaede, a professor in the School of Education and assistant to the president, became chairman of an enlarged Strategic Planning Council. Gaede realized the importance of computers for teaching and institutional research. His council applied statistical research methods to the college's academic programs and public services. Gaede soon realized the importance of the question "Why?" Like most institutions, the college had programs and procedures in place, simply because "that's the way we've always done it." Gaede became inseparable from President Lick who championed change.

When individuals or departments advocated new programs or changes in existing programs, Gaede and Lick discussed the impact on quality. Typically, the president wanted to know whether the innovations would enhance academic excellence. In time that question led to a new motto for the college: *Academic Excellence.* The words became attached to the "new" Georgia Southern, symbolized by the familiar logo.[13]

AFFIRMATIVE ACTION AND ACADEMIC EXCELLENCE

Within a few weeks after beginning his work in Statesboro, Lick met with the regent from Savannah, Erwin Friedman, who told him: "You have the most lily white campus in the whole university system. It is a legal problem, and you need to do something about it."[14]

The college community was familiar with the concept of affirmative action and Title Seven of the Civil Rights Act. Before Lick arrived in Georgia, Regent Friedman had offered a proposal to satisfy federal desegregation requirements. He advocated merging historically black Savannah State College with two predominantly white colleges—Savannah's Armstrong College and Statesboro's Georgia Southern. The new entity, Friedman argued, would satisfy Title VII's requirement to offer equal opportunities to all students and faculty, regardless of race.

Like most observers, Lick believed Friedman's proposal to merge Statesboro's campus with the two smaller colleges in Savannah would not solve the problem. Nevertheless, the new president agreed Georgia Southern had a real problem on its hands. It was not a legal problem, he said, but a moral one.

Lick proposed an office of affirmative action. Then he did the unexpected: he asked a white professor to become the college's first affirmative action officer. "Everyone expected me to bring in a black administrator to handle this 'black' problem. But we did not have a 'black' problem," Lick said, "We had a 'white' problem. We needed to change our attitudes and affirm our responsibility to serve all the people of our region."[15]

He chose Harris Mobley, a professor of sociology and anthropology, because he considered him a rare individual. Mobley had credibility with the local African American community, and his family's roots ran deep into rural southeast Georgia. Vivian Anderson Mobley, his wife, was a native of Bulloch County. Both had served a term as missionaries in Africa.

Lick was impressed that "Harris could walk into Snooky's Restaurant and talk the talk with good old boys. He had credibility with them. At the same time, he was the first college faculty member to join the NAACP. He could attend their meetings and walk the walk with members of the black community. They knew he was for real."[16]

Mobley, known as a friend of students, including the relatively small enrollment of African Americans, accepted the position. He said if the president had described the job as legal window dressing, he would not have accepted it. "The truth of the matter was I didn't know anything about Title Seven. I just supported the concept of equality. So I had a lot of learning to do." Mobley continued:

What impressed me was Lick never said 'keep us out of court' or to 'make sure we abide by the court ruling.' He always talked about 'let's do it, because it's the right thing to do.' What sold me on him was his basic honesty. He said 'I've inherited a bastion of whiteness.' Now a lot of people didn't think he was for real. Neither did I, until he talked about the 'bastion of whiteness.' Lick convinced me he believed strongly in human potential, and my job was to help all citizens realize that potential. So I signed up.[17]

Concerning the "white problem," Mobley admitted some faculty simply did not accept the president's point of view: "They didn't much cotton to him. . . . He caught a lot of flack several times from these people, because he was pushy on that subject. Even when he hired the New York director, Mical Whitaker, he caught flack from PhD's who said Mical was not an academic."

Not all the deans and department heads were eager to support affirmative action. "A lot of them would agree intellectually, but when they got down to it, they wouldn't make the effort. You'd hear things like: 'I'd hire a minority faculty member if I could find one who was qualified.' And so on." Soon that refrain began to wear thin, as many departments maintained the status quo. The president preferred changes to happen from the bottom. In this case, he realized he would need to stimulate change from the top.

Mobley said the president told him to travel widely to identify potential black faculty. Lick, in some cases, "sealed the deal":

I went to Ohio University and found a physicist, Dr. Wil Grant, and his talented wife, Dale. They came here and talked with our Dale. Soon they decided to move to Statesboro at a cut in salary. Why? Because Dale Lick had done his thing. He had convinced them they could help change our students for the better. It was that

HARRIS MOBLEY

A sociologist and anthropologist, Harris Mobley knew and loved the people of South Georgia. The native of Liberty County and former missionary had been foreign student advisor during the Eidson administration. President Lick appointed him as the first Affirmative Action Officer at Georgia Southern. Mobley advised the president and worked on wide-ranging projects.

WIL GRANT

The professor of physics communicated well and inspired the larger student body to pursue academic excellence. Active in community affairs and campus life, Grant was elected Professor of the Year in 1986.

First Ruffin cup, 1982

Professor of English David Ruffiin, *right*, presents the first Ruffin cup for faculty excellence to Barbara Olewine who accepts it for her late husband, the biologist Donald Olewine. Dean of the School of Arts and Sciences Warren F. Jones administered the award.

David Ruffin's estate provided more than $2.8 million dollars to endow scholarships in the humanities for undergraduate students. It is the largest single-donor scholarship endowment at the university.

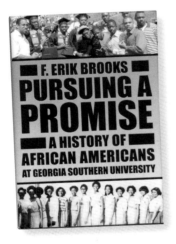

In 2006 Mercer University Press published a volume of 193 pages by F. Erik Brooks, assistant professor of political science at Georgia Southern University. Pursuing a Promise *describes the "defeats, victories, struggles, and developments of blacks at Georgia Southern University."*

old missionary thing. When you believe you are doing the right thing, you can move mountains, and some of them were huge. Getting Wil and Dale Grant was huge.

The appearance of black faculty in different schools and departments on campus encouraged another initiative, Upward Bound. Directed by Randy Gunter, the program involved largely underprivileged black youth in campus activities throughout the year. During summer session, students took classes and participated in activities that encouraged them to aspire to attend college.

The results of the first Affirmative Action Office speak for themselves, Mobley said: "We had one black faculty member when I started in 1978: Dr. Charles Bonds in the education school. When I finished my job, around 1988, we had thirty-eight black faculty and administrators. The most important achievement was the change of culture. The college simply became a more diverse and open community."[18]

ROTC: A MODEL FOR CHANGE

President Lick realized Georgia Southern College lacked programs that characterize a regional university. He initiated changes that quickly altered the look and broadened the appeal of the college. That is why he pursued the Reserve Officer Training Corps.

The college had hosted military programs during World Wars I and II. All male students took classes in military science in 1917–1919. The college hosted a screening unit of the U.S. Army in 1943–44. During peacetime, however, the college had never offered the military curriculum familiar to many campuses.

When he proposed the idea in 1978, the president thought the idea would be an easy sell. In fact, faculty senators made strong arguments against the program for two reasons: First, during the Vietnam conflict, ROTC units at other campuses had become controversial. Second, senators believed a new program would dilute the college's relatively meager budget. Each school had a waiting list of "good ideas" which had been shelved for lack of funding.

In spite of opposition, Lick pursued an ROTC program. At that time Mercer University in Macon, some 125 miles away, had a small unit that could be strengthened by sponsoring a battalion in Statesboro. Lick discovered Mercer was eager to establish a branch of the ROTC at Georgia Southern. Since 1980 the Eagle Battalion has served hundreds of young men and women who became leaders in the United States Army.

Lick realized his alliance with Mercer could benefit Georgia Southern. By becoming an ally of Mercer's ROTC program, Lick felt he would gain Mercer's support of his plan to introduce a nursing program. Over time Lick's scenario unfolded. Mercer University became a friendly party, if not an advocate, of Georgia Southern's efforts to develop a nursing curriculum.

NURSING: A NATURAL NICHE

After Lick accepted the presidency, he made several calls to leaders in adjoining towns. He tallied their major concerns and concluded rural communities shared a common concern: limited or no access to health care. Aware of Lick's initiatives, even as Lick was on the payroll of Old Dominion University, the Statesboro-Bulloch County Chamber of Commerce formally adopted a proposal to support a nursing curriculum at the college.[19]

When Lick officially began his work on July 1, 1978, he immediately requested permission from the Board of Regents to begin an undergraduate nursing program. Two groups resisted the idea immediately: colleges with nursing programs and the Georgia Southern faculty. Both parties opposed Lick's proposal for the same reason. Other colleges feared the new program would dilute funding for their programs. Armstrong College, for example, had a well-established nursing program affiliated with Savannah's hospitals.

Faculty members worried their salaries would be reduced to make way for a nursing faculty. After a long and heated debate, the faculty senate approved a motion to allow a nursing program as long as the program obtained funds beyond those currently in the budget.[20]

"They thought of the college budget as a pie that grew smaller as you added programs. I had to convince them to think of nursing as a way to make the pie larger for everybody."[21] But self-protective thinking was not Lick's major problem as he tried to introduce nursing into the college curriculum. He had to sell the idea to the Board of Regents and the Georgia Board of Nursing.

After the Board of Regents elected him president of the college, Lick asked Harry O'Rear, Vice Chancellor for Health Affairs for the name of someone in Georgia who was interested in rural health and nursing. O'Rear told him about Em Olivia Bevis, a professor of nursing at the Medical College of Georgia and a member of the American Academy of Nursing. Lick called her immediately from his office at Old Dominion. Bevis described what happened next:

I was running late to a meeting. . . . Dr. Lick wanted to discuss with me the possibility of starting a nursing program at Georgia Southern College. . . . When our discussion was over, I was not just running late, I was 45 minutes late to my meeting and didn't even care. A special chemistry had occurred in that long first conversation: I knew something great was about to happen, and I had the opportunity to help make it happen.

As we hung up that first call, I told Dr. Lick, 'I've been waiting for you all of my life.' What was so special, so wonderful, that I would say that to a perfect stranger? I had found someone who believed as I did, that southeast Georgia had unique needs and deserved a nursing program that was designed so that its courses enabled the graduates to be responsive to the unique conditions and ethnic/cultural characteristics of the people of the rural South.[22]

Lick recalled how Em Bevis took on the task as a mission rather than a job: "After we had been working together for a while (she as a consultant), I

Left to right, Martha Coleman, Joyce Murray, and Em Olivia Bevis. They designed the undergraduate nursing curriculum and led the program to accreditation.

The Bluelight at midnight

"Em Bevis and her committee of volunteers often worked until midnight. One of them was going home to Savannah from the meeting in Statesboro. She was driving pretty fast, going 80 or 90 miles an hour. She saw the blue lights in her rearview mirror. The policeman pulled her over, and he asked 'What are you doing?' She answered 'I've been at the college in Statesboro working on a nursing curriculum.'

"The policeman looked at her and said 'Is that part of the new nursing program my wife's been talking about?' She replied: 'Yes, we want better healthcare for rural Georgia.' The officer said, 'Keep up the good work, but slow it down to seventy. Now get on home.'"

Dale Lick, interview

All that you can be on campus

Around 1980 the ROTC's Eagle Battalion built the rappelling tower. Students have used it in two different locations on campus. Soldiers from Fort Stewart helped build it.

Until 1978 the original Snooky's Restaurant was adjacent to Johnson's Minit Mart on the east side of Fair Road. Then Vivian Dake "Snooky" Yawn, left, and his son Bruce, right, built a new restaurant at 11 East Kennedy Street. It became a popular place for students, faculty, and townspeople to eat and to discuss news and sports.

Snooky's as student haven

"I'd hate to guess how many club sandwiches and glasses of sweet tea I enjoyed at Snooky's Restaurant from 1979-1983. More importantly, I can't imagine what my college life would have been without the beloved Statesboro eatery. Spending time there with friends is among my fondest memories at Georgia Southern. I was as comfortable in one of those booths as I was at my family's kitchen table.

DEE MARET

"Most of my buddies and I would buy a Snooky's meal ticket at the beginning of each quarter and would gather for at least two meals a day there—three if we experienced a case of the munchies after a night on the town. Snooky's son, Bruce Yawn, usually worked the late-night shift. He and his waitresses showed a lot of patience putting up with college kids flirting, fussing and generally wasting time."

Dee Maret ('83)

said to her: 'Em, I haven't paid you anything.' And she said, 'Don't talk to me about that. You cannot afford me . . . let's not talk about any money.' She did it all for free. She was such a godsend."[23]

Based largely on the reputation of Bevis, the Board of Regents permitted the college to begin a nursing program with the understanding that the Georgia Board of Nursing would have to give approval before the college offered courses for credit. President Lick required solid research into the region's health needs. Steve Wright, an in-house consultant, conducted regional research, working closely with Lick and Bevis. Wright provided statistical reports and documents for the state and, eventually, the accrediting agencies. However, obtaining approval proved more difficult than either Lick or Bevis imagined:

> About two years after Em had started her great work, she and her advisors felt we were ready to go before the state board. I'll never forget the attitude of folks from Atlanta at that table. They made jokes about the whole idea of rural nursing and health care. 'What's the difference between a rural nurse and an urban nurse?' 'What's a rural appendix?' they asked with a laugh. They turned us down.
>
> They weren't about to let in another nursing program in the state, certainly not one in southeast Georgia. And they politically blocked it. So we went back and regrouped. We got back on their calendar the next moment possible to ask for reconsideration.
>
> Next time we took all our politicians with us—Senator Joe Kennedy, Representative Jones Lane, and Representative Paul Nessmith. They were all local men with rural backgrounds. But they had risen to leadership roles in the legislature. Kennedy was speaker pro tem in the Senate, and both Lane and Nessmith were highly regarded at the capitol.
>
> These gentlemen walked into the room with Em and me. They sat right up at the table and said, 'Let's talk about this.' And we got an honest hearing. The panelists had made jokes at the previous meetings, but they did not find rural nursing funny anymore. They approved it, and boy, were we thrilled.[24]

UNIVERSITY STATUS: REVIVING THE DRIVE

While pursuing the nursing program, Lick also was digesting the work of the Strategic Planning Council. He focused attention on a long deferred dream: university status. As early as 1949, President Emeritus Pittman and the Georgia Teachers College Alumni Association had proposed the regents should recognize the college as a graduate-level institution.

In 1970 President John Eidson named Graduate Dean Jack Averitt chairman of a committee to develop a proposal to the regents. The large book documented the need for advanced graduate study designed primarily for school administrators, but the chancellor's office never responded to the proposal. Even after John Eidson became Vice Chancellor, the college received no response to a revised proposal.

Lick's proposal in 1980 did more than establish the need for university-level offerings at Georgia Southern. It implied the Board of Regents had not engaged in thoughtful planning. Using statistics from other university systems in the southeast, Lick noted that doctoral level universities in adjoining states are evenly distributed to provide public access. Lick noted: "Georgia's universities are centered in North Georgia. . . . South Georgia with approximately two-thirds of the state's land mass and 40 percent of its population has none." [25]

Unlike most states, Georgia had not developed regional universities. The Board of Regents assumed South Georgians could travel to state universities in Athens or Atlanta for doctoral level work. Using a map, Lick demonstrated that universities most convenient to South Georgians, in fact, were Auburn, Florida State, Florida, and the University of South Carolina.

The report to the Regents concluded with a sobering chart about inequitable funding. South Georgia's full-time students attended colleges funded at less than half, per capita, than the University of Georgia. Lick's report concluded with eight points, and each indicated the university system had not served the citizens of Georgia equitably. Lick called for fairness and, more importantly, for better planning by the University System of Georgia.

The campus and community applauded Lick's impressive arguments, based on statistics. Political leaders, including those serving rival South Georgia institutions, thanked him for making a long overdue defense of the region. When politicians asked Lick about the report, he discussed the content and asked for their support. However, the chancellor and some regents regarded the report as controversial and inappropriate. Undoubtedly, the Board of Regents in Atlanta assumed responsibility for determining the needs of geographical regions served by the university system.

Dale Lick threw the spotlight on what he determined to be inequities in both planning and funding. Using diplomatic language, he requested no "drastic modifications," but "refinements" in funding and programming. Yet even Lick acknowledged the boldness of the proposals. He asked for an opportunity to focus on the issue of health care at a future regents' meeting.

A NEW SPORT AS CATALYST

When Lick visited southeast Georgia's communities in 1978, he heard consistently two words: *nursing* and *football*. Some mayors and county commissioners remembered fondly Coach Crook Smith's Professors who played some magnificent games in the 1930s. Rotarians in every town Lick visited joined the chorus: bring back football.

The faculty had not supported the nursing program originally, but he expected them to find football more agreeable. When Lick approached the faculty, he did so only after receiving financial commitments from the community. He also insisted a marching band must be funded at the same time. Originally he said he would not consider beginning intercollegiate football without at least $300,000 in donations.

Karla Redding Andrews remembers a campus with a little bit of soul

KARLA REDDING

"English lit classes helped me forget that terrible algebra grade with the *Iliad* and the *Odyssey* and words from *Romeo and Juliet*. I, like Juliet, was in love with my Romeo, Timothy Andrews, who has been my husband for 20 years! He was a member of Kappa Alpha Psi. Tim and I, along with so many of our friends, spent a lot of time in Sweetheart Circle and had lunch and snacks daily in Sarah's Place. GSC taught me to feel comfortable being me.

"Everyone knew my Dad is the legendary Otis Redding and my brother's songs were at the top of the dance charts. But I was just Karla, trying to pull the grades and impress a professor or two, while having fun and making life-long friends in the best setting. The campus reminded me of home: country living with a little bit of soul. I will be ever grateful to have experienced everything it offered."

Karla Redding Andrews ('85)

A Student encounters the football president –

"I interviewed President Dale Lick in October of 1980, for the *George-Anne*. I happened to notice he was wearing crocodile—Izod®—socks. He talked at length about what it would take for Georgia Southern to have a successful football program. Dr. Lick's final comment (and my final line in the story) was his belief that football at Georgia Southern would be successful. Looking back on this interview years later, I can only say 'How prophetic!'

"We had no picture to illustrate the impending football team, so a cartoonist drew a picture of a fan wearing a raccoon coat with a pennant in hand and a flat brimmed hat. This drawing looked like the stereotypical 'college fan'—from the 1920s and 1930s!

"I remember sweating through a lot of very hot days at Paulson Stadium where it was so warm that even the raccoons were trying to get out of their coats! Speaking of attire, I concluded that Izod® was standard sockwear for successful presidents! "

Hal Fulmer ('81)

David "Bucky" Wagner, left, *became athletics director in 1980. President Lick , right, valued Wagner's experience as a former quarterback and as an athletics administrator at colleges with strong football programs.*

The deciding factor

"Erk would never have come our way if Dale Lick had not put it all on the line. He had regional support, yes, but the person, Dale Lick, was the deciding factor. Oh, the many trips he made to towns all over Georgia, all the late night returns. And the next morning there was Dale in the office looking fresh as a daisy. He was remarkable. Erk realized the president across the table was a man just like himself. They were cut from the same cloth."

Harris Mobley, interview

Morris Lupton, owner of a large chain of convenience stores in South Georgia, pledged $25,000 and committed half of his personal time during the next year to support efforts for football. For several months Lupton and public relations director, Ric Mandes, accompanied Dale Lick on visits to virtually every civic club and boosters group from Savannah to Albany, Georgia. Their message was the same: "Georgia Southern is considering a new football program, and should we begin one, we want it to be a success. What can you do to help with this potential undertaking?" They did a lot, in fact. Soon Lick was moving in on the $300,000 target.

Winning faculty approval, however, proved more difficult, even with evidence of regional support. At the first faculty forum on football in the winter of 1981, the president heard many speeches about academic priorities. He listened and provided answers, based on his research into established programs, such as William and Mary, and fledgling programs at the University of Central Florida and elsewhere. Few skeptics changed their minds. The faculty called for a survey of opinion and a future meeting.

A second forum on April 2, 1981, began with a review of the survey. The results clearly revealed widespread faculty opposition to beginning football (61 percent opposed). But Lick's surveyors did not limit their respondents to faculty. What about staff members and the student body? The staff liked the idea (66 percent favored). In a poll of 1,300 students, nearly 70 percent favored football. The community also clearly wanted to see football at Georgia Southern.

President Lick hoped the faculty senate would approve the motion to renew intercollegiate football. In spite of overwhelming support among students, staff, and the community, the Georgia Southern faculty senate voted against football. The president reluctantly overrode the senate's recommendation.

The president gave credit for implementing Eagle football to his new Athletic Director David "Bucky" Wagner. After the previous Athletic Director, George Cook, stepped down to become golf coach in 1980, Lick hired Wagner, assistant AD at Vanderbilt University.

Wagner, a former Division I quarterback at Ohio University, was youthful and knowledgeable. "He knew how to get the most out of a dollar. He knew how to work with people. He had wonderful skills in terms of promoting. He really was exactly what we needed." [26]

The energetic new athletics director, Bucky Wagner, gave the president's football campaign the appearance of stability. Barbershop quarterbacks and local high school coaches began to speculate about Georgia Southern's first coach. "Candidates quickly came out of the woods—offensive and defensive coordinators. There were some former head coaches who were quite well known," Lick recalled.

One who had not applied happened to be at the top of everyone's list— the charismatic defensive coordinator at the University of Georgia, Erskine "Erk" Russell. Sports writers said he was responsible for the Bulldogs' national championship the previous year. Lick asked Wagner to approach the director of athletics at UGA and ask permission to meet with Coach Russell. "Vince Dooley sort of laughed, 'Sure, go ahead.' He knew we didn't have a prayer," Lick recalled.

What once appeared to be impossible became inevitable:

He came down and they had a day set for him with people from the community . . . and they set up a time for me to have lunch with him over at the Holiday Inn. I knew within five minutes he was my man. This guy is phenomenal! He's a great recruiter, a great teacher, a great communicator, a great coach, and he has tremendous ethics and cares about people. His integrity just jumped out at me.[27]

The obvious question dominated Lick's mind as he sat down with Russell: "Why would you consider coming here?" Russell replied indirectly, as Lick recalled: "'I've had many great experiences in football and even have walked down the celebrated tunnel at the University of Michigan. . . . I've done that.' Then he said: 'I've never started a football program from scratch. I think that would be a wonderful challenge.'"

Thinking Coach Russell would suggest an impossible salary, Lick remembered telling him, "I'm not sure I can afford you; I don't have much money. . . . What will it take to get you here?' His answer floored me: 'it will take $1 more than I'm making right now.'" Knowing Russell's salary and benefits at UGA were modest, Lick shot back: "We can do better than that!"

On a weekend in May, Jean Russell joined her husband on a visit to Statesboro. Lick met with them in his office after they had toured the community and talked with dozens of local citizens, including Snooky Yawn's son, Bruce, who played for the coach at UGA. The Russell family found a nice home they could afford, thanks to efforts by businessman Si Waters, without increasing their current monthly mortgage payment.

On May 23, 1981, Dale Lick and Bucky Wagner introduced the new coach to hundreds of fans who invaded a press conference at Hanner Fieldhouse. Someone mentioned his accomplishments— lettered in four sports at Auburn, beloved coach at Atlanta's Grady High School, Vanderbilt, and Auburn. He had been a mainstay of the Georgia Bulldogs for seventeen years. The coach said, "Just call me Erk." He charmed the crowd with his inimitable banter and self-effacing humor. Spectators and journalists gave him a standing ovation. The gesture touched Erk. He used a handkerchief to wipe away his tears.

Frank Tilton ('67) who was editor of the sports section of the *Savannah Morning News*, told Atlanta author, Lewis Grizzard: "When they landed Erk

Erk Russell spoke from his heart on May 23, 1981. He talked about building a "people's football program," and asked citizens to support the college. The crowd warmly responded to both the coach and the president.

Coach Russell carried a gallon jug of water from a drainage ditch to championship games. He sprinkled the water, infested with gnat larvae, around the endzone. The ritual made players feel at home and, perhaps, kept opponents from scoring. Fans never forgot the meaning of that stream of water Coach Russell named Beautiful Eagle Creek.

A VISION, A LEGACY:
SIX I-AA NCAA CHAMPIONSHIPS

Single Game Records

Rushing Yardage –1998: Adrian Peterson, 1,932

Touchdowns – 1999: Adrian Peterson, 28

Yards Gained – 1999 playoffs: Adrian Peterson vs. Massachusetts, 333

Yards Gained, Freshman – 2005: Adrian Peterson vs. Connecticut, 232

Yards Gained by a Quarterback –1997: Greg Hill vs. Florida A&M, 238

Most Touchdowns: Gerald Harris–five, 1986 vs. North Carolina A&T; Adrian Peterson – five (twice), 1998: vs. The Citadel; 1999 vs. Massachusetts in the playoffs.

Career Records

Yardage: 1998-01–Adrian Peterson, 6,559.
Touchdowns: 1998-01–Adrian Peterson, 84.
Tackles: 1991-94–Paul Carroll, 375
Sacks: 1993-96–Edward Thomas, 30

Eagle national football championship trophies between 1985 and 2000 always came in sets of two: 1985 & 1986; 1989 & 1990; 1999 & 2000. The series of back-to-back wins was unprecedented in NCAA football records.

1985-Eagles 44, Furman 42
Quarterback Tracy Ham earned 419 yards passing and another 90 yards rushing, while the Eagles scored 38 points in the final 21:51 of the game to overcome a 28-6 Furman lead. *Coach: Erk Russell*

1986-Eagles 48, Arkansas State 21
Tracy Ham rushed and passed for 486 yards and scored three touchdowns as Georgia Southern won its second NCAA I-AA National Championship, the first college to ever do so. *Coach: Erk Russell*

1989-Eagles 37, Stephen F. Austin 34
A Paulson Stadium record crowd of 25,725 watched the Eagles win their third national title,and capping off the team's only perfect season. Raymond Gross engineered 17 fourth-quarter points, including the game-winning field goal with 1:41 remaining. *Coach: Erk Russell*

1990-Eagles 36, Nevada 13
Georgia Southern quarterback Raymond Gross rushed for 145 yards as Georgia Southern won its fourth national championship in six years. Great defensive plays from Darryl Hopkins, Mike Dowis and Alex Mash helped the Eagles capture their first NCAA I-AA title without legendary coach Erk Russell. *Coach: Tim Stowers.*

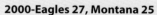

1999-Eagles 59, Youngstown State 24
The Eagles redeemed their 1998 championship loss by pummeling the Youngstown State Penguins and earning their fifth national title. Adrian Peterson rushed for a championship game-record 247 yards on 25 carries with three touchdowns. *Coach: Paul Johnson*

2000-Eagles 27, Montana 25
Georgia Southern won its sixth NCAA I-AA National Championship, behind fullback Adrian Peterson's 148 yards and two touchdowns. *Coach: Paul Johnson*

Research by Kelley Callaway

Russell, they got themselves a franchise."[28] He saw two gritty heroes standing side-by-side: the football coach and the college president.

THE COLLEGE AS LION

On June 9, 1981, Dale Lick presented details of his new proposal, focusing on the need for a university in South Georgia. The normally upbeat president realized members of the Board of Regents appeared preoccupied as he spoke. He began by enthusiastically sharing results of surveys and documenting regional support. He looked around the table and noticed somber faces. Few appeared interested in hearing his comments. Afterwards, a regent spoke, but not about his report.

The chairman of the Board of Regents of the University System of Georgia, O. Torbitt Ivey Jr., complained that President Dale Lick had improperly tried to influence political leaders in Washington, D.C., seeking help for his health care proposals. Soon they debated a motion to dismiss him from his job as president.

The chancellor and some leading members of the Board of Regents were infuriated with Lick's aggressive leadership and wanted to fire him. Regent Erwin Friedman of Savannah cautioned that the public would rise up *en masse*. He suggested a reprimand. Nevertheless, seven of the fifteen regents voted to fire him. After the motion to dismiss Lick failed, the regents agreed to reprimand him for unspecified "inappropriate" activities.

When Lick asked for examples of his behavior that prompted a reprimand, the regents told him to speak with the chancellor. The chancellor also failed to respond to Lick with specific reasons.[29] Thereby the University System clearly indicated its judgment that Dale Lick had overstepped his bounds. The most positive interpretation by his allies was the apparent split within the regents. A majority, albeit razor thin, had expressed confidence in Lick. (Years later, Lick recalled, Ivey apologized for the entire incident.)

The reprimand surprised Lick, because the chancellor earlier had told him "to keep the politicians of our area posted on what we were doing and to solicit their general support for higher education in Georgia." But the chancellor also had warned against divulging "inside information."[30] The president believed he was fulfilling the chancellor's earlier instructions.

At the end of the day, Lick realized, he had encountered an historic, immovable force. Both puzzled and dejected, Dale Lick, accompanied by a member of his planning committee, Owen Gaede, returned to Statesboro to prepare for spring commencement. He had his job, but he worried deeply about the symbolic significance of the encounter in Atlanta.

Lick returned to Statesboro and proceeded to Tiny Hill's pond house, where Ric Mandes and local citizens were hosting a bird supper for Savannah's popular and influential mayor, John Rousakis. Ric waited for the president, as the evening skies grew dark. Then he noticed headlights

Kirbylene Stephens, center, *greets five supervisors whom she served during her career of thirty-seven years.* From left: *Presidents Dale Lick, Nicholas Henry, Pope Duncan; Acting Presidents Harry Carter and Nicholas Quick.*

Kirbylene Stephens made history

When she graduated from Georgia Teachers College in 1955, the native of Waycross was ready to begin a career as a public school teacher. She had majored in English and business education. Then President Henderson asked her to become the secretary to the president, based on her excellent work as a student employee. For the next thirty-two years she served the following presidents:

Zach S. Henderson: 1955–1968
John O. Eidson: 1968–1971
Pope A. Duncan: 1971-1976
Nicholas Quick (acting): 1976-1977
Dale W. Lick: 1977-1986
Harrison S. Carter (acting): 1986-1987

In 1987 she became Director of Special Projects and Associate Director of the Alumni Association. After her retirement in 1992 she continued to volunteer her services to the institution by serving on the Museum Advisory Board and assisting the Alumni Association.

"...YOU KNOW YOUR PLACE NOW STAY IN IT!"

Atlanta Constitution, 12 June 1981

"...A FUNNY THING HAPPENED ON THE WAY TO THE TOP!"

To the surprise of many observers, including the president himself, the public responded favorably toward Dale Lick after the Board of Regents officially reprimanded him. Editorialists and commentators applauded his courage and leadership. Most agreed with Lick's viewpoint that Georgia Southern was ready to provide university-level instruction in South Georgia. The political cartoonist for the Atlanta Constitution, *Clifford "Baldy" Baldowski, presented Lick with his original cartoons.*

bouncing across the field. Dale Lick was at the wheel, taking a short cut to the pond house. He got out, briefly reviewed with Ric what happened in Atlanta and said: "Well, I can always teach high school math." They both laughed, walked inside, and Lick behaved as usual: effervescent, cordial, genuinely interested in each person at the table.

The morning sun shone brightly on the green hill, and Dale Lick was busy inside the Administration Building preparing for the weekend graduation. Throughout the day the ringing telephone told the story that spread quickly across the state: Dale Lick had become Georgia's modern folk hero. Editorials and letters to the editor, all supporting Lick, appeared in newspapers throughout the state. The *Atlanta Constitution* wrote a sympathetic editorial, and the award-winning cartoonist "Baldy" depicted Lick being tossed about by short-sighted regents.[31] Ironically President Lick, not the Board of Regents, represented the aspirations of Georgia's youth in the cartoon.

Responding to public pressure, according to some observers, Chancellor Vernon Crawford announced on July 19, 1981, that Georgia Southern could apply for university status in the future. Simultaneously two other colleges expressed interest in university status: Valdosta State and West Georgia.

A heartened faculty senate unanimously voted to support a proposal the administration prepared, taking into consideration responses Lick had received from various parties, including regents.[32] The year 1982 began with both the faculty senate and general faculty voting to support wholeheartedly President Lick's proposal to transform the college into a university.[33]

The year ended on a bittersweet note, when Savannah's regent, Erwin Friedman, announced on December 12, a "needs assessment . . . calls for no new universities or senior colleges in the state's system." Two reasons for the negative assessment, according to the article, included the financial burden to the state and "that some academicians . . . believed the college is not equipped to become a university."[34]

Nine months after breaking the disappointing news to Statesboro, the chancellor announced the regents had reduced the budget of the college by $259,000.[35] For several years, the regents did not respond favorably to budget requests by Georgia Southern. Some local leaders believed the college suffered undeservedly.[36] Although several facilities were built on campus from private funds and renovations were completed with state money, requests for new buildings floundered, and the regents did not approve a single building project Dale Lick submitted during his entire presidency.

President Lick, perhaps, gained new insight into the "King of the Jungle" tale he shared often in his speeches. Both the president and the college met the elephant that did not reply favorably to the lion's question. Georgia

Southern College had won the hearts of South Georgians, perhaps, but it had not won the minds of the board that determined the region's educational future. For the rest of his tenure, the president, his college, and the region would not gain the prize they sought. Yet there were other prizes, perhaps of greater value.

THE IMPACT OF ERK RUSSELL

With mounting interest and numerous pledges of support, Lick took the next step. He approved Bucky Wagner's proposal to upgrade the athletic fund raising group known as "Big Blue," operated by the GSC Foundation. On December 3, 1981, the college incorporated a new, independent athletic fund raising entity, known as "Southern Boosters." [37] Major donors, in addition to Lupton, began to step forward. Harris Mobley contacted his wife's relative, M. C. Anderson, a contractor. He pledged $250,000 toward the new stadium. That achievement gave the enterprise additional financial credibility.

At that point Lick believed the football program needed a financial coup comparable to its coaching coup. The president enlisted the support of a Georgia Southern alumnus Ronald "Bo" Ginn, congressman from Georgia's First District. Lick knew the president of Gulfstream, Inc., Allen Paulson, was fond of Southern's graduates in technology and business. Lick asked Ginn to approach Paulson with a proposal: give Southern football $1 million and the new stadium will be called "Paulson Stadium." Paulson did not reject the idea but asked Ginn to have Lick call him:

He gave me the time frame and it turned out I was driving to some remote place that day. So I stopped at a gas station and went to a pay phone. I was standing out by the road somewhere. . . . I called him, as he had requested. Paulson told me: 'I've decided to do it now. I'll send you the million dollars before the end of the year.' This was in early December in 1983. The check arrived on the last mail day of the year. It was a personal check for a million dollars. He later did another personal check for $350,000. I gave these cancelled checks to Kirbylene Stephens, my tireless secretary. [38]

On September 29, 1984, the Georgia Southern Eagles played their first home game as a NCAA Division I-AA team in Paulson Stadium, defeating Liberty College, 48-11. On December 21, 1985, playing in the national championship title game in Tacoma, Washington, Erk's Eagles defeated Furman University, 44-42. In 1986 the team successfully defended its national title by returning to Tacoma on December 20, 1986, and beating Arkansas State, 48-21. The Eagles were the first team in NCAA Division I-AA to win back-to-back national championships. The Eagles entered the 2006 season with six national championship trophies, more than any other I-AA team.

Strapped by a small budget, Russell ordered solid blue helmets and asked players to apply a white strip of adhesive tape down the middle. The uniforms

Allen E. Paulson wrote a check on his personal account on December 29, 1983. The postman delivered it to President Lick on Saturday, December 31. This donation made possible what Erk Russell called "the prettiest little stadium in America."

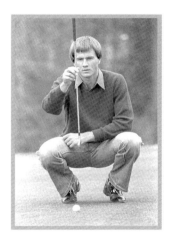

JODIE MUDD

Athletic excellence in 1981-'82

- Jodie Mudd, All American in golf, represents USA in Walker Cup, '81

- Derrell Baker is named to NCAA All American in Division I baseball, '81

- Lynn Ryan, swimmer, is selected to All American squad, '81

- Ellen Evans coaches women's basketball team to second NCAA tournament, '81

- Coach George Shriver's women's tennis team, with four All Americans, ranked fourth in USA, '82

HARRISON SHARPE CARTER

The Lick approach

"Dale Lick always had to be stretching for the next level. Some would say there are times when you need to consolidate your gains. They felt core programs needed shoring up before we took on new things. But Dale was always stretching, even when resources were thin. "

Harrison Sharpe "Harry" Carter, interview

Douglas Graves directing the annual Statesboro-Georgia Southern Symphony concert for school children at Hanner Fieldhouse, a legacy of the Symphony Guild, supported by Marilyn Lick.

were simple: white pants and blue jerseys with numbers but no names. The absence of names encouraged fans to buy programs. Russell said "those kind of things screamed Team."[39]

The successful launch of football sent a message throughout the state, and applications for admissions doubled after the upstart Eagles won the national championship. Occasionally the *Atlanta Constitution* featured the Eagles and their colorful coach on the first page of the sports section.

Lick hired a new director of admissions, charging him to develop a plan for increasing enrollment. While applications increased, the director realized Coach Russell was the college's most successful recruiter. Between 1981 and 1986, the enrollment grew from 6,603 to 7,611, and football, undoubtedly, was a key factor in the subsequent rapid increase in enrollment and quality at Southern. If some students did not always attend the games, they probably enjoyed telling their friends they attended a "football college."

ACHIEVING RESULTS, AWAITING RECOGNITION

The achievement of the administration of Dale Lick rests in significant changes that improved the quality of life for vast segments of citizens previously overlooked. The irony of his tenure is that he experienced acute frustration. The president's proposals for new college programs simply did not gain support he had hoped to obtain from the Board of Regents.

Undaunted, Lick, like his football coach, believed the way the college could change its destination was to function as though it already had arrived.[40] He encouraged Ric Mandes who hosted a talk show, *College Today*, for commercial and public television stations in Savannah, Atlanta, and Philadelphia. Mandes called attention to special visitors, such as Abba Eban, Prime Minister of Israel; Margaret Mead, renowned anthropologist; and Bob Hope, the popular comedian. Mandes' programs suggested properly that Georgia Southern was engaged in major issues of public interest, typical of a first rate university. In 1982-84 Dale Lick hosted a weekly cable TV show that focused on both college and community issues.

President Lick did not pretend Georgia Southern was ready to become a research university. What he proposed was an institution that focused on meeting the needs of people in health care, business, education, science, and technology. Lick organized new programs appropriate for a regional university.

Before he arrived on campus, few understood the implications of the regional university approach to higher education. Many faculty and administrators planned as though the liberal arts controlled the agenda. They had joined the faculty under the presidency of the scholar, John Eidson. Evidence clearly indicated a new era had begun, even before Lick arrived. By 1981, three years after he arrived, only four percent of the student body pursued the Bachelor of Arts degree offered by eighteen departments.

Faculty trained in the liberal arts eventually accepted the trend. They took consolation in the heavy humanities and social science content of the core curriculum that spanned the freshman and sophomore years. The tradition survived in innovative programs, such as the Bell honors program, organized by historian, George "Hew" Joiner, attracting national honors students. This effort grew out of President Eidson's initiatives, developed and implemented later by President Lick, supported by O. B. "Red" Bell.

Almost eighty percent of graduates in the 1980s received degrees in business, education, and technology. Although relatively few students majored in liberal arts and social studies, Lick believed these disciplines had intrinsic importance. He encouraged professors in these fields to pursue grants and organize projects that served the region.

In 1981-82, Georgia Southern received grants of $100,000, funded through the National Endowment for the Humanities. The award supported Project RAFT (Restoring Altamaha Folklife Traditions) that focused on a dozen rural counties in South Georgia. GSC humanities and technology faculty members planned with local citizens a series of festivals of local history, art, music, and story telling. More than 20,000 visitors participated in a series of folk festivals at different sites in the Altamaha River.

Marilyn Lick helped organize "symphony days" at the college. School children from surrounding counties spent a day on campus each year, listening to a live symphony orchestra play selections selected for children. During the Lick years, the art department, led by Richard Tichich, organized an ongoing youth arts festival each spring on Sweetheart Circle. These popular days on campus offer families and children opportunities to paint, sculpt, sing, play, and dance. Groups and individuals returned to the old Rosenwald Library on the campus that Lick transformed into a museum in 1982. By the time he left GSC, the museum had established a family-oriented museum that served 20,000 visitors annually. Later the museum established a science education network supported by two-dozen school systems in southeastern Georgia.

At the end of his eighth year in Statesboro, Dale Lick announced he would become president of the University of Maine, beginning September 1, 1986. Faculty and staff realized the move would benefit both Lick and Maine as he led that state's flagship university. They also hoped the change would encourage the Board of Regents to award much needed improvements to Statesboro's financially strapped college.

Georgia Southern, indeed, found a leader who proved he could "eat the whole watermelon." President Dale Lick led the university into a new era that, like dawn, brightened the horizon. Through its services and programs, Georgia Southern had become a regional university in all but name and budget. The big question about university status no longer began with the word *if* but *when*.

Natural history on campus

The first museum at Georgia Normal School appeared in the late 1920s. Known as the Anderson Memorial Museum, it included shells, bones, and an eclectic assortment of artifacts. Later the library and individual departments exhibited objects.

The Geology Department's fossil collections grew significantly when Professor of Geology Gale Bishop collected a 30-foot Mosasaur skeleton in South Dakota in the late 1970s. The collections in the Herty Building once were called the Herty Museum. Due to the importance of Bishop's discovery, the college organized the Georgia Southern College Museum in 1980, although it did not open until 1982 in what once was the Rosenwald Library.

In 1983 paleontologist Richard Petketwich and Bishop excavated near Augusta, Ga., the oldest fossil whale skeleton found in North America, known as the Vogtle Whale. Both skeletons eventually appeared as permanent museum exhibits—the Mosasaur, *above*, on September 27,1987 and the Vogtle Whale, *below*, on October 1, 1998.

GEORGIA SOUTHERN COLLEGE . . . AND WHERE IS THAT?

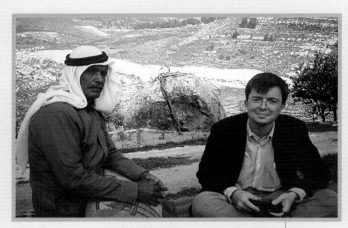

Andrew Shryock recording oral histories from Abd al-Latif al-Shilash, a shaykh of the Adwan tribe, in Jordan, 1990.

ANDREW JOSEPH SHRYOCK

Andrew Shryock is a professor of anthropology at the University of Michigan. His published works include *Nationalism and the Genealogical Imagination: Oral History and Textual Authority in Tribal Jordan* (1997), *Arab Detroit: From Margin to Mainstream* (2000), and *Off Stage/On Display: Intimacy and Ethnography in the Age of Public Culture* (2004). He was a producer of the film, *Tales from Arab Detroit* (1995), and a curator of *A Community Between Two Worlds: Arab Americans in Greater Detroit,* an exhibit held at the Smithsonian Institution (1996). The exhibit toured the U.S. from 1998-2000. Shryock has received numerous awards for his work and has been a fellow at both the Center for Advanced Studies in the Behavioral Sciences (Stanford) and the Institute for Advanced Study (Princeton). In 2005 students at the University of Michigan named Shryock "Professor of the Year." He received a fellowship from the Guggenheim Foundation in 2006.

I left Georgia Southern in 1984, when it was still a college. I'd spent three years there equipping myself to be an anthropologist. I was on my way to Ann Arbor, Michigan, where I'd been admitted to the top anthropology graduate program in the country. I was excited and scared.

My classmates at Michigan had received undergraduate degrees from Harvard, Chicago, Princeton, and Berkeley. There was awkward silence when I told them I was trained at Georgia Southern. "And where is that?" "In Statesboro." "And where is ... that?" "About an hour inland from Savannah." "Oh. Interesting. You don't sound Southern." Faculty and students there had never heard of my alma mater.

It was fitting, perhaps, that I, the budding anthropologist, should become the "exotic Other" in my new department up North. I'd been the "exotic Other" in Statesboro since I moved there at age 14, a Yankee boy who never acquired a local accent or the southern charms. My father, a Christian Church minister, had preached in Missouri, Illinois, and Indiana, before we migrated to the Deep South. Throughout my childhood, I was never a "native." I had to study the local society to understand how it worked.

By the time I entered GSC, I was fascinated by human diversity, and anthropology was a discipline built around this topic. The anthropology program at GSC was new and very small. I was one of only a handful of majors. The professors lavished their time on us. I remember long afternoons in the Newton Building, shuttling between the offices of Richard Persico, Bob Greenfield, Roger Branch, and Sue Moore, whose doors were always open. They shared ideas and books with me, taught me to think in new ways, and challenged me to learn more than they could teach me. In short, they converted me to the scholarly lifestyle I now lead.

Today, I teach at the University of Michigan. I'm happy to say it's still the top anthropology program in the country. My research has taken me to Yemen and Jordan, where I've studied the relationship between nationalism and older, tribal identities. I've lived with Arab immigrants in Detroit, studying their adaptations to American society and how the "War on Terror" is changing their lives. I've written books, made films, and designed museum exhibits. As I interact with students, I apply the lessons I was taught years ago by a few generous professors who convinced me to follow my heart and become a professional anthropologist. I hope, during its second century, that GSU will never be short of faculty who can inspire students to love knowledge and spend their lives pursuing it. "About an hour inland from Savannah" was, for me, the perfect place to start.

Andrew Shryock, BA ('84)

GEORGIA SOUTHERN
UNIVERSITY

GEORGIA SOUTHERN UNIVERSITY
1987-1998

1987 – Board of Regents name Nicholas Llewellyn "Nick" Henry the tenth president of Georgia Southern. (6/11)

1987 – Dow Jones Industrial Average falls by more than 500 points in its biggest one-day drop in history. (10/19)

1987 – Georgia Southern Museum unveils reconstructed skeleton of 30 foot Mosasaur, discovered by faculty geologist Gale Bishop and prepared for exhibition by Richard Petkewich. (9/27)

1988 – Nick Henry is inaugurated as tenth president of Georgia Southern. (4/29)

1988 – President Henry unveils plan to merge regional colleges with Georgia Southern as part of a regional university. (9/16)

1988 – Republican George H.W. Bush wins U.S. Presidential election. (11/08)

1989 – The Regents reclassify Georgia Southern College as Georgia Southern University as part of a union mainly with Armstrong State and Savannah State Colleges, effective July 1, 1990. (9/13)

1989 – Eagles defeat Stephen F. Austin before a record crowd of 25,725 at Paulson Stadium, winning third national NCAA I-AA football championship by a score of 37-34, completing a perfect season of fifteen wins, no losses. (12/16)

1990 – Five thousand people celebrate Georgia Southern University in an outdoor party that began on June 30 and continued until the next morning. (7/1)

1990 – Smithsonian Institution's National Tick Collection arrives at its new home at Georgia Southern. (8/8)

1990 – Erk's Eagles, coached by Tim Stowers, win fourth national football championship, defeating Nevada, 36-13, at Paulson Stadium. (12/15)

1990 – United States Supreme Court Justice Sandra Day O'Connor delivers address celebrating university status. (10/8)

1990 – Georgia Southern Botanical Garden opens on the site of the farmstead of Dan and Catherine Bland, a family associated with GSU since 1908. (9/17)

1991 – The Persian Gulf War begins as the U.S. and allies begin air strikes against Iraq due to Iraq's occupation of Kuwait. (1/17)

1991 – Johns Joseph "Joey" Hamilton, baseball pitcher for Eagles, is drafted in the first round and signs contract with the San Diego Padres. (9/24)

1992 – GSU severs ties with Forest Heights Country Club after the Department of Education finds the club guilty of discriminating against black workers and students. (4/9)

1992 – Democratic candidate William Jefferson Clinton, governor of Arkansas, is elected President of the U.S. (11/03)

1993 – Kara Martin of Statesboro, a math major and Miss GSU, is first runner-up in the Miss America pageant (9/18)

1994 – An earthquake strikes Los Angeles measuring 6.7 on the Richter scale and killing 57 people. (1/17)

1994 – New dormitory opens on Lanier Road, later named for State Senator Joseph Kennedy. (9/20)

1995 – In Oklahoma City, 168 people die when a truck bomb destroys the Alfred P. Murrah Federal Building. (4/19)

1995 – Bulloch County Board of Education votes to close Marvin Pittman Laboratory School by 1998. (11/9)

1996 – The Centennial Summer Olympic Games began in Atlanta and featured two GSU paralympic athletes: Dwight Van Tassell (volleyball) and Tim Willis (track). (8/16)

1997 – Center for Wildlife Education opens under the direction of artist and falconer, Steve Hein. (10/11)

1997 – Diana, Princess of Wales, dies in a car crash in Paris, France. (8/31)

1997 – University System academic calendar changes from quarter to semester system, resulting in massive scheduling and administrative changes. (7/1)

1997 – Freshman enrollment drops by 18 percent as the university begins to eliminate remedial students in "developmental studies" program. (8/15)

1998 – Nick Henry resigns as president, and Harrison Sharpe Carter serves as acting president for the second time in his career. (7/1)

CHAPTER 12

ACHIEVING STATUS

INAUGURATION AS SYMBOL

The crisp morning air on inauguration day enveloped the spring green campus. Beneath the canopy of dogwoods and stately oaks, horticulturist Nancy Trapnell made her rounds. She checked the neat beds of blue, white, and gold flanking the central sidewalk of Sweetheart Circle. She smiled, because the petunias, impatiens, and marigolds had bloomed at just the right moment.

Alumni welcomed the elegant invitation they received weeks earlier, and many returned to the campus for the occasion. The guest list included 3,810 academic delegates, politicians, journalists, regional business leaders, and citizens. A handful of alumni gathered at 7:30 a.m. in the museum rotunda, just fifty yards from the inaugural stage. They talked about the distant past: the old glory days of Professors football and basketball and the new glory days of the Eagles. A few lamented a tough loss in the football playoffs back in December and an early exit from the NCAA regional basketball tournament in March.

Everyone agreed the interim between presidents had been productive. Vice President for Academic Affairs Harrison S. "Harry" Carter, served as acting president. He visited Chancellor Dean Propst and each member of the Board of Regents during his brief tenure, not seeking favors but providing information about Georgia Southern College and allowing them to ask questions.[1] He had a strong ally in Vice President of Business and Finance Richard Armstrong, who made sure the new president inherited a fiscally sound institution.

The really serious talk that morning, however, was about the new leader. Named president by the Board of Regents on June 11, 1987, Nicholas Llewellyn "Nick" Henry had been on campus since the beginning of the academic year. He seemed energetic, and his smile lit up newspapers across the state. What about Henry's wife? Someone who had met her declared Muriel was a charmer who spoke with a soft and pleasant native British accent.

Meeting for coffee at the museum on April 29, 1988, alumni knew the president had skirted the big issue. In fact, he had vowed not to use the *U* word in public. Yet, somehow, loyalists believed the moment had arrived. Could Nick Henry accomplish the mission that eluded his three predecessors? Could this be the president who would bring to Statesboro that long-anticipated, yet always-delayed, change in status?

Presidential background

Nicholas Henry had strong academic credentials: a BA from Centre College of Kentucky, a master's degree in political science from Pennsylvania State University, and both a master's in public administration and a PhD in political science from Indiana University.

While he was an administrator at Arizona State University, he founded the Walter Cronkite School of Journalism and Telecommunication. He added two celebrities to his faculty: Walter Cronkite, the famous news broadcaster, and Arizona's former senator and presidential candidate, Barry Goldwater.

A dancing president and his lady

Nick and Muriel Henry were the first presidential couple who danced publicly and well. Muriel, born and reared in England, often entertained students, faculty, and staff. She was active in civic life and was a member of the Georgia Southern Museum Advisory Board. During the 1990s she helped plan and install dozens of exhibits.

President Henry renewed the quest for university status with a brand new theme: partnership.

The occasion suggested "yes" boldly. A campus accustomed to Spartan austerity revealed elegant touches that morning. Underneath colorful canopies young people wearing white jackets busily worked around long tables covered with crisp linen cloths, flower arrangements, and chafing dishes. They were preparing, hands down, the most elaborate picnic in college history.

Martha Fay Daily, coordinator of facilities, made sure the campus was ready. She used historic buildings on campus as locations for various groups of delegates and guests. Here academicians would don regalia and enjoy refreshments as they waited. Sharon Fell, public relations specialist, provided each reporter individual packets of information, including glossy photographs of the president.[2]

Patsy Bobo, a loyal and talented alumna, helped decorate public places, including the Williams Center, the location of the inaugural ball. Patsy reported with pleasure: "We finally have a president who loves to dance." (After observing him that evening, some celebrants said his moves rivaled those of Fred Astaire.)

Planners made certain everyone on campus that day received the very best impression of the college. The neat grounds usually had that no-nonsense institutional appearance. On this day, however, the place looked not bland, but grand, absolutely grand.

The theme of the day, "Celebrating the Academic Partnership," appeared boldly in print on invitations, programs, and banners. Nicholas Henry had chosen the distinctive typeface for official printed matter. The logo, ornately calligraphed, appeared on all inaugural materials and event signs.

President Henry commissioned two works of art for the occasion: first, a musical composition by college choral director, David Mathew, based on Walt Whitman's poem, "America;" second, a hefty ceremonial mace created by faculty artist and sculptor Pat Steadman.

Visitors and alumni found the occasion the most lavish and impressive event they had attended at Georgia Southern College. The weather cooperated beautifully: a pleasant breeze filtered through the bright green ceiling of pecan and oak trees as the distinguished guests and delegates filed into their respective sections.

Lieutenant Governor Zell Miller and Chancellor Dean Propst represented the State of Georgia and the University System. Regent Jackie Ward extended greetings from the Board of Regents of which she was chairman. Some observers were puzzled when the president of Armstrong State College, Robert Burnett, joined the dignitaries on stage. By the end of the ceremony, however, his presence appeared quite appropriate.

Would he or wouldn't he? That was the question of the hour. Would listeners hear that word of ten letters, beginning with *u* and ending with *y*? What they witnessed, quite frankly, both surprised and impressed them.

In an address of around twenty minutes, the tenth president of Georgia Southern revealed the theme of his administration. He noted the institution's history: "modest yet proud, rough yet reasoned, courageous yet controversial." He also acknowledged the sharp enrollment increases that began before he arrived, making Georgia Southern "one of the most vibrant institutions of higher education in America today." He praised the record of inclusion, noting the number of black students had increased remarkably during the previous decade.

Henry reached the peak of his message at the right moment, with only four minutes remaining. He said "inter-collegial relationships will intensify rather than dilute." He reeled off examples: joint doctoral program with the University of Georgia, off-campus centers, and other cooperative educational projects in the region:

We can anticipate that Georgia Southern College will function at the heart of a union of campuses in South Georgia which will be far more capable of delivering far more programs and services more economically, more efficiently, more effectively, in more places, to more Georgians.

This is the academic partnership that we celebrate today. . . . We all know what Georgia Southern needs to be of even greater usefulness to this region, this state, and this nation. Thanks to a farsighted Board of Regents and a visionary chancellor, we are graced with the leadership that is necessary if we are to use the magnificent resource that is Georgia Southern even more effectively for the economic, intellectual, and cultural benefit of us all.

Immediately the alumni who began the day speculating about university status nodded their heads. Now they realized why Armstrong State's Robert Burnett sat on the stage with Lieutenant Governor Miller and Chancellor Propst. As the president finished his remarks, the true blue Georgia Southern loyalists had not heard the *U* word, but they knew its arrival was at hand. They stood and cheered loudly as their president spoke for them:

> *Georgia Southern has arrived. Georgia Southern is in town.*
> *Georgia Southern has stepped into the arena and is a contender.*
> *Our day is here. Our moment is now.*
> *We will seize this moment—our moment—and we shall prevail.* [3]

Henry's dramatic conclusion left no doubt in anyone's mind. Georgia Southern would become a university, and it would do so in keeping with a new boldness, evoking an "against all odds" tradition. The question remained: how would the pieces of this new "partnership" university fit together? Within two years that question would be answered. Supporters believed the regents already had made a positive gesture toward university status when they appropriated an additional $2 million for the college just as Henry arrived in 1987.[4]

Meanwhile the appearance of the campus changed markedly after the inauguration in 1988. Construction crews fenced off a huge area of land east of the Foy Fine Arts Building. The building boom that extended through the next decade began with the $9 million Fielding D. Russell Student Union, named for the long-serving and popular English teacher, Fielding Russell,

Symbols of change

Professor of Art Patrick Steadman designed the first presidential mace for the inauguration of President Nick Henry. Ceremonial occasions since 1988 typically begin with a processional led by veteran faculty member, carrying the mace.

The inauguration introduced the campus and community to Nick and Muriel Henry's informal and festive approach to life.

During the first two weeks of each December, Muriel and Nick Henry opened their home in the evenings to members of the university family – faculty, staff, and employees of physical plant. International students and student government leaders also participated in the holiday party.

Georgia Southern became a familiar name at the capitol during the Henry administration. From the left: President Henry, Representative John Godbee and Representative Bob Lane, Coach Erk Russell, and Speaker of the House of Representatives Tom Murphy.

brother of Georgia's late Senator Richard B. Russell. In 1989 the auxiliary services division built a state-of-the-art bookstore that made headlines in bookseller's trade journals.[5]

TEMPORARY UNION, PERMANENT UNIVERSITY

At his inauguration, the president spoke of a future Georgia Southern that would function "at the heart of a union of campuses in South Georgia." He was putting into words a concept he had discussed with Robert Burnett, president of Armstrong State College, a senior college in Savannah, and presidents John Teel of Brunswick Junior College and Willie Gunn of Swainsboro's East Georgia Junior College. Within weeks David Menzel, director of the Skidaway Institute for Oceanography, told Burnett his institution wanted to join the alliance.

President Henry and leaders of five other institutions signed the letter to the chancellor, an agreement to combine six institutions into a regional university. Savannah State's president signed the letter, after making clear the historically black institution would continue its identity as a freestanding institution.

In Statesboro Henry encountered some opposition from local community leaders who preferred to think in terms of a single campus. The president enlisted the assistance of his barber, the proprietor of Henry's Haircuts. While trimming the hair of some one hundred clients, the barber asked their opinion about a hub-and-satellite approach to a university, with Statesboro functioning as the hub and colleges in Savannah, Brunswick, and Swainsboro serving as satellite campuses. Henry Doyle, the barber, reported to the president his clients overwhelmingly supported the idea. The president proceeded with confidence.

In preliminary discussions, the five presidents never dealt with the question of the identity of the president of the new university. President Henry believed the discussion might divide the fragile union. "I was prepared to take the risk of not being president," Henry said. "We had a window that would never open again. We had a strong legislative situation, particularly insofar as we had Terry Coleman, a leading state representative, working hard for us. The economy of the state was healthy. . . . We had a respected regent, Arthur Gignilliat, who was in our corner. We had a good chancellor who understood how politics worked, and was open to reason."[6]

Henry credits a politician, speaker pro tem of the Georgia Senate, Joe Kennedy of Claxton, for leading all parties to an agreement. Kennedy invited the chancellor to come to a location near his home in Claxton. Henry explained the circumstances:

We met at the warden's pond house near the Reidsville state prison—a central location for all parties. They had these oval platters for each person, with steaks kind of dripping over the side. Then Senator Kennedy got up there and said 'Chancellor, you are the best thing that ever happened to Georgia.' He was very charming. Then he said 'Chancellor, now we've got to talk about where the water hits the wheel.' That was the moment I knew we had it.[7]

President Henry met with the faculty on September 16, 1988. He announced the following: "The presidents and directors of Armstrong State College, Brunswick College, Savannah State College, East Georgia College, and the Skidaway Institute of Oceanography, along with GSC, presented the regents a regional plan for higher education in southeast Georgia that included an extensive proposal for a multi-campus regional university."[8]

Henry said the regents would consider the proposal in January. The president's announcement, he told the group, was "confidential," but a faculty member divulged the information to the press.[9]

Chancellor Propst informed President Henry the Board of Regents would delay hearing the proposal until the chancellor's staff had studied the proposal. Finally, on September 13, 1989, almost one year after Henry revealed the plan to his faculty, the Board of Regents acted favorably. For the first time in history, the State of Georgia sponsored a public university south of Atlanta.

The party could not begin until July 1, 1990, however, the date for merging the institutions. The fervently hoped-for change of status finally became a date on the calendar. The museum began planning a major exhibit, "From A&M to GSU," scheduled to open in the autumn of 1990. The Georgia Southern Foundation formed a committee to organize the biggest party on Sweetheart Circle since 1911 when 3,000 picnicked there with Governor Hoke Smith.

President Henry commissioned a new university seal, a new presidential medallion, and a new alma mater. The seal departed from the customary oval shape of college medallions featuring State of Georgia icons. He called for local icons—the entrance gate and the administration building. Professor of Art, Pat Steadman, designed and cast the medallion that Henry authorized for presidents to wear at processionals, commencements, and formal academic assemblies. Keenly aware of campus history, Henry emphasized pine trees, especially, and other icons related to the institution's past.

Students had composed earlier school songs that eventually became the official version of the alma mater of 1932. That song with a familiar melody, shared by the University of Georgia, Cornell University and many others, began with words that evoked the local landscape: "Down among the murmuring pine trees."

For the university's new alma mater, President Henry invited local writers to submit lyrics. At the very last minute, Caryl Cain Brown, a member of the Marketing and Communications Department, decided to write a poem—something she had never done before. At the committee meeting the next day, she was astonished and delighted to learn her words, starting with "From humble farm beginnings," would be immortalized in the new alma mater.[10]

Realizing the word *university* would be a central concept, Ms. Brown placed that word at a key point in her poem. David Mathew, professor of music, created an original melody that pleased Brown. He incorporated the

The story behind THE story

"The *Herald's* staff writer, Jim Hite, went to Atlanta on September 13, 1989, to cover the Regents meeting. I stayed in Statesboro to coordinate the news staff. The Regents convened at 9 a.m. that day and within an hour voted 11-2, with one abstention, in favor of university status for Georgia Southern. He called me by telephone (pay, not cell) with the results, some quotes and other details. He reported it, I wrote it, and we both got a byline on the lead story for the 'Extra' edition of the *Statesboro Herald*.

We stood on street corners downtown and yelled things like 'Extra! Extra! Read all about it!' We more than scooped our competition; we became part of their story and part of Georgia Southern history.

The decorations on my office walls have changed a lot since then, but two things that remain the same are my 1987 diploma from Georgia Southern College and a framed edition of the *Statesboro Herald*, vol.19, no. 26. The headline reads, 'University: Yes!'"

Ross Norton ('87)

Not merely a change of signs

For three years Georgia Southern was the state's only regional university. In 1993 Valdosta State became a regional university. In 1996 the Board of Regents changed all four-year colleges to universities.

The party began at 8:00 p.m. on Saturday, June 30,1990. For nearly four hours revelers enjoyed themselves by listening to bands and dancing the night away. At 11:30 p.m. they blocked Highway 301 at the campus entrance. They counted down the last minute in the life of a college. At exactly twelve midnight, President Henry removed the drape from the sign at the entrance: Georgia Southern University. Celebrants yelled themselves hoarse, couples embraced, and more than a few shed tears of joy.

President Henry became friends with Supreme Court Justice, Sandra Day O'Connor, when he was an administrator at Arizona State University. She was eager to help him celebrate Georgia Southern's new status. Many alumni and faculty recall her visit to the campus as one of the most significant events they experienced at the university.

impact of all five syllables in the *u*-word. Some who sing the song follow the music and emphasize each syllable: *u-ni-ver-si-ty*—a tribute to the occasion that produced the new alma mater. Although Brown has not written other poems, she was grateful for her "one hit wonder."

Because many students and faculty were away during the summer and did not experience the transition from college to university, President Henry planned an event for the autumn. In contrast to the big party of the summer, the president planned a week-long emphasis in the fall that celebrated academic excellence and institutional growth. He organized a convocation, and a series of activities for students and faculty starting on Monday, October 8, 1990, just one week after the Supreme Court began its yearly cycle of work.

No one needed an explanation of the event's importance after the president announced his choice for the keynote speaker: United States Supreme Court Justice, Sandra Day O'Connor. Her presence symbolized Henry's aspirations for what he enjoyed calling "South Georgia's first and only university." She spoke eloquently, praising the achievement of Henry whom she knew when both lived and worked in Arizona.

Justice O'Connor noted that Supreme Court justices struggle constantly to interpret the Constitution. She acknowledged her concern about the erosion of individual liberties protected by the Bill of Rights.[11]

EARNING A REPUTATION FOR EXCELLENCE

In other ways the celebration continued during the early nineties when *U.S. News and World Report* ranked Georgia Southern as the fastest growing university in the United States.[12] Vice President of Student Affairs John F. "Jack" Nolen pointed out: "This national recognition is another step in the right direction."[13]

In December of 1990 a new football coach, Tim Stowers, proved the team of Erk's Eagles that won the national championship the year before could repeat the feat. Coach Russell, as a spectator, cheered the Eagles as they easily defeated the University of Nevada at Paulson Stadium on CBS television. Combined with Russell's three trophies, the Eagles ran to an unprecedented Division I-AA first place finish for the fourth time in six years (1985, '86, '89 and '90).

The early 1990s brought other achievements of national significance. The Smithsonian Institution and National Institute of Health in 1990 selected Professor James Oliver as the custodian of the National Tick Collection, consisting of more than one million ticks. President Henry arranged for the additional faculty positions and facilities required to maintain and house the world-class collections. Oliver's Institute of Arthropodology and Parasitology confirmed its research leadership in the field of Lyme disease.

The Georgia Southern Museum followed up by exhibiting an exhibit-in-progress of the oldest fossil whale discovered in North America, donated by the owner of the excavation site near Augusta, the Georgia Power Company. Faculty members in the Department of Geology led the excavation, preparation, and interpretation of this significant collection from 1983–2003: Richard Petkewich, Gale Bishop, James Darrell, Richard Hulbert, and Jonathan Geisler.

Two remarkable educational facilities opened on campus in the 1990s: the Georgia Southern Botanical Garden (1990) and the Wildlife Education Center (1997). The botanical garden of some eleven acres resulted from a gift of property by Dan Bland, a member of the first class at the A & M School.

The Center for Wildlife Education began as a dream of Statesboro businessman, Harry S. Mathews. A great football fan, Mathews wanted to see a bald eagle on the campus of Georgia Southern University. President Henry immediately embraced the project. Mathews and the Statesboro Telephone Company paid for a feasibility study. With the permission of the Georgia Department of Natural Resources and the U.S. Fish and Wildlife Service, the university developed a plan for housing an eagle.

First District Congressman, Lindsay Thomas, assisted the university by securing a grant from the National Fish and Wildlife Foundation. The Robert W. Woodruff Foundation provided a grant of $1 million, its first gift to Georgia Southern University. The Raptor Center began with a contribution by the family of Lamar Q. Ball. The director of the center, Stephen Hein, an expert falconer and artist, profited from on-site advice by the well-known naturalist and TV personality from Albany, Georgia, Jim Fowler.[14]

President Henry put four major buildings at the top of a request to the Board of Regents: the College of Business Administration, the Allen E. Paulson College of Technology, the College of Education, and the College of Science and Nursing. Since President Dale Lick obtained Paulson's support for Erk Russell's football program, Mr. Paulson had followed avidly Georgia Southern and greatly admired Coach Russell.

THE END OF AN EXPERIMENT

Mergers, like marriages, sometimes work better on paper than in reality. This proved to be the case with the experiment of satellite graduate programs involving the three graduate institutions. The presidents of Brunswick Junior College and Savannah State made their reservations public, even as citizens, alumni, and students prepared to celebrate in Statesboro. Students, professors, and the local community seemed oblivious to the partnership issue. They celebrated because Georgia Southern had become what supporters had wanted for the past two decades—a university.

Faculty who lived in Statesboro had been accustomed to teaching at off campus centers for years. They found the transition seamless and simple. Painters installed a Georgia Southern University sign on an office building across the street from Armstrong College. The facility provided office space

Alma Mater of 1990

Lyrics by Caryl Brown, music by David Mathew

From humble farm beginnings
Sprung up from the sandy earth
Among the tow'ring pine trees
stands a treasure of great worth.
Her price cannot be measured
In silver or in gold
But in the love and loyalty
That many hearts enfold

Chorus:
Georgia Southern University.
On Eagles' wings you soar.
We pledge to you our loyalty
And love for ever more.

Through triumphs and through trials
Our Alma Mater's stood
As solid as the oak tree
For justice and for good.
As through these gates we travel
And though our ways must part,
Our Georgia Southern mem'ries
We'll keep within our hearts.

Chorus

After breaking ground for the Wildlife Education Center in 1996, these supporters returned to dedicate the facility on October 10, 1997. From left: David Ball, Nicholas Henry, Harry Mathews, Joe Mathews, Charles Mathews.

President Nick Henry's inaugural theme of partnership grew out of conversations he had with Chancellor Dean Propst, right, and other educators and citizens of South Georgia. Henry genuinely enjoyed working with the chancellor. Propst's previous experience as an administrator at Armstrong State College gave him insight into the region's needs and the aspirations of Georgia Southern College.

On August 8, 1990, two huge semi-trailers arrived on campus, containing the National Tick Collection. James Oliver and his colleagues began unpacking the contents. Two weeks later the fragile specimens had been unpacked and stored in the collection's new headquarters on the campus.

and seminar rooms for graduate programs. The blue and white sign, with the familiar Eagle logo, symbolized the academic equivalent of an arranged marriage. Armstrong's faculty and administrators who had resisted the union constantly remarked about the unwanted presence "over there," on the other side of the four-lane thoroughfare, Abercorn Extension.

Students from Statesboro's campus found it inconvenient to drive to and from Armstrong and Savannah State for proprietary courses, and vice versa. In spite of the "branch office" on Abercorn, faculty from the three institutions experienced little or no collegiality. Letters and public statements by leaders of the Savannah institutions suggested the union was shaky at best.

The three four-year colleges did not coalesce. Armstrong and Savannah State offered graduate courses but could not award master's degrees under their agreement. Furthermore both Armstrong State College and Savannah State College, according to the accrediting agency, had moved from graduate to baccalaureate classification. Both institutions made their complaints public.

In 1995 the Board of Regents of the University System of Georgia restored some master's degrees to Armstrong and Savannah State. Georgia Southern continued to offer its master's of business administration in Savannah, but it could no longer offer its master's of public administration in Chatham County and two adjacent counties.

The five campuses had not become as one. The junior colleges never actively participated in the new university. Armstrong and Savannah State College preferred to disaffiliate and resume their own identities. In 1995 the Board of Regents acknowledged the hub-and-satellite approach to higher education in South Georgia was not successful. But Georgia Southern University in Statesboro was more than successful. President Henry said it had become both exemplary and popular—one of the fastest growing universities in America.

Stephen Portch succeeded Dean Propst as chancellor in 1994. He noted with dismay what he called "mission creep"—the ambition of four-year colleges to become universities. In 1996 Portch decisively ended such future requests, announcing that the Board of Regents had elevated immediately the status of all four-year institutions to universities. Georgia Southern and Valdosta State maintained their previous status as regional universities.

At the same time, Portch limited the scope of the new universities: "We took a very strong stand that only the four research universities would be allowed to offer the PhD degree . . . . That was a bold stand, a quality stand. This country can only afford about a hundred good top research universities. We don't need to create 500 more," Portch maintained.[15]

Georgia Southern's presence in the Coastal Georgia Center for Continuing Education proved to be the most successful byproduct of the

brief partnership. Originally operated by Armstrong State in downtown Savannah near the Convention and Visitors Bureau, the center quickly became a popular site for graduate seminars and educational conferences.

The Savannah business community welcomed the opportunity to organize and attend programs, seminars, and graduate classes offered by GSU faculty. Beginning in 1998, Georgia Southern operated the facility, in cooperation with Armstrong Atlantic State University and Savannah State University. Faculty in the colleges of business administration and education offer around fifty graduate level classes at the center each year.

Nick Henry's work to bring about a union resulted in a permanent presence for the university in Savannah. Residents of the low country of Georgia and South Carolina in 2006 pursue master's and doctoral degrees at Georgia Southern University without driving to Statesboro. The relatively brief merger of graduate programs with Savannah's colleges made possible this important expansion of graduate education.

AMBITION EXTENDED

After Henry successfully led Georgia Southern to university status, he told an interviewer in 1989 he originally believed the process would take five years. He accomplished it in only two. Given the favorable conditions in state government at the time, the president said: "I'm giving myself two or three years for an engineering school . . . a reasonable length of time, but of course it could go on much longer."[16]

The arguments in favor of an engineering school in South Georgia carried weight regionally. The Savannah business community believed President Henry's plan would benefit coastal Georgia by providing firms with engineers who focused on applied rather than theoretical approaches. Henry documented the growing need for personnel who had "applied" engineering degrees. His evidence suggested the low country needed a dependable supply of civil, electrical, and mechanical engineers.

To provide evidence of the university's regional support, Henry made an appointment with one of the university's strongest supporters, Allen E. Paulson, chairman of the board of Gulfstream Aerospace, Inc. Since forming a partnership with Georgia Southern during the presidency of Dale Lick, Paulson had been visible on campus. He absolutely admired the football coach, Erk Russell.

Retired since 1989, Coach Russell joined President Henry on a visit with Allen Paulson. They met at his office at Gulfstream's headquarters in Savannah in 1991. Henry carried a carefully-considered proposal prepared by the dean of the College of Technology, James Manring, and Vice President for Academic Affairs, Harry Carter. Paulson had met Carter in 1987 when the executive gave Georgia Southern $1.25 million for scholarships in engineering technology.

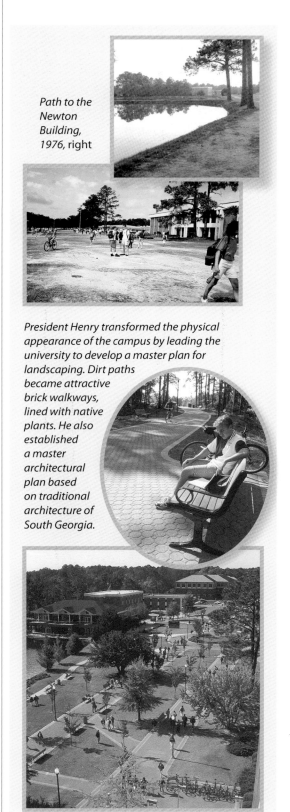

Path to the Newton Building, 1976, right

President Henry transformed the physical appearance of the campus by leading the university to develop a master plan for landscaping. Dirt paths became attractive brick walkways, lined with native plants. He also established a master architectural plan based on traditional architecture of South Georgia.

Nurse practitioner program succeeds

During the 1990s the curriculum in nursing expanded, and the program was a model for rural health training and delivery. It became the only academic program at the university to earn a ranking near the top in a category (nurse practitioner) by *U.S. News and World Report*.

Pittman Lab School closes

The Bulloch County Board of Education voted to end the service of the Marvin Pittman Laboratory School on November 9, 1995. The school finally closed its doors at the end of the spring semester in 1998. Nearly 500 students attended the school that had allowed education majors to learn by assisting in school classrooms for more than seventy years. President Henry had put a brand new school at the top of the university's priority list for construction. On May 16, 1998, the final day of school, Pittman's students and teachers posed for this photograph.

Paulson was proud the college had become a university. He wanted to see in Statesboro a school of engineering that focused on supplying graduates who specialized in applied engineering. The executive especially was glad to see his old friend, Coach Russell. Harry Carter led the discussion of the proposal in a straightforward manner. The president reminded Paulson that this request could lead to the naming of the college of technology, or perhaps, engineering in Paulson's honor. Henry hoped it would be an engineering college.

The trio returned to Statesboro without an outright commitment, but with a "warm and fuzzy feeling." A few weeks later, Carter recalled, Paulson's attorney called President Henry with good news: the aerospace executive had incorporated a $7.5 million bequest to the university in his will.[17]

Paulson's generosity began when First District Congressman Bo Ginn and President Dale Lick convinced him he could take pride in his association with Georgia Southern. That initial gift of $1.35 million to the football program, combined with scholarships of $1.25 million and the $7.5 million bequest, totaled more than $10 million, with more than 85 percent of the funds supporting academics. Officials dedicated the Allen E. Paulson College of Science and Technology in July 1994.

ENHANCING ACADEMICS AND STUDENT LIFE

Great teachers, of course, do not require grand lecture halls or state-of-the-art laboratories. A good education consists of a thoughtful teacher and an eager student. When the future President of the United States, James A. Garfield, was president of Williams College, he famously defended his institution's meager facilities with a folksy but true statement: "The ideal college is Mark Hopkins on one end of a log and a student on the other."[18] (Mark Hopkins, earlier president of Williams College, had taught Garfield.) That manner of thinking applied to Georgia Southern College, particularly during the decade of the 1980s.

The university community took pride in its national recognition for student growth and athletic achievements. However, the enrollment boom that began around 1985 created an instructional crisis. A larger student body demanded additional faculty. Administrators decided to use temporary facilities until the state could provide permanent buildings. Students and faculty grew accustomed to learning and working in pods of oversized trailers.

At Southern, for over a decade, the learning environment sometimes left much to be desired, but great teaching happened in those temporary buildings with creaking floors, uneven walls and drafty rooms. Administrators named the temporary structures "South Building" and "North Building." Students coined more colorful monikers.

The nursing department, the gift of inspired leaders in the early 1980s, organized a curriculum of excellence. The department's faculty and staff worked in trailers parked only a few feet beyond the right field fence of the baseball stadium. During practices and games, instructors grew accustomed to having their lectures punctuated by home-run balls that bounced off the roof of their classroom-on-wheels.

In the tradition of Mark Hopkins, the nursing faculty taught their students well—so well, in fact, that some of the earliest classes passed the stiff nursing certification exam without a single failure. The department also managed to achieve full accreditation and eventually gained a spot in the top twelve nurse practitioner programs in the United States, certified by *U.S. News and World Report*. In 2006 a new chemistry and nursing building houses this exemplary program born in lean times.

A PRESIDENTIAL DECISION

Nicholas Henry led the college to university status by charting a path through a labyrinth of academics and politics. He worked productively with Chancellor Dean Propst, who had advised and sometimes corrected him. Henry freely acknowledged the chancellor's leadership as he sought university status. Before the president could accomplish his second goal—an engineering school for South Georgia—a new chancellor arrived on the scene.

Chancellor Stephen Portch, according to President Henry, did not believe the State of Georgia needed a second university-level engineering program. The chancellor expressed confidence in the ability of the Georgia Institute of Technology to manage engineering education for the entire State of Georgia. The president said these circumstances thwarted his effort to advocate effectively his educational aspirations for the region. Instead of awaiting the inevitable confrontation, the president chose to resign.

President Henry's decision to return to classroom teaching marked a first in the presidential history of the institution.[19] Students in the field of public administration, of course, applauded his decision. As a full-time university president, Henry remarkably had maintained his reputation. He continued to write and speak about his academic field at the national level.

Rejoining the professorial ranks, he resumed his involvement in professional organizations. He turned out numerous articles and books. His professional colleagues elected him to a prestigious honor in his field—membership in the National Academy of Public Administration. They also named him president of Pi Alpha Alpha, the national honor society of public affairs and administration; he also won the Stene Award and Author of the Year prize. In 2003 he won the Burchfield Award. In 2006 Professor Henry was still a familiar and friendly face on campus and a model of the scholar-teacher in action.

Back left to right, *LaTasha Woods, Willgina Montgomery, Niki Morse*. Front, *Shelia Smith and Tamika Cooper.*

"From 1993-96 I lived in those wonderful old fashioned apartments called 'In The Pines.' It was our home away from home. We planned block parties, held sleepovers, and just plain had fun. I was head of the recreation committee in 1994-95, and we encouraged social life and academic excellence."

Willgina Montgomery ('96)

A president's perspective

Political cartoonist for the *Savannah Morning News*, Mark Streeter, interpreted President Henry's resignation by injecting barbed humor in comments by the talking figures on the right.

Savannah Morning News, 24 May 1998.

ELEVEN YEARS: A PRESIDENTIAL APPRAISAL

Professors of the year

Each spring during Honors Day, the Gamma Beta Phi honorary society recognizes an exemplary faculty member as the Wells–Warren Professor of the Year. The award process begins with a campus ballot by students. The award ceremony originated in 1971. Later it was endowed with an annual cash award provided by retired professors Norman and Rosalyn Wells in honor of their parents.

1971 – Fred Richter
1972 – Robert A. Mayer
1973 – David Ruffin
1974 – William Word
1975 – George H. Shriver
1976 – James D. Jordan
1977 – Perry Cochran
1978 – Samuel G. Riley
1979 – Herbert Bice
1980 – Delma E. Presley
1981 – Russell Dewey
1982 – Charles Christmas
1983 – Lloyd Dosier
1984 – Norman Wells
1985 – James Randall
1986 – Wil Grant
1987 – David Heckel
1988 – Lana Wachniak
1989 – Hal Fulmer
1990 – J. Michael McDonald
1991 – David Moskowitz
1992 – Georgene Bess
1993 – Neal Saye
1994 – S. Todd Deal
1995 – Stephen Hale
1996 – Abasi J. Malik
1997 – Debra Sabia
1998 – David Addington
1999 – Donna Hooley
2000 – John B. White
2001 – David Stone
2002 – Craig Roell
2003 – Anthony Barilla
2004 – Lorne Wolfe
2005 – Patrick Novotny
2006 – Darin Van Tassell

Nick Henry's term as president was longer than any presidential term other than Zach Henderson's. Nearing the end of his tenure, he wrote down some of his fondest memories. He incorporated a list of achievements into a typically brief but eloquent address he entitled "Swan Song." The faculty assembled for the spring faculty meeting on May 21, 1998, and heard his remarkable presentation. In a manner both relaxed and dramatic, he moved about the stage, identifying with the faculty and driving home his message.

With clarity and courage, the president said: "The Board of Regents should authorize and fund a second state engineering school at Georgia Southern University. This goal is so affordable, so reasonable, and so beneficial that it should be non-debatable."

"Engineering education," Henry maintained, "is crucial not only to our University's future, but, more importantly, to South Georgia's prosperity and to the larger welfare of all Georgians. . . . Unless South Georgians unite in this cause, fight forcefully for it, and win, we shall slip even further behind the rest of the state."

Rarely does a president speak as boldly as did Henry on this occasion. He acknowledged the conventional wisdom that colleges and universities are subject to the authority of the Board of Regents. Henry declared, however, that the board had not dealt fairly with citizens of South Georgia. "South Georgians deserve more, and they should demand more," he said. "As you and I know, one cannot demand while kneeling. One must stand. It is time for South Georgians to stand up—publicly and proudly, now and from now on—for what is rightfully theirs."

Some members of the audience believed the president's remarks might antagonize the chancellor and Board of Regents. Others, however, believed the candid comments could resonate with some regents and political allies. The speaker, of course, wanted to express the truth as he saw it.

Members of the audience appreciated Henry's words of humility: "I have no doubt that the future greatness of Georgia Southern will be shaped by hands far more skilled than mine. And many hands, far more skilled than mine, have brought us the many successes, and more, that I have mentioned today."

Recalling the dramatic changes of the 1990s, the president took note of major achievements in three areas simultaneously: quality, diversity, and growth. Higher scores on the standardized Scholastic Achievement Test each year could be measured. In his last year, for example, the average advanced ten points. The trend of recent years moved the university nearer the national average, he said. Academically gifted students, measured by the HOPE scholarship program, chose Georgia Southern more than any institution other than the University of Georgia.[20]

Students of color increased from 14 percent to 28 percent, a figure that reflected their percentage in the state population. Faculty of color increased from 4 percent to more than 8 percent. The percentile increase appears more impressive, considering the fact that both the student body and the faculty doubled in size during his tenure. Nick Henry was the first president to employ either a dean or a vice president who was African American.

With good reason the faculty gave President Nicholas Henry a standing ovation at the completion of his valedictory. They realized, no doubt, future generations of faculty, students, and alumni would appreciate his unique leadership and unmistakable accomplishments.

Nicholas Henry achieved a goal earnestly sought by several predecessors: He led the college to become a university. This man who knew how to make the right moves at the right moment managed a critical alliance of educational partners. Although the alliance eventually dissolved, Georgia Southern gained more than status. When he became president in 1987, Georgia Southern was a college identified mainly with South Georgia. When he completed his work in 1998, Georgia Southern was a university with a growing and improving reputation both regionally and nationally.

Nick Henry changed more than the status of Georgia Southern. He worked with a new landscape architect, Charles A. Taylor, to showcase the natural beauty of the campus. During the decade following his presidency, the university continued and enhanced the campus beautification plan begun by President Henry.

The Record: 1987–1998

- Minority student enrollment increased from 14 to 28 percent.
- Minority faculty grew from 5 to 8 percent
- Female faculty increased from 35 percent to 43 percent
- The first doctoral degrees ever awarded by a university in South Georgia
- The University's general campaign for excellence raised $19 million
- A botanical garden and a wildlife education center
- The Smithsonian U. S. National Tick Collection
- A Distance Learning Center teaching one-fourth of all distance learning students in the university system
- A Builders of the University Terrace honoring all retired faculty and staff
- The Executive Planning Council, the Strategic Planning Council, the Personnel Advisory Council, and the Diversity Council
- Staff Awards for Excellence of Performance
- Faculty Awards for Public Service
- Professionally staffed student advisement centers
- The Center for Teaching Excellence
- Two national championships in football and appearances in College World Series and NCAA Division I basketball tournaments
- The fastest-growing university in the nation for seven years
- $125 million for new buildings and a standard architectural style
- Developing and implementing a landscape plan for the campus

THEY CAME HERE TO PLAY

Rolling Stones

Simon and Garfunkel

Ike and Tina Turner

R E M

Many musicians, some who would become entertainment icons, beat a path through the piney woods of South Georgia where college students and townspeople would enjoy their talents.

A musician linked early on to college students was street singer, Blind Willie McTell. The author of *Statesboro Blues* and the man considered to be the master of the blues twelve-string guitar, McTell provided a soundtrack on the sidewalk for those who would listen to his Depression-era tunes.

Other than impromptu performances by itinerate musicians, much of the music performed was for sacred and ceremonial purposes. In those early years, Gospel quartets, singing groups and homespun sing-alongs were popular. From the 1930s until the 1950s, students played and sang in dance bands, conducted by fellow student Carl Collins or Professor Jack Broucek. Dancers knew the bands as the Professors and the Top Tuners. Local pianist Emma Kelly, dubbed by Johnny Mercer as the "Lady of 6,000 Songs," played numerous college engagements either solo or with her combo.

Georgia Southern's first "name" concert was an appearance in 1960 of the Jimmy Dorsey Orchestra for a "Welcome Back Dance" for 800 fans. The big band's big day on campus seemed quaint a few years later when a generation weaned on rock-n-roll enrolled in school.

During spring of 1965, Georgia Southern added to the lore of rock-n-roll by hosting the Rolling Stones for their first collegiate appearance in the U.S. Locals say the Stones lived up to their emerging bad-boys-of-rock image, renting Bragg's Sport's Center, a pool hall downtown, playing pool, and drinking beer all afternoon. A *George-Anne* reviewer credited local bands— the Apollos, the Bushmen, and the Roeman— with saving the evening from the Stones' drunken performance of twenty minutes.

Southern hosted hootenannies and folk-singers in the 1960s. Paul Simon's contemplative folk song, *The Sound of Silence,* remixed with drums and the twang of electric guitars, created a hit sound for Simon & Garfunkel, but that studio concoction was unlike the duo in their 1966 "unplugged" concert—just two voices and an acoustic guitar.

Some performers were on their way up— such as Otis Redding, who appeared here in 1965. He scored a mega-hit *(Sittin' On) The Dock of the Bay* a year later, but perished in plane crash in 1967. His connection to the school continued when the singer's daughter, Karla, enrolled in the 1980s. Students liked rhythm and blues artists such as Dionne Warwick, Percy Sledge, and The Platters. And the "hardest working man in show business," Godfather of Soul, James Brown, played the local armory and campus shows.

Campus culture began to change in 1970. The new activities director, Jack Nolen, named students to a programming council and encouraged them to run the "business" of providing activities. Abandoning the "free admission" policy, Nolen agreed to give "paid admission" a try. He hoped proceeds would pay for future performances.

Mountain, a heavy metal group whose tune *Mississippi Queen* was riding the charts, appeared on their first national tour with Boston rockers, J. Geils Bands, as an opening act. The concert was a less expensive "stopover" show between gigs in bigger cities. Despite using such cost-saving measures, the total expense— estimated at $4,000—was a sizable portion of that year's activities budget for the whole school. The decision was a gamble for the young activities director, but Nolen's faith in his student programmers paid off as 3,500 bought tickets, covering costs and providing money for future shows and other activities.

More great shows followed. Fleetwood Mac appeared in 1972 with its hard-driving British blues. Z Z Top brought its Texas brand of electric boogie to Hanner in 1973. Students recall the 1970s as an exciting time for concerts by Kenny Rogers and the First Edition, Linda Rondstadt, the Hollies, Ike and Tina Turner, Badfinger, REO Speedwagon, B.B, King, Jimmy Buffett, and more.

A GROWING LIST OF PERFORMERS

Allman Brothers Band	Tony Arata with Pat Alger and Jellyroll Johnson	Section	Roy Buchanan	Cherish the Ladies	Orchestra	Fifth Dimension	Thermos Greenwood and the Colored People	Bob Hope Show
Gregg Allman		Backstreet Society	The Buckinghams	The New Christie Minstrels	The Dovells	Mac Frampton		Freddie Hubbard
Anthony and the Imperials	The Association	Badfinger	Jimmy Buffet	Cornelius Brothers	The Downright Brothers	The Four Freshmen	Grinder's Switch	Killer Mike
The Apollos	Atlanta Rhythm	Blackwood Brothers	The Bushmen	Critical Mass	The Drifters	Mother's Finest	Bruce Hampton and the Hampton Grease Band	Kinchafoonee Cowboys
		Norman Blake Trio	Jerry Butler	Mike Cross	The Elements	J. Geils Band		B. B. King
		Bloodrock	Ciara	Taylor Dane	Eli	Vince Gill		The Kingston Trio
		Booger	Albert Collins	John Davidson	Elohsa	Goose Creek Symphony	The Heath Brothers (Jimmy & Percy)	Leo Kottke
		Breaking Benjamin	Arthur Conley	Dixie Dregs	Eric Quincy Tate	Grapes of Wrath		Kudzu
		Brick	Chad and Jeremy	The Jimmy Dorsey	Fleetwood Mac	Lee Greenwood	The Hollies	Myron Lefevre and Holy Smoke
		James Brown	The Chambers Brothers					

Some shows became footnotes in rock-n-roll lore. The Jacksonville-based band, Lynyrd Skynyrd, had achieved a sort of cult status with their mix of Southern Rock, red necks, and blue-collar attitude with hits like *Free Bird,* and *Sweet Home, Alabama.* They were a sought-after act when they agreed to appear in the fall of 1977. The show was a break-even event; however, the business of putting on concerts was overshadowed by tragedy. The last words of a *George-Anne* story—"there seems to be no stopping them now"—would soon echo as a promise left unfulfilled. Just days after departing Statesboro, the band's plane crashed in Mississippi, claiming the lives of three musicians, their road manager, and severely injuring five. Skynyrd's performance at Georgia Southern proved to be the original band's last college show.

Not all the emphasis at this time was on staging big events. Mississippi John's Coffeehouse on the ground floor of the Williams Center hosted "mini-concerts" by diverse groups from the region. Some of those players would achieve iconic status. Bruce Hampton and the Grease Band brought an avant-garde performance to this space, while the New Grass Revival, featuring bluegrass virtuosos Sam Bush and Béla Fleck, introduced "new" acoustic music to a student audience.

The string of successes, however, did not last. The union board could have called a Chic concert "Death by Disco" in 1979 when only 500 bought tickets and the board lost $12,000. Even a mainstream act, such as a solo appearance by Stephen Stills (of Crosby, Stills, Nash & Young fame), could prove disappointing. A faulty sound system caused Stills to cut his set short as he tromped off stage in disgust.

After being idle as a venue for several years, Hanner Fieldhouse was the site of a 1986 performance by Athens' alternative rock native sons, REM. It would be fourteen more years before what might prove to be Hanner's final rock show. Jam band Widespread Panic played to a full house in 2000; however, their tie-dyed, die-hard fans, the "Spread Heads," set-up smoky pre-concert "campsites" in the Hanner parking lot, to the chagrin of some college officials.

Bands like Widespread Panic and many others can trace musical roots to Southern Rock. But the group that virtually invented the genre in 1969 was the Allman Brothers Band. The tie between Statesboro and the Brothers provides another link to rock history. The Brothers' arrangement of *Statesboro Blues* has become a Southern Rock anthem. The six founding musicians—including bassist Berry Oakley who performed on campus in the '60s with Tommy Roe's backup band, The Roeman—had many connections to audiences in the area; however, once they became the Allman Brothers Band, word spread quickly about this exciting musical juggernaut based in Macon.

This fan excitement led the Interfraternity Council to sign the band for an appearance at Hanner Fieldhouse in January 1971. Band leader, legendary guitarist Duane Allman, leaned into the microphone and opened the show that night by saying, "Somehow this song seems apropos. It's called 'Statesboro Blues.'" He then pulled a glass bottleneck slide across the strings of his electric guitar and sounded the opening riffs of *Statesboro Blues.* From that electric moment and for most of the next two hours, the Brothers rocketed through a blistering set that would be recorded in New York later that spring as one of rock's greatest live recordings, "Live at the Fillmore East."

When WVGS signed on the air in 1974 as a student-run radio station, the first song played was *Statesboro Blues.* The Brothers' music was a favorite of station deejays. Gregg Allman, reprising *Statesboro Blues,* made a solo appearance in 1990 at Paulson Stadium as halftime performer for a national championship football game. In June 2005, when the university transferred WVGS to an academic department, the last song played by request was *Statesboro Blues.*

In some ways, *Statesboro Blues* was a song cycle that had come full circle. From performances by street musician McTell to a rock-n-roll rebirth by the Allman Brothers, the song connected a street musician to mainstream American rock music.

William G. Neville III ('73)

Atlanta Rhythm Section

Mountain and signed 8-track

Marshall Tucker Band

Allman Brothers Band

B B King

The Lettermen
Lighthouse
Little River Band
Patty Loveless
Taj Mahal
Marshall Tucker Band
Kathy Mattea
Middleground
Ronnie Milsap
Chris Mitchell Band

Chad Mitchell Trio
Mountain
New Grass Revival
Nickel Creek
Nitty Gritty Dirt Band
Harry O'Donoghue
Danny O'Keef
Glenn Phillips
Pieces of Eight
The Platters

Four Preps
Preservation Hall Jazz
  Band
Pure Prairie League
Raspberry
Otis Redding
REM
Daryl Rhodes & the
  Hahavishnu Orchestra
The Righteous Brothers

Rock Mountain
The Roeman
Rooftop Singers
Kenny Rogers and the
  First Edition
Linda Ronstadt
Sister Rose
Ricky Skaggs &
  Kentucky Thunder
Rolling Stones

Earl Scruggs Review
Sea Level
Silvertide
ShaNaNa
Simon and Garfunkel
Lynyrd Skynyrd
Sky Boat with Mac
  Gayden
Percy Sledge
Soul Miner's Daughter

(Jennifer Nettles)
REO Speedwagon
Jim Stafford
Hovie Lister's
  Statesmen Quartet
Stephen Stills
Stoutbeats
Starbuck
Stompin' Suede
Greasers

Doug Supernaw
Swinging Medallions
Billy Taylor Trio
The Tams
Rufus Thomas
B. J. Thomas
3 Doors Down
John Tillotson
Aaron Tippin
Ike & Tina Turner

McCoy Tyner
Bobby Valentino
Rhonda Vincent and
  the Rage
Frankie Valli and the
  Four Seasons
The Vogues
Wallace Green
Tom Waits
Dionne Warwick

Wheatstone Mission
Bryan White
Wet Willie
Widepsread Panic
Stevie Wonder
Betty Wright
Younger Brothers
Dennis Yost and the
  Classics IV
Z Z Top

GEORGIA SOUTHERN UNIVERSITY
1999-2006

1999 – Board of Regents appoints Bruce F. Grube, president of St. Cloud University in Minnesota, as the eleventh president, effective July 1. (3/11)

1999 – Dow Jones Industrial Average closes above 10,000 for the first time. (3/29)

1999 – Track and field coach Todd Lane announces signing of first ever women's track athletes to scholarships at Georgia Southern: Stefanie Anderson, Keyonia Collins, Heidi Gholston, and Jennifer McCalla. (4/21)

1999 – A GSU flag returns from the Discovery space shuttle mission to the International Space Station. (6/6)

1999 – Grube administration begins with a student enrollment of 14,476, an all-time high. (8/15)

1999 – Eagle fullback Adrian Peterson is the first sophomore to win the Walter Payton Award as the best player in Division I-AA college football. Later he stars in Eagles' fifth national title victory vs. Youngstown State. (12/20)

2000 – Georgia Southern meets rules for "Y2K" with 99 percent success rate. (1/1)

2000 – University holds first commencement at Paulson Stadium and awards 1,500 diplomas, following an address by Governor Roy Barnes. (5/6)

2000 – Coach Paul Johnson's Eagles defeat the University of Montana 27-25, winning sixth national football title. (12/16)

2000 – Republican George W. Bush, with 500,000 fewer votes than Democrat Albert Gore, is elected president of the U.S. after the U.S. Supreme Court stops Florida's recounting of ballots. (12/12)

2001 – Ten older dormitories converted to wireless internet access, setting the pace for campus information technology. (11/1)

2001 – Terrorists attack the U.S. with hijacked commercial airplanes demolishing New York's World Trade Center, damaging the Pentagon, and killing approximately 3,000 people. (9/11)

2001 – Lucindia Chance is new dean of the College of Education, and Katherine Conway-Turner is dean of the College of Liberal Arts and Social Studies. (7/1)

2002 – Lieutenant Governor Mark Taylor helps break ground for the State of Georgia's first College of Information Technology, costing $33 million, to be completed in less than two years. (4/11)

2002 – The School of Nursing's Family Nurse Practitioner Program is ranked 11th in the nation by *U.S. News and World Report*, while maintaining its position in the top tier of programs of its type in the nation. (10/1)

2002 – Former U.S. President Jimmy Carter wins the Nobel Peace Prize. (12/10)

2003 – College of Education receives grant of $1.3 million from the Microsoft Innovative Teachers Program. (1/1)

2003 – Oxford dormitory and In The Pines apartments give way to Southern Courtyard and Southern Pines, with places for 1,100 students. (8/1)

2003 – Space Shuttle Columbia disintegrates as it returns to the Earth's atmosphere, killing all seven members of the crew. (2/1)

2004 – Zach S. Henderson Library undergoes expansion that will double its size by the completion date of 2008. (7/1)

2004 – President George W. Bush wins re-election as President of the U.S. (11/03)

2004 – After leading the Eagles to an eighth Southern Conference football title, Coach Mike Sewak is named conference Coach of the Year. (12/15)

2005 – Pope John Paul II dies at the age of 84. (4/02)

2005 – Auxiliary Services introduces a solution to parking problem: a campus transit system, using modern passenger buses that make stops every fifteen minutes. (8/1)

2005 – Eagle Village, a new residence hall located on the site of Knight Village, opens, providing lodging for 782 freshmen. (8/1)

2006 – The Carnegie Foundation raises GSU to Doctoral/Research status. (4/19)

2006 – New head football coach Brian Van Gorder drops Eagles' famous option offense for a multiple scheme. (8/1)

CHAPTER 13

AMBITION AND MEMORY

A QUESTION OF IDENTITY

The seven years leading up to the end of the first century reflected an active university. Almost daily the local and regional media described new programs, outstanding faculty members and interesting students. The players walked the stage constantly, living out the current story of Georgia Southern.

The historian, like the coroner, should not conduct a postmortem exam prematurely. Time's passage provides perspective. In the meantime, contemporaries, including this writer, should observe the news and try to report it accurately.

When Bruce F. Grube took control of Georgia Southern in 1999, he became the first president since the 1960s that did not need to advocate university status. He believed earlier efforts to gain university status and an engineering school, perhaps, had left some parties wounded. He assumed the role of healer, at least temporarily. In some ways he began his presidency in the manner of President Zach Henderson who in 1948 viewed himself as a reconciler.

"I'm in the center of a web," Grube said, reflecting on his task. "I've got these strands of the web going out into all these very important constituencies and many of them internal and many external. And I'm trying to move the whole web forward without severing any of those strands."[1]

Seven years into his tenure, he gave the annual "state of the university" address to the faculty in 2006. He said he and his leadership team had been "setting the stage for a new Georgia Southern University."[2] Listeners who heard this announcement might have recalled events since 1980. How do these years fit into the larger story? To ask the question another way, what does it mean to be Georgia Southern University?

Really there are two Georgia Southerns: One is that fixed-in-time Georgia Southern of Memory. The other is that ever-restless Georgia Southern of Ambition. Each version of this place accurately depicted the university over which President Grube presided in 2006.

The Georgia Southern of Memory always will be "the people's school," brought to life by those fifty founders who rode that train to Savannah and placed the winning bid on December 1, 1906. Throughout the institution's history, people have kept the faith, as they did a century later, lending support through thick and thin.

Bruce Grube is twelfth president

Born in Arizona, on November 8, 1942, Bruce F. Grube grew up in California, living in several places as his father completed military service and, afterwards, moved throughout the state with his company. He completed an undergraduate degree in political science at the University of California, Berkeley, and a PhD at the University of Texas, Austin, in American government, politics, and public administration.

After completing his degree and teaching briefly at the University of Texas, he taught at John Jay College in New York, the University of Southern California and California State University. While working in California, he married Kathryn, a student whom he had met when he was an instructor at the University of Texas. He joined the faculty of California State University at Pomona, a comprehensive university, moving through the ranks to become a full professor.

One year's experience as head of the Political Science department convinced Grube he enjoyed administrative work, and his superiors recognized his interest and abilities. In 1987 the university named him Provost and Academic Vice President. In 1992 he moved to Colorado State where he was provost for three years. From 1995 until 1999 he was president of St. Cloud State in Minnesota, a master's level, NCAA Division II University, with more than 14,000 students. Bruce Grube was the first leader in Georgia Southern history who had previous experience as president of a four-year college or university.

Alumni regard the Georgia Southern of Memory fondly and in much the same way. They share the same mental landscape—the stately pines, majestic oaks, peaceful lakes, and dozens of buildings, including those of red brick and white columns on Sweetheart Circle. Here they lived, learned and loved. Here they also found their way into life, gaining a sense of direction that led them to a career.

The Georgia Southern of Ambition, on the other hand, forever reaches beyond itself, seeking a higher level of performance. This is the institution of tireless and enthusiastic leaders. It is Guy Wells landscaping and Marvin Pittman transforming Culture Hill into the state's Teachers College. It is Crook Smith, J. B. Scearce, J. I. Clements, Jack Stallings, and Erk Russell lifting the name to national prominence in athletics.

This Georgia Southern is John Eidson reorganizing and inspiring the college academically. It is Dale Lick working day and night for programs and projects that reshaped the institution. It is Nick Henry, with energy and imagination, finding a way to achieve status as South Georgia's first public university. It is President Grube's twenty-first century effort to enhance the university's national reputation. From the start this university has been a work in progress, with emphasis upon the latter.

SEEKING NATIONAL DISTINCTION

The chairman of the presidential nominating committee in 1998, Luther "Trey" Denton, believed the members wanted to see the university continue to move forward as a comprehensive university. After months of intensive searching and screening, the committee submitted to the Board of Regents the names of three finalists. The committee received reviews from several constituencies: the faculty, student body, community, and alumni. Denton was surprised that one candidate rose to the top of each review: the man who had been president of St. Cloud State University in Minnesota for only three years. His name was Bruce F. Grube.[3]

Chancellor Steven Portch critiqued the three and especially liked what he saw in the candidate from Minnesota: here was an experienced administrator who had been a successful president of an institution similar to Georgia Southern. The chancellor realized Bruce Grube, in his late fifties, had entered his prime years of productivity. For these and other reasons, Portch selected Grube. "When Georgia Southern found Bruce Grube, it hit a homerun," the chancellor remarked.[4]

During the interim, Harrison Sharpe Carter made history by serving for the second time as acting president.[5] (Near the end of the Henry administration, Carter had resigned as vice president, returning to the College of Business as a professor.) Denton, agreeing with the chancellor, said conditions were right for the new president to "hit the ground running."[6]

The chancellor appreciated Grube's breadth of experience as an academic leader in institutions similar to Georgia Southern. He noted the candidate's ability to develop strategies for helping universities implement change.[7]

Chancellor Portch perceived Georgia Southern to be a much better university than its reputation. Even though the institution had shown remarkable progress since the 1970s, the chancellor considered it an under-achiever. He believed Georgia Southern resembled most four-year institutions in the university system. Grube said he knew he "had been appointed by the regents and the chancellor to engage Georgia Southern in an effort to jump up a level in quality. That was very clear. I was here as a change agent."[8]

While he was a candidate for the presidency, Bruce Grube came to Statesboro to participate in an open question and answer forum. One of his major points impressed both students and faculty: "You will move forward as a university if you create a very student-centered university." He said a president should teach a class regularly because it "reminds me of why we are all here, and it's fun."[9]

Editors of the *George-Anne* and student government leaders discovered the president lived up to his words. He paid a personal visit to the campus newspaper office. He scheduled meetings monthly with the editor and leaders of student government. He taught a class, GSU 1210 (a brief introduction to the university), as recently as 2004.

UNDERSTANDING THE GOAL

When he became president, Bruce Grube realized this position would probably be his last before retirement, barring unforeseen circumstances. A decade is the common standard of measurement of institutional progress. "I would rather be known as the person . . . who was president when our quality and facility improved more so than in any other ten year period in our history."[10]

Hearing the clock in the bell tower chime the hours away, Grube immediately convened the Strategic Planning Council. He said he did not review with them the university's strengths and/or evaluate existing goals. Rather, the president revealed his ambitions for the university. He asked the committee to develop a strategic plan.

In the fall of 1999, the new president absolutely "charged up" the council, according to some of its members.[11] After adding two student representatives to the group, the president led the discussion about the future Georgia Southern. By the spring the president and the council had developed a major goal and a list of strategies for reaching it. This became a vision for the next ten years: "Georgia Southern will gain a national reputation as one of the best comprehensive universities."

Comprehensive universities typically focus on teaching rather than research. Comparisons between comprehensive universities are not easy,

The President's lady

Kathryn met her future husband, Bruce, when she was completing her undergraduate program at the University of Texas. The young political science instructor, Mr. Grube, worked part time as a university counselor. Kathryn asked her counselor for advice about whether to accept a "full ride" graduate fellowship in sociology. The counselor urged her to "go for it." Kathryn, fascinated by the counselor, had other ideas. The Grubes spend four or five evenings a week attending college and community functions, including a variety of sporting events—from football to volleyball.

BRUCE AND KATHRYN GRUBE

The Chancellor's appraisal

"Bruce Grube's experience and leadership are a perfect match for GSU. I'm truly excited about his appointment. He is a skilled leader, with a deep appreciation for the role of a regional university within a state system. He is also a people person, with strong interpersonal skills that will serve him well."

Stephen Portch, Chancellor
George-Anne, 11 March 1999

Top six SAT scores, 2005

Georgia Institute of Technology 1,328
University of Georgia.....................1,237
Southern Polytechnic Institute...........1,124
Georgia College & State University.......1,120
Georgia Southern University 1,098
Georgia State University.................1,085
Average for 18 four-year universities.....1,107

Charts of enrollment figures from 1906–2005 and SAT scores from 1960–2005 appear in the appendix.

President Grube & his vice presidents

Left to right: Teresa Thompson, student affairs; William Griffis, university advancement; Linda Bleicken, academic affairs; Joseph Franklin, business & finance; Marilyn Bruce, executive assistant.

"One of the Best" – The strategic plan

Vision:

Georgia Southern University will be recognized as one of the best public comprehensive universities in the country within the next ten years.

Strategies:

Academic Distinction
Student-Centered University
Technological Advancement
Transcultural Opportunities
Private and Public Partnerships
Physical Environment

"Academic distinction is the core of our vision of greatness, and . . . we must focus all our energies on an uncompromising expectation of excellence and the nurturing of an intellectual community. When that is achieved, our greatness will be validated."

because, unlike Georgia Southern, some do not offer doctoral degrees. Comprehensive universities enroll some 3.2 million students and have more graduates than any other academic institution, with the exception of community or junior colleges.[12] They may have enrollments as small as 4,000 or as large as 30,000. Many states classify their universities as either research or comprehensive.[13] Some have more rigorous entry requirements than others.

According to the council, in order to achieve the goals by the year 2009, the faculty and staff should concentrate on six strategies: 1) excellent teaching, 2) putting students at the center of campus life, 3) using technology productively and innovatively, 4) providing cross-cultural learning, 5) utilizing public and private support, and 6) improving the appearance of the campus environment.

At his inaugural address on Sunday afternoon, April 2, 2000, President Grube focused on academic excellence and said the university would stop admitting students who did not meet minimal admission requirements by 2001, even if this decision created a temporary enrollment shortfall. Thereby he accelerated an existing timetable for ending remedial studies (called "Learning Support").

He said he would begin discussions to speed up the university's plan to raise admissions standards. The university would concentrate on improving its academic environment. Emphasizing the importance of a student-centered campus, the president also reiterated a traditional Georgia Southern theme: excellence in teaching.

Within months of the inauguration, the president launched a capital campaign drive to coincide with the quest for national distinction. Early in 2006, he was confident the university would surpass its goal of $40 million well before the official 100th birthday on December 1, 2006.

President Grube designed his cabinet of four vice presidents to help shape policies and implement them uniformly. Two are alumni: Vice President for University Advancement William Griffis, ('69) and Vice President for Business and Finance Joseph Franklin, ('75). Griffis, appointed in 2004, supervised the capital campaign and ongoing fundraising efforts. The president also asked him to manage the university's communications.

Franklin, named in 2006, monitored the budget of $216 million and took responsibility for the buildings, grounds, auxiliary affairs, and athletic programs. He described the campus of 650 acres as a community with a combined population of around 18,000 students, faculty, staff, and employees. "This community requires the same level of service as any community, and we want to provide the very best," Franklin said.[14]

Before leaving to become a university chancellor in Illinois in 2004, Provost and Vice President for Academic Affairs Vaughn Vandegrift enhanced the academic environment and implemented standards for the faculty as scholar-teachers (a familiar concept in higher education). Linda Bleicken, formerly an associate professor of management, served briefly as acting provost and vice president for academic affairs before succeeding Vandegrift in 2005. She understood clearly her primary task: to build a team focused on achieving national distinction.

Teresa Thompson joined the staff of Georgia Southern in 2000 as director of admissions. In 2005 President Grube named her permanent vice president for student affairs, after she had served one year as acting vice president. Thompson focused broadly on the students' home-away-from-home. She managed a wide variety of student services, including health, entertainment, and information. She also sought to attract and retain highly motivated and well-qualified students who could take advantage of the learning experience and also contribute to it.

FULFILLING HISTORIC ASPIRATIONS

Trey Denton, a professor in the College of Business Administration was a co-chairman of the Strategic Planning Council when his term of service expired in 2006. He said the plan of twenty-four pages "put Georgia Southern's ideals into an action plan." For example, the rise in SAT scores began accelerating during President Henry's administration. Earlier strategic planning councils had placed a priority on improving academic standards. The plan of 2004 also focused on the faculty's history of good teaching and outlined in detail what it means to be a scholar-teacher.[15]

In the year 2000 the university finally caught up with the national average of SAT scores for entering freshmen. By then junior colleges had taken over all remedial or "learning support" programs. In 2006 freshmen had higher scores than the national average. SAT scores of entering freshmen in the fall averaged 1103, increasing five points above 1098 in 2005. The upward trend continued a pattern over the past dozen years.[16]

This record of consecutive improvement, Grube noted, was an accomplishment unmatched in the university system. In 2005 the university only slightly trailed the statewide SAT average among eighteen four-year institutions. The enrollment in 2006 of around 16,550 was virtually unchanged from 2005.

Minority students in the state continued to express interest in attending Georgia Southern. With a minority enrollment of 22 percent, the university ranked 27th nationally for the number of degrees awarded to African American students by traditionally white institutions.[17] This achievement reflects well on the institution's past.

The roots of positive racial attitudes run deep into the heart of Georgia Southern. A young musician, John Bradley, became the first African American student in 1965. He had never heard the names of Guy Wells, Marvin Pittman, or those editors of the *George-Anne* who, decades earlier, challenged prejudice and exposed racial intolerance. Between 1980 and 1997, the percentage of blacks enrolled rose from less than 8 percent to 28 percent, while the university simultaneously increased SAT scores.[18]

Stephen Portch and Bruce Grube

“ Wayne Gretsky said he was good, because he goes where the puck will be, not where the puck is. That applies to being the president of a university. Grube will go where the puck will be, not where it already is. ”

Chancellor Stephen Portch

Chancellors of the University System of Georgia

Charles M. Snelling, 1932-33
Philip Weltner, 1933-35
Steadman V. Sanford, 1935-45
Raymond R. Paty, 1946-48
Harmon W. Caldwell, 1949-64
George L. Simpson, 1965-79
Vernon Crawford, 1979-85
H. Dean Propst, 1985-1993
Stephen R. Portch, 1994-2001
Thomas C. Meredith, 2002-2005
Erroll B. Davis Jr., 2006 –

Provost and deans

Left to right, **row one:** Saundra Murray Nettles (graduate school), Lucindia Chance (education); **row two:** Linda M. Bleicken (provost), Charles J. Hardy (public health), Jane Rhoades Hudak (liberal arts, social sciences); **row three:** Amy Heaston (associate provost), Ronald E. Shiffler (business administration); **row four:** Virginia Samiratedu (assoc. to provost); **row five:** James Bradford (information technology), Gary E. Means (continuing education, public services), Frederick K. Whitt (health & human sciences), W. Bede Mitchell (library).

Original public health faculty

On January 1, 2006, six faculty members officially began the work of the new Jiann-Ping Hsu College of Public Health. Transferring from the College of Health and Human Sciences where the program began, the faculty included, *left to right,* Stuart Tedders, Anthony Parrillo, Robert Vogel, Charles Hardy, Laura Gunn, and Karl Peace.

THE LEADERSHIP TEAM OF 2006

Provost Bleicken took note of a "change in culture. We are certainly pursuing a slightly different pathway than we did before." Georgia Southern could not embark on a quest for national distinction without faculty support. She emphasized the importance of faculty-administration "connectivity."

The Grube administration, Bleicken said, introduced a new sense of identity. "Here people value the relationships they have with one another. I think people that don't buy into that culture or don't adopt it don't do well here. I think it's just a very frustrating place for them." As provost, Bleicken saw her task as building and nourishing the academic team. She said the deans who work with her pursue excellence in ways unique to each college.[19]

THE NEWEST COLLEGE:
JIANN-PING HSU COLLEGE OF PUBLIC HEALTH

At a time when no school or college of public health existed in the University System, Karl Peace found a way to support the beginning of one at Georgia Southern. The faculty member and scientist donated $2.5 million to establish the Jiann-Ping Hsu College of Public Health. The curriculum included programs for doctoral degrees in five areas. The name honored Peace's wife, who died of cancer in 2004.

Dean Fred Whitt of the College of Health and Human Sciences endorsed the proposal and collaborated with the former Dean of the Graduate College Charles Hardy. The result is the Jiann-Ping Hsu College of Public Health.

Dean Hardy said the university's newest college could become a major resource for improving the health of rural areas. This role would complement the highly successful rural health and nursing programs begun in the 1980s. Few public health programs in America focus on this neglected area of the population.

Hardy spent much of his time recruiting and mentoring highly qualified faculty who previously studied or taught in America's leading colleges of public health. Many new faculty members previously had been professors in some of the thirty-eight accredited colleges of public health in the nation.

COLLEGE OF HEALTH AND HUMAN SCIENCES

In the 1950s Georgia Southern established a reputation for offering the leading undergraduate program in Health, Physical Education, and Recreation in the State of Georgia. Graduates found jobs in schools and especially community recreation programs. In truth, the groundwork for this achievement began in 1935 when President Pittman created the Division of Physical Education. For decades public schools in Georgia depended on Teachers College to supply qualified PE teachers and coaches.

By 1980 new leadership led to the creation of the School of Health, Physical Education, Recreation and Nursing. With the addition of Home Economics and the Center for Rural Health and Research in 1987, the school continued to evolve and became the School of Health and Professional Studies. The Board of Regents upgraded Georgia Southern to university status in 1990, and two years later the unit became the College of Health and Professional Studies.

In 2006 under a new name, the College of Health and Human Sciences included a School of Nursing, the Department of Health and Kinesiology, and the Department of Hospitality, Tourism, & Consumer Sciences. The highly successful School of Public Health, which began in the College of Health and Human Sciences under Dean Fred Whitt, became an independent college in an effort to gain national accreditation. Dean Whitt, who began leading the college in 1992, gave credit to his high-achieving faculty.

The dean took special pride in the more than 2,500 students enrolled in undergraduate and graduate programs in the College of Health and Human Sciences. Each year and in growing numbers they prepare for a variety of occupations, such as nursing and health care, recreation, tourism, hotel and restaurant management, interior design, sports management, nutrition, exercise science, sports medicine, child development, and fashion merchandising and apparel design.

COLLEGE OF LIBERAL ARTS AND SOCIAL SCIENCES

The College of Liberal Arts and Social Sciences grew out of the School of Arts and Sciences, organized in 1968. The college helps provide the foundation for the student's entire university education—the core curriculum. Ten departments and five interdisciplinary centers compose CLASS.

Dean Jane Rhoades Hudak, formerly a professor of art, administered a college of some 3,000 students in 2006. She said the "humanities, social science, and fine arts engage the students" in subjects relevant to one's life and work. Hudak talked with corporate executives who said their companies needed employees who could communicate well and use research and critical thinking skills. They told her to send CLASS graduates "into the world of work where they were needed."

CLASS majors specialize in subjects that prepare them to think independently and for the public good. Hudak adds that at Georgia Southern majors in her college learn how to think internationally.[20]

Departments in the liberal arts and social sciences typically produce the largest share of the university's faculty publications and scholarly presentations each year.[21] In 2006, dozens of professors were well-known

Lonice C. Barrett ('65)

Selected by *Georgia Trend* magazine in 2004 as Georgia's "Top Public Servant," Barrett graduated from Georgia Southern in 1965. A recreation major, he worked at all levels of government, beginning as director of the Statesboro Recreation Department and including a lengthy and distinguished tenure as Commissioner of the Georgia Department of Natural Resources. Organizations at the state and national level have honored Barrett for his effective leadership in the fields of recreation, tourism, and conservation. In 2006 he was director of implementation of the Commission for a New Georgia.

Music majors sing and dance through a Gilbert and Sullivan show in the Performing Arts Center. They experience a stage and orchestra that meet standards for Broadway productions.

Professor of Biology Lorne M. Wolfe is featured on the cover of a magazine published by the University of Lausanne, Switzerland. Wolfe, right, works with a biologist from the University of Virginia, Professor Douglas R. Taylor, and with numerous GSU undergraduate and graduate students. Wolfe, supported by major federal grants, monitors how invasive plants threaten global biodiversity.

authors, musicians, artists, speakers, and thinkers. She said CLASS professors focus on their reason for being: to inspire and prepare students for the future.

THE ALLEN E. PAULSON COLLEGE OF SCIENCE AND TECHNOLOGY

This college goes by the acronym of COST. It is a dynamic consortium of science departments (biology, chemistry, mathematics, physics, geology and geography) and applied departments (engineering technology, construction, graphic communications, industrial manufacturing, and military science). Students pursing careers in medicine, pharmacy, environmental research, or engineering fields tend to gravitate toward this college.

Interim Dean Bret Danilowicz said COST's location is an advantage. Statesboro lies near the center of a corridor linking southeastern and coastal Georgia. Regional leaders developed an economic plan known as the S4 Technology Corridor Initiative, designed to attract technology industries to the region. Georgia Southern could become the intellectual and technical hub of this region, he noted, because of the strong academic programs and historically active connections between the college and industries, such as Gulfstream Aerospace Corporation. Southern's new College of Information of Technology and COST could provide significant leadership for developing industries in the region.

In 2006 southeastern and coastal sections of Georgia continued to attract industries and build residential communities. Some COST professors conducted research into the impact of development on water quality, biodiversity, and natural habitats. Both undergraduate and graduate students conducted internships and research experiences related to the sustainability of resources. Dean Danilowicz said COST graduates were ready to help plan for a sustainable environment.[22]

The first stand-alone information technology college in the University System of Georgia opened in 2001. Graduates of the program serve industries and businesses that depend upon digital communication.

COLLEGE OF INFORMATION TECHNOLOGY

According to a widely circulated story, the state's only stand-alone College of Information Technology began as a dinner-table conversation at an Atlanta restaurant around the year 2000. Those at the table included the Governor of Georgia, Roy Barnes, an influential state politician, Terry Coleman, and the founder and president of Dell Computers, Inc., Michael Dell. When the governor asked the computer magnate what the state should do if it wanted to play a larger role in the important new field of information technology, Dell replied with words like these: "First, you need a good college of information technology to provide the intellectual leadership." Governor Barnes and

Representative Coleman had good reasons to consider placing the college in Statesboro, because of the university's growing influence in the state and nation.

The new College of Information Technology quickly established links with industries such as NCR, or National Cash Register. Using a gift of NCR software and rights valued at almost $3 million, professors have taught students to become communications consultants and entrepreneurs. Georgia Southern students designed and tested programs for scanning and tracking devices that NCR used worldwide.

One of among only forty colleges of information technology in America, the CIT at Georgia Southern installed state-of-the-art equipment. Funded by a special grant from the legislature, contractors designed the technology into the building itself. Behind the walls a vast fiber optics network connects classrooms and offices with the world's information infrastructure.

The program does not focus only on computer technology, said Founding Dean James Bradford. It produces leaders and innovators who find good jobs when they earn their degrees. Georgia Southern's graduates should be models of creativity and character.

Instead of a single-discipline approach to learning, Bradford organized a program based on the bedrock curriculum of the university. Students specialize in software development, computer science, information systems, or information technology. A student who majors in information technology likely will have a career in the corporate world. Bradford said his students should be aware of the social implications of I T.[23]

Students spend some class time discussing ethical dilemmas created by the information age. Those who major in I T also specialize in an "outside" field. Some choose business, education, health science, technology, or one of the liberal arts or social sciences. This interdisciplinary approach has become a hallmark of information technology at Southern.

COLLEGE OF EDUCATION

The College of Education in 2006 offered the oldest professional degree at Georgia Southern: the bachelor's degree education. From 1924 to 1955 the entire college focused exclusively on preparing future teachers. Students at Georgia Southern commonly intended to teach, although they sometimes chose careers outside of education. Having offered the doctoral degree for the past decade, the College of Education in 2005 enrolled 1,218 graduate students; more that one-third pursued doctoral degrees.

Dean Lucindia "Cindi" Chance came to Georgia Southern in 2001 and began to lead the college to form partnerships with local schools. She wanted to improve teaching and learning at all levels—pre-school through doctoral. Georgia Southern is the only unit in the university system to hold

Above: *Maria Teresa de Jesus Mendoza de Vasquez, a graduate student from Mexico, is part of the GSU's Veracruz Teacher Project, an effort to share bilingual and cultural expertise. Both the university and area schools benefit from the exchange program.*

Below: *GSU education major, Jessica Warnock, right, demonstrates a science activity with British students at the Deptford Green Secondary School in East London in 2004.*

membership in the National Network for Educational Renewal. Founded by John Goodlad of the University of Washington, this organization seeks to restore public education to the role envisioned by the founders of the nation. Schools should prepare citizens to make judgments about democracy's core values—compassion, freedom, and responsibility.

The COE in 2006 was the only college of education in the United States involved in the International Networking for Educational Transformation, an organization that began as a network of 2,700 English schools in 2004; now it includes schools and universities from around the world. Georgia Southern hosted their international conference in 2006, the first time on U.S. soil.

As a founding partner of the International Learning Community, the College developed a plan for majors to fulfill their student teaching assignments in partner schools in England. Unlike typical exchange programs, college faculty organized this project as a way for students to become immersed in an international school with a single focus—improved teaching and learning. Teachers from other countries usually work with Georgia Southern students on the campus and with peer teachers and public schools of South Georgia.[24]

THE COLLEGE OF BUSINESS ADMINISTRATION

Led by Dean Ronald Shiffler, the College of Business Administration grew out of the business education division established in the 1930s. In 2006 COBA was the university's largest college, enrolling more than 3,000 undergraduate and nearly 300 graduate students. Students typically major in management, marketing, finance, and accounting. COBA also hosts the School of Economic Development, an extension of the Department of economics. Graduates of the school help communities develop their economic resources. Some also find rewarding careers in international business.

Dean Shiffler built programs relevant to the region's needs. For example, the university in 2006 was about an hour's drive from a major port in Savannah and just ten minutes from one of the largest distribution centers operated by America's leading retailer. Shiffler suggested the obvious: COBA should focus on major business activities in the region. The logistics major has become one of the university's most productive new programs, and the transportation industry began to look to COBA for guidance and support.[25]

Another program extended the influence of the college into America's corporate arena. In 2005 the college enrolled its first class of students in a new major, forensic accounting. Led by the director of the School of Accountancy, J. Lowell Mooney, this interdisciplinary program joined the study of ethics with sophisticated analyses of financial record

Professors teach business administration through real-life boardroom experiences. Left to right: *Brooke Smith, student; Ronald Shiffler, Dean; Cheryl Metrejean, professor; and Ayanna Luke, student.*

keeping. News headlines of corporate accounting scandals made obvious the relevance of this innovative new program. The forensic accounting program at Georgia Southern University was one of the first of its kind in the nation.[26]

Through the College of Graduate Studies, COBA organized at Savannah's Coastal Georgia Center an evening MBA program. Working professionals in the low country liked the arrangement from the start. Another educational solution for this adult population, the WebMBA, began in the year 2000. COBA helped organize a consortium of five Georgia institutions of higher education to create and deliver this wholly online MBA program.

JACK N. AVERITT COLLEGE OF GRADUATE STUDIES

In 2006 the provost and the deans of the colleges pursued national distinction through their undergraduate programs as well as the Jack N. Averitt College of Graduate Studies, administered by Interim Dean Saundra Murray Nettles.

The college anticipated new doctoral degrees, in addition to those in education and psychology. Most academic departments offer graduate classes and masters degrees in thirty-eight major areas. A popular offering through the years has been the specialist degree in education.

Students enroll in graduate classes on the campus in Statesboro and in off campus centers at Brunswick, Augusta, Dublin, and Savannah, where the university operates a spacious mini-campus called the Coastal Georgia Center. Other graduate-level courses appear in the list of classes offered by the Continuing Education Center.

The College of Graduate Studies was named for the founding dean of the division of graduate studies, Jack Nelson Averitt. This longtime administrator and faculty member taught history and social science to thousands of students during his career from 1945-1979.

ZACH S. HENDERSON LIBRARY

The university's intellectual storehouse has a name: the Zach S. Henderson Library, named for the longest-serving administrator and president of Georgia Southern. A new addition/renovation was underway in 2006. Planners designed the building to double the space for materials and research.

Bede Mitchell, dean of the libraries, projected this state-of-the-art facility would store 1.1 million books. In 2006 the library held 588,997 volumes. The new space provided computer services that link readers to libraries and other learners across the globe. The library celebrated the centennial year by introducing to the State of Georgia an automated system for locating books. Known as ARC (for "automatic retrieval collection"), the new machinery eliminates the need for readers to search the stacks for books. A click of the

Honoring the longtime history professor and administrator and first dean of the graduate school, the Jack N. Averitt College of Graduate Studies offers a broad range of programs leading to master's and doctoral degrees.

Zach S. Henderson Library

Named for President Zach Suddath Henderson, dean from 1927-1948 and president from 1948-1968, the library is located in the heart of the campus near the scenic lake built by President Guy Wells in 1933. An expansion begun in 2004 doubled the size of the original structure.

Pop & rock at PAC & Paulson

"Since 2002 the Performing Arts Center has provided an intimate venue for performers and musical groups. Some acts featured 'roots'musicians like those who appeared at coffeehouse bookings in Williams Center years earlier. PAC performers have included Ricky Skaggs, Little River Band, Rhonda Vincent and the Rage, Nitty Gritty Dirt Band, Nickel Creek, Kathy Mattea, Preservation Hall Jazz Band, and Tony Arata (award-winning songwriter and 1980 alumnus).

"Big outdoor shows arrived at Paulson Stadium from 1995 through 1997 with a series of spring concerts featuring such country acts as Vince Gill, Lee Greenwood, Aaron Tippins, and Doug Supernaw. Stadium shows returned in 2005 with a spring concert by 3 Doors Down attended by about 7,000 wildly enthusiastic fans; however, urban artist Ciara's show later that year only drew 1,000."

William G. Neville III

Located in the heart of the Georgia Southern University campus among the pines, the Center for Wildlife Education and the Lamar Q Ball Jr. Raptor Center provide educational opportunities for families and school groups throughout the year.

An early 20th century farm of eleven acres is the home of the Georgia Southern Botanical Garden. Visitors of all ages can glimpse a unique view of the cultural and natural heritage of the southeastern coastal plain, an area rich in unique and endangered plants.

computer mouse quickly dispatches the requested book to the circulation desk, where the reader can check it out.

CONTINUING EDUCATION AND PUBLIC SERVICES

The Continuing Education Center opens the university's doors to all who want to learn. Young adults contemplating a career join retired seniors to learn new skills or to seek knowledge in general. This unit provides college-level learning opportunities for thousands of people who otherwise could not attend. The university offers courses in the Nessmith-Lane Building on campus and in university centers in Dublin, Brunswick, and Hinesville, as well as the Coastal Georgia Center in Savannah.

Gary Means, an experienced public education leader in the California State University system, became Dean of Continuing Education and Public Services during the summer of 2006. Immediately he began working on two projects to link excellent teachers with eager learners: 1) offering undergraduate and graduate-level classes for CE credits that, in some cases, can be transferred into academic credits; 2) implementing a program that permits high school students to obtain academic credits in a variety of subjects.

Huge audiences each year benefit from other public services provided by the Continuing Education Center. Families and individuals of all ages make a combined audience of more than 100,000 visitors each year at the Wildlife Education Center, the Botanical Garden, the Georgia Southern Museum, and the Performing Arts Center. At each venue visitors experience the joy of informal learning and the pleasure of professional productions.

PRESIDENT GRUBE ANNOUNCES DISTINCTION

On April 19, 2006, President Grube delivered an announcement he considered evidence of national distinction. The "classification body for American universities has elevated Georgia Southern to Doctoral/Research University status, up from its previous Masters I ranking." [27]

The Carnegie Foundation for the Advancement of Teaching decided to reclassify Georgia Southern, President Grube explained, because the university had made progress toward achieving the goal of "rising to the top tier of national ranking among comprehensive universities." [28]

The president also offered as evidence of distinction some important news from the Capitol. On the previous day, April 18, 2006, the Board of Regents authorized the university to grant a doctoral degree in psychology, the institution's second doctorate. The College of Education awarded the university's first stand-alone doctorate in education in 1996. [29]

As the president spoke, the Board of Regents was reviewing the university's request for a doctoral degree in public health. Within a few short years, Grube said, the university planned to offer several doctorates, all in practical or applied areas.

Previously the Carnegie Foundation had classified Georgia Southern as one of 350 "Masters Level I" institutions, a category including a number of four-year colleges and universities in the University System of Georgia. The move forward made Georgia Southern the only university in Georgia in a category of 84 Doctoral/Research Universities nationwide, public and private. The change recognized the growing number of EdD degrees the university had granted each year since 1996.

Within the university system, only three public universities had achieved higher Carnegie rankings: Georgia State University was one of 103 "high research" universities. Both Georgia Tech and the University of Georgia were among 96 "very high research" universities.[30] Using its own nomenclature, the University System of Georgia listed Georgia Southern and Valdosta State as "regional universities."

President Bruce Grube announced on April 19, 2006, the university had moved from a master's category to a doctoral/research category, based in part on the number of doctoral degrees it had granted since 1996.

EVALUATING NATIONAL DISTINCTION

The authors of the Strategic Plan incorporated the president's ambition for the university with words such as *distinction, greatness, reputation, national,* and *international.* These words appear sixty-seven times in the text of twenty-four pages.[31] The plan, however, did not include a yardstick for measuring national distinction.

How will the university know when the nation regards it as distinctive? Annual rankings, such as those by *U.S. News and World Report,* provide national benchmarks. Provost Linda Bleicken points out "It would be nice, but before we ever get a high ranking, the people who are out there need to know how good we are. People need to somehow understand that this takes time."[32]

One of the architects of the Strategic Plan, Trey Denton, said the mark of distinction would appear "whenever universities like Appalachian State, James Madison, and Northern Iowa consider Georgia Southern as a peer institution."[33] The plan listed these and similar universities as "aspirational models."

The College of Liberal Arts and Social Sciences Dean Jane Rhoades Hudak said the institution will achieve distinction when others regard it as the "go-to place. That is when we will know. When people start to say 'Georgia Southern is the place to go' to find the best program in communications, clinical psychology, anthropology, and other liberal arts and social sciences." In some cases, Hudak maintained, people already regard Georgia Southern as the "go to" place.[34]

Dean Charles Hardy of the Jiann-Ping Hsu College of Public Health suggested a method for determining the university's ultimate distinction.

The Nessmith-Lane Continuing Education Building offers the ideal location and facilities for adult learning, below. The center offers a full schedule of training, programs, conferences, workshops, seminars, symposia, and business meeting. The building honors the contributions of two outstanding local legislators of the twentieth century, Paul Nessmith and Jones Lane.

Students learn more than biostatistics in Professor Peace's classroom, right.

Putting his life where his heart is

In 2000 Karl Peace surprised many research professionals when he decided to leave his extremely lucrative job and join the faculty of Georgia Southern University. Right away he founded the Center for Biostatistics. Because of his experience and reputation as a scientist, the College of Health and Human Sciences received major grants from the Georgia Research Alliance and the Georgia Cancer Coalition. These funds allowed Georgia Southern to establish a center for biostatistics.

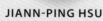

JIANN-PING HSU

Later the GCC recognized Peace as the Georgia Cancer Coalition Distinguished Cancer Scholar at this university, the only biostatistician in the State of Georgia to hold this title.

When his wife, Jiann-Ping Hsu, knew she was dying of cancer, Karl Peace approached Provost Vaughn Vandegrift and explored the possibility of endowing a college of public health. The Board of Regents approved the request on January 14, 2004. The university dedicated the college twelve days later while Peace's wife courageously lived with her terminal illness. The Jiann-Ping Hsu College of Public Health became Peace's main interest and workplace.

"When knowledgeable people mention rural public health education, what will be the name that first comes to mind?" Hardy said, "When they answer, at first breath, 'Georgia Southern University,' we will have achieved distinction."[35]

Professor Karl Peace, a biostatistical scientist, provided by far the most ambitious criterion for distinction: "When students in my field—public health—turn down admission to Harvard or Emory and choose Georgia Southern, then we will know the university has arrived."[36]

AN ALUMNUS ADDS DISTINCTION

Karl Peace left his home in rural southwest Georgia in 1959, having borrowed money to attend Georgia Teachers College. The son of an illiterate tenant farmer, Peace found a future at what then was a much smaller and less ambitious institution.

Within a year the college wore a new name, Georgia Southern. Here he found his intellectual home in the world of mathematics and science. After earning a PhD at the Medical College of Virginia, he applied his love of statistics to medical research. When he began his career as a researcher, Peace's ambition sprang from a deeply personal motive: He was supporting his mother, a cancer patient, as well as his younger brother and sister.

Peace enjoyed his career in the pharmaceutical industry, rising swiftly to become Vice President of Worldwide Technical Operations at Parke-Davis/Warner Lambert. After a few years, he started his own company, Biopharmaceutical Research Consultants, Inc.

He engaged in pace-setting research, quickly making pivotal contributions in the development of drugs for treating hypertension, Alzheimer's disease, and panic attacks. He introduced preventive medications for gastric and peptic ulcers. The company grew from one to sixty-five employees, mostly scientists, before he gave it to his wife, Jiann-Ping Hsu, a fellow medical researcher who received her PhD from the University of California at Berkeley, graduating at the head of her class.

Peace realized he owed so much of his success to the opportunities he had as a student at Georgia Southern. He endowed two scholarships in 1996, one to honor his mother and another to assist needy and high-achieving students. By the year 2006 his scholarships had assisted a dozen students. Willie I. "Bill" Golden told Peace about the Board of Regents' matching funds for endowed professorships. He responded with the Karl E. Peace Chair in Biostatistics—the first Eminent Scholar Chair at the university.

Meanwhile, the College of Health and Human Sciences under the leadership of Dean Fred Whitt, had begun to explore the possibility of organizing a School of Public Health. Peace found an especially helpful colleague in Charles Hardy, head of the Department of Kinesiology and, later, Dean of the College of Graduate Studies. They planned the Master's of Public Health degree in Biostatistics.

With his gift of $2.5 million to establish the institution's newest college, the Jiann-Ping Hsu College of Public Health. Peace gave something else of great value. He gave a part of himself: this man who began his path through life as a barefooted tenant farmer's son. His students got the point of this story. They realized they were beginning their journey precisely where their professor began his—Georgia Southern University, their university. [37]

Karl Peace wrote the entering class in 2006 a letter that encouraged them to aspire toward achievement and service. He reminded them of the "power of human will over circumstances" as well as the "noble principles of initiative, work ethic, honesty, integrity and fair play, being selfless and always striving to elevate the human condition of others." In this case the students realized the author had followed his own advice.

STUDENTS GAVE IT TO THE FUTURE: THE RAC

The tradition of intramurals began in the earliest days of the A&M School. Students wanted to play sports in 1909, so they bought a football and began practice. Soon women divided into teams and began intramural basketball. Baseball, softball, tennis, soccer, volleyball and boxing followed. By 1935 the division of physical education offered these sports as intramural activities.

Beginning in the 1950s, campus intramurals involved large numbers of students. In 2005, the Office Campus Recreation and Intramurals reported more than 400,000 participations in league sports or fitness activities. This level of activity is unusually heavy for a student body of less than 17,000 students. The point is clear: students typically engage in sports and fitness at Georgia Southern.

For decades, students depended on athletic playing fields and indoor courts whenever Eagle athletic teams were not using them. In 1990 CRI Director William Ehling and Assistant Dean of Students George Lynch began discussing ways to provide facilities dedicated solely for recreational purposes. Soon students and administrators together planned a new Recreation Activity Center. They called it the RAC, and the name stuck. The college could not use state funding for this facility, so the student body voted to raise their activity fee by $20 to pay off bonds for a new structure of some 85,000 square feet.

On April 18, 1998, President Nick Henry pulled himself to the top of the climbing wall and came back down to dedicate

Building a RAC for tomorrow

The Recreation Activities Center is one of the most popular places to gather for exercise and intramural athletics. Because the original red brick building was so heavily used, students invested their own money to build an expansion. The new addition, *shown below*, created a massive structure of more than 200,000 square feet.

The retired jerseys: No. 8, No. 3

Tracy Ham # 8—The quarterback who defined the powerful triple option scheme led the Eagles to two Division I-AA champions in 1985 and 1986. He was

the only player in college football history to rush for more than 3,000 yards and pass for more than 5,000. Although the Los Angeles Rams drafted him, he shifted to the Canadian Football League where he became a superstar. In 1989, after rushing for 1,005 yards and passing for a career-high 4,366 yards as an Edmonton Eskimo, Ham was named the CFL's Most Outstanding Player. The CFL named him MVP of the Grey Cup after he led Baltimore to a championship win over Calgary. After thirteen years in the CFL he retired in 2000.

Adrian Peterson # 3—While attending GSU, Peterson broke most of the school's offensive records and led the team to three national championship appearances. The quick, powerful fullback played a key role in back-to-back wins of 1999 and 2000. After winning the Walter Payton Award in 1999, Peterson was drafted by the Chicago Bears in 2002 and continued to play for them in 2006. He scored his first NFL touchdown in 2002, and he had his best professional season in 2005, playing in 16 games, earning 391 yards and scoring two touchdowns.

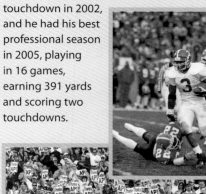

the RAC. Students cheered loudly for what they had contributed – three full-length courts marked for basketball and volleyball, and badminton. There were state-of-the-art fitness machines, table tennis courts, and an indoor walking track. The climbing walls featured three elevations of varying degrees of difficulty.

Within three years the facility had become so popular, students voted to increase its size by 120,000 square feet. The addition includes both an indoor and an outdoor swimming pool, extended walking trails, more exercise machines, huge saunas, and a new Southern Adventures Center where students can schedule the use of outdoor equipment such as canoes, tents, and hiking equipment. The expansion also renovated fields for flag football, softball, and soccer. Scheduled for completion by the end of 2006, the facility cost some $32 million, all paid for by an additional fee of $43 per student.

The vision of the student body amazed many outsiders. Those who voted to build the original RAC in 1991 taxed themselves to build something they would never enjoy. Likewise, upperclassmen that voted for the expansion in 2003 would not use the new facility. They gave a wonderful present to the next generation of students.

THE LENGTHENED SHADOW

At the dawn of its second century, this institution reflected the irreversible effects of change. In spite of setbacks, roadblocks, and, yes, mistakes, Georgia Southern ended its first century. The first day of December in 2006 was not a nostalgic ending but a moment filled with promise. This was the Georgia Southern of Ambition in full form. Yet there is another institution that always catches up with the future: The Georgia Southern of Memory.

Ralph Waldo Emerson in 1841 memorably said, "An institution is the lengthened shadow of one man." Most who quote the phrase identify the shadow with the president of an organization. The Georgia Southern of Memory, however, casts a shadow composed of untold numbers of individuals.

Marvin Pittman suggested that students—future alumni—actually carried forward the image of Teachers College. He made that point in several articles he wrote for the *Alumni Quarterly* in 1950-1952.

Georgia Southern's destiny is nothing less than the lengthened shadow of its alumni and those who influenced them. The shadow includes professors, administrators, and coaches. Yes, coaches also belong on the list of mentors.

In 2006 the Athletic Department was responsible for some 370 student-athletes. The way they compete, according to Athletics Director Sam Baker, sends a message to a vast audience.[38] The influence of coaches extends far beyond the athletes under their charge.

At Georgia Southern some of the great instructors of its first century went by the name of "Coach." They taught fans lessons about life's adversities and challenges. They inspired them with great victories and demonstrated how to overcome defeat on the playing field and in the larger game of life.

On Sunday afternoon, September 10, 2006, the university opened its football stadium for a memorial service honoring Coach Erk Russell who died two days earlier at the age of eighty. A crowd of around three thousand, larger than any church or auditorium in town could hold, gathered at Paulson Stadium. There they remembered one of the university's great teachers who led the Eagles to three national championships and a record of 83-22-1. The service of forty-five minutes featured comments by some of his friends and former players. Rev. Claude McBride, chaplain emeritus of the University of Georgia Bulldogs football team, delivered the eulogy. Each speaker recalled Russell's great gift: he loved his subject, and he loved his students.

President Emeritus Pittman wrote interesting paragraphs about former students who had become teachers, school administrators, doctors, ministers, lawyers, businessmen, journalists, and so forth. He sketched the history of the college in outline form. Clearly he loved to define the institution, but he knew only the next generation could give it momentum.

In 1952, two years before he died, Pittman passed the revitalized association into the capable hands of Alumni Director Georgia Watson. Perhaps the most unselfish and lengthy alumni volunteer in history was Newelle DeLoach Anderson, an alumna of the 1930s who for decades kept in touch with fellow alumni from the twenties and thirties. In 2006 the Georgia Southern Alumni Association, led by Director of Alumni Relations Frank Hook, kept in touch with 59,505 living alumni, including those who attended as early as the 1920s. He became director in 1995 when Gene Crawford retired after completing sixteen years of service as director of alumni development.

A SHARED JOURNEY THROUGH TIME

More than anyone else, alumni experience a common journey into the larger world. Most recall the day they first traveled up that hill of memories on the south side of Statesboro. Perhaps they remember the road through stately pine trees, bordered by dogwoods.

Most of the original pines remained and appeared healthy in 2006. In general the scenery had improved as the institution entered its second century. The campus in 2006, by any measure, was the most beautiful in the University System of Georgia. President Bruce Grube said he had made a priority of continually improving the appearance of the campus. The master plan of 2002 protects and enhances historic sections of the campus, including the Herty Pines and the original buildings.

The spectacle of 2006 exists, because President Grube and several earlier presidents invested time and effort. President Nick Henry authorized those red brick walkways that now direct students beneath the reaching arms of stately oaks. The paths lead walkers beside the still waters of neatly coupled

Fabled coach of the Blue Tide, Teachers, and Professors football teams, Crook Smith, left, realized his fondest wish when Erk Russell restored football at Georgia Southern in 1981, after an absence of forty years.

The Quotable Erk

- The harder I work, the luckier I get.
- When you don't have the best of everything, make the best of everything you have.
- There is no "I" in Team.
- If I do, they will. If I don't, they won't.
- The brotherhood of football is the strongest known to man.
- If you want to get to the top, start playing like you're already there.
- Communication is the most important technique in teaching. Not memos, not bulletin boards, not announcements, but one-on-one.
- Do right, say your prayers, and after you die, if you're lucky, you'll wake up in . . . Statesboro.

Erk Russell (1926–2006)
Collected

ponds. Students in the 1930s called them Lake Wells and Lake Ruby. The signature oaks, another legacy of President Wells, descend directly from historic landmark trees of Colonial Georgia.

When he retired from a long presidential career elsewhere, Guy Wells moved back to Statesboro. On summer mornings in the late 1950s, he returned to the campus and stood in the shade, enjoying the taste of cool, red, ripe watermelon, sliced expertly by Zach Henderson, the man he once appointed dean. Like those oaks he nurtured from tiny acorns, his college had grown sturdily and impressively. Proudly and thankfully he remembered.

A LIGHT ON THE HILL

An honorable image of this place appears at the beginning of chapter seven. Drawn by a member of the student body, the scene depicts the heart and soul of the institution: It is a light on the hill.

The familiar buildings at the peak represent the historic Georgia Southern campus. Here the light of learning shines beyond the known to the unknown. Seekers arrive from all parts of the world and every walk of life. As they approach the top, they see an ideal image of themselves reflected in the eyes of a student.

This image depicts the true story of Georgia Southern. On day one the college was a gift of hope. The founders and early leaders would not let it perish. They always managed to keep the light burning.

Those who made the first century—founders, faculty, staff, students, administrators, and supporters—forever reside in the Georgia Southern of Memory. Their voices from the past, like a gentle breeze, renew and inspire all who will listen.

Those who climb the hill of memory can hear voices of yesterday echo around Sweetheart Circle and across the lakes. Alumni who return for homecoming weekend may recall the names of classmates with whom they shared the treasure of youth. Here they reflect on those women and men who taught them well. What never seems to die is the influence of people who care, who love both learning and learners.

The past lingers among the pine and the dogwood, the oak and the willow. The truth about this university endures into its second century. Herein lies the distinction of Georgia Southern University: It is still the people's school. Each autumn this wonderful story begins anew on that bright green hill south of Statesboro.

Acknowledgments

This work reflects the encouragement and assistance of so many generous and thoughtful people. When Regina "Gina" Neville accepted the task of managing the production and design of this book, I was pleased. Having worked with her on other publications, I knew she would bring to bear a great deal of experience in printing and design. In very important ways she identified with the author's commitment to prepare the best history within our ability. She constantly found ways to translate ideas and images into effective page layouts, as the pages of the book make clear. The appearance of this very ambitious book, including more than five hundred images, is a tribute to Gina's handiwork.

Gina and I determined quite early that an illustrator could portray the landscapes of memory and provide continuity. We found a GSU alumnus and artist, Lawrence Smith, who was interested in assisting us. His work is visible on the upper right hand corner of the pages of each chapter. Each of the book's four sections begins with his art, and more than a dozen pages reflect the skillful presence of Smith's hand.

Because photographs of the university play such an important role in this book, we turned to the files of Georgia Southern's gifted photographer and media expert, Frank Fortune. Negatives from the 1970s and early 1980s reflect the work of his talented predecessor, Steve Ellwood, and we were lucky to have these at our disposal. For the final chapter, Fortune provided some outstanding images of the university in the year 2006. Frank and his able assistant, Suzanne Oliver, helped us locate hard-to-find pictures that add much human interest.

Another key team member throughout, Marvin Goss, a librarian and assistant professor, prepared a highly useful index. He worked with speed and accuracy as we completed the project. For three years he was a phone call or a click-of-the-mouse away, handling many dozens of requests for sources of information and images. He read and critiqued each chapter of the book, and the text reflects his corrections and suggestions. On occasion he helped our cause by combining archival research with personal travel plans. I cannot forget Marvin's unique eagerness to find solutions to difficult research problems.

Kelley Callaway, our in-house copy editor, began her publications career as editor of the *George-Anne*. In 2006 she received her MA degree in English. We are fortunate that she was able to assist us at this time in her life. She handled corrections and instructions made by Kelly Caudle, our consulting editorial supervisor. Like Gina, Kelley bonded with the project and found ways to fill in many blanks in my research and writing. Gina, Kelley, and I are so glad we were able to work with Kelly Caudle, an experienced and talented professional.

At key moments, friends stepped forward to lend a hand. Kirbylene Stephens donated many hours reading proofs of the last half of the book, making suggestions and correcting factual errors. Ric Mandes also helped by reading chapters, locating photographs, and recalling anecdotes from his long career at Georgia Southern. David Thompson, editor of the *Georgia Southern Magazine*, read most of the text and contributed some anecdotes that appear in the text. He also contacted alumni whose words appear on the pages of this volume.

Before I accepted the task of preparing this history, I talked with my friend and mentor, Jack Averitt. At one time I had thought he might be my co-author, but he convinced me I could do it alone. He discussed my research plans and reviewed some of my findings, filtering them through his personal knowledge of three-fourths of the university's history. I brought to his home on many occasions bare outlines that, after a few hours of his thoughtful analysis, became the framework for several chapters. I know to take his advice seriously, and this book reflects both his knowledge and wisdom.

I was fortunate to be able to interview four former presidents. Each one took time to review his years of service, and several commented helpfully on early drafts of chapters. Pope Duncan received me at his home in Deland, Florida, in the spring of 2003. He talked with me at length and candidly, even though he was suffering from an illness that claimed his life later that year. Judson Ward, well into his nineties, met me twice at his office at the Miller-Ward Alumni House at Emory University. He recalled many key players of Georgia Southern's history, and I am grateful for his sharp analysis of politics and personalities in the 1940s.

Dale Lick spoke with me for nearly four hours without repeating a single episode. This remarkable man helped me understand much better a presidency that I observed as a member of the faculty. Nick Henry not only allowed me to interview him twice, but he also indulged my frequent e-mail requests for information and photographs. Fortunately for Georgia Southern, he continues to contribute to this university's history as a productive member of the faculty. Bruce Grube, the current president, responded graciously to my request and granted a very helpful interview. He also had an opportunity to read sections of the book.

Interviews are not useful until a transcriber makes a faithful printed copy of conversations. At the beginning, Lavada Sykora, secretary to the provost, volunteered to make transcriptions of my interviews. She completed several in a professional manner. As the tapes mounted, the project identified Sherry Hoffman, who served as the project's transcriber. She worked quickly and accurately during her after-hours and weekends. I wish to thank Sherry for her conscientious and most helpful assistance.

Katharine Branscomb Kelley, granddaughter of Guy Wells, read and commented on material concerning her grandfather's years here. When I thought we would never find key photographs of his time, Katharine, better known as "Kc" (big "K," little "c") came through, and I am so grateful for her interest in helping us better understand one of this institution's early presidents.

I deeply appreciate the generous help and hospitality provided by I. M. Destler, who allowed me to interview him and to use his collection of letters and papers of his father, the late Chester McArthur Destler, a faculty member at Georgia Teachers College who played a significant role here from 1934 until 1941. Because the collected papers of Marvin Pittman apparently no longer exist, the Destler collection provides the best glimpse into the life and work of this president of the 1930s–40s.

Patrick Novotny, a member of the faculty in 2006, specializes in the social and political life of Georgia during the 1930s-1950s. A political scientist, Novotny was the first faculty member to compile for the library the writings of and about Marvin Pittman and his role at this institution.

Patrick has been especially generous, providing news items, correspondence, and other helpful material. I benefited from his keen insight into both politics and American history.

A local physician and Statesboro native, Robert Benson Jr., knew I was struggling to locate photographs of the institution from 1908 until the 1930s. He worked very hard to find them or to put me in touch with people who could help. Dr. Benson's collection of deeds, records, photographs, and manuscripts makes the early chapters come to life, and I want to take note of his unselfish interest in the centennial history project.

Two local historians also realized I needed help at various times. They did more than answer my calls. They anticipated my needs in advance. Kemp Mabry and Smith Banks for years have helped me understand Statesboro and Bulloch County. They stood by me in this truly exhaustive project and gave me benefit of their wealth of knowledge and friendship.

I acknowledge with sincere appreciation the following archives that provided information and materials useful for this publication:

Bulloch County Courthouse, Clerk of Court Records
Department of Archives and Records Management, Georgia Southern University
Division of Behavioral Science Research, Tuskegee Institute
Georgia Department of Archives and History
Georgia Historical Society
Hargrett Rare Book and Manuscript Library, University of Georgia
Museum and Archives of Georgia Education, Georgia College and State University
Southern Historical Collection, Manuscripts Department, Wilson Library, The University of North Carolina at Chapel Hill
Special Collections and Archives, Bruce T. Halle Library, Eastern Michigan University
Special Collections Unit, Robert Muldrow Cooper Library, Clemson University
Special Collections, Dunn Library, Simpson College, Indianola, Iowa
Special Collections, Georgia College and State University
Special Collections, Henderson Library, Georgia Southern University
Statesboro Regional Library

I hesitate to list names of individuals, because literally hundreds have assisted this project. The following provided unique materials or interpretations of events that helped me prepare this book. I mention them, knowing that I surely forgot someone whose name belongs here:

Elizabeth Cato Albers, Norma Allen, China Altman, Betty Altman, Pamela Altman, Urkovia Jacobs Andrews, Karla Redding Andrews, Jean Bartels, Sara Bennett, Dan Biggers, Barbara Bitter, Linda Bleicken, Parrish Blitch, Emory Bohler, Charles Bonds, LaShawn Bonds-Myers, Stella Vanlandingham Boswell, James Bradford, John and Winnette Bradley, Loretta Brandon, Lewis M. Branscomb, June Strickland Brantley, Nancy Davis Bray, Michael Braz, Clavelia Love Brinson, Erik Brooks, Caryl Brown, Jane Perkins Brown, Kelly Stratton Brown, Ed Brown, Marilyn Bruce, Nona and Isaac Bunce, Jo Starr Callaway, Harrison S. Carter, Jessie Zeigler Carter, Lucindia Chance, Genevieve Guardia Chenault, Eliza Clark, Martha Coleman, Chester Curry, Bret Danilowicz, Nancy Kerves Dart, Alton Davis, Larry Davis, Inman Davis, Catherine Davis, Maria Davis, Michael Deal, Cookie Deal, Michael Dean, Steve Denenberg, Trey Denton, Juanita Doss, Gay Kimbrough Dull, Margaret Duncan, Mitchell Dunn, William Duren, Frederick Dyer, Kent Dykes, Yolanda Eppes, Fran Florian, Cynthia Frost, Hal Fulmer, Owen Gaede, Jerry Smith Gentry, Daniel Good, Larry W. Gordon, Ruth Green, Eric Greimann, Thomas Grovenstein, William Grovenstein, Donald Hackett, Theresa Hackle, Bertha and Ida Mae Hagin, Robert Haney, Charles Hardy, Patrick D. Harrison, Tanya Harrison, Deborah Harvey, Greg Haynes, Ben Hayslip, Stephen Hein, Gene and Laquita Henderson, Edwin Hendricks, Mary Henderson Hobbs, Carolyn Milton Hobbs, Carl Hodges, Mark Holland, Frank Hook, Harold Howell, Jane Rhoades Hudak, Page Hungerpiller, Robert Latimer Hurst, Warren F. Jones, Catherine Davis Joyce, Beth Joyner, Donald King, Mary Thomas Perry King, Kathy Moore Kline, Betty Lane, Ruth Quarles Langston, Earl Lee, Betty Lewis, Kelly Lewis, Evelyn Mabry, Esther Mallard, Ginger Malphrus, Dee Maret, Victor Martinez, Gary Means, Peggy Miley, Terry Miller, Kaye L. Minchew, Mary Margaret Minter, Bede Mitchell, Harris Mobley, Willgina Montgomery, Charlton Moseley, Eloise Smith Nessmith, Saundra Nettles, Amy Neville, William Gesmon Neville III, William Josiah Neville, Doris Warnock Niblett, Cathy Norton, Ross Norton, James Oliver, James Orr, Patrick Osterman, Connie Palfy, Leo Parrish, Karl Peace, Wade "Scotty" Perkins, Myron Powell, Susan Presley, Joseph D. Purvis, Robert Randolph, George A. Rogers, Cherrell Williams Rose, Virginia Russell, John and Mary Sanders, R. Frank Saunders, Donna Saye, Anna Cone Seyle, Jane Seabolt Shellmyer, Ronald Shiffler, George Shriver, Susan Shryock, Andrew Shryock, Dorothy Durrence Simmons, Barry Slay, Libba Smith, Betty Watson Spaid, Sandra Wiggins Stange, Julian Stanley, Lewis Stewart, John "Bud" Stone, Rosina Tammany, Reginald Terrell, Brent Tharp, Teresa Thompson, Wendell Tompkins, Christy Trowell, Pat Vail, Lane Van Tassell, Ralph Walton, Angela Walton, Gene Washington, Chester Webb, Randy Weldon, Mrs. Guy Wells Jr., Guy Wells III, Janice West, Jan and Don Whaley, Michael Whitaker, Curtis Whitaker, Fred Whitt, Chester Williams, Keith Willis, Paul Wilver, Gary Witte, Lorne Wolfe, Frances Worden Wood.

A following section of credits acknowledges those who provided photographs or other graphic materials.

Finally, I acknowledge personally and professionally the support and assistance provided by my wife, Beverly. Since our marriage in 1961, she often has worked wholeheartedly as my colleague. She has become such a part of this centennial history project that we often find ourselves conversing avidly about nearly forgotten historical figures. Together we worked in archives and strolled through quaint cemeteries as we rediscovered the Georgia Southern of Memory. I will always be grateful.

D. E. P.

ENROLLMENT - SAT SCORES

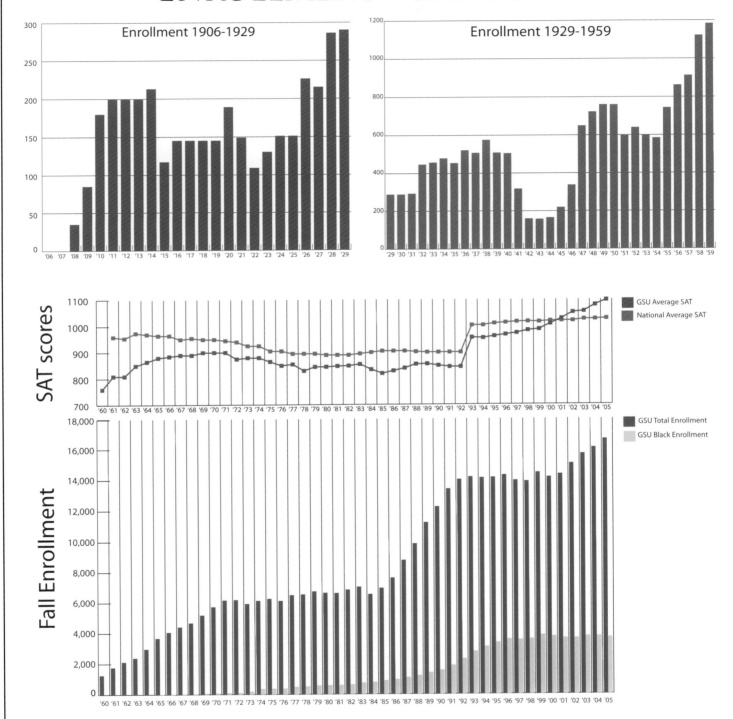

SAT scores reflect a new formula adopted nationwide in 1993.

Enrollment chart in green, *top left*, reflects the sharp increases in enrollment after the A&M School became a junior college in 1924. The chart in brown, *top right*, vividly shows the impact of political interference in 1941 as well as the influx of veterans after World War II.

The lower chart at the top demonstrates the gradual improvement of SAT scores of entering freshmen, beginning around 1991. By the year 2000, the

university had stopped admitting remedial students and raised admission standards. In 2006 the university's SAT scores crossed the 1100 mark for the first time with three points to spare.

The lower chart at the bottom shows trends of enrollment, including the gradual increase of students of color from 0 percent in 1964 to a peak of 28 percent in 1998.

Warren F. "Spike" Jones suggested the format of the chart at the bottom of the page.

NOTES

1. THE MEANING OF THE FIRST DAY

1. *Statesboro News*, 6 December 1904.

2. Ray Stannard Baker, "What Is a Lynching? A Study of Mob Justice, South and North," *McClure's Magazine* (January 1905), reprinted in *Statesboro News*, 30 December 1904.

3. *Ibid*. The church's administrative board supported the minister's actions in writing. For the text of a resolution by the official board of the church, reiterating the leadership of Whitley Langston, see *Statesboro News*, 6 September 1904.

4. Charlton Moseley and Frederick Brogdon, "A Lynching in Statesboro: The Story of Paul Reed and Will Cato," *Georgia Historical Quarterly* 65, no. 2 (1981): 104-18.

5. Joseph M. Terrell, *Message of the Governor of Georgia to the General Assembly* (Atlanta: Geo. W. Harrison, 1902), 6.

6. Oscar H. Joiner, *A History of Public Education in Georgia* (Columbia, S.C.: R. L. Bryan Co., 1979), 159.

7. John Hillison, "Congressional District Schools: Forerunner of Federally Supported Vocational Agriculture," *Journal of Agricultural Education* (Winter 1989): 7. The author notes that Virginia was the third and last state to develop a network of A&M schools based on congressional-district boundaries.

8. Ibid, 8.

9. "Plans for Georgia's Agricultural Schools," *Statesboro News*, 16 October 1906.

10. Dorothy Brannen, *Life in Old Bulloch: The Story of a Wiregrass County in Georgia* (Gainesville, Ga.: Magnolia Press, 1987), 386-87. Public education for black children did not begin before 1903. It gained support, especially when William James moved to Statesboro in 1907 and began the Statesboro High and Industrial School on land adjacent to Blitch Street (renamed Martin Luther King Jr. Boulevard in 2003).

11. Ibid.

12. *Savannah Morning News*, 2 December 1906, 1, 15.

13. Kenyon L. Butterfield, *The Farmer and the New Day* (New York: Macmillan, 1920), 11.

14. Delegates at the Savannah bidding contest ultimately rejected both the Mikell lands and the Gould estate in favor of the Brannen property that was located on a hill and nearer town.

15. Smith C. Banks, interview with author on 28 March 2006. Banks consulted with members of the Gould and Mikell families.

16. "General Presentments of the Grand Jury of Bulloch County, October Term, 1906," *Statesboro News*, 30 October 1906.

17. Ibid. Editor James R. Miller wrote in an editorial, "When this college is complete the students will roll in from every section of the state. . . . The action of the grand jury is universally commended by all well-meaning citizens of the county. There is no reason why we should fail to land this school."

18. Anderson found the railroad business profitable, and by 1906 he had developed a plan to expand the S&S. On 26 August 1906, he wrote his wife, "I got back from Statesboro about eleven o'clock this morning and have spent the rest of the day in closing up the S&S Ry books for the year and getting up my annual statements . . . I have evolved a plan which seems to me a good one for building myself an extension of the S&S road so that I will own and control the extension and without having to actually expend more than from 3 to 5 thousand dollars myself . . . First thing you know sweetheart I will be a railway magnate on a small scale." J. Randolph Anderson to his wife, Page Anderson, 28 August 1906, file 1255, Wilder and Anderson Family Papers, Southern Historical Collection, University of North Carolina Library, Chapel Hill.

19. Marvin S. Pittman, "A Calendar of Progress of Georgia Teachers College," *Georgia Teachers College Alumni Quarterly* 3 (June 1952): 3. Governor Joseph M. Terrell championed the A&M bill and encouraged Senator Henry H. Perry of Hall County to introduce the bill when signed by the governor on 18 August 1906.

20. Miller, editorial, *Statesboro News*, 24 August 1906.

21. Miller, editorial, *Statesboro News*, 9 November 1906.

22. Miller, editorial, *Statesboro News*, 31 October 1906.

23. Miller, editorial, *Statesboro News*, 9 November 1906.

24. *Statesboro News*, 30 November 1906.

25. Pittman, "Calendar of Progress," 3. Governor Terrell endorsed Stewart's proposal and made the A&M system one of the major objectives of his administration. Henry H. Perry of Hall County introduced the A&M bill on Tuesday, 11 July 1906.

26. "Bulloch Lands District College," *Savannah Morning News*, 2 December 1906, 1, 15.

27. *Ibid*, 1.

28. For some reason, the photograph did not appear with the article on 2 December.

29. Despite stiff competition from Pelham, Camilla, Turner County, and Dougherty County ,"Tifton paid $60,000 in cash and 300 acres of land and free lights, water, sewerage and telephones for ten years, the total being equivalent of $95,000." Editorial, *Bulloch Times*, 21 November 1906.

30. "According to the government *Gin Report*, Bulloch County is the biggest Sea Island Cotton producing county in the world, and . . . Statesboro is the biggest Sea Island Cotton market in the world," *Statesboro News*, 19 June 1903. Subsequent issues between 1903 and 1908 of the *Statesboro News* and *Bulloch Times* repeated this claim. An historical account of the cotton market in Statesboro appears in Leodel Coleman, *Statesboro, a Century of Progress: 1866–1966* (Statesboro, Ga.: *Bulloch Herald*, 1969), 363-67.

31. "Bulloch Lands District College," *Savannah Morning News*, 2 December 1906, *20*.

32. While news accounts did not itemize Tattnall's total initial bid, David Turner reported the amount was "somewhat ahead of us (about $5,000), and upon request the various counties were granted an opportunity to supplement their bids." *Bulloch Times*, 5 December 1906.

33. Henderson Library Special Collections, Georgia Southern University. Copies of deeds used in the original bidding later served as collateral for several loans. In addition to major holdings by J. Ewell Brannen, Richard Brannen, Glen Bland, and T. E. Fields, the following individuals turned over deeds to adjoining property: J. T. Rogers, T. L. Hiers, Edward Kennedy, Mikell Bland, and J. S. Brannen. The combined value of the property approached $60,000.

34. Turner, editorial, *Bulloch Times*, 5 December 1906.

35. Turner, editorial, *Bulloch Times*, 5 December 1906.

36. Editorial from *Savannah Press* reprinted by *Statesboro News*, 7 December 1906.

37. J. C. Bonner, Myron W. House, and James W. Matthews, *From A&M to State University: A History of the State University of West Georgia* (Carrollton, Ga.: State University of West Georgia Foundation, 1998), 14.

38. I. S. Ingram, "*The History and Significance of the A. and M. Schools in Georgia,*" (master's thesis, Emory University, 1933), 62, 157-61.

2. AN ASPIRATION SET IN A PINE FOREST

1. Dorothy Brannen, *Life in Old Bulloch: The Story of a Wiregrass County in Georgia* (Gainesville, Ga.: Magnolia Press, 1987), 73-75.

2. Germaine M. Reed, *Crusading for Chemistry: The Professional Career of Charles Holmes Herty* (Athens: University of Georgia Press, 1995), 19-21. Reed notes that Herty's initial contact was J. P. Williams, an entrepreneur who made one fortune as a naval stores developer and another as a railroad magnate.

3. *Statesboro News*, 18 December 1906.

4. Contract of trustees with Nicholas Ittner, Georgia Southern University Historical and Legal Documents, 1903-1951, Henderson Library Special Collections, Georgia Southern University.

5. *Statesboro News*, 29 January 1907.

6. *Statesboro News*, 12 February 1907. At the time of his appointment, he was teaching at the Southern Normal Institute in Douglas, Georgia, a position he had held since 1900. During the preceding five years he had served as principal of the institute.

7. *Millen News*, 12 February 1907.

8. *Statesboro News*, 19 February 1907.

9. *Bulloch Times*, 27 February 1907.

10. *Thirty-Ninth Annual Report of the Department of Education to the General Assembly of the State of Georgia for the School Year Ending December 21, 1910* (Atlanta: Georgia Department of Education, 1911), 157-58.

11. *Statesboro News*, 19 March 1907.

12. J. C. Bonner, Myron W. House, and James W. Matthews, *From A&M to State University: A History of the State University of West Georgia* (Carrollton, Ga.: State University of West Georgia Foundation, 1998), 14.

13. J. Walter Hendricks, *The Autobiography of Elder James Walter Hendricks* (Columbus, Ga.: Columbus Office Supply, 1960), 36. Hendricks, writing about these events some fifty-eight years later, recalled that trustees had delayed the opening in order to allow Hendricks to recruit students while Harper, the agriculturalist, prepared the farm.

14. Edwin Hendricks (grandson of J. Walter Hendricks), interview with author, Demorest, Georgia, 30 July 2003, Henderson Library Special Collections, Georgia Southern University. J. Walter Hendricks's friendship with Roland Harper continued throughout their lives, and it

was Roland who introduced his brother, Otto, to J. Walter. Otto Harper became the first faculty member of the First District A&M School. His field was agricultural science.

15. *Oxford English Dictionary*, 2d ed., s.v. "normal school." Normal schools in the United States began in the late 1830s. Horace Mann had advocated systematic training of elementary teachers especially. Normal schools introduced the "norms" or "standards" governing appropriate subject matter and teaching methods.

16. Valparaiso University, "About Valpo: University Presidents," *http://www.valpo.edu/about_valpo/history.htm* (accessed 3 May 2006). Henry Baker Brown became president of Northern Indiana Normal School and Business Institute at Valparaiso, Indiana, in 1873. He remained president after the trustees changed the name to Valparaiso University in 1900 and ended his career as president in 1917.

17. Hendricks, *Autobiography*, 35. His autobiography, published when he was eighty-six years old, is notable for factual details about his family life and his mission as a Primitive Baptist preacher. The book reveals relatively little about his career at the First District A&M School, with the exception of his decision to leave during his second year.

18. Hendricks, interview. According to Hendricks, his grandmother, Nina Lively Hendricks, "stood about four feet, nine inches, was very thin . . . and she was a staunch Methodist, which was always a sore spot for [her husband]. In fact, one time when he was off itinerant preaching down in Waycross, and she took [their children] to the Methodist church and had them baptized. When he came back, he was livid, you know, but she could always settle him down."

19. *Savannah Morning News*, 27 October 1907. In addition to the scholarly Roland Harper, Otto Harper's other brother, Francis, received his Ph.D. in zoology at Cornell University and became a well-known American naturalist and interpreter of William Bartram. See Francis Harper and Delma E. Presley, *Okefinokee Album* (Athens: University of Georgia Press, 1981).

20. Frank M. Rowan, "Reminiscences," *Reflector* (1933), 29.

21. Miller, editorial, *George-Anne*, 17 April 1933; *Webster's Unabridged Dictionary*, 3d ed., s.v. "brick." The term is slang for a "good hearted or selfless" person.

22. Miller, editorial, *George-Anne*, 17 April 1933.

23. *Savannah Morning News*, 2 February 1908.

24. Rowan, "Reminiscences," 29.

25. *Savannah Morning News*, 6 February 1908.

26. "In Interest of District College," *Savannah Morning News*, 15 May 1908.

27. Hendricks, *Autobiography*, 36.

28. Marvin S. Pittman, "A Calendar of Progress of Georgia Teachers College," *Georgia Teachers College Alumni Quarterly* 3 (June 1952), 3.

29. "First District Agricultural and Mechanical School . . . Records from Prof. J. Walter Hendricks' Record Book – End of the 2nd Month of School – March 25, 1908 – Earliest Available Record," Bulloch County education file, Genealogy Section, Statesboro Regional Library. At the beginning of the list the following notation appears: "Troy Anderson entered on April 1, 1908."
Concerning residents in the girls dormitory: "Mr.

[Dan] Bland . . . remembers that Elma Smith, Mamie Newsome and Annie Waters were the only three girls to live in the dormitory that first term. They were under the care of Mrs. Nina Hendricks, the wife of the principal, J. Walter Hendricks." *Bulloch Herald,* 27 February 1958.

30. Rowan, "Reminiscences," 29.

31. C. H. Lane and Dick J. Crosby, *The District Agricultural Schools of Georgia* (Washington, D.C.: Department of the Interior, Bureau of Education, 1916), 20-21.

32. Hendricks, *Autobiography*, 36.

33. J. Walter Hendricks, "Reminiscences," *Reflector* (1933), 26.

34. Hendricks, interview. Recalling his childhood relationship with his grandfather, Hendricks spoke kindly of a man whose identity appeared to him inseparable from his role as a Primitive Baptist elder.

35. Hendricks, "Reminiscences," 36.

36. Ibid., 35.

37. *Savannah Morning News*, 15 June 1908.

38. *Bulloch Times*, 13 May 1908.

39. *Bulloch Times*, 19 August 1908.

40. *Savannah Morning News*, 26 August 1908.

41. Rowan, "Reminiscences," 29.

42. *Savannah Morning News*, reprinted in *Bulloch Times*, 26 August 1908.

43. Ibid.

44. *Savannah Morning News*, 30 August 1908.

45. *Bulloch Times*, 2 September 1908.

46. *Savannah Morning News*, 1 October 1908.

47. *Webster's Unabridged Dictionary*, 3d ed., s.v. "*culture.*" The first meaning refers to tilling the soil, the second to education.

48. *Statesboro News*, 6 September 1901.

49. Julian Quattlebaum, interview with Esther Mallard and Charlton Moseley, ca. 1986, Henderson Library Special Collections, Georgia Southern University. Dr. Quattlebaum was born in 1896 and died in 1987.

50. *Bulloch Herald*, 23 April 1970. The newspaper printed excerpts from Quattlebaum's talk at a ceremony to change the name of East Hall (the girls dormitory on the circle) to Anderson Hall. Quattlebaum graduated in 1913, so he could have played during the fall football seasons of 1910-12. The game he described probably took place in the autumn of 1910, because the boys of A&M began football practice in the autumn of 1909, according to *Statesboro News*, 4 December 1909.

51. Dan Bland, interview with author, April 1972. James Miller later recalled how farmers reacted to the "proper" Harper. Writing in the student newspaper, Miller, the original secretary of the A&M school, wrote, "[The] farm head came with a 'biled' [laundered] shirt and a standing collar. The neighboring farmers looked him over and shook their heads. They looked at our tall Jerusalem weeds and proclaimed us a farm failure. We put a subsoil plow into an old, poor, worn-out sandy field by the side of the road, broke it up thirteen inches deep, the farmers looked at us and said that we had gone crazy. . . . We made a bale of cotton to the acre on this land and it was an eye opener to the farmers." *George-Anne*, 17 April 1933.

52. *Savannah Morning News*, 2 September 1908; 20 October 1908.

53. *Savannah Morning News*, 20 October 1908.

54. *Bulloch Times*, 9 December 1909.

55. R. J. H. DeLoach file, Henderson Library Special

Collections, Georgia Southern University. DeLoach wrote four articles on cotton breeding for the *Georgia Experiment Station Bulletin and University of Georgia Bulletin in 1908-9*. In 1910 he and A. M. Soule published "Suggestions on Cotton Cultivation and Fertilization" in the *University of Georgia Bulletin*.

56. The name of the debating society is interesting. Persephone was the Greek mythological goddess of the underworld. She also was the harbinger of spring and rebirth. Her name suggests an introspective, intelligent person.

57. *Statesboro News*, 3 February 1909. The news story also reveals the role of Albert Deal on the campus and in the community. In the 1908 gubernatorial race, Deal had supported Hoke Smith, who lost to Joseph M. Brown. Deal introduced Governor-elect Brown with these words: "We were all so glad to have Mr. Brown with us that we all felt like we would like to have him in our arms hugging him." Governor Brown followed with self-effacing comments about his small stature and limited strength. Deal played a leading role in local politics, and he represented Bulloch County as a state representative and senator.

58. J. Walter Hendricks, "Advice to Farmers," *Statesboro News*, 13 February 1909.

59. "Brooklet Plays at Agricultural School," *Statesboro News*, 3 April 1909. This articles includes the first reference to extramural sports at the school.

60. *Statesboro News*, 17 June 1909.

61. *Statesboro News*, 20 April 1909.

62. *Statesboro News*, 3 June 1909.

63. *Bulloch Times*, 2 June 1909.

64. "School Scandal Explained," *Bulloch Times*, 9 June 1909.

65. *Statesboro News*, 8 June 1909.

66. *Statesboro News*, 18 July 1909.

67. Hendricks, "Reminiscences," 26.

68. Hendricks, interview. The grandson of J. Walter Hendricks recalled that one of his grandfather's favorite self-descriptions was the term "tenant of the Lord."

3. The View from Culture Hill

1. *Bulloch Times*, 7 December 1910.

2. E. C. J. Dickens, *Annual Report to the Georgia Department of Education, 1911-1912 (n.p.)*, Henderson Library Special Collections, Georgia Southern University.

3. *Savannah Morning News*, 4 November 1909.

4. *Atlanta Georgian*, 16 December 1909, reprinted in *Statesboro News,* 19 December 1909.

5. *Statesboro News*, 16 November 1909; *Bulloch Times*, 17 November 1909; *Statesboro News*, 27 November 1909.

6. *Statesboro News,* 4 December 1909.

7. *Statesboro News*, 23 December 1909. "The boys have recently purchased a foot ball [sic]. With a little practice we expect to have a team that will be a credit to the school."

8. *Statesboro News*, 30 December 1909.

9. Marvin S. Pittman, "A Calendar of Progress of Georgia Teachers College," *Georgia Teachers College Alumni Quarterly* 3 (June 1952), 3.

10. S. L. Lewis, "Historical Sketch of the District Agricultural Schools," *Thirty-Ninth Annual Report of the Department of Education to the General Assembly of the State of Georgia for the School Year Ending December 31, 1910* (Atlanta: Georgia

Department of Education, 1911), 158.

11. *Bulloch Times*, 31 May 1911. The "conservative" estimate of the crowd size, according to David Turner, was more than 1,500. The *Statesboro News* of 30 May 1911 offered a more liberal estimate of 3,000. Miller described the impact of the event both politically and logistically, "Perhaps the greatest day in the history of the First Congressional District Agricultural School was that of today, when three thousand enthusiastic friends of the great school and admirers of Georgia's great governor-elect, gathered to pay their respects and listen to the closing exercises and hear the splendid address of Gov. Smith . . . Men and women stood up for two hours to hear the great speech of the Governor. "

12. *Statesboro News*, 30 May 1911.

13. Dorothy Brannen, *Life in Old Bulloch: The Story of a Wiregrass County in Georgia* (Gainesville, Ga.: Magnolia Press, 1987), 337.

14. Frank M. Rowan, "Reminiscences," *Reflector* (1933), 30.

15. An expanding student body in the late 1950s persuaded the Board of Regents to authorize a student union and dining hall. The college razed Anderson Hall in 1959 to accommodate the Frank I. Williams Student Center. In 2006 the Builders of the University Terrace stands on the site of "Old Anderson."

17. Jimmy Jones, "Old Bell in Anderson Hall," *George-Anne*, 27 January 1941.

18. E. C. J. Dickens, *Annual Report, 1913*, 76. Henderson Library Special Collections, Georgia Southern University.

19. James Arthur Bunce, "Three Years after Graduation," Bulletin Issued by the *First District Agricultural and Mechanical School* (n.p., 1913), Henderson Library Special Collections, Georgia Southern University.

20. T. Ray Shurbutt, *Georgia Southern: Seventy-Five Years of Service and Progress* (Statesboro: Georgia Southern College Foundation, Inc., 1982), 17. Harper served on the faculty for six years,1908-14, before accepting his new job. He was succeeded by Henry L. Debbink, who joined the faculty in 1912 and taught until 1915. See *Statesboro News*, 11 May 1916.

21. *Bulloch Times*, 6 February 1914.

22. J. Randolph Anderson, letter to his wife, Page Anderson, 6 October 1914, file 1255, Wilder and Anderson Family Papers, Southern Historical Collection, University of North Carolina Library, Chapel Hill.

23. Ibid.

24. *Statesboro News*, 15 April 1915.

25. *Statesboro News*, 3 June 1915.

26. Ibid.

27. *Bulloch Herald*, 16 January 1964.

28. *Statesboro News*, 18 May 1916.

29. James Alonzo Brannen, letter to J. Randolph Anderson, 23 November 1916, Henderson Library Special Collections, Georgia Southern University.

30. "List of Claimants," 2 December 1916, Henderson Library Special Collections, Georgia Southern University.

31. Rowan, "Reminiscences," 31.

32. *Statesboro News*, 30 September 1915.

33. *Statesboro News*, 6 April 1916.

34. *Statesboro News*, 2 November 1916.

35. *Bulloch Times*, 25 January 1917.

36. Rowan, "Reminiscences," 31.

37. Bertha Hagin, interview with author, April 1996.

38. Bertha Hagin, "Class History '20," Horace and Maggie Simmons Hagin school papers, 1915-45, Henderson Library Special Collections, Georgia Southern University.

39. *Bulloch Times*, 20 March 1919.

40. The first two stanzas of the University of Georgia's alma mater reveal similarities to the first published *alma mater* of the First District A&M School. A later version of the local *alma mater* in 1932 substituted "murmuring pine trees" for cypress, reminiscent of the popular song of the University of Georgia, the "parent institution" of A&M schools. The first two stanzas of the UGA song are:

From the hills of Georgia's northland
Beams thy noble brow,
And the sons of Georgia rising
Pledge with sacred vow.

'Neath the pine tree's stately shadow
Spread thy riches rare,
And thy sons, dear Alma Mater,
Will thy treasure share.

References to the "sons of Georgia rising" appeared "inappropriate" to members of the faculty senate of the University of Georgia on 2 March 1989, according to their official proceedings: "The Senate of the Franklin College of Arts and Sciences supports changing or removing inappropriate gender-specific language from the official *alma mater* of the University." See "Archived Resolutions, Recommendations, Expressions of Opinion, and Petitions of the Faculty Senate, Franklin College of Arts and Sciences," *http://www.franklin.uga.edu/deans/hruppers/Resolutions.pdf* (accessed 3 May 1906). The university added an "inclusive" third stanza in 1990:

And thy daughters proudly join thee,
Take their rightful place,
Side by side into the future,
Equal dreams embrace.

See UGA Factbook, *1996, http://www.uga.edu/irp/fb96/01gen18.htm* (accessed 3 May 2006).

41. "Annual Report," 17 January 1920, typescript, Henderson Library Special Collections, Georgia Southern University.

42. Frank M. Rowan, "First District Agricultural and Mechanical School," *Annual Report to the Georgia Department of Education, 1919-1920*, 223. Henderson Library Special Collections, Georgia Southern University.

43. *Bulloch Times*, 12 February 1920.

44. *Bulloch Times*, 8 April 1920.

45. *Bulloch Times*, 29 April 1920.

46. *Bulloch Times*, 6 May 1920.

47. Bulloch County native Hendricks was succeeded in 1909 by trustee E. C. J. Dickens, who retired at the end of 1914, allowing the promotion of a member of the original faculty, Frank M. Rowan.

48. "Georgia Normal College," Ernest V. Hollis, *Reflector* (1933), 32.

49. Hollis returned to the customary name of the institution on the bulletin cover for 1924-25, even as he made "plans to convert this school into a Teachers College." Hollis entitled the publication "Old Culture" – Bulletin of First District State A&M School. The theme of the book, however, reveals his ambition. In 1921-22, the bulletin had focused on the training of

"future leaders of Georgia Agriculture." The 1924-25 bulletin boldly proclaimed,"We are educating the future leaders of Georgia."

50. *The State Agricultural School: 1921–1922, 1st District, Statesboro* (Atlanta: Index Printing Co., 1921), 34.

51. Ada Lou (Rowe) Waters, letter to the editor, *Georgia Teachers College Alumni Quarterly* 1 (June 1950): 2.

52. *The First District Agricultural and Mechanical School, Statesboro, Georgia, 1919–1920* (Macon, Ga.: J. W. Burke Co., 1919), 11.

53. *State Agricultural School*, 36-37.

54. Ernest V. Hollis, "First District Agricultural and Mechanical School," *Annual Report to the Georgia Department of Education, 1920–1921*, 273. Henderson Library Special Collections, Georgia Southern University.

55. Howell Cone, letter to Guy Wells, 14 January 1943, presidential correspondence, Special Collections, Georgia College and State University Library.

56. *Savannah Morning News*, 23 May 1923.

57. *Bulloch Times*, 29 May 1924.

58. *Savannah Morning News*, 12 August 1923. "President Hollis and the board of trustees are gratified at having this type of man direct a field of the school's activities that is so epoch making in the life of the students. Possibly no one member of the faculty exerts so large an influence over the student body as the coach. He will build his ideals into the lives of his charges."

59. *Bulloch Times*, 14 February 1924. "State Superintendent N. H. Ballard has designated the First District A&M School as the training place for teachers of the First District under the direction of the state department of education." The article noted that during the program's first year, only teachers of grades one through seven would be eligible. "The state department of education will furnish the faculty of the school with the questions to be asked on the state examination."

60. "Old 'Culture" – *Bulletin of First District State A&M School, 1924 – 1925* (n.p.), Henderson Library Special Collections, Georgia Southern University.

61. Selected from Ernest V. Hollis's introduction and conclusion to the last bulletin of the First District A&M School, *"Old 'Culture."*

62. *Bulloch Times*, 14 August 1924. Note: Turner wrote the headline and article after the bill was passed but before the governor signed it on 18 August.

63. W. T. Anderson, editorial, reprinted in *Bulloch Times*, 11 September 1924.

64. Guy Wells observed the work of Hollis, the trustees, and the legislature shortly before he was named president in the summer of 1926. Wells recalled that the legislature had passed a bill that guaranteed payment of the loan. After Wells became president, the legislature, prodded by Senator Cone in 1927, paid in full the balance of $45,000. Wells, editorial, *Reflector* (1933), 33.

65. *Bulloch Times*, 6 November 1924.

66. Bulloch County School Superintendent B. R. Olliff wrote, "We have now for the first time in our entire history a college in Southeast Georgia, . . . a section which comprises about two-fifths of the entire state . . . Since the creation of the Georgia Normal College at Statesboro, it is a duty and privilege of the citizens of this section to support and boost the institution until it surpasses all other such institutions in the South, and we must." *Bulloch Times*, 9 July 1926.

67. Two representative columns appeared in the *Bulloch Times*, 9 April 1925 and 16 April 1925.
68. *Bulloch Times*, 28 January 1926.
69. *Bulloch Times*, 3 December 1925.
70. *Bulloch Times*, 23 July 1925. Lota Trapnell was president of the Candler County Club, a student organization. She commented on the instruction as well as social occasions that local citizens had sponsored.
71. *Bulloch Times*, 15 April 1926.
72. *Bulloch Times*, 23 October 1924.
73. *Bulloch Times*, 1 April 1926.
74. *Bulloch Times*, 24 June 1926.
75. *Bulloch Times*, 19 April 1934.
76. Helen Mathews Lewis, interview with author, Milledgeville, Georgia, 11 November 2004. Lewis said she admired both Mr. and Mrs. Wells, even though they did not always exhibit "cultivated judgment." She recalled the time a visitor from India dined with the Wells family at the historic governor's mansion: "They had a dinner at the mansion house and we were invited, and what did they serve but a big steak! . . . And I remember seeing the Indian's face, like, 'What do I do?' And it was just kind of very embarrassing."
77. William Ivy Hair, with James C. Bonner and Edward B. Dawson, *A History of Georgia College* (Milledgeville, Ga.: Georgia College, 1979), 171.
78. Ibid.
79. Judson C. Ward, interview with author, 7 July 2003 and 22 September 2005.
80. Pittman, "Calendar of Progress," 6.
81. *Bulloch Times*, 17 June 1926.
82. *Bulloch Times*, 19 August 1926.
83. Alyson Bennett, "*George-Anne* Has Interesting Past," *George-Anne*, 31 January 1984, 6.
84. "Senior Diary," 17 September 1926: "All our fun was destroyed, for Mr. Anderson informed us all 'hazing' must stop. Oh, horrors!," *Reflector* (1927), 82.
85. Leonard Powell, "Autobiography of Leonard Powell," Henderson Library Special Collections, Georgia Southern University. Powell, from Lyons, Georgia, was a student in the late 1920s. He wrote about the initiation of freshmen "rats" and described in some detail the practice of hazing. When he arrived, initiation involved male but not female freshmen. A female high school and college student of this era (1928-34), Stella Vanlandingham of Wrightsville, Georgia, did not recall any hazing activities involving coeds. Stella Vanlandingham Boswell, interview with author, Brunswick, Georgia, 4 March 2006.
86. *Bulloch Times*, 21 April 1927. Turner provided personal details about the death of the popular dean: "Taken to the hospital in Macon, he was operated upon for 'adhesions of the intestines' and died Friday morning. President Wells journeyed to be at his side when Mr. Anderson died. . . . His popularity as an educator was attested by the fact that he brought with him to the school here a large number of young people who had been students under him at Graymont-Summit . . . Besides his wife, he is survived by two small children."
87. *Bulloch Times*, 16 June 1927.
88. *George-Anne*, 29 June 1927.
89. Brannen, *Life in Old Bulloch*, 2. William Cone, who died in 1816, was an early leader in Bulloch County, which was formed in 1796. Cone rose from the rank of private to captain during the Revolutionary War. Newspapers of the day described how he attacked a group of Tories, led by the infamous Dan McGirt, forcing them to abandon claims to lands in southeast Georgia.
90. Wells, presidential correspondence, Special Collections, Georgia College and State University Library. These observations about the relationship between Howell Cone and Guy Wells are based on the Wells-Cone "personal and confidential" correspondence of approximately one hundred pages.
91. Wells, presidential correspondence, Special Collections, Georgia College and State University Library. Letters of 12 November 1940, 22 July 1941, and 29 March 1944.
92. Guy Wells, first address to the faculty and students at Georgia State College for Women in Hair, *A History of Georgia College*, 171.
93. Boswell, interview.
94. *George-Anne*, 12 April 1927.
95. *George-Anne*, 18 July 1927.
96. U.S. Post Office correspondence in possession of Daniel B. Good, Statesboro, Georgia.
97. Pittman, "Calendar of Progress," 7.
98. *Columbus Ledger*, reprinted in *Bulloch Times*, 21 November 1929.

4. DEFINING THE ROLE

1. John A. Beineke, *And There Were Giants in the Land: The Life of William Heard Kilpatrick* (New York: Peter Lang, 1998), 43-46. Professor Kilpatrick and Wells shared similar social and, perhaps, theological beliefs. Kilpatrick became an advocate of racial equality long before the Supreme Court rendered its decision, *Brown vs. Board of Educaiton* in 1954. He refused to agree with traditional Baptist doctrines, such as the virgin birth, and he did not accept the Bible as either literally true or historically accurate. For these reasons officials at Mercer University subjected Kilpatrick to a heresy trial and found him guilty.
2. Morgan Blake, *Atlanta Journal*, 6 March 1941; *George-Anne*, 28 October, 1935; 2 December 1935.
3. Chester Williams, Statesboro, interview with author, 28 April 2005.
4. Ibid.
5. *George-Anne*, 18 December 1929.
6. *George-Anne*, 20 June 1930.
7. Chester Williams, interview.
8. Stella Vanlandingham Boswell, Brunswick, Georgia, interview with the author, 4 March 2006.
9. Chester Williams, interview.
10. *George-Anne*, 16 April 1930
11. *George-Anne*, 8 May 1930.
12. *Bulloch Times*, 12 December 1929.
13. Martha Cone Benson, Statesboro, interview with the author on 10 May 2003.
14. *Bulloch Times*, 24 April 1934.
15. Jack Nelson Averitt, Statesboro, Georgia, interview with the author, 7 April, 2006.
16. *Bulloch Times*, 19 January 1933.
17. *George-Anne*, 12 December 1932
18. Invoice to South Georgia Teachers College by John T. Ragan, Henderson Library Special Collections, Georgia Southern University.
19. Jack Nelson Averitt, Statesboro, interview with the author, 1 July 2003.
20. *Reflector*, 1932.
21. The renovation of Sunnyside School into the science building was completed during the spring of 1934, just before Mr. Wells learned the new Board of Regents had reassigned him to another presidency in the system. *George Anne*, 12 March 1934.
22. *Bulloch Times*, 17 December 1931.
23. *Atlanta Journal*, 20 February 1933; reprinted in *Bulloch Times*, 23 Febuary 1933.
24. *Reflector*, 1933.
25. *Bulloch Times*, 21 April 1932.
26. *Bulloch Times*, 23 November 1933. Written upon the occasion of the funeral of Mr. Knight, the article notes that a letter to Mrs. Lane explained the donation of volumes was influenced by his long friendship with her. "Only a few days before his death, probably among the last personal communications penned by him, Dr. Knight again wrote Ms. Lane: 'I have always esteemed you one of my best and dearest friends.'"
27. *George-Anne*, 13 February 1933.
28. *Bulloch Times*, 26 July 1934.
29. *Bulloch Times*, 2 February 1933.
30. *Reflector*, 1931, 61.
31. *Bulloch Times*, 14 July 1932.
32. Fleming D. Roach, interview. Mr. Roach recalled "a county agent man" living on the top floor of West Hall in 1932 –1933. For Mrs. Dyer's role in the physical education department, see *George-Anne*, 13 November 1933.
33. *George-Anne*, 3 July 1933
34. *Bulloch Times*, 23 April 1933. Horticulturalists at the University of Washington also cultivated cuttings from the Bonaparte willow, and these historic trees play an important part in the landscape of this university in Seattle. See: *http://depts.washington.edu/~uweek/archives/2001.03.MAR_29/_article6.html*
35. *Bulloch Times*, 2 May 1929.
36. "*Our History*," YMCA Web Site: *Eliminating Racism, Empowering Women*: *http://www.ywca.org/site/pp.asp?c=dJISI6PIKpG&b=281379*
37. Chester Williams, interview.
38. Joseph D. Purvis, *Back to Folklore: Selected Columns from Savannah Morning News*. Savannah, Ga. Published by the author, 2006, 162.
39. *George-Anne*, 6 November 1931.
40. Letter of Benjamin F. Hubert to George W. Carver, 26 September 1933. Microfilm Roll 14, Division of Behavioral Science Research of the Carver Research Foundation of Tuskegee Institute.
41. Ibid.
42. S. D. Groover, letter to George W. Carver, 21 September 1932. Microfilm Roll 14, Division of Behavioral Science Research of the Carver Research Foundation of Tuskegee Institute.
43. Fleming D. Roach, M. D., Jacksonville, Florida, attended SGTC from 1932–1934. Interview with the author on 10 October 2005.
44. Samuel Hill Morgan, letter to George Washington Carver, 9 November 1933. Microfilm Roll 14, Division of Behavioral Science Research of the Carver Research Foundation of Tuskegee Institute.
45. Benjamin Hubert, letter to George W. Carver, 30 April 1934. Microfilm Roll 14, Division of Behavioral Science Research of the Carver Research Foundation of Tuskegee Institute.
46. Benjamin Hubert, letter to George W. Carver, 30 April 1934. Microfilm Roll 14, Division of Behavioral Science Research of the Carver

Research Foundation of Tuskegee Institute.

47. S. H. Morgan to Guy H. Wells, 23 November 1934. Presidential Correspondence, Special Collections at Georgia College and State University.

48. Guy H. Wells, letter to S. H. Morgan, 30 March 1935. Special Collections, Georgia College and State University Library.

49. *Union Recorder*, 18 October 1934.

50. *Bulloch Times*, 19 April 1934.

51. *Bulloch Times,* 31 May 1934.

52. *George-Anne*, 27 May 1937.

53. William Ivy Hair, James C. Bonner, Edward B. Dawson, Robert J. Wilson III, *A Centennial History of Georgia College* (Milledgeville, Ga.: Georgia College),173.

54. Beineke, 369.

55. Ibid.

5. THE DREAM, THE DRAMA

1. Carlton Carruth and Edward Carruth, "Biographical Sketch of Joseph E. Carruth," 2001, typescript, Henderson Library Special Collections, Georgia Southern University.

2. David S. Flower, ed., *A Scrapbook History of Lincoln Consolidated School* (Ypsilanti, Mich.: privately printed, 1999), 2-4.

3. "Ypsilanti to Lose Educator Who Dared Be a Democrat," *Detroit Free Press*, 18 June 1934, 4. This newspaper earlier that year reviewed Pittman's leadership role in the Michigan Democratic Party, 28 January 1934, C12.

4. *Ann Arbor Tribune*, reprinted in *Bulloch Times*, 10 May 1934.

5. Marvin Pittman, letter to Chester Destler, 12 May 1934, Papers of Chester McArthur Destler, collected by I. M. Destler, Great Falls, Virginia.

6. Chester Destler, letter to Guy Wells, 3 October 1942, presidential correspondence, Special Collections, Georgia College and State University.

7. I. M. Destler, interview with author, Great Falls, Virginia, 13 July 2005.

8. Julian Stanley, letter to Marvin Goss, 3 November 2004, Henderson Library Special Collections, Georgia Southern University.

9. Salaries paid members of faculty and staff at colleges and universities appear in annual reports to the Board of Regents of the University System of Georgia.

10. *Bulloch Times*, 28 June 1934.

11. Marvin Pittman, interview and deposition with M. C. Huntley, typescript report to the Southern Association of Schools and Colleges, November 1941, 76-77. Hargrett Rare Book and Manuscript Library, University of Georgia.

12. Chester Williams, interview with author, Statesboro, Georgia, 28 May 2005.

13. *ibid.*

14. R. J. H. DeLoach, *Rambles With John Burroughs* (Boston: R. G. Badger, 1912). Upon completing his undergraduate studies at the University of Georgia, DeLoach taught school in Oklahoma at an Indian reservation and briefly served as principal of the Statesboro Institute. As a young man, he met John Burroughs and traveled with him regularly.

15. *Bulloch Times*, 13 June 1935. The paper's editor, David Turner, described the event: "Governor Talmadge was in fine fettle, and his address, less than an hour in duration, was replete with pleasantries and philosophy. Only once did he refer to politics, and that was in a spirit of humor."

16. *Bulloch Times*, 17 November 1934. The local newspaper reprinted an article that appeared in Milledgeville's newspaper, the *Union-Recorder*. After only a few months in Georgia, Guy Wells invited Pittman to speak to the students and faculty of the Georgia State College for Women. Pittman said he favored liberalization of politics, religion, and public education: "States are disregarding party lines as never before. Another interesting change is toward denominational religion; the doctrinal sermon [is] becoming almost obsolete. . . . Our broader and newer conception of education has made this age in which we are living the greatest that the world has yet known." He considered all these trends positive indicators for the future of America.

17. William Heard Kilpatrick, "What Do We Mean by Progressive Education?" *Progressive Education* (December 1930): 383-86. Reprinted in John A. Beineke, *And There Were Giants in the Land: The Life of Williams Heard Kilpatrick* (New York: Peter Lang, 1998), 227.

18. "T. C. and Progressive Education," *George-Anne*, 4 March 1946.

19. *George-Anne*, 5 November 1934.

20. *Bulloch Times*, 28 August 1934.

21. *Bulloch Times*, 27 September 1934; *George-Anne*, 28 October 1934.

22. *Bulloch Times*, 3 December 1936. The local newspaper announced the regular meeting of the AAUW for 8 December 1936. The topic was the role of black people in southern society. The organization's membership included faculty and staff of the college as well as college-educated women who lived in Bulloch County.

23. *Bulloch Herald*, 16 November 1938. President Katharine Destler later presided at an AAUW program entitled "Should America Surrender Europe to Hitler?"

24. *Bulloch Herald,* 18 April 1940.

25. Pittman, letter to Destler, 21 December 1934, Destler Papers.

26. Pittman, letter to Destler, 18 July 1941, Destler Papers.

27. *Bulloch Times*, 17 January 1935. The broadcast date was 18 January 1935.

28. Marvin S. Pittman, "Industrial Arts at Georgia Teachers College," *Georgia Teachers College Alumni Quarterly* 3 (June 1951): 1,3.

29. Claude A. Bell, *Biographical Dictionary of American Educators* (Westport, Conn.: Greenwood Publishing Group,1978), s.v. "Hoyt Hobson London."

30. *Bulloch Times,* 28 May 1936.

31. J. D. Purvis, *Growing Up in Willachoochee* (Savannah, Ga.: privately printed, 2002), 84-86.

32. *Bulloch Herald*, 21 March 1940.

33. *George-Anne*, 17 November 1947.

34. "Some Professional Developments," *Georgia Teachers College Alumni Quarterly* 3 (June 1952), 8.

35. *Bulloch Times*, 13 September, 1934. The FERA workshop for teachers included instructions on how to establish local leisure arts programs, a lecture on the New Deal by Chester Destler, and other presentations. Details on the mattress factory appear in *George-Anne*, 22 October 1934 and *Bulloch Times*, 14 March, 1935.

36. *Bulloch Times*, 26 August 1937.

37. H. L. Mencken, "The Sahara of the Bozart," in *The American Scene: A Reader*, ed. H. L. Mencken (New York: Knopf, 1977), 161.

38. *Bulloch Times*, 7 March, 1935. The newspaper printed the program in advance of the 22-23 March meeting.

39. *George-Anne*, 1 February 1937.

40. *Bulloch Times*, 14 March 1937. Destler balanced the program with representatives of various interests: "[Couch's] address will be followed by an informal platform discussion with the following outstanding Southerners taking part: Dr. T. F. Abercrombie, of the State Department of Health; Dr. Charles H. Herty, noted chemist; Dr. J. T. Wheeler, of the State College of Agriculture; H. H. Carswell, well known LaGrange industrialist; Miss Gay B. Shepperson, state director of WPA; Tom Wisdom, state auditor; Thomas Askew, dean of Armstrong Junior College of Savannah, and Henry McIntosh, editor of the Albany Herald."

41. Chester Destler, letter to the American Hospital Association of Chicago, 7 February 1938, Destler Papers: "Our county, Bulloch, is one of the largest in the state. It is fairly prosperous and more diversified than most agricultural counties in the state. With a set of unusually well trained and forward-looking officials in charge, it should be a favorable location. Furthermore, we have a number of progressive doctors who would, I believe, support such an experiment." Zach S. Henderson, letter to Chester Destler, 19 August 1938, Destler Papers. Destler was conducting research in Wisconsin when Henderson wrote, "I was talking to John Mooney yesterday, and he said the plan passed the Medical Association unanimously. I think all of the people who would have voted against it were absent from the regular meeting."

42. *Bulloch Herald*, 18 April 1940.

43. Stella Vanlandingham Boswell, interview with author, Brunswick, Georgia, 4 March 2006.

44. Williams, interview.

45. Fred Sturges Beers, letter to Chester Destler, 2 June 1937, Destler Papers.

46. Judson C. Ward, letter to Chester Destler, 25 June 1940, Destler Papers.

47. Destler, letter to Pittman, 8 January 1941, Destler Papers.

48. Destler, typescript of notes for WSB interview, Destler Papers.

49. R. J. H. DeLoach, letter to Guy Wells, 9 August 1942, presidential correspondence, Special Collections, Georgia College and State University Library.

50. R. J. H. DeLoach, letter to Eugene Talmadge, 6 June 1942, governor's correspondence, Eugene Talmadge Papers, Georgia Archives. Although written after the crisis of 1941, the letter reveals familiar opinions of DeLoach.

51. Homer Cling Parker, letter to Eugene Talmadge enclosed with letter to Guy Wells, 21 May 1941, presidential correspondence, Special Collections, Georgia College and State University Library.

52. Guy Wells, letter to Howell Cone, 14 July 1944, presidential correspondence, Special Collections, Georgia College and State University Library.

53. Wells, letter to Cone, 12 November 1940, presidential correspondence, Special Collections, Georgia College and State University Library.

54. *Bulloch Times*, 5 June 1941.

55. Judson C. Ward, interview with author, Atlanta, Georgia, 22 September 2005.

56. William Josiah Neville, interview with author, Statesboro, Georgia, 11 May 2006.

57. *Savannah Morning News*, 28 July 1941.

58. Marvin Pittman, WSB radio address, *Atlanta Journal*, 2 August 1941.

59. Wells, letter to Cone, 5 August 1941, presidential correspondence, Special Collections, Georgia College and State University Library.

60. Ward, interview.

61. Williams, interview. Other alumni from the 1930s made similar observations.

62. Emory Bohler, interview with author, 18 October 2005.

63. Ward, interview.

64. *George-Anne*, 22 May 1944.

65. *We Remember Marvin Pittman: The Testimony of Twenty-Two Alumni,* comp. Marvin Goss (Statesboro, Ga.: Bulloch County Historical Society), 2001.

66. Ralph McGill, editorial, *Atlanta Constitution*, reprinted in *Bulloch Times*, 17 July 1941.

67. DeLoach, letter to Talmadge, 23 October 1941, governor's correspondence, Eugene Talmadge Papers, Georgia Archives.

68. *Bulloch Times*, 12 December 1941.

69. Evelyn Darley Mabry, interview with author, 7 December 2005. She attended the college in the late 1930s and early 1940s. She recalled, "The war was about to break out, you know, and some people circulated rumors about him. They said he was a communist sympathizer, maybe a German. But my memories are about him as a very fine, conscientious, and dedicated member of the faculty."

70. M. C. Huntley, typescript report to the Southern Association of Schools and Colleges, November 1941, 65-67. Hargrett Rare Book and Manuscript Library, University of Georgia.

71. Ibid., 38.

72. Ibid., 42.

73. Steadman V. Sanford, letter to Board of Regents, 19 November 1941, Board of Regents minutes, Georgia Archives.

74. *Savannah Morning News*, 30 August 1942.

75. Huntley, 42, 81-82.

76. "Lynching in Georgia," *Time,* July 28, 1941, 37.

77. Guy Wells, letter to Curtis Dixon, 18 August 1941, presidential correspondence, Special Collections, Georgia College and State University Library. Wells wrote, "Dear Curtis, I have your note about Destler. He is, perhaps, the greatest loss of any teacher that is going. If I learn of anything, I shall communicate with you at once."

78. James F. Cook Jr., "Politics and Education in the Talmadge Era: The Controversy over the University System of Georgia, 1941-1942" (PhD diss., University of Georgia, 1972). Cook suggests Sanford could have influenced the regents or crafted a compromise, and that his failure to do so was lamentable. Another historian has defended the inaction of Sanford, arguing he was silent because he realized the futility of attempting to speak on behalf of academic freedom in the governor's presence. See Stephen Gurr, *The Personal Equation: A Biography of Steadman Vincent Sanford* (Athens: University of Georgia Press, 1999).

79. Affidavit of Chester McArthur Destler and William A. Bowen, notarized by Harry S. Akin, 11 September 1941, Destler Papers.

80. Chester Destler, letter to Katharine Destler, 2 August 1941, Destler Papers.

6. PERFORMANCE POSTPONED

1. *Bulloch Times*, 21 August 1941.

2. William H. Crouse, letter to Carlton Mobley, 5 February 1941, governor's correspondence, Georgia Archives. Elder Crouse had encouraged the talented Coleman brothers to organize the *Herald* and asked Mobley, the governor's assistant, to obtain state printing contracts for the Colemans' printing firm.

3. *Bulloch Herald*, 31 July 1941.

4. Zach Henderson, letter to Chester Destler, 2 August 1941, Papers of Chester McArthur Destler, collected by I. M. Destler, Great Falls, Virginia.

5. Chester Destler, letter to Ralph E. Himstead, General Secretary of the American Association of University Professors, 11 September 1941, Destler Papers.

6. Hester Newton, letter to Katharine Destler, 12 August 1942, Destler Papers.

7. William Henderson, letter to Chester Destler, 14 February 1942, Destler Papers.

8. Evelyn Baggett, letter to Chester Destler, 17 March 1942, Destler Papers. Baggett wrote, "G.T.C. is a hopeless mess. I can see no hope for the college until it hits bottom and then the wreck may be beyond repair. . . . Now Gates has just fired Miss Michael." Baggett earlier had led alumni in an unsuccessful effort to organize a special session of the legislature to reverse Governor Talmadge's actions.

9. Guy Wells, letter to Howell Cone, 2 July 1942, presidential correspondence, Special Collections, Georgia College and State University.

10. Cone, letter with attachment to Wells, 4 July 1942, presidential correspondence, Special Collections, Georgia College and State University.

11. Wells, letter to Cone, 29 July 1942, presidential correspondence, Special Collections, Georgia College and State University.

12. Cone, letter to Wells, 3 June 1941, presidential correspondence, Special Collections, Georgia College and State University.

13. Cone, letter to Wells, 7 July 1942, presidential correspondence, Special Collections, Georgia College and State University.

14. R. J. H. DeLoach, letters to Eugene Talmadge, Georgia Archives, and Henderson Library Special Collections, Georgia Southern University.

15. Crouse, letter to Mobley, 5 February 1941, governor's correspondence, Georgia Archives. Crouse, appointed by Talmadge to head the old-age benefits program, died during the spring of 1941.

16. Hester Newton, letter to Katharine Destler, 12 August 1942, Destler Papers.

17. *Savannah Morning News,* 30 August 1942. The Associated Press dateline is 29 August 1942.

18. Ralph McGill, "One More Word," *Atlanta Constitution*, 31 January 1943, reprinted in *George-Anne*, 8 February 1943.

19. *Bulloch Times*, 11 February 1943. The *Times* devoted a major story to the brief program and reprinted the text of Pittman's remarks.

20. Chester Destler, letter to Marvin Pittman, 15 February 1943, Destler Papers.

21. Newton, letter to Katharine and Chester Destler, 22 March 1943, Destler Papers.

22. *Bulloch Times*, 3 June 1943.

23. Charles Stephen Gurr, *The Personal Equation: A Biography of Steadman Vincent Sanford* (Athens, Ga.: University of Georgia Press, 1999), 213. Gurr finds those statements "difficult to reconcile" with Sanford's support of Franklin D. Roosevelt, but the biographer does not discuss the intellectual implications of Chancellor Steadman's statements.

24. "Six to One—Imagine That!" *George-Anne*, 30 April 1954.

25. Board of Regents of the University System of Georgia Minutes, 13 October 1943, Georgia Archives.

26. *George-Anne*, 17 January 1944; John "Bud" Stone, interview with author, 28 April 2005. Stone confirmed this story, which became a part of campus folklore.

27. *George-Anne*, 11 January 1943. *Look* magazine's description of the heroism of Paine appeared in the campus newspaper.

28. *Bulloch Times*, 9 May 1946.

29. Pittman, letter to Destler, 5 March 1945, Destler Papers.

30. Pittman, letter to Destler, 26 March 1945, Destler Papers.

31. Destler, letter to Pittman, 2 April 1945, Destler Papers.

32. Pittman, letter to Destler, 26 March 1945, Destler Papers.

33. Pittman, letter to Destler, 7 April 1945, Destler Papers.

34. Judson Ward, letter to Destler, 31 January 1942, Destler Papers. Ward wrote, "Miss Veazey wrote me last week and among other things she said that she really feared for Mrs. Pittman's mind. She cannot seem to throw the thing off."

35. Board of Regents of the University System of Georgia Minutes, 20 February 1947, Georgia Archives.

36. I. M. Destler, interview with author, Great Falls, Virginia, 13 July 2005.

37. Judson Ward, interview with author, 25 June 2003.

38. *George-Anne*, 23 October 1947.

39. *George-Anne*, 31 May 1948.

40. Ibid.

41. Judson Ward, paper prepared for the author, 17 July 2003; Ward, interview with author, Emory University, 22 September 2005.

42. Ward, paper; Ward, interview.

7. THE LAST YEARS OF MARVIN PITTMAN

1. Marvin S. Pittman, "A New Publication is Born," *Georgia Teachers College Alumni Quarterly* 1 (March 1950): 2.

2. "TC Alumni Association Protests Pay Difference," *Bulloch Herald*, 3 June 1948.

3. Ibid.

4. Ibid.

5. Marvin S. Pittman, "Joyous Living for Fifty Years," *Georgia Teachers College Alumni Quarterly* 3 (June 1952): 2.

6. *Bulloch Herald*, 19 January 1950.

7. Judson C. Ward, "Marvin Pittman School Dedicatory Address," *Georgia Teachers College Alumni Quarterly* 7 (June 1955): 4-6.

8. "Founder Returning," *Lincoln Highlight* 7, no. 2

(8 November 1949). This is a publication of the Lincoln Consolidated School, originally affiliated with Eastern Michigan University in Ypsilanti, Michigan.

9. Jack Nelson Averitt, "The Mentor and the Protégé," typescript of speech given at the dedication of the Marvin Pittman Administration Building, 18 April 1999.

10. Ward, "Marvin Pittman," 4.

8. THE FINAL DECADE

1. Board of Regents, University System of Georgia, Minutes, 11 February 1948. Georgia Department of Archives and History.

2. *Bulloch Times*, 12 February 1948, *Bulloch Herald*, 12 February 1948.

3. *Bulloch Herald*, 19 February 1948.

4. "Final Registration Hits All-Time High at 723," *George-Anne*, 11 October 1948.

5. "Enrollment Increases 10% Over Last Fall," *George-Anne*, 9 October 1958.

6. George A. Rogers, interview with author, Rincon, Ga., 14 June 2006.

7. Ralph Walton, "Making History," a statement prepared for the author, 10 December 2005.

8. *Bulloch Times*, 19 February 1948.

9. Marvin Pittman, "The Masters Degree at Georgia Teachers College," *Georgia Teachers College Alumni Quarterly*, 3 (December, 1951), 2.

10. "Regents Award Graduate Program to GTC," *Georgia Teachers College Alumni Quarterly* 9, (1 December 1957), 3.

11. Ibid.

12. *Savannah Morning News*, 12 January 1958, excerpted in two stories, including Joyce Kirkland, "English Has Bright Outlook, In Spite of Article," *George Anne*, 17 January 1958, 1, 2. The student newspaper quoted Fielding Russell, division head, who claimed the *News* report was misleading.

13. Donald Hackett, interview with the author, Statesboro, Ga., 6 June 2006. In the field of technology, he said, courses in methods of teaching and organizing shops and laboratories "should have continued to be taught in that division."

14. Jack Nelson Averitt, telephone interview with the author, 12 June 2006.

15. Donald Hackett interview.

16. Libba Smith, "The Older Coed: Hackett Has Been Innovator," *The Eagle* (27 June 1984), 4.

17. Donald Hackett interview.

18. Ibid.

19. Charles Stewart, interview with author, Hinesville, Ga., 26 April 2005.

20. Bobby R. Presley, interview with the author, Toccoa, Ga., 24 September 2004.

21. Interview with Mary Henderson Hobbs, Gene and Laquita Henderson by the author, Warner Robins, Ga., 12 November 2005.

22. Donald Hackett, interview.

23. *Bulloch Times*, 23 November 1944.

24. *Bulloch Times*, 10 January 1946.

25. Bill Sarratt, editorial, *George-Anne*, 1 November 1948.

26. "English Club Has Stormy Re-election," *George-Anne*, 8 November 1948.

27. Alton Davis, "Letter to the Editor," *George-Anne*, 8 November 1948.

28. Remer Tyson, editorial, *George-Anne*, 16 October 1953.

29. R. L. Smith, Angus L. Strickland, and Bruce Inman Abbott, "Letter to the Editor," *George-Anne*, 28 May 1954.

30. Charlton Moseley, interview with author, 22 May 2005.

31. Cherrell Williams Rose, letter to author, 8 February 2006.

32. Cathy Holt Norton, statement prepared for author, 20 June 2006.

33. Carlton Humphrey, "The People Forget," *George Anne*, 23 March 1956. At the time of this editorial, Guy Wells had returned to Statesboro, where he resided until his death. His was a familiar face on campus and around town, even as he traveled widely and represented the Southern Interracial Council and, later, the Peace Corps.

34. Taylor Branch, *Parting the Waters: America in the King Years, 1954–63* (New York: Simon and Schuster), 167-68, 181.

35. Ellen Blizzard, "Does Georgia Need Wilson as a Leader at This Time?" *George-Anne*, 13 April 1956.

36. John Stone, interview with author, 23 April 2005.

37. George A. Rogers, letter to the author, 15 June 2006.

38. Donald Hackett, interview.

39. Ibid.

40. *Savannah Morning News*, 31 December 1952, reprinted in *Bulloch Herald*, 1 January 1953.

41. Scot Perkins, interview with author, Statesboro, Ga., 21 October 2005.

42. J. B. Scearce, interview with Esther Mallard, n.d. Special Collections, Henderson Library, Georgia Southern University.

43. "Was Webb First? A Busy Bisher Zips up Zippy," *George–Anne*, 3 February 1956, 1. The University of Georgia insisted Zippy Morocco was the first basketball All American in Georgia. Furman Bisher studied the claim in 1956 and wrote: "This is intended to take nothing away from Zippy Morocco, who was no less than great with a basketball at Georgia, but contrary to Athens' contention he is not listed among Helms Foundation's All Americans of '53 . . . Morocco must have been a second or third team selection, and though Chester Webb's was a small college citation, it's still an authentic, first-class first-team A-A."

44. Chester Webb, interview with author, Statesboro, Ga., 21 October 2005.

45. Albert Howard, "Home, Home of the Strange," *George-Anne*, 3 March 1946.

46. Chuck Hutcheson, "Dr. Neil Sees Passing of Rock 'n Roll Fad," *George-Anne*, 18 April 1958.

47. Chester Curry, "Inquiring Reporter," *George-Anne*, 18 April 1958.

48. "Dr. Robert Strozier, FSU President, Delivers Opening Address," *George Anne*, 17 January 1958. Two days of festivities included alumni luncheons, a tree planting by the Veterans Club, a beauty review, homecoming parade downtown, and a concluding basketball game vs. Erskine College. On Sunday the churches of Statesboro recognized the college's origins through announcements and comments.

9. FROM PROFESSORS TO EAGLES

1. "Profs Beat Tech 72-64," *Bulloch Herald*, 4 December 1958.

2. Tom Coffee, "Professors Open Season With a Bang, Whip Georgia 82-73," *Savannah Morning News*.

3. "Board of Regents Authorizes Georgia Southern College As New School Name," *George-Anne*, 14 December 1959.

4. *Bulloch Herald*, 14 June 1962.

5. *Bulloch Herald*, 18 April 1963, 15 October 1964.

6. Frances Worden Wood, paper prepared for author, 18 May 2006.

7. *Bulloch Herald*, 2 February 1961.

8. *Bulloch Herald*, 3 January 1962. The fastest growing unit in the university system was the School of Nursing at the Medical College of Georgia.

9. *Bulloch Herald*, 14 January 1965.

10. *Bulloch Herald*, 30 September 1965.

11. *Bulloch Herald*, 5 March 1964.

12. *Bulloch Herald*, 10 October 1964.

13. "Foundation Drive in Bulloch County," *Bulloch Herald*, 29 November 1962.

14. "GSC Foundation Seeks Matching Funds," *Bulloch Herald*, 21 November 1963.

15. Kent Dykes, e-mail message to author, 22 August 2005.

16. Ibid.

17. *Bulloch Herald*, 2 May 1968.

18. *Bulloch Herald*, 9 August 1962.

19. David Thompson, interview with the author, 25 October 2005.

20. David Thompson, interview.

21. *Bulloch Herald*, 2 November 1957.

22. Leonard Powell, "Memoirs," Special Collections, Henderson Library, Georgia Southern University.

23. "Freshmen Speak," *George-Anne*, 7 October 1940.

24. *Bulloch Times*, 6 May 1943.

25. "Frosh Suffer Rat Day Antics," *George–Anne*, 6 November 1953.

26. "Students Hang Keefer in Effigy," *George-Anne*, 8 November 1957.

27. George A. Rogers, interview with author, Rincon, Ga., 14 June 2006. Rogers and Scearce made efforts to expose students who ruined a long jump pit and caused fellow students to miss an important examination. They relentlessly pursued the culprits for weeks. Finally the anonymous guilty parties hung the professors in effigy.

28. "Keefer Makes Proposals on Rat Standards," *George–Anne*, 8 November 1957.

29. Frances Worden Wood, email message to author, 19 May 2006. She wrote: I do vaguely have an impression that we may have been the last freshman class [1966] to go through Ratting."

30. Elaine Thomas, "Rat Day Activities Should Be Revived," *George-Anne*, 29 September 1967.

31. John Bradley, Augusta, Ga., telephone interview with the author, 16 December 2005. Later Bradley earned a doctoral degree from another institution; his wife, Winnette Bradley, a principal in Augusta, Ga., was pursuing a doctorate in education at Georgia Southern University in 2006.

32. John Bradley, interview with the author, 28 June 2006.

33. Ibid.

34. Catharine Davis Joyce, interview with author, 27 June 2006.

35. Ibid.

36. Jessie Zeigler Carter, interview with author, 30 June 2006.

37. Clavelia Love Brinson, interview with the author, 10 July 2006

38. Ibid.

39. Carolyn Milton Hobbs, interview with author, 30 June 2006.

40. Ibid.

41. Adam Crisp, "Proving Herself, Paving a Path," *George-Anne*, 9 February 2005, 1.

42. Hobbs. For additional information, see F. Erik Brooks, *Pursuing a Promise: A History of African Americans at Georgia Southern University* (Mercer University Press, 2006). The book deals at length with the quest for inclusion.

43. J. B. Scearce, interview with Esther Mallard, no date, Special Collections, Henderson Library.

44. Ibid.

45. Ibid. Scearce returned to graduate school to work on his doctorate in 1967.

46. At the beginning of the 1964 academic year, 42 percent of the faculty had earned doctoral degrees. *Bulloch Times*, 15 October 1964.

47. Carl Hodges, letter to the author, 18 August 2005.

48. "Four Campus Facilities Will be Dedicated Oct. 26," *George-Anne*, 24 October 1985.

10. ORGANIZING FOR QUALITY

1. Kent Dykes, email message to author, 22 August, 2005.

2. "Dr. John O. Eidson is New President," *Bulloch Herald*, 14 December 1967, 1. Donald Hackett and George A. Rogers provided information about the presidential advisory committee. Hackett, interview with the author, Statesboro, Ga., 6 June 2006; Rogers, interview with the author, Rincon, Ga., 14 June 2006.

3. Pope A. Duncan, interview with author, Deland, Fl., 24 February 2003.

4. Barbara Bitter, email message to the author, 28 June 2006.

5. "Dr. Eidson Appoints Callaway Professor," *George-Anne*, 18 April 1969, 2.

6. "Two Administrative Positions Filled," *George-Anne*, 25 April 1969, 2.

7. "College Begins New Department," *George-Anne*, 20 January 1970, 6.

8. George Shriver, interview, 30 June 2006. Barbara Bitter, email.

9. President Carrie Mitchell in 2005 reported the organization has awarded twenty scholarships since 1985. *A.G.S.W. Yearbook*, 2005-2006 (Statesboro, Ga.: Association of Georgia Southern Women, 2005), 2.

10. "Time to Consider University Status," an editorial, *Bulloch Herald*, 5 June 1969.

11. Reprinted in the *Bulloch Herald*, 21 June 1970.

12. "Homecoming," editorial, *Bulloch Herald*, 3 February 1971.

13. Pope A. Duncan, *Memoirs of a Peripatetic Educator* (DeLand, Florida: Legacies and Memories, 2005), 190.

14. Jack Averitt, interview with the author, Statesboro, Ga., 23 April 2005.

15. *Bulloch Herald*, 20 May 1971

16. William Blankenship, "Non-Violence, Peace Exhibited at Memorial Service for King," *George-Anne*, 11 April 1969, 3. Editor Blankinship wrote: "There were no jeerers, no agitating onlookers and evidently no trouble makers."

17. "Charles Kelly 149th Vietnam Death," *Bulloch Herald*, 16 July 1964, 1.

18. "Vietnam Moratorium Observed Nationally by Foes of War: Rallies Here Crowded, Orderly", *New York Times*, New York, October 16, 1969, 1.

19. Bill Neville, "Students & Faculty March in Support of Grievances," *George-Anne*, 26 May 1970, 2, 12.

20. Larry Davis, interview with author, 31 January 1906.

21. *Bulloch Herald*, 11 September 1969, 2 February 1971.

22. "Eagles Bow," *George-Anne*, 3 December 1971, 10.

23. Harris Mobley, interview with the author, Savannah, Ga., 2 November 2005.

24. Duncan, 202.

25. Duncan, 203-04.

26. Duncan, 212.

27. Duncan, 213.

28. Bulloch Herald, 30 July, 1970.

29. David Thompson, interview with author, Statesboro, Ga., 25 October 2005.

30. Ibid.

31. Pope Duncan, interview.

32. Duncan, *Memoirs*, 216-17.

33. Duncan, *Memoirs*, 219.

34. Duncan, *Memoirs*, 214-15.

35. Duncan, *Memoirs*, 217.

36. Duncan, 216-17.

37. Duncan, 226.

38. Margaret Duncan, interview with the author, Statesboro, Ga., 5 October 2005.

39. Margaret Duncan.

11. TOWARD A REGIONAL UNIVERSITY

1. Leo Parrish, interview with the author, Statesboro, Ga., 20 December 2005

2. Ibid.

3. Dale W. Lick, interview with the author, Savannah, Ga., 6 May 2005.

4. Dale W. Lick, "Address to the Faculty," Georgia Southern College, 15 September 1978, Special Collections of the Henderson Library, Georgia Southern University.

5. Kirbylene Stephens, interview with author, 18 July 2006, confirmed by a copy of Quick's report to the chancellor for 1987-88, Department of Archives and Records Management, Georgia Southern University.

6. E-mail message from James Orr, 4 September 2006. The corporation purchased twenty-two acres from Grady Johnson in 1977 and five acres from Buford Knight in 1988. The average cost per acre was $2,400. James Orr was Associate Dean of Students from 1977 until he retired in 1996.

7. Dale W. Lick, interview.

8. Dale W. Lick, interview.

9. Dale W. Lick, "Address to the Faculty."

10. Libba Smith, "Mrs. Lick – Still a Cheerleader," *The Eagle*, 9 May 1984, 4.

11. Warren F. Jones, interview with author, 18 April 2006.

12. Harrison Sharpe Carter, interview with the author, 29 December 2005.

13. Owen Gaede, interview with the author, 26 July 2006.

14. *Statesboro Herald*, 17 May 1978.

15. Dale W. Lick, interview.

16. Dale W. Lick, interview.

17. Harris Mobley, interview with the author, Savannah, Ga., 2 November 2005.

18. Ibid.

19. *Statesboro Herald*, 22 March 1978.

20. Handwritten faculty senate motion, no date, in 1979 folder of presidential correspondence, Department of Archives and Records Management, Georgia Southern University.

21. Dale Lick, interview.

22. Web site, Georgia Southern School of Nursing, "Overview," *http://chhs.georgiasouthern.edu/nursing/overview.html*.

23. Dale Lick, interview.

24. Ibid.

25. Dale W. Lick, "A Perspective on Higher Education in Georgia," 11 November 1980, 25.

26. Dale Lick, interview.

27. Ibid.

28. Lewis Grizzard, "Southeast Georgia Discovers That Pride Has a Bald Head," *Atlanta Weekly*, a supplement to the *Atlanta Journal-Constitution*, 30 August 1981, 44.

29. Dale W. Lick, interview. He recalled the Chairman of the Board of Regents, O. Torbitt Ivey, who led the effort to fire him on June 9, 1981, confessed a few years later that he wrongly had accused Lick of inappropriate conduct. He said he was "sorry for all that happened to you [Lick] as a result."

30. Dale W. Lick, summary report in memorandum to "The File," June 18, 1980.

31. *The Atlanta Constitution, 12 June 1981, A-4*.

32. Charles H. Brown, letter to Scott Candler, Jr., 25 August 1981, Department of Archives and Records Management, Georgia Southern University. On August 24, 1981, attorney Charles Brown visited regent Scott Candler, Jr., whose father, as a regent, voted to fire President Marvin Pittman. In a note to George Hanson and Dale Lick, Brown said Candler "expressed 'chagrin at Dale's not 'following directions to stop making political contacts.' I tried to explain to him the dynamic in the community for university status and my opinion that Dale was merely providing effective leadership . . . Based on what he said, I should think he would be most sympathetic to a proposal for university status. Time will tell."

33. "GSC Faculty Backs Lick's Plan," *Savannah Morning News*, 24 February 1982.

34. "Georgia Southern Not to Get University Status in 1983," *Statesboro Herald*, 12 December 1983.

35. *Statesboro Herald*, 13 October 1983.

36. Harrison S. Carter, interview.

37. "Report of the Principal Committee on Organization and Administration," *Institutional Self-Study Program With the Southern Association of Colleges and Schools*, 1983 (Statesboro: Georgia Southern College, 1983), 50.

38. Dale Lick, interview.

39. Joe Kovac, Jr., "Coach Erk Russell, 79, Football Wizard," *Macon Telegraph*, 28 August 2005, F, 1, 9.

40. Dale Lick, interview.

12. ACHIEVING STATUS

1. Harrison Sharpe Carter, interview with author, 29 December 2005.

2. Sharon Fell, "Georgia Southern College Decks Out for Inauguration," *Southern Traces* 2 (Spring, 1988), 8-9.

3. Nicholas Henry, Inaugural Address, 29 April 1988, Special Collections, Henderson Library, Georgia Southern University.

4 *Statesboro Herald*, 4 July 1987.

5 Larry Davis, interview with the author, 31 January 2006.

6 Nicholas Henry, interview with Esther Mallard, 10 October 1990, used with permission of Nicholas Henry.

7 Nicholas Henry, interview with the author, 10 October 2005, 17 October 2005..

8 *George-Anne*, 22 September 1988.

9 Nicholas Henry, interview with the author.

10 Caryl Brown, interview with the author, 15 August 2006.

11 *George-Anne*, 9 October 1990.

12 "America's Best Colleges," *U.S. News & World Report*, 16 October 1989, 81.

13 *George-Anne*, 10 October 1989.

14 For more history of the Center for Wildlife Education, see the following: *http://welcome. georgiasouthern.edu/wildlife/history.htm*.

15 Beth Roberts, "Of flagships, admissions, and affirmative action: Chancellor discusses broad issues during his visit," *The University of Georgia Campus News*, 27 October 1997, *http://www.uga. edu/columns/102797/camp2.html*.

16 Nicholas Henry, interview with Esther Mallard.

17 Harrison Sharpe Carter, interview.

18 Alan Peskin, *Garfield: A Biography* (Kent, Oh.: Kent State University Press, 1978), 34.

19 The resignation of J. Walter Hendricks in 1909 allowed him to become a full-time farmer. Hendricks held the position of principal of the First District A&M School.

20 Nicholas Henry, "Swan Song: Remarks to the Spring Faculty Meeting, May 21, 1998," Department of Archives and Records Management, Georgia Southern University.

13. AMBITION AND MEMORY

1 Bruce Grube, interview with the author, 12 January 2006.

2 *Statesboro Herald*, 10 August 2006.

3 Trey Denton, interview with the author, 8 September 2006.

4 *George-Anne*, 11 March 1999.

5 Carter continued his unique career when he joined the faculty of the Citadel. There he served as provost, acting provost and professor.

6 Ibid.

7 Ibid.

8 Grube, interview.

9 *George-Anne*, 11 March 1999.

10 Grube, interview.

11 Linda Bleicken, interview with author, 22 March 2006.

12 "What is the Comprehensive University?" Council on Undergraduate Research, *http://www. cur.org/wp_recpr.html*.

13 In the State of Washington, there are two research universities – Washington and Washington State. Four comprehensive universities—Eastern, Central, Western, and Evergreen—do not offer doctoral degrees. In California, on the other hand, some well-known universities, like California State University at Los Angeles, define themselves as comprehensive universities. *http://www.hecb.wa.gov/Links/colleges/ collegesindex.asp* and Council on Undergraduate Research web page.

14 Joseph Franklin, interview with the author, 2 August 2006.

15 Bruce Grube, "The Campaign for National Distinction," booklet, 2004, inside cover.

16 The Fact Book, Georgia Southern University, *http://services.georgiasouthern.edu/osra/fb0506.pdf*, 21-22 .

17 Victor M. H. Borden and Pamela C. Brown," The Top 100: Interpreting the Data," *Diverse: Issues in Higher Education* 23 (June 1, 2006), 44.

18 Nicholas Henry, interview with the author, 10 October 2005, 17 October 2005.

19 Linda Bleicken, interview with the author.

20 Jane Rhoades Hudak, interview with the author, 8 September 2006.

21 Annual Report for 2006, College of Liberal Arts and Social Sciences, Georgia Southern University.

22 Brett Danilowicz, interview with the author, 4 August 2006.

23 James Bradford, interview with the author, 28 July 2006.

24 Lucindia Chance, interview with the author, 1 August 2006.

25 Ronald Shiffler, interview with the author, 2 August 2006.

26 Lowell Mooney, letter to author, 18 October 2005.

27 "Georgia Southern achieves national research university status," a press release, Office of Marketing and Communications, 19 April 2006, *http://www.georgiasouthern.edu/news/2006_ PressRels/Apro6/research.htm*

28 Bruce Grube, interview with the author, 12 January 2006.

29 Four individuals received doctoral degrees in educational administration on June 8, 1996: Lynn Futch, Brenda Riley, Jody Woodrum, and Linda Wright. All pursued the doctorate while serving as teachers or administrators in southeast Georgia schools. Michael Richardson, "First Doctoral Degrees Awarded," *Southern Educator* 9 (Fall 1996), 2.

30 The Carnegie Foundation for the Advancement of Teaching Web Site. *http://www. carnegiefoundation.org/classifications/index. asp?key=807* .

31 In a document of twenty-four pages, the word "distinction" appears twenty-five times, "greatness" seven, and "national" or "international" twenty. "Recognized" or "recognition" show up fifteen times. Georgia Southern University Strategic Plan, Fall of 2004, 5. *http://services.georgiasouthern.edu/osra/councils/spc/ stratplan.pdf*

32 Bleicken, interview.

33 Trey Denton, interview with the author, 8 September 2006.

34 Jane Rhoades Hudak, interview with the author, 8 September 2006.

35 Charles Hardy, interview with the author, 27 July 2006.

36 Karl Peace, interview with the author, 25 July 2006.

37 Ibid. The university recognized Peace's contributions by awarding him the first Presidential medal. More important than personal recognition, Peace said, is the future of this institution as an innovative resource for improving public health. During his first six years on the faculty, he could have made some $10 million in his previous job. Thinking in the longer term, however, Peace realized he made the right decision to invest his life and resources into this bold effort at his alma mater.

38 Athletic Director Sam Baker in 2006 used the term "student athlete" for approximately 370 who participate in intercollegiate sports. Coaches at Georgia Southern prefer the term, because it expresses clearly the role of athletics in collegiate life. In addition to athletes under their charge, coaches also teach untold thousands of spectators and fans. The continuing appeal of deceased coaches, such as legendary figures Crook Smith and Erk Russell, was their ability to communicate clearly the human meaning of athletic competition.

Miss Myrtle Smith (later Mrs. C. P. Olliff Sr.) toured Culture Hill on a Sunday afternoon with Percy Averitt in 1907. Averitt owned one of only a few automobiles in Bulloch County at the time this of this photograph. Builders completed the three main buildings of the original campus later that year.

ILLUSTRATION CREDITS

TO BUILD THE PEOPLE'S SCHOOL

Chapter 1: The Meaning of the First Day
p1-2 illustration: Lawrence B. Smith; **p3**: Delma E. Presley and Smith Banks; **p4p1**: Statesboro Regional Library; **p4p2**: Statesboro Regional Library; **p4p3**: City of Statesboro; **p5**: Presley & Banks; **p6**: Georgia Historical Society; **p7p1**: Henderson Library Special Collections; **p7p2**: Presley & Banks; **p8**: Presley & Banks; **p9**: Rand McNally & Co. map, 1910; **p10p1**: Henderson Library Special Collections; **p11p1**: Mrs. James "Cookie" Deal; **p12 images**: Georgia Historical Society; **p13p1**: Statesboro Regional Library; **p13p2**: Georgia Historical Society; **p14 images**: Georgia Historical Society; **p15**: Georgia Historical Society; **p17p1**: Betty Moore Kline; **p17p2**: Henderson Library Special Collections; **p18**: Robert M. Benson Jr.; **p19 images**: Robert M. Benson Jr.; **p21**: Lawrence B. Smith; **p22p1**: Rand McNally & Co. map, 1910; **p22p2**: Henderson Library Special Collections; **p23 images**: GSU Photo Services

Chapter 2: An Aspiration Set in a Pine Forest
p24: Lawrence B. Smith; **p25p1**: GSU Photo Services; **p25p2**: Henderson Library Special Collections; **p26p1**: Lawrence B. Smith; **p26p2**: Robert M. Benson Jr.; **p27p1**: GSU photo archives; **p27p2**: Henderson Library Special Collections; **p27p3**: Lawrence B. Smith; **p28 images**: Henderson Library Special Collections; **p29 images**: Statesboro Regional Library; **p30p1**: Edwin M. Hendricks; **p30p2**: Sarah Waters; **p31 images**: Henderson Library Special Collections; **p32p1**: Henderson Library Special Collections; **p32p2**: Homer Miller; **p33p1**: Henderson Library Special Collections; **p33p2**: Statesboro Regional Library; **p34-37 images**: Henderson Library Special Collections; **p38 images**: Robert M. Benson Jr.; **p39 images**: Henderson Library Special Collections; **p40**: Statesboro Regional Library; **p41-42 images**: Henderson Library Special Collections; **p44**: Edwin M. Hendricks; **p45**: GSU Archives and Records; **p46 images**: Henderson Library Special Collections

Ch. 3: The View from 'Culture Hill
p50: Presley & Banks; **p51**: Henderson Library Special Collections; **p52p1**: Henderson Library Special Collections; **p52p2**: Reflector; **p53**: images from Reflector except for Bell Tower from Robert Muldrow Cooper Library; **p54-55 images**: Henderson Library Special Collections; **p56**: drawings from Henderson Library Special Collections, picture from Statesboro Regional Library; **p57**: Presley & Smith; **p58-59 images**: Henderson Library Special Collections; **p60**: images from Robert Muldrow Cooper Library, except Cromartie from Henderson Library Special Collections; **p61**: Robert M. Benson Jr; **p62**: images from Henderson Library Special Collections; lower left from Robert Muldrow Cooper Library and lower right from Statesboro Regional Library; **p63**: top images from Robert Muldrow Cooper Library; bottom images from Henderson Library Special Collections; **p64**: image from Robert M. Benson; medals and ring from Henderson Library Special Collections; **p65**: basketball image from Reflector; others from Robert Muldrow Cooper Library; **p66p1**: William & Thomas Grovenstein; **p66p2**: Henderson Library Special Collections; **p67**: Anna Cone Seyle; **p68p1**: Reflector; **p68p2**: Robert M. Benson Jr.; **p69p1**: Reflector; **p69p2**: Smith Banks; **p70-71 images**: Reflector; **p72**: Robert M. Benson Collection; **p73p1**: Henderson Library Special Collections; **p73p2**: T. Ray Shurbutt; **p74**: Anderson image from Reflector; others from Henderson Library Special Collections; **p75**: Reflector; **p76p1**: GSU Botanical Garden; **p76p2**: Reflector; **p77**: Reflector; **p78 images**: GSU Photo Archives; **p79-80 images**: Reflector; **p81**: Henderson Library Special Collections

TEACHERS COLLEGE

Chapter 4: Defining the Role
p83-84 illustrations: Lawrence B. Smith; **p85**: Georgia College & State University Library; **p86p1**: Mrs. Don Whaley; **p86p2**: Henderson Library Special Collections; **p86p3**: Reflector; **p87**: Mary Henderson Hobbs; **p88**: Lawrence B. Smith; **p89**: Henderson Library Special Collections; **p90-91 images**: Reflector; **p92p1** Frederick Dyer; **p92p2**: Reflector; **p93**: images from Reflector, except team meeting from Henderson Library Special Collections; **p94**: Presley & Banks; **p95 images**: Reflector; **p96**: Lawrence B. Smith; **p97p1**: Eloise Nessmith; **p97p2**: Katherine Branscomb Kelly; **p97p3**: Reflector; **p97p4**: Reflector; **p98p1**: The George-Anne; **p98p2**: Reflector; **p99**: Reflector; **p100p1**: Tuskegee Institute Archives; **p100p2**: GSU Archives; **p102**: Lawrence B. Smith; **p103p1**: Katherine Branscomb Kelly

Chapter 5: The Dream, The Drama
p105p1: Bruce T. Halle Library; **p105p2**: GSU Museum; **p106p1**: I.M. Destler; **p106p2**: GSU Museum; **p107**: Reflector; **p108**: Henderson Library Special Collections; **p109p1**: Henderson Library Special Collections; **p109p2**: Presley & Banks; **p110**: Mrs. James "Cookie" Deal; **p111**: The George-Anne; **p112 images**: Reflector; **p113-144 images**: Reflector; **p115**: GSU Photo Services; **p116**: Reflector; **p118**: images from Mary Thomas Perry King, except top photo from Reflector; **p119**: Reflector; **p120p1**: Elizabeth Cato Albers; **p120p2**: Reflector; **p122**: Henderson Library Special Collections; **p123**: William G. Neville III; **p124p1**: Reflector; **p124p2**: Anna Cone Seyle; **p124p3**: Reflector; **p124p4**: Reflector; **p124-125**: images from Henderson Library Special Collections, except bottom photo from The George-Anne; **p126**: Reflector; **p127**: Henderson Library Special Collections; **p128**: Georgia Department of Archives; **p129**: Reflector; **p130**: The George-Anne; **p131**: Reflector

Chapter 6: Performance Postponed
p133 images: Henderson Library; **p134-136 images**: Reflector; **p137p1**: Henderson Library; **p137p2**: Mary Thomas Perry King; **p139-140 images**: The George-Anne; **p141-148 images**: Reflector; **p149**: images from Reflector, except top picture from Judson C. Ward

Chapter 7: Vigorously Taking Leave
p150-151 images: Reflector; **p152**: Georgia Teachers College Alumni Bulletin; **p153**: Reflector; **p154p1**: Bruce T. Halle Library; **p154p2**: GSU Photo Services; **p155p1**: Bruce T. Halle Library; **p155p2**: GSU Photo Services; **p155p3**: Victor Martinez; **p155p4**: Victor Martinez

Chapter 8: The Final Decade
p157: Reflector; **p158p1**: Reflector; **p158p2**: The George-Anne; **p159p1**: Reflector; **p160p1**: images from Reflector, except Blitch from Mary Margaret Menter; **p161p1**: Reflector; **p161p2**: Jo Starr Callaway; **p161p3**: Reflector; **p162**: Reflector; **p163p1**: Henderson Library Special Collections; **p163p2**: Reflector; **p163p3**: Reflector; **p164p4**: Gay Kimbrough Dull; **p164p1**: Reflector; **p164p2**: Dan Biggers; **p165p1**: Gay Kimbrall Dull; **p165p2**: Sandra Stange; **p165p3**: GSU Museum; **p165p4**: Reflector; **p165p5**: Juliet Oliver Tarver; **p165p6**: The George-Anne; **p166p1**: Reflector; **p166p2**: GSU Photo Services; **p167 images**: China Altman; **p168p1**: Reflector; **p168p2**: GSU Photo Services; **p169 images**: Reflector; **p170p1**: Reflector; **p170p2**: Juanita Doss; **p171p1**: The George-Anne; **p171p2**: Reflector; **p172p1**: T. Ray Shurbutt; **p172p2**: Lawrence B. Smith; **p173**: images from Reflector; except invitation from Kirbylene Stephens

GEORGIA SOUTHERN COLLEGE

Chapter 9: From Professors to Eagles
p175-176 illustrations: Lawrence B. Smith; **p178-179**: images from Reflector, except eagle from The George-Anne; **p180**: patches from Frances Warden Wood, picture from Reflector; **p181 images**: GSU Photo Services; **p183**: Reflector; **p184p1**: Steve Denenberg; **p184p2**: Steve Denenberg; **p184p3**: William Griffis; **p185-186 images**: The George-Anne; **p187**: Betty Spaid; **p188-190**: images from Reflector except Bradley from John Bradley; Brayboy and Dickerson from The George-Anne; **p191p1**: GSU Photo Services; **p191p2**: Reflector; **p192p1**: Reflector; **p192p2**: GSU Archives & Records; **p193**: Reflector

Chapter 10: Organizing for Quality
p195p1: Reflector; **p195p2**: Margaret Duncan; **p196**: The George-Anne; **p197**: James H. Oliver Jr.; **p198**: Beverly Presley; **p199p1**: GSU Archives & Records; **p199p2**: Reflector; **p200**: images from Reflector, except float from The George-Anne; **p201**: images from The George-Anne and Reflector; **p202-203**: images from Reflector, except alumni house from GSU Photo Services; **p204p1**: images from The George-Anne, except sign from Kent Dykes; **p205p1**: Reflector; **p205p2**: Ric Mandes; **p206p1**: Delma E. Presley; **p206p2**: Georgia Southern University; **p206p3**: Georgia Southern University; **p206p4**: Reflector; **p207p1**: GSU Photo Services; **p207p2**: Reflector; **p208p1**: Reflector; **p208p2**: The George-Anne; **p208p3**: William G. Neville III; **p209-211 images**: Reflector

Chapter 11: Toward a Regional University
p213: GSU Photo Services; **p214 images**: Reflector; **p215-216 images**: GSU Photo Services; **p217 images**: GSU Vice President of Business and Finance; **p218**: GSU Photo Services; **p219 images**: Reflector; **p220p1**: GSU Photo Services; **p220p2**: F. Erik Brooks; **p221p1**: Martha Coleman; **p221p2**: Reflector; **p222**: images from GSU Photo Services, except Maret from Reflector; **p223**: The George-Anne; **p224**: GSU Photo Services; **p225p1**: GSU Photo Services; **p225p2**: Lawrence B. Smith; **p226 images**: GSU Photo Services; **p227**: Kirbylene Stephens; **p228 images**: Dale Lick; **p229p1**: Kirbylene Stephens; **p229p2**: GSU Photo Services; **p230p1**: Reflector; **p230p2**: GSU Photo Services; **p231 images**: GSU Photo Services; **p232p1**: A. J. Shryock; **p232p2**: GSU Alumni Association

GEORGIA SOUTHERN UNIVERSITY

Chapter 12: Achieving Status
p233-224 illustrations: Lawrence B. Smith; **p235**: GSU Photo Services; **p236**: image from Nicholas Henry; invitation from Kirbylene Stephens; **p237 images**: GSU Photo Services; **p238 images**: Nicholas Henry; **p239p1**: Ross Norton; **p239p2**: GSU Photo Services; **p240-242 images**: GSU Photo Services; **p243**: images from GSU Photo Services, except top one from Reflector; **p244p1**: GSU Photo Services; **p244p2**: Beth Joyner; **p245p1**: Willgina Montgomery; **p245p2**: Nicholas Henry; **p247 images**: GSU Photo Services; **p248-249**: Rolling Stones from GSU Student Media Archives; Simon & Garfunkel from Reflector; Ike & Tina Turner, REM, Allman Brothers and BB King from The George-Anne, ticket from Thomas Grovenstein, Mountain pic and 8-track from William G. Neville III, Atlanta Rhythm and Marshall Tucker from GSU Photo Services

Chapter 13: Ambition and Memory
All images from GSU Photo Services, except **p257** Barrett from Reflector; **p258** *uniscope* from University of Lausanne; **p259** both from College of Education; **p261** library rendering from Henderson Library Special Collections; **p264** images from Karl Peace

INDEX

Bold page number indicates the subject appears in a photograph.

Printed in Canada
on Acid-Free Paper

Friesens
The Yearbook Company

Printed in Canada
on Acid-Free Paper